Việt Nam

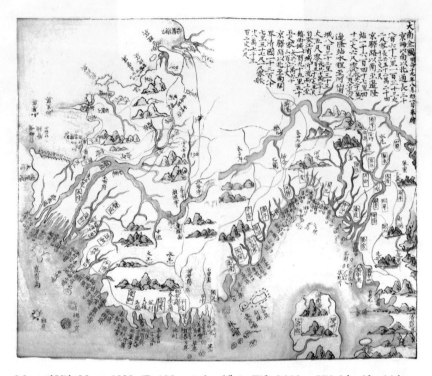

Map of Việt Nam, 1839. (Đại Nam toàn đồ, in *Tiền Lê Nam Việt bản đồ mô bản*, manuscript from the Bibliotèque de l'École Française d'Extrême-Orient—Paris. Reference: Viet/A/GEO/4.)

Việt Nam
Borderless Histories

Edited by
NHUNG TUYET TRAN
and
ANTHONY J. S. REID

THE UNIVERSITY OF WISCONSIN PRESS

$22.95
B & T
10/06

The University of Wisconsin Press
1930 Monroe Street
Madison, Wisconsin 53711

www.wisc.edu/wisconsinpress/

3 Henrietta Street
London WC2E 8LU, England

5   4   3   2   1

Printed in the United States of America

Library of Congress Cataloging-in-Publication Data
Việt Nam : borderless histories / edited by Nhung Tuyet Tran and Anthony Reid.
p.   cm. — (New perspectives in Southeast Asian studies)
Includes bibliographical references and index.
ISBN-13: 978-0-299-21770-9 (cloth: alk. paper)
ISBN-13: 978-0-299-21774-7 (pbk.: alk. paper)
   1. Vietnam — History.   I. Tran, Nhung Tuyet.   II. Reid, Anthony, 1939–   III. Series.
DS556.5.V544   2005
959.7 — dc22   2005032883

This book was published with the support of the Anonymous Fund for the Humanities of the University of Wisconsin–Madison and the Center for Southeast Asian Studies at the University of Wisconsin–Madison.

Contents

Preface

This volume has been made possible by a new generation of Việt Nam scholars, much richer in both numbers and diversity than their predecessors. The idea for a conference to bring together international Việt Nam scholars grew out of one held at the University of Pennsylvania in April 2000: "Moving beyond the War: New Directions in the Study of Việt Nam." The Department of History and the Center for East Asian Studies at the University of Pennsylvania, and in particular, then Chair Lynn Lees, provided the support necessary to hold the event. At that conference, we both recognized the excitement that this inquiry brought and decided to provide a more directed forum to continue this dialog.

A new Center for Southeast Asian Studies at UCLA seemed a fitting place for many scholars to reconvene. "Việt Nam: Beyond the Frontiers," held in May 2001, tested the limits of the possible, with a younger generation of scholars engaging in dialog with the pillars of the field. We are grateful to those who contributed thoughtful papers to the conference program, including Jessica Breiteneicher, Micheline Lessard, Ngô Đức Thịnh, Nguyễn Thị Hiền, Nguyễn Xuân Thu, Panivong Norindr, Douglas Padgett, Melissa Pashigian, Minh Hoa Ta, Angie Ngoc Tran, Caroline Valverde, and John Wills. Our thanks go also to the scholars who served as discussants at the conference: Cường Tự Nguyễn, Thu-Hương Nguyễn-Võ, Linda Võ, John Whitmore, and Peter Zinoman. At UCLA the staff of the Center for Southeast Asian Studies, including David Deltesta (then acting codirector), Jennifer Winther, Elmer Almer, and Paul Nguyen and Thao Nguyen (conference assistants) made the logistical planning all the easier. Christine Cao, Catherine Greene-Husbands, and Hueybin Teng's assistance ensured that the conference ran smoothly.

The conference was made possible through the generous funding of the following UCLA programs and departments: Center for Southeast Asian Studies, Comparative and Interdisciplinary Research on Asia (CIRA) Program, the Department of History, and the International and Area Studies Program (ISOP). Gary Larsen, through the Asia Society of Southern California and Cathay Pacific, arranged the air travel for participants from Việt Nam.

During the conference we realized that the advances in historical analysis were particularly important and that Vietnamese history would be the subject of this book. In the efforts that followed, we acquired further debts, notably to our contributors, who wrote and rewrote to ever higher levels and waited patiently for the outcome. We also thank two anonymous readers for the Center of Southeast Asian Studies Publications who provided insightful comments on our manuscript and revisions. In the final editing task we were much assisted by Tan Ying Ying, Kamalini Ramdas, and Connie Teo Eng Seng from the Asia Research Institute in Singapore.

Toronto and Singapore, 2005

A Note on Terminology/ Transliteration

To ensure consistency, we decided to maintain Vietnamese terms with complete diacritics in the text. Chinese terms have been rendered in the contemporary romanization standards in Hán-Việt or pinyin next to the English translation. A glossary of Chinese terms used in each essay is provided for readers who are familiar with characters and wish to consult the phrases in the original.

Proper names are rendered with or without diacritics according to standard Vietnamese and/or Western convention. Of greater controversy is the rendering of the term "Việt Nam." Although the separation of the term with diacritics is still hotly debated in Vietnamese studies, we have decided to render it in the original. For the pre-nineteenth century, we have avoided referring to the different states as "Việt Nam." The authors in this volume have also used Đàng Trong to refer to the southern realm of Nguyễn rule in the pre–Gia Long period. When discussing colonial literature, we have tried to use the terms the authors use in their discussion.

Việt Nam

Introduction

The Construction of Vietnamese Historical Identities

NHUNG TUYET TRAN AND ANTHONY REID

Few historiographies have borne such a strong national imprint as that of Việt Nam in the twentieth century. Engaged through much of that century in a fierce battle for national identity and survival, Vietnamese historians and their international sympathizers focused intently on the grand narrative of national struggle against China, France, and America. Only recently has a new generation of historians been able to explore the political and cultural complexities of relations between the myriad peoples who have inhabited the Indo-Chinese peninsula without having to consider the effect of their words on national struggle.[1] This volume represents another step for that generation.

The book opens new insights into the ways in which a Vietnamese identity interacted over a thousand years with Chinese, Cham, Khmer, French, and stateless peoples of the peninsula. It reveals a history that not only is the point of intersection of East and Southeast Asia but also is itself variegated and open to multiple possibilities. There is another sense in which this book transcends borders. A generation ago Western historiography on Việt Nam was completely

separate from Vietnamese historiography, even if often sympathetic
to it, and shied away from engaging French-colonial historiography.
What was written in China and Japan was largely unknown to Western scholars. This book represents a continuing dialogue between historians trained or partly trained in Việt Nam, China, Japan, Korea,
and Australia as well as in the United States. A key figure in the dialogue is Professor Phan Huy Lê, doyen of Vietnamese historians and
heir of a famous literati family, whose career has spanned the evolution of independent Việt Nam's historiography. The other representative of an older generation is Korea's leading Việt Nam scholar, Yu
Insun, whose training in Vietnamese and Southeast Asian history in
Japan and the United States offers a unique perspective on the
sources. Without contrivance this volume demonstrates the way in
which research on Vietnamese history has necessarily, at last, become
an international conversation.

Of course, this broadening of the agenda of Vietnamese history to
some extent follows a global trend. Although the pressures of nationalism were extreme in Việt Nam, especially in the third quarter of the
last century, the interest in redeeming nonnational actors, networks,
and movements from obscurity has been proceeding everywhere.
Prasenjit Duara's work on modern Chinese history and the work of
Partha Chatterjee and others of the subaltern school for India have
already sought to distinguish historical experience from national narratives.[2] In Southeast Asian studies Thailand has produced the most
interesting debates of this kind, perhaps because the nationalist history writing that peaked there as elsewhere in the middle of the twentieth century did not have the same legitimizing aura of overturning
colonialism. As historian Thongchai Winichakul has recently argued,
"The validity of writing 'national history' in Asia is now disputed and
the need to 'rescue' its 'casualties' advocated. The nation as historical
subject, a natural and given assumption glorified by many great
thinkers from the eighteenth to the early twentieth century, is now in
trouble."[3]

His plea is for "writing history from the interstices of cultures,
from the limits, the edges, the margins that are no longer marginal."
This book does not stand alone. The following overview of the historiography of precolonial Việt Nam places the new work in this
volume within the context that preceded it.

The Historiographical Debate with China

Vietnamese history writing was born out of the millennial grappling with the problem of its stronger neighbor, erstwhile colonizer, and literary model to the north. The literati of the Trần and Lê dynasties (thirteenth and fifteenth centuries) dealt with this problem by seeking an ancient genealogy for Vietnamese autonomy. As the essay by Yu Insun shows, Lê Văn Hưu and Ngô Sĩ Liên both sought a point of origin for the southern state before Chinese colonization, though their solutions differed. Lê Văn Hưu focused on Triệu Đà's establishment of power in the second century BCE to highlight Đại Việt's equality with China. Ngô Sĩ Liên went further, tracing the origins of Vietnamese autonomy back to the Hồng Bàng, when Lạc Long Quân, a descendant of the Shen Nong Emperor, and his fairy bride gave birth to a hundred boys in 2789 BCE. By tracing Vietnamese origins to the Shen Nong (Thần Nông) Emperor, the second of the three golden rulers of heaven,[4] and creating a mythology of creation independent of the Hán, Ngô Sĩ Liên constructed an identity of Vietnamese that was equal if not superior to the Chinese. Even the Catholic convert Bento Thiện, the first to write a *quốc ngữ* history of Annam (1659) at the request of the Jesuit Francis Marini, traced the origins of the country to this Shen Nong emperor.[5] When Europeans themselves were writing the story, however, following the lead of another seventeenth-century Jesuit, Alexandre de Rhodes, they sought the origins of "Tonquinese" society no earlier than its separation from the Middle Kingdom in the tenth century.[6]

The imposition of French authority in the nineteenth century brought the beginnings of modern Western constructions of Vietnamese linear history by colonial scholars. The earliest French scholars to tackle this task were preoccupied, like their Vietnamese predecessors, with the China connection but offered the opposite interpretation of it as derivative, "colonial," and second rate, adopting Sinic institutions without innovation. Adrien Launay, historian of the Missions-Étrangères, suggested that "the Annamites conserved a certain number of their customs, but in the most fundamental ways, Annamite civilization followed that of the Chinese." He continued, "The complete absence of progress that the Annamites had on Chinese civilization and the negligible development in the arts and sciences, far inferior to that of the Chinese, [demonstrates] that without

Chinese domination, *Giao-chỉ* of old times would have rested in savage tribal communities, just like the Mường who live on the frontiers of their country."[7]

With varying degrees of sophistication, other assimilationist scholars, such as Eliacin Lurô and Paul Ory, echoed Launay's characterization, depicting Vietnamese society as a dimmer version of its northern model.[8] Others of this generation pointed toward future new Orientalist trends in allowing some Vietnamese initiative in the appropriation of Chinese institutions. Camille Briffaut, whose *La cité annamite* sought to locate Vietnamese uniqueness in the village, nevertheless traced its origins to the Chinese village. However, he argued that it was the success of the "Annamites" in adapting this Chinese institution that made possible Vietnamese colonization of the western and southern realms. The early "civilizing mission" policies before the shift to associationist ideas were justified by depictions of Vietnamese history as static, derivative, and savage.

The institutional history of France's scholarly arm in Indochina from 1898, the École Française d'Extrême Orient (EFEO), parallels that of colonial attitudes more generally. One of its charges was to supplant the dominance of the Confucian scholar sympathetic to political revivalism of the *Cần vương* sort with a model of a "disinterested intellectual."[9] Its younger generation of Orientalists challenged the assimilation policies built into its original purposes as detrimental to French colonial goals. Louis Finôt, first director of the EFEO, proposed that a better policy would be that of "discovering the origins, explaining the anomalies, and justifying the diversity" of the colonies.[10]

The discourses on Vietnamese identity in the *Bulletin de l'EFEO* (*BEFEO*) reflected this shift in EFEO colonial recommendations as scholars began to highlight institutions they regarded as uniquely "Annamite," challenging the scholarship of Briffaut and older Orientalists.[11] This changing discourse on Vietnamese identity reflected a broader desire by the colonial authorities and scholars to separate "their" colony from China or from Indianization associated with the British. Key figures in this endeavor were the Maspéro brothers, whose scholarship helped to distinguish China and the Southeast Asian polities. Henri Maspéro wrote prolifically on Chinese history and institutions, while his younger brother, Georges, produced scholarship identifying Annamite, Cambodian, and Cham uniqueness.[12] As part of this endeavor, the *BEFEO* also published Raymond Déloustal's translation of the Lê Code and proclaimed it as the embodiment of ancient Annamite (read pre-Chinese) customs.[13] A later generation of scholars of the EFEO, represented by its director in the 1940s, Georges Coedès, moved closer to scholars in Java, Burma, and Malaya, developing a model of Southeast Asia as a whole that was "hindouisé" without entirely losing its own character. Champa and Cambodia were emphatically part of this Southeast Asia, while the Vietnamese state had a more complex and ambivalent relationship to it.[14]

History as Nation Building

The EFEO's model of Việt Nam-centered Orientalist scholarship, intended to offset the influence of anti-Western movements in China and Japan, ironically assisted Vietnamese nationalists in their construction of their narrative.[15] By highlighting the colony's non-Chinese characteristics, EFEO scholars unwittingly constructed a model of "indigenousness" that nationalists would soon appropriate in their construction of the inevitability of the Vietnamese nation. The dominant themes became a distinct, non-Chinese origin, the homogeneity of Vietnamese culture, and the southward-expansion (*nam tiến, nan jin*) explanation for the development of national borders. Although Vietnamese nationalists created this narrative, the first generation of Việt Nam historians in America built on it for their own reasons.

The first generation of Vietnamese scholars to write in *quốc-ngữ* script and in a nation-centered historical idiom drew deeply on both the French colonial writings and the older imperial chroniclers while being influenced by reformist and nationalist models in China and Japan. A crucial transitional figure in this and other respects was Phan Bội Châu, Confucian scholar and anti-French nationalist, whose political philosophy evolved from dynastic reformation to national liberation. His 1909 work, *Việt Nam quốc sử khảo* [A Study of Việt Nam's National History], was still written in the Chinese of his classical training but followed Chinese, Japanese, and French nationalist models in providing a history centered on the nation.[16]

Far more influential in the classrooms of the 1920s through the 1950s was *Việt Nam sử lược* by Trần Trọng Kim (1887–1953), first published in 1920, which provided a chronological account from

Vietnamese mythical origins to the establishment of French authority in 1858. Kim critically examined the dynastic histories, conceding that Lê Văn Hưu and Ngô Sĩ Liên's creation of a Vietnamese historical identity predating the Shang emperor was inconsistent with rational understandings of historical process. Although Kim disavowed this particular narrative, he rationalized the need for it, adding that "one must understand that [such a construction] happens in every country. When [the country] is in its incipient stage, everyone wants to trace his origins to mythical gods to highlight his [people's] uniqueness."[17] Keenly aware of the historical claims of the Chinese national movement to the north, Trần Trọng Kim carefully traced the history of the Vietnamese polity to the third century BCE, just predating the Han invasion. He located the origins of modern Việt Nam in the Âu Lạc Kingdom, whose founders were not from the Chinese empire, he insisted, lest anyone mistakenly perceive Việt Nam as a province of the Middle Kingdom.[18]

Vietnamese scholars trained in Western social-scientific thought and influenced by Orientalist constructions of Annamite identity continued the quest to locate Vietnamese genius and homogeneity of culture. Many of these scholars appropriated the EFEO scholars' elevation of the Lê Code as Vietnamese genius and used these constructions to demonstrate that the colony was just as civilized as the West.[19] Others, like Việt Nam's premier socialist-national historian, Nguyễn Văn Huyên, identified Vietnamese uniqueness in racial features, architectural structures, and eating habits.[20] Like his counterparts in the legal profession, Huyên appropriated French Orientalist constructions of Annamite mentalities and transformed them into national characteristics. The importance of the village in Vietnamese society and the people's resistance to foreign invaders became key signifiers of a unique Vietnamese national spirit.

From 1954 to 1975, scholars from the North and the South each continued to produce histories claiming their respective countries to be legitimate heirs of the great national tradition. One issue dividing them was the role of the Tây Sơn uprising in the eighteenth century. For the most part, northern historiography depicted the Tây Sơn as a peasant movement "guided by leaders with a devotion to the nation, its defense and unity," while southern scholars either continued the Nguyễn dynasty's refusal of legitimacy to the Tây Sơn or, like Trần Trọng Kim, accepted the legitimacy of Nguyễn Huệ as emperor after

1788 (to preserve order after the Lê had fled to China) but not as rebel.[21]

Partition in 1954 brought polarization in institutions and ideologies without questioning the unity of the national past. In the Democratic Republic of Việt Nam (North Việt Nam, DRV) the Research Committee of 1953 bifurcated in 1959 into separate entities, the Institute of History and the Institute of Literature, the former dedicated to harmonizing debates into "a smooth and seamless narrative," authored by committee, revealing the progression of the ancient Vietnamese nation through slave, feudal, and bourgeois stages to culminate in the Party's successful struggle.[22] In the South individual authors continued to vie with one another and the North in finding ancient roots for Vietnamese identity. Phạm Văn Sơn's magnum opus, *Việt sử tân biên*, echoed Ngô Sĩ Liên's findings in tracing Vietnamese origins to 2789 BCE, Lạc Long Quân, and the founding of the Hồng Bàng dynasty. Phạm Văn Sơn, however, added a further dimension to his story to distinguish Vietnamese origins even more from the Chinese. For Sơn, the Thần Nông emperor from whom Ngô Sĩ Liên had declared the Vietnamese descended was a peasant genie, who ruled over a land no less magnificent than the Chinese Shen Nong.[23] The Hồng Bàng society of Lạc was no less brilliant than that of the Yao and Shun emperors.[24]

The major links between these internally influential nationalist writers and the postwar world of Western scholarship were Lê Thành Khôi in France and Trương Bửu Lâm in the United States.[25] Khôi's *Histoire du Việt Nam: des origins à 1858* incorporated a Braudelian environmental perspective and a Southeast Asian context (he was the first Vietnamese to write a history of Southeast Asia, in 1959) into the national narrative.[26] He claimed that a fusion of Mongoloid and Austronesian characteristics had created a distinctive Vietnamese people.[27] Khôi acknowledged that the founder of Âu Lạc was of Chinese origin, though he became Vietnamese through absorption of local custom. The ability of the Lạc to resist complete domination and to fuse the best of Chinese culture with local custom paved the way for independence and the unique Vietnamese culture that developed in the tenth century, Khôi argued.[28] Lâm, who left the Institute of Historical Research in Sài Gòn for the United States in 1964, opened American eyes to what he called "the link with the past" of Vietnamese nationalism. The expressions of Vietnamese resistance to China and France that he translated seemed strikingly modern in their evocation of centuries-long national struggle.[29]

A Contested Frontier of Western Academic Discourse

English-language historiography largely discovered Việt Nam in the era of conflict between 1945 and 1975. The reaction against first French and later U.S. military operations against communist-led Vietnamese nationalism created an environment in which qualifications and nuances to the linear national narrative seemed tantamount to aiding the CIA. In seeking to explain to a bewildered U.S. public the tenacity of Vietnamese resistance, a unique identity that could be traced back to the third century BCE and the long resistance to Chinese occupiers, represented a considerable advance on international communist conspiracy theories.[30] Although the logic underlying the internal nationalist historiography and the sympathetic Western one differed, the resulting historical models look strikingly similar. Both portrayed particular characteristics of Vietnamese culture, including resistance to foreign invaders, as signifiers of the people's identity.

The more scholarly discourse in English on Việt Nam's historical identity, following the debates begun in French, approached the country either from the East Asian or the Southeast Asian area studies enterprises that took shape in the 1950s. Harvard University's China historian John Fairbank identified Việt Nam as a member of the East Asian cultural world, a place it retains today at that university. This understandable attempt to exploit Confucian commonalities did not become widespread, despite the popularization of an "East Asian" identity by Joseph Buttinger.[31] Việt Nam was eventually corralled into the Southeast Asian realm by the growing uniformity of area studies boundaries in the United States and, it must be acknowledged, by the centuries-long anxiety of Việt Nam's leaders and foreign sympathizers about absorption into the northern giant. Even scholars with training in classical Chinese, such as Alexander Woodside, O. W. Wolters, and his student John K. Whitmore, found characteristics of Vietnamese political organization and culture that resembled observed commonalities in the rest of Southeast Asia. Wolters has argued that Đại Việt political organization in the Lý dynasty reflected the shifting political centers, the *mandala,* characteristic of other Southeast Asian polities.[32] Other early Vietnamese cultural practices that were indicative of Southeast patterns included cognatic kinship patterns and the dominance of "men and women of prowess" in politics during the Trần dynasty.[33]

John Whitmore likewise found Southeast Asian characteristics in his studies of Đại Việt in the fourteenth and fifteenth centuries.[34] He has argued that following the destruction of the Mongol regime, Vietnamese political organization again began to resemble that of the rest of Southeast Asia.[35] With the eclipse of Trần power in the late fourteenth century, political organization became increasing loose, as the throne and regional princes held power by administering blood oaths.[36] Within this context, Whitmore argues, Hồ Qúy Ly, a Vietnamese man of prowess, emerged in the Thanh Hóa area and resurrected Đại Việt power.[37] The condemnation of Ly's role as a usurper by Confucian-oriented Lê dynasty historians (described by Yu Insun in this volume), "deprived history of a true rendering of the role of Hồ Qúy Ly," who saved a weak Vietnamese state from Cham aggression.[38] Esta Ungar carries Whitmore's research further, linking Hồ political theory to governmental reforms of the later Lê dynasty. She argues that Nguyễn Trãi and Lê Lợi were profoundly influenced by Hồ administrative reforms, and their vision of government based on moral righteousness conflicted with indigenous visions of leadership and order. The latter vision, embodied by the *quân thần* hereditary nobles from the Lâm Sơn area, soon triumphed, as dueling factions allowed the Mặc, Nguyễn, and Trịnh to seize power and to epitomize much of later Vietnamese imperial history.[39] Wolters, Whitmore, and Ungar well represent the school that attributes a Southeast Asian identity to political and cultural patterns observed in Vietnamese history.

Harvard's East Asian Studies approach eventually brought a fuller understanding of Chinese legal and governmental methods to the task of understanding Việt Nam's mixed heritage. Alexander Woodside's *Vietnam and the Chinese Model* nevertheless argued that Vietnamese ingenuity outlasted neo-Confucian attempts to suppress it. Even the Nguyễn court of the nineteenth century, Việt Nam's most centralized and Sinophile, was never able fully to apply the blueprint of the Qing dynasty, its avowed model. The dynasty's founder, Nguyễn Ánh, had only a weak mandate to rule because of his controversial method of using Thai and French power to defeat the Tây Sơn rebels and unify Việt Nam in 1802. His personal mystique ended with his death, and his successor faced a fracturing of power. Emperor Minh Mạng (1820–41) concluded, in Woodside's summary, "that the comprehensive application of long-descended Chinese bureaucratic techniques and formulas were the historic key to the restoration of a unified, centrally-ruled political society after centuries of disunity."[40] In tracing this process, Woodside acknowledged that the Nguyễn adaptation reflected a disjunction between a high-center affinity for Chinese cultural influence and a Vietnamese population attached to its local practices. Describing Việt Nam as a crossroad of the Southeast Asian crossroad, Woodside highlights the means by which the Nguyễn rulers refined the Chinese model to fit local circumstances, particularly in foreign relations.[41] Although Woodside framed Việt Nam as a part of Fairbank's Chinese World Order, his meticulous research and nuanced analysis has given the study a durability bearing testimony to his refusal to reify any one of Việt Nam's varied heritages.[42]

The first of the important post-1975 studies of premodern Việt Nam, Keith Taylor's *Birth of Vietnam*, strongly influenced by sympathy with the nationalist model, traces Việt Nam's evolution from a "preliterate society within a 'South Sea' civilization into a distinctive member of the East Asian world."[43] By tracing the emergence of a unique Vietnamese identity in the tenth century, Taylor mediated between Vietnamese historians' conceptions of the timeless character of their own history and Sino-centric understandings of Việt Nam as a variation on the Chinese theme. He highlighted the emergence of a new Vietnamese consciousness during the period of Chinese rule, the success of this consciousness in ejecting the Chinese in the tenth century, and the distinctive cultural forms that were later manifest.[44] Although careful to document the gradual emergence of national self-consciousness, this early writing can be read as interpreting non-Chinese norms that survived the Chinese period as timeless "Lạc-Việt" characteristics that lay dormant during Chinese rule.[45]

The Vietnamese Nation and the *Nam Tiến* Paradigm

Early in the twentieth century, Phan Bội Châu characterized Vietnamese society as one with "numbers of talented [men] who, since the beginnings of the country, all had the heart and soul that made possible the progression southward."[46] This *nam tiến* (southward movement) narrative, generally stated, describes the fulfillment of the destiny of the S-shaped Vietnamese nation through gradual conquest and village migration southward.[47] As Vietnamese moved southward, they brought with them their unique culture, which was protected by the villages and ensured the homogeneity of the country. The neatness of this *nam tiến* narrative, however, was undermined by the fact that much of this expansion was attributable to the Nguyễn family during a period of civil war.

Nationalist and socialist historians of the older school tended to portray the early Lê period (1428 to 1527) as the pinnacle of Vietnamese imperial history and the following period of division between de facto Trịnh rulers in the north and Nguyễn in the south as a (two-century-long) aberration. This genre of writings by both Vietnamese and Western scholars claims the massive territorial expansion of the southern kingdom (Cochin China, or Đàng Trong) in the seventeenth and eighteenth centuries as a collective Vietnamese achievement, even while condemning or marginalizing the southern rulers as schismatic. The *nam tiến* framework was destiny, the political fragmentation only temporary. The Lê success in the fifteenth century in driving out the Ming, establishing centralized control, reorganizing the state on a new fiscal basis, and acquiring Cham land through military victories distinguished this dynasty as the greatest in Vietnamese history.[48] However, the period of its glory was virtually restricted to the fifteenth century, while the ruinous civil wars of the sixteenth century and the regional fragmentation of the seventeenth and the eighteenth appear to contradict the grand narrative. Part of the logic behind the veneration of the Lê dynasty in nationalist historiography has been to condemn the southern Nguyễn rulers of Đàng Trong. The seventeenth and eighteenth centuries were typically portrayed as a period in which the rival Trịnh and Nguyễn families usurped imperial power. Trần Trọng Kim described the period as one in which the Trịnh and Nguyễn each "stole a direction. . . . From then on, the mountains and the rivers were separated, South and North divided—that was a distinct period in the history of [the] country."[49] Socialist historians likewise condemned the period of division but did not resolve the tension between a positive view of the *nam tiến* narrative and a negative one of the Nguyễn family, which had presided over most of it.

During the modern civil war between the North and the South, historians from the southern Republic of Việt Nam (RVN) resolved this tension in favor of the Nguyễn, depicting the family's role as strictly defensive. The perpetrators of the division of the lands and the waters were not them but the Trịnh and the Mạc families. The Nguyễn ancestors fought bravely to rescue the Lê from the Mạc only to have the Trịnh seize power and eject the Nguyễn from the north. Nguyễn Hoàng went south because of Trịnh Kiểm's greed; he wanted to send the talented young man away to "remove the thorn in his eye."[50] Not long after Hoàng's arrival, Phạm Văn Sơn argued, "Thuận hóa had markets, the streets and aid societies were prosperous in business, and it became a society in which countries from near and far (even countries in the West) came to trade. Under Hoàng's regime taxation also was light; [the people] could breath easily. Because of that, the people gave Hoàng the appellation the 'Ephemeral Lord' [chúa tiên]."[51] In this southern version of the nam tiến narrative, the Trịnh were the usurpers, and the Nguyễn family was merely reacting to Trịnh aggression. Similarly, Phan Khoang's Việt sử xứ Đàng Trong (The Southward Movement of the Vietnamese People), the first historical study of the southern realm, defended Nguyễn family actions in Đàng Trong.

To justify nationalist understandings of the uniqueness of Vietnamese culture and society, Vietnamese and Western scholars created an identity myth that transcended time and space. The notion that a multiethnic southern realm developed apart from the northern state contradicted the myth that Việt Nam was a distinct whole since time immemorial, only torn asunder by poor administration and voracious regents and generals. Thus, even southern scholarship sympathetic to the Nguyễn family's contribution to the nam tiến movement necessarily wrote the multiethnic dimension of southern history out of the narrative. Cham and Cambodian history ended where Vietnamese history began.[52] Western scholars writing almost half a century after the Vietnamese nationalists could not ignore the context of a war widely seen as anti-imperial. The defeat of technologically advanced American forces by Vietnamese guerilla fighters suggested a cultural cohesiveness Western historical writings sought to explain and celebrate.[53] Although Vietnamese and Western scholarship might have been manifested in different forms, their products built and supported a national narrative appropriated by the contemporary government.[54]

Revising the *Nam Tiến* Narrative: Australian and American Perspectives

The last two decades have witnessed a reaction against this grand narrative of the nation, most evident in Australia and the United States. A third generation of historians trained at Cornell and the Australian National University cautiously deconstructed the framework their teachers had done much to build. More distant from the war, they were more open to multiple understandings of Việt Nam's historical identity and the *nam tiến* narrative. A key figure in promoting the new revisionism has been Keith Taylor, both through his own scholarly transition and the students he has influenced at Cornell University. The 1991 symposium that led to the publication of Taylor and Whitmore's *Essays into Vietnamese Pasts*, debating various texts and their messages, was instrumental in this transition process. This group of essays "undermined the idea of a single Vietnamese past," in Taylor's words.[55] Meanwhile in Việt Nam, France, and Australia, other scholars, drawing from local sources and Chinese and Southeast Asian discourses, began to rewrite the *nam tiến* paradigm.

A consequence of this emphasis on the localization theme in Vietnamese history has been the revision of dynastic orthodoxy and the *nam tiến* narrative, taken yet further in several chapters of this book. Đinh Khắc Thuân, a Paris-trained Việt Nam scholar based in Hà Nội, rehabilitates the Mạc as a dynasty of great importance in Vietnamese history. Using a corpus of stele inscriptions and Chinese and Vietnamese sources, Thuân's PhD dissertation thoughtfully highlights the administrative and governmental contributions of the Mạc period, including the collecting and promulgation of the various statutes and cases in the [*Book*] *of Good Government* (*Hồng Đức thiện chính [thư]*).[56] Significantly, Thuân is one of the first scholars to use stele inscriptions in historical research.[57] His meticulous use of these sources enables a nuanced understanding of local factors in early modern Vietnamese history.

The work of contemporary scholars on the development of the southern domain in the seventeenth and eighteenth centuries pioneered a dynamic and positive picture of the southern realm, symbolized by the adoption of the name it had called itself: *Đàng Trong* (inner region).[58] In the first Western-language studies to reintegrate the history of the southern state as a successful state experiment, Yang

Baoyun and Li Tana argue convincingly that the two hundred years of the family's rule provided a stable foundation for their imperial successors.[59] Yang's study highlights the ways in which the Nguyễn family successfully drew on Chinese, Southeast Asian, and local religious and governmental influences to establish a dynamic, internationally engaged state in the South.[60] In her study, Li Tana demonstrated the pluralistic and Southeast Asian economic, social, and cultural features of Đàng Trong society. She argues that Nguyễn Hoàng's successful localization mechanisms enabled the family to develop "a new way of being Vietnamese."[61] On the one hand, Nguyễn ability to localize indigenous traditions allowed for territorial and financial success. On the other hand, the Nguyễn inability to establish a centralized bureaucratic system like that of their successors in the nineteenth century led to the collapse of Đàng Trong society. Li Tana's Canberra colleague Nola Cooke pushes further the analysis of Đàng Trong society as the basis for much of the strength of the nineteenth-century Vietnamese state.[62]

Another strand in revisionist scholarship was a critical deconstruction of colonial and nationalist narratives of Vietnamese identity. Cooke applies Edward Said's theories in a critical examination of colonial perceptions of Vietnamese cultural identity, which she calls the "little China fallacy."[63] Most recently Patricia Pelley, in *Postcolonial Vietnam: New Histories of the National Past* (2002), traces the foundations of the historical institutions of the Democratic Republic of Việt Nam to the need to create an independent history of the new nation. In the most vigorous challenge to existing perceptions of the Vietnamese past, Keith Taylor links a revision of the *nam tiến* narrative with a historiographical deconstruction in an article subtitled "Beyond Histories of Nation and Region." Taylor suggests that the histories of speakers of Vietnamese should be studied as "correlations between the specificities of time and place and the vicissitudes of human thought and practice."[64] Through examining six different military conflicts since the Lê uprising against the Ming forces in the fifteenth century, Taylor provides a complex critique of the ways in which events in individual Vietnamese lives were incorporated into a national myth in the twentieth century.[65] Some of the problems inherent in thus dethroning nation and region in the study of Vietnamese quickly emerge in his suggestion that one focus instead on those who spoke Vietnamese across time and space, despite the great variations found in the spoken and written vernacular, *chữ nôm*.[66]

Borderless Histories

This book features multiple voices of several generations sharing a concern to broaden the agenda and incorporate new sources from a multiplicity of provenances. Most essays in this book are marked by an interest in crossing borders and exploring ambiguities. They seek to document voices that have been ignored or marginalized, whether those of women, subalterns, or cosmopolitan misfits. They consult the official documents of the state narrative but also exploit local, legal, Buddhist, Christian, Chinese, Thai, and a variety of European documents. They build gratefully on the foundations laid by their predecessors and teachers, but their interpretive frameworks leave more open ends, windows, and adjoining corridors than previous work.

In chapter 1, Phan Huy Lê provides a masterful summary of the existing scholarship on land-holding patterns in the village over several centuries. As he demonstrates, the role of the village as both a revolutionary base and a symbol of Vietnamese identity make it a suitable focus for historians. The most substantial precolonial records at village level in Southeast Asia in turn make innovative work possible.

The first group of essays, "Constructing Việt against a Hán World," revisit Vietnamese relations with Chinese influence, challenging traditional historiographic narratives of identity and power. Insun Yu uncovers prenationalist understandings of Vietnamese history and identity by examining the differing perspectives of the two most influential chroniclers of Đại Việt, Lê Văn Hưu and Ngô Sĩ Liên. Although both writers were preoccupied with themes of independence from China, the fifteenth-century Ngô Sĩ Liên was more concerned with Confucian orthodoxy while the thirteenth-century Lê Văn Hưu emphasized defending the country from the Mongols and asserting equality with China. Sun Laichen traces the basis for Đại Việt's remarkable fifteenth-century expansion as far as the Irrawaddy to the effective adoption of Chinese-derived military technology. He challenges the accepted notion that the Chinese adopted gunpowder technology from the Vietnamese, arguing instead that Đại Việt's manipulation of Chinese military technology enabled its expansion into the southern and western realms. Nhung Tuyet Tran's chapter subverts contemporary constructions of Vietnamese womanhood based on inheritance provisions in the Lê Code. She argues that the notion of woman as the embodiment of Vietnamese national identity relies on ahistorical constructions of Chinese women's history and a distortion of the property provisions in the code. By introducing new local empirical evidence, she demonstrates the nuanced character of the inheritance regime in the Lê Code.

The second group of essays, "Southern Pluralities," explores the particular complexity of the new territories (Đàng Trong) into which Vietnamese migrated in the sixteenth and seventeenth centuries, fragmenting the state into two while introducing new interactions with Cham, Khmer, Chinese, and Montagnard. Li Tana, whose *Nguyễn Cochinchina* blazed the trail for such studies, here argues the case for seeing the southern part of the Indochinese peninsula as a contested, open "water frontier" before the nineteenth century. The history of this "most complex and vigorous part of Việt Nam," she argues, is profoundly distorted by projecting modern national borders back into the past. This region was a world of multiple competing ports until the late eighteenth-century rise of Bangkok gave it supremacy in the gulf, while Sài Gòn became more securely part of the Vietnamese world. Charles Wheeler shows the value of uniting the usually separated histories of Cham, Vietnamese, and Chinese to understand the long-term history of an economic zone in what is today central Việt Nam. He demonstrates how Cham and Vietnamese coexistence in the eighteenth century renders a relentless *nam tiến* narrative inappropriate. Wynn Wilcox exposes the pluralism at the heart of the period in which a unified Việt Nam was constructed under Gia Long. Although colonial, nationalist, and area studies "allegories" of the period have all assumed a dichotomy between French and Vietnamese, he firmly resists temptations to read these boundaries back in time.

The last section examines "Vietnamese-European Encounters" in the fresh light of borderless history. Two of the essays reverse the Orientalist paradigm by exploring Vietnamese discoveries of Europe. George Dutton introduces us to the remarkable life of Father Philiphê Bình, a prolific Vietnamese Jesuit who spent half his life in Portugal in the early nineteenth century. Bình's writings represent the fullest precolonial Vietnamese portrayal of Europe as well as the largest surviving body of precolonial *quốc ngữ* writing. Dutton rescues Bình from the pathos of lost causes and sees him as a tireless literary innovator and recorder who explained Europe and the modern world in words he believed ordinary Vietnamese could understand. Kimloan Hill explores the participation of almost one hundred thousand Vietnamese during the First World War in Europe and the extraordinary impact this had on their lives. Hill shows how their daily experience eroded their perception of the civilized French as they witnessed firsthand racist attitudes and French military humiliation. Moreover, her meticulous research on the Vietnamese soldiers' perceptions of Americans in contrast to their French allies on the battlefield adds another dimension to Mark Bradley's seminal study of Vietnamese/American constructions of each other.[67] Finally, Pigneau de Behaine (Bá Đa Lộc), the missionary bishop who acquires a Vietnamese character in Wilcox's chapter, is revisited in J. P. Daughton's final chapter. Daughton is concerned with the use made of the Bishop of Adran after his death, as successive missionary and colonial writers forgot the ambivalence of his cosmopolitan life and turned him into an icon of colonial nationalism.

This last group of chapters suggests some of the complexity of the early encounters and mutual discoveries between Vietnamese and Europeans. Individual narratives may color national ones but can also subvert them. The histories of this tormented but richly fascinating part of the world cannot be constrained by the purposes of the present.

Notes

1. The principal landmarks for this generation of historians include Taylor and Whitmore, *Essays into Vietnamese Pasts*; Li Tana, *Nguyễn Cochinchina*; and Taylor, "Surface Orientations in Vietnam," which will all be discussed later in this volume.

2. Duara, *Rescuing History from the Nation*; Chatterjee, *Nation and Its Fragments*.

3. Thongchai Winichakul, "Writing at the Interstices," 3–4.

4. See Hucker, *China's Imperial Past*.

5. Bento Thiện, "Lịch sử nước Annam," 248–50.

6. Rhodes, *Histoire du royaume de tunquin*, 5.

7. Launay, *Histoire ancienne et moderne de l'Annam*, 37.

8. Lurô's *Cours d'administration annamite* and *Le pays d'Annam* typify the more moderate position. In these two studies Lurô argued that the Vietnamese had adopted important Chinese governmental institutions and maintained them to the eve of colonization. Likewise, Paul Ory argued that the

village in Annam was a copy of that of the Chinese and organized similarly. See also Schreiner, *Les institutions annamites*, vol. 1. For a more thorough examination of early colonial discourses on Vietnamese society as derivative of the Chinese, see Cooke, *Political Myth and the Problem of the Other*.

9. Singaravélou, *L'école française d'Extrême-Orient*, 72.

10. Louis Finôt, "Les études indochinois," 232.

11. Claude Maître, "Critique sur M. Briffaut."

12. Maspéro, *Un empire colonial français*.

13. Déloustal, "La justice dans l'ancien Annam"; Maître, "Introduction à l'ouvrage du M. Déloustal."

14. Coedès, *Histoire ancienne des états hindouisés d'Extrême-Orient*.

15. See, for example, the discussion of Nguyễn Văn Huyên later in this chapter.

16. See also Phan Bội Châu, *Việt sử vọng quốc*.

17. Trần Trọng Kim, *Việt Nam sử lược*, 27.

18. Ibid., 43. The particular venom of early DRV writers against Trần Trọng Kim arose partly because their generation had been so influenced by him; see Pelley, *Postcolonial Vietnam*, 36–40.

19. See, for example, Nguyễn Mạnh Tường, *l'individu dans la vieille cité annamite*, and Trần Văn Chương, *Essai sur l'esprit du droit*.

20. Nguyễn Văn Huyên, *La civilisation annamite*, 19–71.

21. Dutton, *Tây Sơn Uprising*, 27; Pelley, *Postcolonial Vietnam*, 37–38.

22. Pelley, *Postcolonial Vietnam*, 20–28. The most authoritative work of the institute was Viện Sử Học, *Lịch sử Việt Nam*.

23. Phạm Văn Sơn, *Việt sử tân biên*, 1:78. This work ran to seven volumes, the last published in 1972.

24. Ibid., 83.

25. Legal scholars such as Nguyễn Ngọc Huy and Tạ Văn Tài, former professors from the Sài Gon Law School and later resident at Harvard Law School, were also important transitional figures.

26. Lê Thành Khôi, *Histoire du Việt Nam*, 19. Cf. his *Histoire de l'Asie du Sud-Est*.

27. Lê Thành Khôi, *Histoire du Việt Nam*, 80.

28. Ibid., 121.

29. Trương Bửu Lâm, *Patterns of Vietnamese Response to Foreign Intervention*.

30. Among the most influential works of history in the war period were Marr, *Vietnamese Anticolonialism*; Fitzgerald, *Fire in the Lake*; and McAlister and Mus, *Vietnamese and Their Revolution*.

31. Drawing on French trends mentioned earlier, Buttinger characterized Việt Nam as a replica of the larger dragon, evident in "all aspects of Vietnamese life: in its political institutions, the people's philosophy, in literature and art, and even in the legends that attempt to describe the origins of the Vietnamese people and state." Although Buttinger also acknowledged Việt Nam's Southeast Asian origins, his narrative implied that centuries of Chinese rule transformed the Vietnamese polity into a passively Confucian one until aroused by the struggle for independence; see *Dragon Defiant*, 35.

32. Wolters, *History, Culture and Region in Southeast Asian Perspectives*, 19.
33. Ibid.
34. Whitmore, *Vietnam, Ho Quy Ly and the Ming*.
35. In the twelfth and thirteenth centuries the Trần dynasty had tried to establish a centralized bureaucratic state based on the examination system.
36. Whitmore, *Vietnam, Ho Quy Ly and the Ming*, 15.
37. Ibid., 38.
38. Ibid., vii.
39. Ungar, "Vietnamese Leadership and Order," 22.
40. Woodside, *Vietnam and the Chinese Model*, 103.
41. Ibid., 283.
42. Woodside's second Việt Nam book, *Community and Revolution in Modern Vietnam*, is yet more complex in its weaving of diverse influences and responses.
43. Taylor, *Birth of Vietnam*, xvii.
44. Ibid., especially comparing chaps. 1 and 7.
45. Note also Taylor, "Early Kingdoms," 137–81; and idem, "Authority and Legitimacy in Eleventh-Century Vietnam," 140–73, which examined the incorporation of syncretic Buddhist practices into a unique style of Lý kingship.
46. Phan Bội Châu, *Việt Nam vong quốc sử*, 73.
47. For a summary of the *nam tiến* model, see Nguyễn Thế Anh, "Le Nam Tien dans les textes vietnamiens," 121–22; and Marr, *Vietnamese Anticolonialism*, introduction.
48. Lê Thành Khôi, *Histoire du Vietnam*, chap. 5.
49. Trần Trọng Kim, *Việt Nam sử lược*, 293.
50. These are Phạm Văn Sơn's exact words: "Có ngay cái lợi là nhổ được cái gai trước mắt." Phạm Văn Sơn, *Việt sử tân biên*, 3:78.
51. Ibid., 80. Emphasis in the original.
52. See Charles Wheeler, "One Region, Two Histories," this volume. In a 1996 article, "The Vietnamization of the Cham Deity Po Nagar," Nguyễn Thế Anh explores Cham influence on Vietnamese religious practices.
53. See, for example, Taylor's preface to *Birth of Vietnam* and Marr's preface to *Vietnamese Tradition on Trial*.
54. For example, reprintings of early scholarship, including Trần Trọng Kim, and Vietnamese translations of Keith Taylor's *Birth of Vietnam*.
55. Taylor and Whitmore, *Essays into Vietnamese Pasts*, 5.
56. Đinh Khắc Thuân, *Contribution a l'histoire de la dynastie des Mặc au Việt Nam*.
57. Although Thuân's PhD dissertation was only recently filed in Paris, his methodological and historiographical impact dates at least a decade. See, for example, Nguyễn Tri An's use of Thuân's findings in his study of Vietnamese Buddhist revivalism in the seventeenth century, Nguyễn, "Ninh Phúc Temple." See also Đinh Khắc Thuân, *Văn Bia Thời Mặc*.
58. The first published use in English of the Đàng Trong terminology was in Li Tana and Reid, *Southern Vietnam under the Nguyễn*.

59. Yang Baoyun, *Contribution à l'histoire de la principauté des Nguyên*; and Li Tana, *Nguyễn Cochinchina*.

60. Yang Baoyun, *Contribution à l'histoire de la principauté des Nguyên*, 185.

61. Li Tana, *Nguyễn Cochinchina*, 99.

62. Cooke, "Regionalism and Nguyen Rule in Seventeenth-Century Dang Trong (Cochinchina)"; and idem, "Myth of the Restoration," 269–95.

63. Cooke, "Political Myth and the Problem of the Other."

64. Taylor, "Surface Orientations in Vietnam."

65. Ibid., 954.

66. Methods of writing the vernacular differ; those who wrote the vernacular in the disparate regions wrote *nôm* characters differently.

67. Bradley, *Imagining Vietnam and America*.

1

Research on the Vietnamese Village

Assessment and Perspectives

PHAN HUY LÊ

Việt Nam is an agricultural country with the majority of its population living in rural communities throughout the countryside. The village (*làng*) has played an important role in the country's historical development and remains significant in its economic transition.[1] Even with the gradual shift toward industrialization, agriculture still accounts for over a quarter of economic production in Việt Nam.[2] As the primary communities in which farmers live and work, villages play important social and cultural roles: they are the settings for major agricultural activities such as land reclamation, dike construction, water resource planning, agricultural and handicraft industry development, the preservation of local customs, and resistance. They have also played an important symbolic role in Vietnamese history. In scholarly studies as well as in the popular imagination, the village remains one of the most important symbols of Vietnamese uniqueness. The village's importance as a social and political institution in Việt Nam's historical development and its power as a sign of Vietnamese identity have interested social scientists and scholars internationally. This essay will trace the origins of the village studies field and assess the major contributions of the scholarship.

Development of the Field

Village studies began as an imperial endeavor in the late nineteenth and early twentieth centuries, when French officials identified rural areas as the key to controlling the colony and protectorates of Cochin China, Annam, and Tonkin. Recognizing that Vietnamese rural life was organized around villages, colonial officials commissioned studies that would enable the state apparatus to reach the lowest levels of society.[3] Although ostensibly studies of Vietnamese villages, the earliest French works reified Vietnamese village life based on contemporary European conceptions of Western and Eastern rural lives.[4] Limited as they were within the polarity of East and West, the studies emphasized the similarities between Vietnamese and Chinese villages. Such studies portrayed the village as a static, insular community that sharply contrasted with the dynamic European one. Though remaining within the Sinocentric framework, Camille Briffaut's more sophisticated model emphasized Vietnamese success in adapting Chinese village administration to expand its southern boundaries in the seventeenth and eighteenth centuries.[5]

In the first two decades of the twentieth century, rural unrest and administrative difficulties in the northern realms convinced colonial administrators of the importance of village control in their imperial endeavor. Vietnamese village studies were thus catalyzed by the colonial government's desperate attempt to implement rural reforms through the agrarian reform programs of 1921 and 1927.[6] On the administrative side of the reform initiatives, village conventions (*hương ước*) were required to be rewritten to conform to a standardized model.[7] On the intellectual side of the experiment, the colonial authorities encouraged and trained local scholars to identify and preserve village tradition and customary practice.[8] Perhaps unaware of French intentions, local scholars began to publish their findings in journals such as *Nam Phong* (Southern Wind), *Annam Nouveau,* and *Đông Dương Tạp Chí* (The Indochinese Journal), which formed a locus for the emergence of the public sphere in colonial Việt Nam.[9]

The proliferation of village studies in the 1930s and 1940s transformed the field as scholars diversified their inquiries into environmental factors, architectural styles, and socioeconomic, cultural, and religious subjects. Based on meticulously collected village surveys, Pierre Gourou's *Les paysans du delta Tonkinois* pioneered the anthropological study of village life. His overview of lineage, organization, and cultural and religious practices in the Red River Delta included full-color ethnographic and climatic maps, which served as an important resource for future scholars. Other local and French social scientists trained in the French tradition produced studies on land ownership, village organization, and the village economy.[10] Young local anthropologists and historians trained by the École Française d'Extrême-Orient (EFEO), notably Nguyễn Văn Huyên, Đào Duy Anh, and Nguyễn Văn Khoan, focused on the cultural life and beliefs of peasants in the Red River Delta, while southern scholars studied villages in the Mekong Delta.[11]

The end of the Second World War and the establishment of a new Vietnamese state in the North enabled Vietnamese village studies to develop under local leadership, but the French war restricted field research greatly. Between 1954, when the country was partitioned, and 1975, Vietnamese scholarship on the village diverged sharply along geographic lines. In North Việt Nam, scholarship on land ownership and village socioeconomic structures proliferated as historians linked the evolution of the economic exploitation of peasants to the emergence of the Vietnamese nation and stressed the peasants' seminal role in the historical development of the nation.[12] Other works emphasized the importance of the social revolution and resistance to foreign domination, whether Chinese, Mongol, French, or American.[13] During the same period in South Việt Nam researchers focused primarily on the annexation of the Mekong Delta and on the settlement and development of Vietnamese villages in the area.[14] Southern scholars of northern origin drew from their own memories in writing about customs and traditional beliefs.[15] Western researchers also began to produce rural case studies based on anthropological and sociological research on particular villages in the South.[16]

Following reunification in 1975 and the renovation process in 1986, two factors spurred the development of Vietnamese village studies: the opening of archival materials and interaction across state and methodological boundaries. For the first time scholars began to explore interdisciplinary approaches to village study. Changes in Việt Nam's rural areas have attracted scientists from the disciplines of

history, economics, ethnology, anthropology, and sociology. The increased flexibility of conducting field research has encouraged collaboration with foreign social scientists. The wealth of empirical
sources, such as printed Hán-Nôm books, stone stele inscriptions,
conventions, genealogies, land registers, and the Imperial Archives of
the Nguyễn dynasty, have opened new research opportunities in village studies. The opening of these sources has allowed scholars to
reach new understandings of the village in Việt Nam. Moreover, interdisciplinary methods have enriched the study of the field. For example, the incorporation of oral and folk sources into village studies
has provided new insight into rural cultural and religious life.

In state-sponsored social-science programs in Việt Nam, village
studies are intimately connected with rural studies; agricultural work
and cultural issues occupy an important place in such studies.
Between 1991 and 1995, 153 studies were produced by the ten state-
sponsored social-science and humanities programs. One such program, "The Comprehensive Development of Rural Social Economy,"
produced 11 works.[17] Although there was no separate program for
rural and village studies in the 1995–2000 period, a number of works
did address various economic, cultural, and social changes in rural
areas that affect village studies. Finally, village studies in Việt Nam
have diversified and expanded greatly. Gradually the field has
opened its doors to research on ethnic minority villages in the mountainous areas as well as on the plains.[18] The growth of Vietnamese
village studies has expanded beyond state borders as an increasingly
large number of foreign scholars continue their studies of the village,
often collaborating with local scholars in their research and rural surveys. Over the years many rural research projects conducted by foreign researchers have been published, contributing to the scholarship
on the Vietnamese village.[19] In recent years a younger generation of
foreign scholars has continued the study of the village, culminating in
several doctoral theses defended in Europe, Japan, Korea, and the
United States.[20]

Vibrant interdisciplinary collaboration in Vietnamese village
studies was manifested in a series of seminars held in Hà Nội, rural
provinces, and other cities since 1970.[21] At the First International Conference on Vietnamese Studies held in Hà Nội in July 1998, over six
hundred local and foreign social scientists presented papers, a large
number of which were devoted to village studies.[22] International

cooperation on village studies initiated a number of large-scale research projects. At Hà Nội National University, the Center for Vietnamese and Intercultural Studies continues to collaborate with Japanese researchers on a ten-year interdisciplinary research project on Bách Cốc village.[23] Initiated in 1994, the program brings together scholars from fields as disparate as geography, hydro-meteorology, biology and botany, archaeology, history, sociology, anthropology, economics, literature, and art to provide a detailed analysis of historical-social developments. Also in Hà Nội the National Center for Social Sciences and Humanities and the École Française d'Extrême-Orient (EFEO) have collaborated on village-based research projects in the Red River Delta. In the Mekong Delta scholars from the Social Sciences Institute in Hồ Chí Minh City, various southern universities, and foreign institutions are currently collaborating in rural research projects.

Advances in village studies in the last few decades question earlier models of Vietnamese villages and highlight new frontiers of research. Advances made in the study of village development, socioeconomic history, and cultural development foreshadow research opportunities yet to be explored. To place these opportunities in perspective, the remainder of this essay outlines the contributions of Vietnamese village studies in recent years and the questions this research raises for the future.

Village Establishment and Development

In popular discourse and in contemporary scholarship, two terms, *làng* (village) and *xã* (commune), are used to express the English term "village." Although the two are closely related, the difference between them is important. Under Tang rule the *xã* (commune) emerged as a basic administrative unit in the eighth century. In this period Tang rulers used the terms *hương* (*鄉*) and xã for the two major rural administrative units, the former being the larger of the two. A third rural unit, the *thôn* (*邨*), can be dated to the tenth century.[24] From the tenth to the fifteenth century, the terms *hương, giáp, xã*, and *thôn* were used to describe administrative units. How these institutions related to one another, however, remains unclear and continues to be debated by scholars. From Lê dynasty sources we know that in fifteenth-century Đại Việt one or more *thôn* could be found within a *xã* (commune), suggesting that the *thôn* would have been the smaller rural community unit.[25] In southern and central Việt Nam, the *thôn* and *ấp* were smaller units within a xã. The dynastic annals and village regulations (*hương ước*) also listed the following administrative units: *phường, sách, trang, động, trại, man, thuyền,* and *nậu.*

The word *làng* is generally found in folk songs, proverbs, and vernacular literature, but is not used in official papers such as village registries or contracts.[26] It is generally presumed that the *làng* emerged from ancient rural communities. Other terms predating *làng* include *kẻ, chạ,* and *chiêng.*[27] A defining characteristic of these villages was the virtual absence of private lands: all the land within each *làng* belonged to the village and was parceled out to each family for cultivation. Within each village lineages (*họ* or *tông*) preserved the long-term survival of the family line; sometimes villages with particularly strong lineages are termed *làng-họ.*[28]

The definitions of a *làng* vary: some consider it a community, others a residential unit in a particular area. Based on Lê and Nguyễn dynasty sources, it seems that the *làng* (Vietnamese village) was a residential community with the following general characteristics: (1) Spatially each village was comprised of a residential area, a cultivation area, and natural resources such as rivers, mountains, and ponds shared by the community. Before the imposition of state control, villages were defined by natural borders such as rivers, streams, and mountains. The extension of centralized control over villages led to the defining of borders along ownership lines. Although land registries delineated property boundaries, village borders often shifted because of the flexibility of the property regime: land could be and was sold to outsiders for cultivation. (2) Residents in a village are members of a community closely linked by blood relations, proximity, occupation, handicraft, religious beliefs, and cultural practices. (3) Each village contained a communal house for worship of village tutelary genies and an architectural complex of temples and pagodas, which together served as a center for cultural activities, the expression of shared beliefs, and village festivals. (4) Each village community was led by a council comprised of elder village notables (*hương lão*), state officials (*quan viên*), and a village headman (*xã trưởng* or *lý trưởng*) who was responsible for all village administration.

Historical change and geographic diversity have created variations of these criteria among northern, central, and southern villages in Việt

Nam. In general, however, the *làng* corresponds to one *thôn/ấp*. In the earliest villages each *xã* consisted of one *làng*, as reflected in the familiar phrase "one commune, one *thôn*" (*nhất xã, nhất thôn*), so that each administrative unit had one *thôn* (i.e., village). However, in some cases a residential unit is separated from a certain village and is not considered a *làng*.[29]

Land Ownership and Socioeconomic Structure

Recent research using new documentary evidence such as stele inscriptions, genealogies, and land registries challenges long-held assertions of village autonomy and insularity. Long described by the adage "the king's law loses to the custom of the village," (*phép vua thua lệ làng*), the traditional Vietnamese village that emerges from this research is far more complex. The village here is one in which local or community, state, and private interests influenced the transfer of authority to village, state, and private hands during the Lê and Nguyễn dynasties. This devolution of authority paralleled the almost complete transfer of communal (i.e., village-owned) lands into private hands. The frequent exchange of private property between residents of different villages suggests the relatively flexible character of the property regime and contrasts with popular notions of village insularity and endogamy. The regional variation of this process offers historical insight into the migration and integration of the Vietnamese populace in the peninsula. In particular population growth, village splintering, and the expansion of Vietnamese populations to the western and southern realms and coastal areas created differences not only in the level of land transfer but also in the kinds of villages that emerged.[30] These processes are detailed more fully in recent studies of villages in the Red River Delta and the Mekong River Delta.[31]

In 1092 the Lý dynasty (1009–1225) established land registries (*điền tịch*), marking the first time that the government penetrated the village structure and managed village communal land. During the Trần dynasty (1226–1400), the state expanded its authority over villages even further by reclassifying communal land as state land (*quan-điền*) and reserving the authority to distribute it to imperial officials. State ownership of village land was thus established, and in the ensuing years village authority over the former communal lands was relegated to management and distribution. In theory all land within the realm was now the property of the king, and the village only reserved the authority to manage it. In the fifteenth century land allocation had to comply with government stipulations (*chế độ quan điền*), and cultivators became subject to head and labor taxes, including corvée and military service for the state. The emergence of private ownership of land diminished village authority even further as property concerns governed the relations of private individuals toward the village community.[32]

With the establishment of formal control over the entire peninsula in the nineteenth century, the Nguyễn emperors instituted the land registry system.[33] These records indicate that by the nineteenth century private ownership of land was the norm, while only 20 percent of land continued to be publicly owned in Tonkin. As table 1.1 illustrates, the proportion of land that had become privately owned dwarfed public lands. The exception is Thừa Thiên; its location as the center of Nguyễn power helps to explain why such a large proportion of the land remained in imperial hands. By contrast, in the Red River and Mekong deltas, a much smaller proportion of land was still under state ownership. Data from the Mekong Delta reveals the most significant disparity between state and private lands, with only 6.41 percent still in state hands in 1838. The settlement of the Mekong Delta in the seventeenth and eighteenth centuries and rapid expansion of the southern commodities and cash-crop industry likely kept the lands in private hands through the nineteenth century.

Data from the land registries also suggest other remarkable features of landholding patterns in the nineteenth century. First, private ownership of land was generally confined to small lots, averaging

Table 1.1. Nguyễn dynasty distribution of private/public lands

Region	Year	Percentage of public lands	Percentage of private lands	Percentage of other lands
Hà Đông	1805	14.59	65.34	20.07
Thái Bình	1805	31.43	53.24	15.33
Thừa Thiên	1815	60.87	32.10	7.03
Mekong Delta	1836	6.41	92.43	1.16

Sources: Phan Huy Lê, Vũ Minh Giang, and Phan Phương Thảo, *Địa bạ Hà Đông,* 640; Phan Huy Lê, Nguyễn Đức Nghinh, and Philipe Langlet, *Địa bạ Thái Bình,* 464; Nguyễn Đình Đầu, *Nghiên cứu địa bạ Triều Nguyễn: Thừa Thiên,* 112–13; Nguyễn Đình Đầu, *Tổng kết nghiên cứu địa bạ,* 151.

around one *mẫu* per male registered member. Second, approximately
20 percent of the landholders were women (21.79 percent in Hà Đông
and 17.52 percent in Thái Bình) and/or outsiders (19.01 percent in Hà
Đông and 21.26 percent in Thái Bình). The share held by women suggests that they were not simply disenfranchised with the advent of
the Nguyễn monarchy, and that they retained control over a sizeable
amount of private property.[34] More surprisingly, "outsiders" (*phụ
canh*) owned almost one-fifth of all private lands (22.98 percent in Hà
Đông and 22.51 percent in Thái Bình).[35] Finally, the fact that only 56.49
percent of village notables owned land suggests that local authority
and prestige were not based solely on land ownership. The preceding
patterns suggest that village hierarchies and boundaries were not
rigidly maintained but rather subject to constant negotiation.

Originally subsistence communities dependent on wet-rice agriculture, Vietnamese villages adapted to social and economic change by
combining various handicraft and trade specialties with subsistence
agriculture.[36] Gradually the processes of labor division and the development of a commodities economy differentiated villages by craft:
handicraft villages emerged alongside agricultural and trading villages.[37] Many villages were mixed: in some agricultural villages
handicraft work and minor trading provided supplementary income,
while in other villages families often cultivated land as an additional
form of production. The majority of villages fit this mixed-trade
model of agrarian-handicraft-trading village.[38] Between the seventeenth and the nineteenth century, large local markets emerged in
areas where a number of village market places intersected. These local
markets provided meeting places and satisfied the commercial needs
of daily life in rural Việt Nam.[39] The proliferation of these local
markets reflects the broadening of migration flows and economic
interaction in the last centuries of imperial rule.

Ideally villages were structurally divided into four social strata, determined by occupation and institutionalized by a local council.[40]
These four groups, the scholars (*sĩ*), peasants (*nông*), craftsmen (*công*),
and traders (*thương*), were tied together by a complex web of hierar-
chically based community relationships.[41] Mekong Delta villages,
however, differed in the level of community cohesiveness because of
the recent settlement of the area and its economic and cultural
features.[42] In the Red River Delta and areas immediately south of it,
village cohesiveness was maintained through the social institution of

the *giáp*. As the major intravillage group that organized all adult male
residents in the village, the *giáp* played an important role in village
sociocultural and religious life.[43] As a cultural institution, this *giáp*
should be distinguished from the administrative *giáp*, which historical
documents record as resembling its Chinese counterpart more closely,
particularly with respect to surveillance. In the tenth century the *khúc*
authorities renamed the Tang *hương* to *giáp*: this particular institution
was a smaller unit within the administrative *xã*. During this period
the state was divided into 314 *giáp*, some of which survived throughout the Lý, Trần, and Lê periods. In the nineteenth century the *giáp*
was once again transformed. In newly established districts such as
Kim Sơn in Ninh Bình province and Tiên Hải in Thái Bình province,
the *giáp* became a unit of the same rank as *xã*, *ấp*, and *trại*, to be
administered by the *lý trưởng*.[44] In 1890 it was formally renamed *xã*.

Administrative Apparatus

Historical research and ethnographic field work suggest that villages
were formerly autonomous entities headed by a *gia làng*, a male
leader who naturally emerged because of his experience and the prestige he enjoyed in the surrounding areas.[45] As the monarchy developed, however, the state used this natural community as a basis for its
new basic rural administrative unit, the *xã*, and replaced the *làng* with
the *thôn*. Since the imposition of state power onto the village, village
autonomy has fluctuated according to the infrastructural power of the
state. The complexity of village-state relations is manifest in the various mechanisms implemented in the past few centuries, suggesting
that cooperation and confrontation characterized the relationship.
Under the Lê and the Nguyễn, the management structure involved
two parallel systems selected at the local and state level. The first,
consisting of the village head (*xã trưởng*, renamed *lý trưởng* in 1828),
was elected by villagers in compliance with government regulations.
These leaders were then subject to approval by the district magistrate
and then granted a certificate and given a seal. Their duties included
village administration, tax collection, and the administration of corvée
and military services. The community council overseeing local
administration, called the *hội đồng kỳ mục* (literally, "council that
leads"), was a board of village notables presided over by the *tiên chỉ*,
the premier notable, and it served as the representative organ of the

community. This dual mechanism of village administration comprising an official and nonofficial system produced tension in successive state regimes, the most dramatic issue of which related to the village regulations (*hương ước*). Though represented as a convention among all members of the village community, the regulations were likely mediations between village custom, state law, and the interests of different social strata within the community.[46]

In the colonial period the French authorities identified control of the villages as the key mechanism for consolidating their power throughout the countryside and ensuring efficient tax collection. The legal reform movements of the early twentieth century advocated the reorganization of villages along "traditional" lines. The Village Reform Program had multiple goals. As its name implied, it was intended to correct the excesses of Nguyễn bureaucratic reform but also to make villages more compliant to colonial rule and to ensure the efficient extraction of resources. This political agenda was realized in 1921 with the replacement of the Board of Notables with the Board of Lineage Heads (*hội đông tộc biểu* or *hội đồng hương chính*), headed by a mutually acceptable representative, the *chánh hương hội,* and his assistant, the *phó hương hội.* Although swift protests from village notables forced the colonial authorities to reestablish the Board of Notables in 1927, the Board of Lineage Heads remained in place, duplicating the village management structure and creating confusion. Finally, to correct this confusion the colonial government replaced the former two boards with the Board of Seniors (*hội đồng kỳ hào*) in 1941.[47]

Following the August Revolution in 1945, Việt Nam's new government replaced the former institutions with the Administrative Committee (Ủy Ban Hành Chính), then the Resistance Committee, and finally the People's Council (Ủy Ban Kháng Chiến and Hội Đồng Nhân Dân) in 1954. As part of the new rural reforms of 1955–56, villages throughout the North were reorganized into grand communes. During the collectivization program of the 1950s, the cooperative movement, initially limited to the *thôn,* was progressively applied at higher levels up to the *xã* or federations of *xã.* This led to the overlap of economic management between the cooperative and the People's Committee. In the renovation (*đổi mới*) period, the state's administrative powers were transferred to the local People's Committees and disassociated from the economic aspects of production. The People's Committees' administrative powers were subsequently disassociated from economic functions in the rural areas. At the same time, the village heads (*trưởng thôn, trưởng ban* in the delta, *già làng* in the mountainous areas) were reintroduced.[48]

Cultural Life and Beliefs

In the last decade the study of village cultural and religious life has dominated anthropological research on Việt Nam as emphasis on architectural styles of communal houses (*đình*) and the worship of tutelary genii (*thành hoàng*) gained prominence.[49] Research indicates that the worship of tutelary genies was likely borrowed from Chinese practices during the Tang period, though significant distinctions exist. In China these genies often protected castles and small towns, while in Việt Nam they protected the village as an institution.[50] In many Vietnamese villages an architectural complex of temples (*miếu* and *đền*), pagodas, and the *đình* constituted the infrastructure of village cultural and religious life.[51] The presence of these varied structures within one cultural-religious complex demonstrates the symbiosis of popular religious practices and the imported faiths of Buddhism, Taoism, and Confucianism in the North as well as the integration of Cham and Khmer influences in the central and southern regions. For example, the cult of the Mother Goddess (Thánh Mẫu), especially that of Mother Goddess Liễu Hạnh, developed rapidly after the seventeenth century.[52] Village festivals celebrated in local pagodas, temples, or communal houses were celebrations of syncretic religious traditions. Organized by one or multiple villages or regionally, these festivals sometimes attracted a large number of participants annually. In recent years scholars across disciplines have contributed greatly to our understanding of these festivals.[53] As such, it may be said that the village played and continues to play an integral role in the preservation and development of cultural life.

Recent Changes in Village Structure

Almost half a century of warfare and land reform programs, including collectivization and the renovation process, has dramatically changed rural life in Việt Nam. This transformation of rural life and institutions constitutes a major area of research, with field surveys highlighting the following processes: the replacement of the cooperative program with product-based contracts (*khóan*); the emergence and development of a farm economy; increasing socioeconomic differentiation; and the resurgence of "traditional values" in village life.

Although many social scientists have explained the economic reforms in Russia and China in terms of the gradual replacement of agricultural cooperatives with small family farms and product-based contracts, research in Việt Nam indicates that internal socioeconomic factors triggered these reforms. In particular the impetus seems to have been peasants' initiatives. Collective labor as well as egalitarian distribution drove the peasants to poverty, leading to a serious socioeconomic crisis in the late 1970s and early 1980s.[54] Under these circumstances villagers secretly handed over the field plots to households on a contractual basis. This form of confidential contract, officially authorized in 1981 by directive no. 100 to become "product-based contract 100" and then in 1988 by resolution no. 10 to become "product-based contract 10," gave land to peasants for long-term use and reestablished the household economy as a production unit with business initiative.[55] Just one year after implementing "contract 10," agricultural production was restored and developed rapidly, supplying not only enough food for the population but also rice for export. Việt Nam quickly became the second largest rice exporter in the world. The Land Law issued in 1993 (with amendments and supplements made in 1998) ensured the right of peasants to long-term use, which facilitated the growth of household productivity.[56]

The emergence and development of a farm economy attracted particular attention during Việt Nam's transition toward an industrialized economy. Despite the expansion of the industrial economy since the 1990s, the number of large household farms (*trang trì*) seems to be increasing. The farm economy has grown rapidly, with individual farms averaging five hectares on the plains and tens of hectares in the highlands. Figures from 1994 indicate that there were 93,343 registered farms of three to four hectares; 18,572 farms of five to ten hectares; 1,832 farms over ten hectares; and several farms hundreds of hectares in size.[57] This concentration of commercial farming emerged as government transferred land away from forest or commercial use and from waste reclamation or topsoil leasing from poor peasants. The farm economy became quite varied, including timber and forest products, fruit trees, industrial crops, animal husbandry, fisheries, combinations of production and processing, and the use of machinery and of science and technology. Farms became small- and medium-sized commodity factories contributing to agricultural production in the period of national modernization and industrialization. Vietnamese villages are changing from a small peasant economy to one combining the small peasants with commercial farmers. This combination has a higher commodity manufacturing character and defies simple industrialization models.

Social problems have accompanied modernization.[58] Currently the government has initiated campaign programs targeting hunger elimination, poverty alleviation, and unemployment in rural areas. Sociological surveys sponsored by both government and nongovernmental agencies have tried to evaluate the extent of these social problems and to implement solutions.

Finally, the tendency of rural village communities to reinvent traditional forms of cultural, religious, and social conventions in a transnational context presents an exciting area to be researched. Traditional festivals have been reestablished nationwide, drawing celebrants and patrons from the local and international community. Family relationships have strengthened through the building or rebuilding of houses for ancestor worship. This in turn has renewed the relationship between clan branches and triggered the rewriting of genealogies in romanized Vietnamese (*quốc ngữ*). Often these endeavors are funded by overseas remittances, as local and international actors rediscover and rearticulate old traditions in a new Việt Nam. These opportunities and research themes present an exciting area of observation and scholarship.

The village's importance in Vietnamese history as the major cultural, social, and religious institution and a base of revolutionary activity underscores the importance of continued research in the field. The opening of archival resources, interdisciplinary influences, and local-foreign scholarly cooperation have ensured quality research, particularly over the past two decades. Much progress has been made in Vietnamese village studies, but recent research has raised more questions than it has answered. Although the village has often been seen as a microcosm of Vietnamese culture and society, more comparative studies of the Vietnamese village are needed, particularly regarding its relation to other Southeast Asian and East Asian villages. Việt Nam's position at the crossroad of these two cultural worlds has caused great controversy in historiography and will likely continue do so. Comparative research will only help to illuminate this complexity.[59]

Notes

1. According to the 1999 census, 76.5 percent of Việt Nam's population resides in rural areas (Cục Thông Kê, *Niên giam thông kê 1999*).

2. In 1999 agricultural production (including farming, forestry, and aquaculture) accounted for 25.43 percent of GDP. Industrial goods accounted for 34.49 percent, and the service industry accounted for 40.08 percent (ibid.).

3. One of the more notable studies was written by a scholar-official as a manual to train future administrators (Lurô, *Cours annamite*).

4. Ory, *La commune annamite au Tonkin*; Briffaut, *La cité annamite*.

5. Briffaut, *La cité annamite*.

6. Gueyfier, *Essai sur le régime de la terre en Indochine*; Rouilly, *La commune annamite*; Ngô Vi Liễn, *Nomenclature des communes du Tonkin*.

7. Bùi Xuân Đính

8. Singaravélou has argued that this project was aimed at cultivating a "disinterested intellectual."

9. Đặng Xuân Viễn, "Hương chính cải lương"; Đỗ Thiện, "Cải lương hương chính"; Hoàng Hưữ Đôn, "Cải lương hương tục"; Nguyễn Văn Vĩnh, "Le village annamite"; Nguyễn Như Ngọc, "Bàn góp về vấn đề cải lương hương chính''; Phan Kế Bính, "Phong tục Việt Nam." *Đông Dương Tạp Chí*. For more on the emergence of the public sphere in Việt Nam, see McHale, *Printing and Power*.

10. Regarding land ownership, see Vũ Văn Hiền, *La propreté communale du Tonkin*, and Vũ Văn Mẫu, *Les successions testamentaires en droit vietnamien*. For village organization, see Nguyễn Hữu Khang, *La commune annamite,* and Nguyễn Văn Huyên, *Recherche sur la commune annamite*. Regarding village economy, see Y. Henry, *L'économie agricole de l'Indochine*.

11. Examples of southern scholarship include Kresser, *La commune annamite en Cochinchine*. Regarding significant work by EFEO-trained scholars, see Nguyễn Văn Huyên, *Les fêtes de Phủ Đông*; idem, *Contribution à l'étude d'un génie titulaire annamite Li Phu Man*; idem, *Le problème de la paysannerie annamite au Tonkin*; and idem, *Le culte des Immortels en Annam*; Đào Duy Anh, *Việt Nam văn hóa sử cương*; Nguyễn Văn Khoan, *Essai sur le Dinh et le culte du Génie titulaire des villages au Tonkin*.

12. Regarding landownership and socioeconomic structures, see Phan Huy Lê, Vũ Minh Giang, and Phan Phương Thảo, *Chế độ ruộng đất và kinh tế nông nghiệp thời Lê sơ,* and Viên Kinh Tế Học, *45 Năm kinh tế Việt Nam, 1945–1990*. Regarding the peasant and historical development, see Nguyễn Hồng Phong, *Xã-thôn Việt Nam* and *Tìm hiểu tính chất dân tộc*.

13. See, for example, various articles in the Institute of History's journal, *Historical Research*. Viện Sử Học, *Tổng mục lục tạp chí Nghiên cứu lịch sử* and *Nông thôn Việt Nam trong lịch sử*.

14. Regarding annexation, see Phan Khoang, *Việt Sử xứ Đàng Trong*, and Nguyễn Văn Hầu, *Thoại Ngọc hầu và những cuộc khai phá miền Hậu Giang*. On settlement and development, see Sơn Nam, *Đồng bằng sông Cửu Long hay văn minh miệt vườn*, and Đồng Phố, *Lịch sử khẩn hoang miền nam*.

15. Nhất Thanh, *Đất là quê thói*; and Toan Ánh, *Con người Việt Nam, Nếp cũ xóm làng, Nếp cũ tín ngưỡng Việt Nam*, and *Nếp cũ hội hè đình đám*.

16. Donoghue, *My Thuan*; J. B. Henry, *Small World of Khanh Hau*; Gerald Hickey, *Nghiên cứu một cộng đồng thôn xã Việt Nam, xã hội học* and *Village in Vietnam*; Sansom, *Economics of Insurgency*; Schell, *Village of Ben Suc*; and Woodside, *Community and Revolution in Modern Vietnam*.

17. Hội Đồng lý luận tung ương, *Các chương trình khoa học xã hội cấp nhà nước 1991–2000*.

18. Bế Viết Đẳng and Nguyễn Khắc Tụng, *Người Dao ở Việt Nam*; Cầm Trọng, *Người Thái ở Tây Bắc Việt Nam*; Đặng Nghiêm Vạn and Cầm Trọng, *Các dân tộc Gia-Lai Công Tum*; Đặng Nghiêm Vạn et al., *Những nhóm dân tộc thuộc ngữ hệ Nám Á ở Tây Bắc Việt Nam*; Đặng Văn Lung, Nguyên Sông Thao, and Hoàng Văn Trụ, *Phong tục tạp quán dân tộc Việt Nam*; Ma Khánh Bằng, *Người Sánh dìu ở Việt Nam*; Mặc Đường, *Các dân tộc miền núi bắc Trung Bộ*; Ngô Đức Thịnh and Chu Thái Sơn, *Luật tục Êđê*; Nguyễn Khắc Tụng, *Nhà của các dân tộc ở trung du Bắc Bộ*; Phan Xuân Biên, *Văn hóa và xã hội người Raglai ở Việt Nam*; Phan Xuân Biên, Phan An, and Phan Văn Dốp, *Văn Hóa Chàm*; Bế Viết Đẳng, *Các Dân tộc ít người ở Việt Nam*; Viện Nghiên Cứu Văn Hóa Dân Gian, *Luật tục Mường* and *Luật tục Thái ở Việt Nam*; Viện Văn Hóa, *Văn hóa người Khmer vùng đồng bằng sôn Cửu Long*.

19. Fforde, *Agrarian Question in North Vietnam*; Houtart, *Sociologie d'une commune Vietnamienne*; Hy Van Luong, *Revolution in the Village*; Jamieson, *Understanding Vietnam*; Kerkvliet, *State-Village Relations in Vietnam* and *Land Struggles and Land Regimes*; Kerkvliet and Porter, *Vietnam's Rural Transformation*; Kleinen, "Village as Pretext" and "Sự đáp ứng với việc chuyển biến kinh tế ở một làng Bắc Bộ Việt Nam"; Nguyễn Tùng, *Mong Phu*; Sakurai Yumio, *Betonamu sonorakai no keisei*.

20. M. Grossheim, "Das traditionelle Dorf im vorkolonialen Vietnam und seine Transformation in der französichen Kolonialzeit" and "Kontinuität und Wandel in nord-vietnamesischen Dorfgemeinschaften vom Beginn der Kolonialzeit bis zum Ende der Vietnam Kriege"; Malarney, "Ritual and Revolution in Vietnam"; Misaki Shigehisa, "Nghiên cứu làng Tran Liệt"; Miyazawa Chihiro, "Nghiên cứu làng Diềm Xá"; Sim Sang Joon, "Gia đình người Việt ở châu thổ sông Hồng và mối lien hệ của nó với các cộng đồng xã hội"; and Song Jeong Nam, "Làng Yên Sơ, truyền thống và đổi mới."

21. Viện Sử Học, *Nông thôn Việt Nam trong lịch sử*; idem, *Nông thôn và nông dân Việt Nam thời cận đại*; and *Tổng mục lục tạp chí nghiên cứu lịch sử 1954–94*.

22. Đại Học Quốc Gia Hà Nội; Trung Tâm Khoa Học Xã Hội và Nhân Văn Quốc Gia: *Hội thảo quốc tế về Việt Nam học (Tóm tắt báo cáo)* / *International Conference* and *Việt Nam học, Kỷ yếu hội thảo quốc tế lần thứ nhất*.

23. Thắng Lợi commune, Vũ Bản district, Nam Định province.

24. A verse carved on a brass bell in Nhật Tảo Đông Ngạc commune, Tây Hồ district, dates to 948 CE. Phan Văn Các and Saumon, *Épigraphie en Chinois du Vietnam*.

25. Phan Huy Lê, Vũ Minh Giang, and Phan Phương Thảo, *Chế độ ruộng đất và kinh tế nông nghiệp thời Lê sơ*.

26. *Làng* is a Vietnamese term and written in the demotic script.

27. Each ethnic group also refers to this rural community with local terms such as *bản* or *mường* in northern mountainous areas and central Việt Nam, or *buôn, plây,* or *palây* in the central highlands.

28. The terms *tổng* and *họ* are the Sino-Vietnamese and *nôm* equivalent of "lineage."

29. Bùi Xuân Đính, "Bàn về mối quan hệ giữa làng và xã qua qui mô cấp xã thời phong kiến."

30. Li Tana, *Nguyễn Cochinchina*.

31. Regarding the Red River Delta, see Hy Văn Lương, *Revolution in the Village*; Trần Đức, *Nền văn minh song Hồng xưa và nay*; Vũ Tự Lập, *Văn hóa và cư dân đồng bằng song Hồng*. Regarding the Mekong River Delta, see Huỳnh Lứa, *Lịch sử khai phá vùng đất Nam Bộ* and *Góp phần tìm hiểu vùng đất nam bộ các thế kỷ XVII, XVIII, XIX*; Nguyễn Công Bình, Lê Xuân Diễm, and Mạc Đường, *Văn hóa cư dân đồng song Cửu Long*; Thạch Phương Hồ, Lê Huỳnh Lứa, and Nguyễn Quang Vinh, *Văn hóa dân gian người Việt ở nam bộ*.

32. Trương Hữu Quỳnh, *Chế độ ruộng đất ở Việt Nam thế kỷ XI–XVIII*; Vũ Huy Phúc, *Tìm hiểu chế độ ruộng đất Việt Nam nửa đầu thế kỷ XIX*.

33. Of these registries, 1,044 volumes with 16,884 registers are preserved in National Archives I (Hanoi) and 526 volumes with 1,635 registries at the Institute of Hán-Nôm Studies. See Nguyễn Đình Đầu, *Tổng kết nghiên cứu địa bạ: Nam Kỳ lục tỉnh*; idem, *Nghiên cứu địa bạ triều Nguyễn*; and Phan Huy Lê, Vũ Minh Giang, and Phan Phương Thảo, *Địa bạ Hà Đông*.

34. Tran highlights the larger size of average lots registered to women (upward of four *mẫu*) vis-à-vis men (less than one *mẫu*). She argues that the difference in average size suggests that women did not inherit property equally, as sons did (except in instances when the son was the sole heir), thus explaining the larger average property owned. In contrast, men's property holdings were smaller because of the legal mandate that families divide property equally (*quân phân*) between sons. See chap. 3, "The Gender System," and chap. 5, "The Property Regime," in Nhung Tuyet Tran, "Vietnamese Women at the Crossroads: Gender and Society in Seventeenth- and Eighteenth-Century An Nam."

35. Phan Huy Lê, Vũ Minh Giang, and Phan Phương Thảo, *Địa bạ Hà Đông*; and Phan Huy Lê, Nguyễn Đức Nghinh, and Philippe Langlet, *Địa bạ Thái Bình*.

36. Bùi Huy Đáp, *Văn minh lúa nước và nghề trồng lúa Việt Nam*.

37. Regarding handicraft villages, see Bùi Thị Tân, *Về hai làng truyền thống Phú Bài và Hiền Lương*; Bùi Văn Vượng, *Làng nghề thủ công truyền thống Việt Nam*; Chu Quang Trứ, *Tìm hiểu làng nghệ thủ công điêu khắc cổ truyền*; Phan Huy Lê, Đình Chiến, and Nguyễn Quang Ngọc, *Gốm Bát Tràng / Bát Tràng*

Ceramics; Tạ Phong Châu, Nguyễn Quang Vinh, and Nghiêm Đa Văn, *Truyện các ngành nghề*; Tăng Bá Hoành, *Nghề cổ truyền*; Trần Quốc Vượng and Đỗ Thị Hảo, *Nghề thủ công truyền thống và các vị tổ nghề*; Vũ Ngọc Khánh, *Lược truyện văn hóa truyền Việt Nam*; and Vũ Từ Trang, *Nghề cổ nước Việt Nam*. Regarding their emergence alongside agricultural and trading villages, see Nguyễn Quang Ngọc, *Về một số làng buôn ở đông bằng Bắc Bộ thế kỷ XVIII–XIX*.

38. Bùi Xuân Đính, *Lịch sử xã Đông La*; Diệp Đinh Hoa, *Làng Nguyễn*; Hồ Sĩ Giàng, *Từ thổ Đôi Trang đến xã Quỳnh Đôi*; Phan Huy Lê, Vũ Minh Giang, and Phan Phương Thảo, "Kẻ Giá, một làng chiến đấu tiêu"; and idem, "The Vietnamese Traditional Village: Historical Evolution and Socio-economic Structure"; Phan Huy Lê, "Làng xã cổ truyền của người Việt: tiến trình lịch sử và kết cấu kinh tế xã hội."

39. Nguyễn Đức Nghinh, "Chợ chùa ở thế kỷ XVII"; idem, "Mấy nét phác thảo chơ lang qua những tư liệu của các thế kỷ XVII–XVIII"; and Nguyễn Quang Ngọc, *Về một số làng buôn ở đồng bằng Bắc Bộ thế kỷ XVIII–XIX*.

40. Phan Văn Các and Salmon, *Épigraphie en Chinois du Vietnam*; Phan Huy Lê, Vũ Minh Giang, and Phan Phương Thảo, "Structure des villages vietnamiens traditionels."

41. Nguyễn Quang Ngọc, *Cơ cấu xã hội trong quá trình phát triển của lịch sử Việt Nam*; "Le village traditionel," *Études Vietnamiennes* 61 (1980) and 65 (1981); Phan Huy Lê, Vũ Minh Giang, and Phan Phương Thảo, "Vietnamese Traditional Village"; and Phan Huy Lê, "Làng xã cổ truyền của người Việt: tiến trình lịch sử và kết cấu kinh tế xã hội," in *Tìm về cội nguồn*, vol. 1.

42. Huỳnh Lứa, *Góp phần tìm hiểu vùng đất Nam Bộ các thế kỷ XVII, XVIII, XIX*; Li Tana, *Nguyễn Cochinchina*.

43. Trần Từ, *Cơ cấu tổ chức của làng Việt Nam cổ truyền ở Bắc Bộ*.

44. Nguyễn Cảnh Minh and Đào Tố Uyên, *Công cuộc khẩn hoang thành lập huyện Kim Sơn*.

45. This image of the village head resembles a phenomenon that Wolters has termed "men of prowess" in other Southeast Asian polities. See his *History, Culture and Region*.

46. Bùi Xuân Đính, *Lệ làng phép nước* and *Hương ước và quản lý làng xã*; Đỗ Khải Đại, *Hương ước xã Nam Trung*; Hồ Đức Thọ, *Lệ làng Việt Nam*.

47. This reform process is recorded in 3,360 village regulations compiled during the Rural Reform Program (*Cải lương hương chính*) (Viện Thông Tin Khoa Học Xã Hội, *Thư mục hương ước Việt Nam thời cận đại*.

48. Học Viện chính trị quốc gia Hồ Chí Minh, *Cộng đồng xã Việt Nam hiện nay*.

49. Nguyễn Duy Hình, *Tín ngưỡng thành hoàng Việt Nam*; and Nguyễn Thị Phương, *Bảng tra thần tích theo địa danh làng xã*.

50. Hà Văn Tấn, *Đình Việt Nam*; and Huỳnh Ngọc Trang, Trương Ngọc Tường, and Hồ Tường, *Đình Nam Bộ*.

51. Chu Quang Trú, *Kiến trúc dân gian truyền thống Việt Nam* and *Sáng giá chùa xưa*; Đặng Nghiêm Vạn et al., *Về tín ngưỡng tôn giáo Việt Nam hiện nay*; Hà Văn Tấn, *Chùa Việt Nam*; Trần Lâm Biền, *Chùa Việt*; Trần Quốc Vượng, *Văn hóa Việt Nam, tìm tòi và suy ngẫm*.

52. Ngô Đức Thịnh, *Đạo Mẫu ở Việt Nam.*

53. Đinh Gia Khánh and Lê Hữu Tầng, *Lễ hội truyền trong đời sống xã hội hiện đại;* Lê Tấn Nẫm, *Lễ hội cổ truyền; Kho tang lễ hội cổ truyền Việt Nam;* Viện Nghiên Cứu Văn Hóa Dân Gian, *Lễ hội truyền thống.*

54. Chử Văn Lâm, *Hớp tác hóa nôn nghiệp Việt Nam.*

55. Kerkvliet, *State-Village Relations in Vietnam.*

56. Đằng Cộng Sản Việt Nam: Ban Nông nghiệp trung ương, *Kinh tế xã hội nông thôn Việt Nam ngày nay;* and Đào thế Tuấn, *Khảo sát các hình thức tổ chức hợp tắc xã của nông dân nước ta hiện nay;* and *Kinh tế hội nông dân.*

57. Chu Hữu Quý, "Trang trại gia đình một hiện tương kinh tế xã hội mới xuất hiện trên một số vùng nông thôn nước ta."

58. Đỗ Nguyên Phương, *Những vấn đề chính tri—xã hội của cơ cấu xã hội—giai cấp ở nước ta;* and Nguyễn Phương Đỗ, *Thực tràng và xu thế phát triển có cấu xã hội nước ta trong giai đoạn hiện nay.*

59. For a Vietnamese view of Việt Nam's position in Southeast Asia, see Trung Tâm Nghiên Cứu Việt Nam Đông Nam Á, *Văn hóa Nam Bộ trong không gian xã hội Đông Nam Ă.*

Constructing Việt against a Hán World

2

Lê Văn Hưu and Ngô Sĩ Liên
A Comparison of Their Perception of
Vietnamese History

YU INSUN

Until the mid-1980s, historians in Hà Nội usually characterized Vietnamese history as a "struggle for national independence." Vietnamese history was portrayed as a fight to preserve national independence against an onslaught of foreign aggression: Chinese, French, or American. Although Vietnamese historians began to take a serious interest in reformist movements in Vietnamese history after the adoption of Đổi Mới in 1986, the "struggle for national independence" continues to be the mainstream of their perception of Vietnamese history.

The question arises, how did premodern Vietnamese view their history? There is a dearth of systematic scholarly research on this topic both within and outside Việt Nam. O. W. Wolters has published three articles on premodern Vietnamese portrayals of history.[1] A collection of articles on Ngô Sĩ Liên was recently published in Hà Nội, but most of these offer no detail on his perception of Vietnamese history.[2] To begin to address this issue, I will examine and compare the historical perspectives of two of the best-known historians in premodern Việt Nam: Lê Văn Hưu, the compiler of the *Đại Việt sử ký,* and Ngô Sĩ Liên, the compiler of the *Đại Việt sử ký toàn thư* (hereafter referred to as the *Toàn thư*).

According to the *Toàn thư*, Lê Văn Hưu received the order from Trần Thánh-Tông (r. 1258–78) to revise a certain history book, and he completed the thirty-volume *Đại Việt sử ký* in 1272. This work, which followed the format of the *Zi zhi tong jian,* by Si Ma Guang, covered Vietnamese history from the beginning of Triệu Đà's reign in the late third century BCE to the end of the Lý dynasty (1225).[3] However, considering that the *Toàn thư*, which was based mainly on the *Đại Việt sử ký*, comprises only fifteen volumes, Japanese scholars tend to think that the *Đại Việt sử ký* was most likely much smaller than the reported thirty volumes. It is unlikely that Ngô Sĩ Liên would have edited a thirty-volume *Đại Việt sử ký* down to a mere fifteen-volume *Toàn thư*.[4]

The *Toàn thư*, which was modeled after Si Ma Qian's *Shi ji*, provides a chronological historical narration beginning with the legendary Hồng Bàng dynasty (2888 BCE?) and continuing to the founding of the Lê dynasty in 1428. In 1460 Lê Thánh-Tông (1460–97) issued a royal edict ordering Confucian officials to compile an official national history. The edict called for the collection of all unofficial histories and historical materials held in private collections; these documents were to be brought to the palace, where they would be edited by Confucian officials into an official national history and stored in the Eastern Pavilion (Đông Các). Although Ngô Sĩ Liên initially participated in the compilation of these documents, his father's death forced him to leave his post temporarily. When he returned, the compilation had already been completed. Ngô Sĩ Liên compiled his own national history by editing Lê Văn Hưu's *Đại Việt sư ký*, comparing Vietnamese royal historical records with unofficial histories and referencing Chinese documents. The new fifteen-volume *Đại Việt sư kỳ toàn thư*, which is composed of the "Ngoại Kỷ" (Preliminary Part), the "Bản Kỷ" (Principal Part), and the "Lê Thái Tổ Kỷ" (Record on Lê Thái-Tổ), was presented to Thánh-Tông in 1479. Unfortunately the official national history stored in the Eastern Pavilion was lost; only the *Toàn thư* was passed on to future generations.[5] The history of the Lê dynasty (1428–1788) was written by subsequent historians, the book being titled the *Đại Việt sử ký tục biên* (A Sequel to the *Toàn thư*).

The *Đại Việt sử ký* and the *Toàn thư* provide very useful source materials for understanding the premodern Vietnamese view of history, since they were compiled by single authors. Just like Si Ma Guang in the *Zi zhi tong jian* and Si Ma Qian in the *Shi ji*, Lê Văn Hưu and Ngô Sĩ Liên express their own opinions about historical incidents and historical figures. Through such commentaries and evaluations the historical perspectives of Lê Văn Hưu and Ngô Sĩ Liên become clear. The other historians who wrote the *Đại Việt sử ký tục biên* inserted no personal comments.

Lê Văn Hưu has included 30 commentaries in his work, while Ngô Sĩ Liên wrote approximately 170 such commentaries. Ngô Sĩ Liên included 86 commentaries on Vietnamese historical events up to the Lý dynasty—56 more than Lê Văn Hưu in his *Đại Việt sử ký*. There are fifteen cases where Lê Văn Hưu and Ngô Sĩ Liên wrote commentaries on the same historical incident. A comparison of such cases can be very instructive. In general there are more differences than similarities between the two authors' historical perspectives, differences deriving mainly from the different historical context in which Lê Văn Hưu and Ngô Sĩ Liên lived.[6]

Several questions also arise in relation to the compilation of the *Đại Việt sử ký* and the *Toàn thư*. Why did Lê Văn Hưu choose Triệu Đà as the starting point for his narrative of Vietnamese history? Why did Ngô Sĩ Liên, in contrast, go all the way back to the Hồng Bàng period when choosing a starting point for his historical work? Furthermore, why did Ngô Sĩ Liên write the *Toàn thư* when an official national history had already been compiled in accordance with Thánh-Tông's edict?

Lê Văn Hưu

Lê Văn Hưu was born in Thanh Hóa province in 1230 and died in 1322 at the age of ninety-three. He passed the *tiến sĩ* at the national examination in 1247 when he was eighteen years old. After serving at several different governmental posts, Lê Văn Hưu became the director of the Office of Historiographers (*chưởng sử quan*), while at the same time serving as minister of war. Here we should raise the question, What was going on in the Trần dynasty between 1230 (the year of Lê Văn Hưu's birth) and 1272, when Lê Văn Hưu completed the *Đại Việt sử ký*?

One of the most important historical events during this period was the Mongol invasion in 1257. Although the Mongol forces captured the capital of Thăng Long (located on the site of present day Hà Nội), the Trần court drove them back with the help of Trần Quốc Tuấn, who was later known as Hưng Đạo Vương. With the Mongol appointment of Trần Thánh-Tông in 1261 to the post of An Nam Vương and other such acts, the relations between the Mongols and the Trần dynasty were normalized, and diplomatic envoys were frequently exchanged between the two countries. Nevertheless, the Trần dynasty continued to be seriously concerned about the possibility of another Mongol invasion. In 1271 the Mongols, who had adopted the dynastic name Yuan, demanded that Trần Thánh-Tông visit and pay his respects directly to the Yuan emperor. The following year Mongol ambitions were further revealed when a Yuan diplomatic envoy was dispatched to inquire about the "bronze post" that was said to have been set up by General Ma Yuan of the Later Han as a marker for the Han southern territorial boundary after the general had suppressed the resistance by the Trưng sisters in 42 CE.

Trần Thánh-Tông, who had experience fighting the Mongol invasion as a crown prince, could not help but be concerned about future invasions. Furthermore, the decision of Trần Thái-Tông (r. 1225–58) to pass the throne to Thánh-Tông in 1258 and to restrict himself to the supervision of important issues as "senior emperor" was probably directly related to the Mongol threat. The earlier introduction of the senior emperor system by Trần Thủ Độ, in many ways the real founder of the Trần dynasty, had been motivated by concern that disputes over royal succession could cripple the country during times of national crisis.

The Trần dynasty was essentially an oligarchy of the Trần clan, which practiced intermarriage among its members to prevent other clans from acquiring power. The governing ideology of the Trần dynasty was Buddhism, while Confucianism was used as a tool in the selection of government officials.

Ultimately the royal edict ordering Lê Văn Hưu to compile a national history must be understood in terms of the Trần clan's efforts to solidify its power and learn something from Việt Nam's past history to preserve the dynasty's independence. It is natural then, given the impending threat of the Mongol invasion, that Lê Văn Hưu would decide to focus his work, the *Đại Việt sử ký*, on Việt Nam's equality with and independence from China.

Lê Văn Hưu's choice of Triệu Đà's Nam Việt as the starting point for Vietnamese history is directly related to this theme of Việt Nam's equality with China. This is illustrated by the following historical legend. In 196 BCE, after Gao Zu of the Han dynasty had unified China, a Chinese emissary named Lu Jia was sent to invest Triệu Đà with the title King of Nam Việt. When Triệu Đà met the emissary, he asked, "Who is greater, me (Triệu Đà) or Gao Zu of the Han?" When Lu Jia replied that Gao Zu of the Han, who governs a vast empire, is surely the greatest, Triệu Đà said, "Had I been born in China would I not be just as great as the Gao Zu?"[7] After the empress Lu took control of the Han dynasty, relations between the Han dynasty and Nam Việt became strained. In 183 BCE Triệu Đà changed his title to Vũ Đế (emperor) and asserted his equality with the Han emperor. After Wen Di was enthroned in the Han, Triệu Đà officially paid proper respects as a vassal of China, but he did not abandon his view that Nam Việt was equal to China. Inside Nam Việt, Triệu Đà continued to call himself "emperor." Even though Nam Việt was officially a vassal of China, it was so in name only. Nam Việt agreed to this designation simply to avoid unnecessary conflict with the Han dynasty.

Lê Văn Hưu, who was living in a Đại Việt menaced by the potential invasion of Yuan China, undoubtedly was troubled over how the country could maintain its independence and avoid humiliation in diplomatic relations. Thus Triệu Đà must have seemed like an ideal historical figure to Lê Văn Hưu.[8] Triệu Đà had handled the threat of Han China without sacrificing his belief in Việt Nam's equality with China or unnecessarily ruffling any diplomatic feathers. Indeed, Triệu Đà would have appeared to be the true founding father of Việt Nam. Of course, Lê Văn Hưu would have known about other legendary Vietnamese leaders who ruled long before Triệu Đà. Yet these early figures would have appeared pale in comparison to Triệu Đà because of his adept defiance of China. These early Vietnamese rulers were content with the title of king and did not pursue the rank of emperor.

In one of his commentaries on Triệu Đà, Lê Văn Hưu writes that the most important attribute of a ruler is not how much land he controls or where he was raised but whether he possesses "virtue" (đức).[9] Lê Văn Hưu is refuting the emissary Lu Jia's notion that the amount of land and the number of vassals a ruler controls are important factors in evaluating his merits. Here, the "virtue" to which Lê Văn Hưu refers is not really a Confucian notion of virtue. Instead it is the virtue of a sovereign who called himself "emperor"; the virtue of a ruler who can maintain a relatively equal relationship with China while at the same time humbling himself to protect his country. When Lê Văn Hưu insists that Vietnamese rulers, including Thánh-Tông of the Trần dynasty, should follow the example of Triệu Vũ Đế, he means that, just like Triệu Đà, Vietnamese rulers should protect the sovereignty of Việt Nam while at the same time skillfully responding to Chinese power.

The historical date that Lê Văn Hưu sets to mark Việt Nam's independence from China clearly reflects his underlying interest in the theme of equality with China. Lê Văn Hưu did not select the year 939, when Ngô Quyền designated himself as king after defeating the army of the Southern Han a year earlier. Instead Lê Văn Hưu chose 966, when the Period of the Twelve Lords ended with Đinh Bộ Lĩnh's unification of the country and his ascension to the throne. The name of the resultant country was Đại Cồ Việt, and its capital was set in Hoa Lư.[10] Lê Văn Hưu recognizes Ngô Quyền's noteworthy accomplishments in expelling the Southern Han army and stopping any subsequent Chinese advances into Vietnamese territory. However, Lê Văn Hưu criticizes Ngô Quyền for being content with the position of king.[11] Specifically Ngô Quyền did not institute a reign title or raise himself to the rank of emperor. Lê Văn Hưu concludes that Ngô Quyền was unable to completely restore Nam Việt's legitimacy. For Lê Văn Hưu, Đinh Bộ Lĩnh, not Ngô Quyền, is the courageous sage sent down from heaven to help Việt Nam. Đinh Bộ Lĩnh was talented enough to force the twelve lords into submission with a single stroke, while he rose to the rank of emperor and restored the legitimate tradition of Triệu Vũ Đế.[12]

Since Lê Văn Hưu prized Vietnamese independence so highly, it is not surprising that he would criticize historical figures who were in any way responsible for the loss of such autonomy. Nam Việt's prime minister Lư Gia is a prime example of the kind of figure Lê Văn Hưu targeted for criticism. The prime minister started an insurrection when Ai Vương (112 BCE) and his mother Empress Dowager Cù would not heed his advice. (Lư Gia had advised the king not to allow Nam Việt to become a feudal vassal of Han China.) Lư Gia assassinated the king, the empress dowager, and China's senior representative and placed his own son-in-law on the throne. However, Lư Gia's insurrection became a pretext for China's first forceful invasion of Việt Nam. Lê Văn Hưu praises Lư Gia's advice that Việt Nam should avoid becoming China's vassal. However, he describes Lư Gia's killing of the king and his failure to sacrifice his own life to protect the country as unpardonable sins.[13] Lê Văn Hưu's critical evaluation of Lư Gia clearly reflects his concern with independence.

Even historical figures who struggled fiercely against China but did not ultimately achieve independence received adverse comment from Lê Văn Hưu. An example is Lý Bổn, who attempted in vain to win independence from Chinese control. In 541 Lý Bổn led a resistance movement against the tyrannical governor of Giao Châu during the Liang dynasty's occupation of Việt Nam. In the name of recovering the legitimate tradition of Emperor Triệu Đà, Lý Bổn designated himself emperor of Nam Việt, and named his country Vạn Xuân. However, Lý Bổn was defeated by the Liang general Chen Ba Xian and escaped to live among remote ethnic minorities. He eventually died of natural causes.

Contemporary Hà Nội scholars hold Lý Bổn in high esteem; Lý Bổn's struggle is said to have enhanced Vietnamese nationalism and opened the door for future independence movements.[14] Lê Văn Hưu, however, criticizes Lý Bổn rather harshly. Even though he commanded fifty thousand troops, Lê Văn Hưu points out, Lý Bổn could not protect his country. In the end, he quips, Lý Bổn was just an "average" general.[15] Nevertheless, Lê Văn Hưu seems to express genuine regret that Lý Bổn did not win Vietnamese independence, writing that it was the rebel's misfortune that he had to face a skilled military tactician like General Chen Ba Xian.

Lê Văn Hưu's evaluation of Trưng Trắc and Trưng Nhị is an exception to this rule. Even though these two sisters' fight against the Chinese ended in defeat, Lê Văn Hưu reserves high praise for them. In 40 CE the Trưng sisters led the first large-scale movement against Chinese rule; their revolt spread throughout the country as the people responded to their call. Lê Văn Hưu likens the Trưng sisters' deeds to the great works of the supreme ruler.[16] More likely than not, he was thinking about the possibility of Yuan China's aggression when he wrote this commentary about the Trưng sisters. Furthermore, the Confucian scholar Lê Văn Hưu may have been implying that if women struggled fiercely for Việt Nam's independence, men should be doing even more to protect the country from invasion.

Lê Văn Hưu's serious concern for the preservation of an independent Việt Nam can be seen in his comparison of the Former Lê dynasty's founder Lê Hoàn (r. 980–1005) and the Lý dynasty's founder

Lý Công Uẩn (r. 1009–28). When Lê Hoàn decided to expand his role beyond that of regent of the Đinh dynasty's young emperor Đinh Toàn to include the position of viceroy, Prime Minister Nguyễn Bặc and another high official, Đinh Điền, became suspicious of his intentions. They took up arms against Lê Hoàn but were removed from power. Capitalizing on Việt Nam's internal strife, China's Song dynasty decided to invade. However, after Lê Hoàn ascended to the throne in 980, he confronted and crushed the Chinese at Bạch Đằng River the following year. Lê Hoàn is often compared favorably with Lý Công Uẩn because he resolved domestic strife promptly while at the same time strengthening the country and repelling the Chinese with a spectacular show of force. On the other hand, those who prefer Lý Công Uẩn point out that he was chosen by the people to be their ruler because of his good deeds and commanding dignity. Although Lê Văn Hưu would not comment on which ruler was "better," he believed that Lý Công Uẩn's dynasty lasted much longer than Lê Hoàn's because of Lý Công Uẩn's virtues.[17] Here Lê Văn Hưu is implying that even in a difficult situation (like that of the Trần dynasty under the threat of Mongol attack), it is crucial for a ruler to have the support of his people if the dynasty is to last.

From Lê Văn Hưu's perspective, Lê Hoàn's inability to extend his reign over a long period of time is a significant shortcoming. One of the main reasons Lê Hoàn's dynasty was cut short was that he did not choose a successor early on. After Lê Hoàn died, a struggle for the throne ensued that eventually destabilized the country.[18] Trung-Tông, who managed to capture the throne after a political struggle, had been king for only a few days when he was killed by his younger brother, Long Đĩnh, whose reign was called Ngọa Triều (1005–9). Lê Văn Hưu concluded that Long Đĩnh's atrocious acts cut short the lifespan of the Former Lê dynasty.

Indeed, Lê Văn Hưu criticized the Lý dynasty sovereigns for not selecting their heirs early in the reign, thereby failing to counter internal political strife.[19] It was customary that a Lý emperor designate on his deathbed "the most talented courageous person" to succeed him.[20] The practice of primogeniture did not become established until the subsequent Trần dynasty. Even then its practice was largely restricted to the royal family and remained virtually unknown among commoners.

Criticizing Đinh Bộ Lĩnh for having had five queens, Lê Văn Hưu lamented that the influence of this "bad precedent" continued through the dynasties of the Former Lê and the Lý.[21] Of course, Đinh Bộ Lĩnh and Lê Hoàn, as well as earlier rulers in the Lý dynasty, had deliberately married many queens in an attempt to consolidate power through marriage alliances with powerful local clans.[22] Even though Lê Văn Hưu was probably aware of the intentions underlying Đinh Bộ Lĩnh's multiple marriages, the historian nevertheless criticized his actions. It is likely that Lê Văn Hưu was concerned about political instability during succession crises.[23]

Lê Văn Hưu also criticized Lý Công Uẩn for merely bestowing "king" status on his father.[24] Since Tai Zu of China's Song dynasty had given his father "emperor's status," Lê Văn Hưu asserted that Lý Công Uẩn was engaging in self-demeaning behavior and should have bestowed higher status on his own father. Underlying these criticisms is the historian's continuing concern with the issue of equality with China.

Since Lê Văn Hưu's main concern was the preservation of a strong independent Việt Nam, any act that jeopardized these goals was condemned. This is undoubtedly the reason he criticized Ngô Quyền's son Xương Văn. Xương Văn was given good marks for forgiving his maternal uncle Dương Tam Kha, who had once usurped the throne, and for being tolerant of the arrogance of his elder brother, Xương Ngập. Yet when Xương Văn invited back Xương Ngập, who had been in exile during Dương Tam Kha's reign, to rule the dynasty jointly, Lê Văn Hưu was critical, arguing that Xương Văn's overly forgiving and lenient actions were the very reason the dynasty could not properly succeed.[25] Lê Văn Hưu's criticism of Lý Thái-Tông (r. 1028–54) for his lenience to Trí Cao, son of the Tai chief Nùng Tồn Phúc, can also be understood in this light.[26] Lý Thái-Tông had executed Nùng Tồn Phúc for instigating a rebellion in 1042 but out of pity allowed Tri Cao, who had been captured alive, to retain his official post. In spite of all this Trí Cao rebelled again the following year. Lê Văn Hưu concluded that Lý Thái-Tông's failure to execute or exile Trí Cao was the result of the Buddhist concept of "lesser benevolence" (*xiao ren* in Chinese).[27] He says that Lý Thái-Tông had been oblivious to what should have been his ultimate concern: protecting the dynasty. Lê Văn Hưu's negative evaluation may in part spring from a concern that China could have taken advantage of the Lý dynasty's internal conflict and launched an invasion.

Lê Văn Hưu's criticism of Lý Anh-Tông (r. 1138–75) was also centered on that ruler's harm to the dynasty.[28] Anh-Tông sent his army to invade Champa and installed a new king there. When he heard that his new king had been expelled by a rival, Anh-Tông immediately gave full recognition to this rival king. This act, according to Lê Văn Hưu, ultimately caused severe damage to the Lý dynasty because it was this rival who later invaded Việt Nam.

On the other hand, Lê Văn Hưu gave a favorable evaluation of anyone, even Chinese, who contributed to the stability of Việt Nam. His treatment of Shi Xie (Sĩ Nhiếp in Vietnamese) and Gao Pian is a case in point. As the prefect of Chao Chi of the Wu dynasty, Shi Xie prevented Sun Quan's direct intervention in Việt Nam by sending him valuable products from the southern sea. Lê Văn Hưu commented that even though Shi Xie did not have the strength of Triệu Vũ Đế and was forced to serve the Wu, he was wise enough to protect the territorial autonomy of Việt Nam.[29] In yet another example the historian praises Gao Pian, who saved Việt Nam from Nan Zhao's invasion during the turbulent period of the late Tang dynasty. He proclaimed that Gao Pian was the wisest person of his time.[30]

In addition to his concern for the stability and autonomy of Việt Nam, Lê Văn Hưu's comments reveal his Confucian values. A case in point is his claim that Lý Công Uẩn did not place high enough priority on building the ancestral temple (tông miếu) and honoring the guardian deities of the state (xã tắc) after moving the capital to Thăng Long. Instead, Lê Văn Hưu lamented, Lý Công Uẩn built and restored numerous Buddhist temples in both the capital and the countryside.[31] According to Lê Văn Hưu, Lý Công Uẩn wasted valuable resources and manpower during a time when he should have been frugally engaged in empire building. Was Lê Văn Hưu unaware that Lý Công Uẩn rose to the throne with the strong support of the Buddhists, or did he make such comments despite such knowledge? It is most likely that he understood the stakes involved. Although there had been bureaucrats selected through a Confucian examination process since the beginning of the Trần dynasty, their role in the court had been limited. Bureaucrats, however, became more prominent when they proved necessary during diplomatic contacts with Yuan China after the latter's first invasion. These bureaucrats eventually came to oppose the Trần dynasty's Buddhist-oriented policy, and they began to search for a new ruling paradigm.[32] Taking these trends into consideration, one can construe Lê Văn Hưu's criticism of Lý Công Uẩn as an indirect attack on the powerful Buddhist influence in the Trần court.

Support for this interpretation can be seen in Lê Văn Hưu's commentary on Lý Thần-Tông's (1128–38) reaction to the Vietnamese triumph at Nghệ An.[33] When Thần-Tông learned that Lý Công Bình had repelled the Cambodian army at Nghệ An, he paid tribute by visiting Buddhist and Taoist temples. Lê Văn Hưu says that Thần-Tông should have first announced the victory to the ancestral shrine (thái miếu) and then given distinguished service awards to the meritorious subjects who had served the dynasty with valor. By merely attributing the victory to Buddhism, Thần-Tông had failed to reward those who rendered distinguished service. Lê Văn Hưu warned that if valiant subjects were not properly rewarded, they might not serve the dynasty in the future.

Lê Văn Hưu pointed out it was wrong for Lý Thái-Tông to have his subjects refer to him as "Court" (triều đình) instead of "Your Majesty" (bệ hạ). He noted that it was a violation of Confucian ethics for Lý Thánh-Tông to call himself "A Man Having Ten Thousand Carriages" (vạn thừa), and for Lý Cao-Tông (r. 1176–1210) to presume himself to be a Buddha.[34] With these comments Lê Văn Hưu was covertly promoting Confucianism while arguing against Buddhism. On numerous occasions he criticizes court proceedings and rituals, blaming the lack of "appropriately Confucian-educated" court officials and retainers for these inadequacies. Lê Văn Hưu also disapproved of references to Lê Hoàn by the title of Đại Hành Hoàng Đế since his proper posthumous title had not yet been determined.[35] Other lapses in court etiquette included Lý Thần-Tông's wearing mourning dress for only one month, not three years, after the death of Nhân-Tông (1072–1128).[36] Lê Văn Hưu's criticism of the Lý dynasty's court officials is a cloaked attack on the powerful Buddhist influence in the Trần court. Even though there were Confucian scholar-officials, they had very little influence at the time.

Occasionally Lê Văn Hưu pointed out the "misdeeds" of the emperor and his subjects from a purely Confucian point of view. For example, he criticized Lý Thần-Tông, Nhân-Tông's adopted son and heir to the throne, for appointing his biological father and mother as senior emperor and empress dowager. He argued that this designation should have been given to Nhân-Tông.[37] Nevertheless, considering that Thần-Tông was only a child, he concluded that these mistakes were the fault of ignorant advisers. Furthermore, Thần-Tông's awarding of government posts to two subjects who presented him with a white deer was judged an abuse of privilege. Since the subjects received an office without performing any merit, "they were deceiving of the emperor."[38] Lê Văn Hưu's criticism of rulers from a Confucian ethical perspective and his indirect attacks on Buddhism suggest that Confucianism was steadily gaining power despite the strong Buddhist influence both in and out of the court.

Ngô Sĩ Liên

Originally from Sơn Nam province (present-day Hà Sơn Bình province), Ngô Sĩ Liên is said to have participated in Lê Lợi's struggle against the Ming occupation.[39] After the establishment of the Lê dynasty, Ngô Sĩ Liên passed the *tiến sĩ* at the national examination in 1442, during Thái-Tông's rule (1434–42).[40] Under Nhân-Tông's rule (1443–59) he held the position of censor-in-chief (*đô ngự sử*). During Thánh-Tông's reign, Ngô Sĩ Liên became vice-minister of rites and director of studies at the National University (*quốc tử giám ty nghiệp*) and participated in the project to compile an official national history. The exact years of his birth and death are unknown, but he is said to have died at the age of ninety-nine. We may speculate that he was born around 1400 and lived until the late period of Thánh-Tông's reign.

Ngô Sĩ Liên's early years were marked by the collapse of the Trần dynasty and Hồ Quý Ly's establishment of the Hồ dynasty (1400–1407). With the Ming occupation of Việt Nam, a policy of cultural assimilation was carried out. Other important historical events of the time were Lê Lợi's independence struggle and his founding of the new dynasty. With the establishment of the Lê dynasty, Confucianism came to replace Buddhism, which had been the ruling ideology in Vietnamese thought up through the Trần dynasty. However, Confucianism did not really secure a firm hold until Thánh-Tông's enthronement. There were continuing conflicts between the predominantly Buddhist "meritorious subjects" from Thanh Hóa, who held most major court posts after the struggle with the Ming, and the new

Confucian bureaucrats from the Red River Delta. Because Thánh-Tông gained the throne through a military coup d'état, he could not at first ignore the influence of the predominately Buddhist court. However, several years later, with the promotion of Confucian scholars from the delta and Thánh-Tông's encouragement of Confucian learning, Confucianism came to enjoy its most prosperous time in Vietnamese history. It was in this context that Ngô Sĩ Liên wrote the *Toàn thư*.

One cannot help but wonder why Ngô Sĩ Liên decided to write his own national history. As we have seen, the Confucian scholar-officials had already, in response to Thánh-Tông's edict, completed a national history, which was stored in the Eastern Pavilion.

Even though he did not have access to this official history, Ngô Sĩ Liên would have known from his previous experience participating in the compilation project that it was different from what he had envisioned. Although exactly what was different is not clear, it is likely that the national history in the Eastern Pavilion focused on the listing of objective facts, since it had been compiled by a group of scholars. Perhaps it was Ngô Sĩ Liên's dissatisfaction with this kind of history that prompted him to start compiling his own. Perhaps Ngô Sĩ Liên wanted to express his own opinions just as Lê Văn Hưu did. More specifically, being a Confucianist, Ngô Sĩ Liên wrote the *Toàn thư* because he keenly felt the need to promote Confucian ideology; he had seen enough of the overwhelming influence of Buddhist court officials who wielded power up until the later years of the Trần dynasty. Ngô Sĩ Liên, no doubt, had felt uneasy about the intense confrontation between the Buddhist powers from Thanh Hóa and the rising Confucian bureaucrats from the Red River Delta.

Wolters has recently proposed that Ngô Sĩ Liên wrote the *Toàn thư* as a record firmly grounded in Confucianism that would be a resource for the Vietnamese, especially in times of national crisis. Through the compilation of the *Toàn thư* he hoped to contribute to the maintenance of national order and stability. Fully aware of the instability of his times, he wrote the *Toàn thư* as a warning to his contemporaries. This is one reason Ngô Sĩ Liên focused on critiquing the preceding Trần dynasty, still palpable to his readers in contrast to the distant Lý dynasty of the eleventh and twelfth centuries.[41] Of the 170 commentaries by Ngô Sĩ Liên in the *Toàn thư*, 72 refer to the Trần dynasty and 12 to the Hồ dynasty and the Ming occupation period, while 86 relate to the period from ancient times to the Lý dynasty. Clearly Ngô Sĩ Liên was interested in the Trần dynasty's governing institutions. He was also concerned with safety from Chinese invasion, even though the Lê dynasty was not under any threat after coming to power by defeating the Ming army.

Since Confucianism, especially neo-Confucianism, heavily influenced Ngô Sĩ Liên's thinking, his comments often center on family ethics and the ruler-subject relationship.[42] He thought that the nation should be governed in accordance with proper Confucian ethics. Only then, he believed, could the foundation of a dynasty be solid. In 1320, when Trần Anh-Tông (r. 1293–1314) died, Ngô Sĩ Liên, drawing on Mencius's thought, proclaimed: "The empire has its basis in the state, the state in the family, and the family in one's own self." He added that the family must be properly governed if the nation was to be well regulated. This was true in the times of Yao and Shun (legendary rulers in China's golden age) just as it was true in his own day.[43] He harshly criticized anyone who violated these principles.

Ngô Sĩ Liên reserved high praise for Trần Anh-Tông: Anh-Tông was quick to mend his mistakes, sincerely revered his parents, maintained a harmonious relationship with his relatives, in addition to paying sincere tribute to his ancestors. Indeed, Anh-Tông's family was said to be a model for others to follow. According to Ngô Sĩ Liên, Anh-Tông's reign was righteous, and the common people enjoyed a peaceful life. However, despite these favorable comments, Ngô Sĩ Liên blamed Anh-Tông for not properly conducting a burial ceremony at the death of the senior emperor, Nhân-Tông (r. 1278–1293) in 1310.[44]

In general Ngô Sĩ Liên harshly condemns the immorality of Trần dynasty rulers. This response may be seen as an inevitable reaction to the Buddhist ruling ideology of the Trần. First of all, Ngô Sĩ Liên stressed the immorality of Trần Thái-Tông's marriage practices. At the insistence of his uncle Trần Thủ Độ, Thái-Tông married his elder brother's pregnant wife, because his wife, the first empress, had failed to produce an heir. Ngô Sĩ Liên lamented that this "bad precedent" led Dụ-Tông (r. 1341–69) to commit a similar misdeed. Moreover, the first empress was demoted to "princess status," and twenty-one years later she was given to a subject who had rendered distinguished service during the Mongol invasion. Making matters even worse in Ngô

Sĩ Liên's view, Thái-Tông, who had originally planned on giving his daughter in marriage to a member of a royal family, Trung Thành Vương, ended up marrying her to a cousin who coveted her. Ngô Sĩ Liên claimed that the Trần royal family had sullied the husband-wife relationship and proper marriage customs beyond recognition.[45] He concluded that a sovereign without virtue could not properly govern his country.

Ngô Sĩ Liên believed that the emperor's legitimate first son should succeed to the throne. If the empress did not bear a son, a son of the emperor's concubine could be provisionally appointed crown prince. However, if the empress did give birth to a son later, this provisional heir must step down. This is why Ngô Sĩ Liên lamented the death of the empress's father, Trần Quốc Chẩn, who was killed by opponents during Trần Minh-Tông's reign (r. 1314–29) after he objected to the appointment of a provisional crown prince and insisted on waiting until the empress bore a son.[46] He also found fault with Lý Thần-Tông for having initially made a concubine's elder son the crown prince instead of the empress's young son.[47] Ngô Sĩ Liên thought that the empress's second son should succeed to the throne only if there was something wrong with the eldest son. Hence he attacked Ngô Quyền's eldest son, Xương Ngập, for having abused authority by accepting an invitation, offered by his younger brother Xương Văn, to jointly rule the country. He argued that since Xương Ngập did not have any merit, it was his duty to decline the offer.[48] Ngô Sĩ Liên also criticizes Đinh Bộ Lĩnh for having a concubine's young son, Hạng Lang, succeed to the throne instead of the capable and legitimate first son, Đinh Liễn.[49] He concluded that this mistake harmed both Đinh Bộ Lĩnh and his son.[50] Even so it was not a break from common Vietnamese practice to appoint a concubine's younger son crown prince. The practice of primogeniture and discrimination against concubines' sons was not prevalent until the late Lê dynasty.

Ngô Sĩ Liên stipulated that if an emperor had no son, one should be adopted from the royal family. He points to the Lý dynasty's precedent of Nhân-Tông adopting one of his nephews, who then succeeded to the throne. He opposes the succession of women to the throne, notably the enthronement of Huệ-Tông's (r. 1211–24) daughter, Phật Kim, who became Chiêu-Hoàng (r. 1224–25).[51] In Ngô Sĩ Liên's view, Huệ-Tông was the main culprit responsible for the fall of the Lý dynasty to the Trần because he made the major mistake of having his daughter succeed to the throne. He believed that Huệ-Tông should have followed Nhân-Tông's precedent.

As previously mentioned, the Lý dynasty did not rely on a prede-termined primogeniture system but appointed successors judged to be the most capable. To prevent disputes over succession, the senior emperor system was introduced during the Trần dynasty. Although Ngô Sĩ Liên probably understood this system, he criticized it from a patriarchal perspective.[52] The father should not be relieved of his power during his lifetime, he believed.

Ngô Sĩ Liên also criticized the Trần clan's practice of same-surname endogamy. He judged the clan's complete disregard of exogamy to be a grave violation of ethics.[53] Trần Thủ Độ had used intermarriage among the royal family to prevent the diffusion of power to other clans, ensuring the power of the Trần family. Since restrictions on marriage such as surname exogamy were not practiced in Việt Nam at that time, royal intermarriage would not have been considered "immoral" in the sense that Ngô Sĩ Liên insists. Indeed, one factor contributing to the fall of the Trần dynasty was the political maneu-verings of an in-law clan of the royal family, who gained power after the demise of the royal intermarriage system.[54]

A proponent of wives' submission to their husbands, Ngô Sĩ Liên upheld a stern view of wifely chastity. He suggested that rather than giving simple prizes, the court should bestow an "emblem" on a chaste wife. Such a system, Ngô Sĩ Liên argues, would set an example for later generations. He believed that Lý Huệ-Tông's widow, the empress Linh Từ, should have remained a chaste widow instead of marrying Trần Thủ Độ.[55] Similarly, he concludes that Lê Hoàn's tak-ing the former dynasty's empress Dương as his own empress was a shameful action that degraded the ethics of the husband-wife rela-tionship.[56] Ngô Sĩ Liên, who was immersed in Confucian ideology, must have had difficulty understanding Lê Hoàn's attempt to legiti-mize his authority by using a bilateral kinship system and taking ad-vantage of the high social status of a woman. On the other hand, he praised Champa's queen who during Lý Thái-Tông's reign, decided to drown herself instead of losing her chastity when she was taken prisoner by captors who intended to force her to service the em-peror.[57] Here the Cham queen's suicide can be likened to the uphold-ing of the Confucian ethic that a loyal subject would never serve two kings.

As an advocate of neo-Confucian ethics, Ngô Sĩ Liên demanded that subjects be loyal to their ruler under any circumstances. In 1285, when the Yuan invading army was defeated, its chief general was killed. On seeing the general's decapitated head, Trần Nhân-Tông remarked, "This is what a subject must do for his lord." He then covered the head with his own clothes. Ngô Sĩ Liên praised these words as those of a true emperor, adding that subjects who are loyal to their lord shall never be forgotten.[58] Indeed, Ngô Sĩ Liên heaped praise on any subject, Vietnamese or not, who was loyal to his ruler. When Champa invaded in 1378, Lê Giốc was taken prisoner and killed after refusing to humble himself before another lord. Lê Giốc reportedly stated, "Since I am a subject of a great country, how can I possibly bow before you?" Ngô Sĩ Liên praised Lê Giốc for his un-yielding loyalty as a "gentleman" (jun zi in Chinese).[59] Referring to Su Qian, who had led the Song army's invasion into Việt Nam in 1075, Ngô Sĩ Liên said his loyalty and valor matched those of Lý Thường Kiệt even though Su Qian was defeated and killed by the latter's troops.[60]

Even though Ngô Sĩ Liên often referred to Mencius's thought when commenting on events, he did not accept Mencius's concept of "smit-ing and banishing a sovereign" (fang fa in Chinese). He must have felt that this concept would open the door to protest against the Lê dy-nasty. He advocated instead the neo-Confucian ethic of demanding a subject's absolute loyalty to his ruler. Apparently this is why Ngô Sĩ Liên harshly criticized Lê Hoàn, Trần Thủ Độ, and Hồ Qúy Ly for usurping the throne, arguing that when Lê Hoàn designated himself viceroy, he harmed the ruler, a crime worthy of death. Even though Đinh Toàn of the Đinh dynasty was young, he was still a king. There-fore, it was right for Nguyễn Bặc and Đinh Điền to take up arms against Lê Hoàn in an effort to preserve the sovereignty of Đinh Toàn.[61] Ngô Sĩ Liên's criticism of Trần Thủ Độ was especially caus-tic.[62] Ever since China's Zhou dynasty, feudal lords had agreed not to threaten the sovereignty of other countries. Nevertheless, Trần Thủ Độ had robbed another dynasty of its sovereignty and murdered Lý Huệ-Tông. Trần Thủ Độ's actions, Ngô Sĩ Liên remarked, should be compared to those of dogs and pigs.

Ngô Sĩ Liên thought that Hồ Qúy Ly also deserved the death pen-alty since he murdered Trần Thuận-Tông (r. 1388–98) and usurped the Trần throne two years later. Hồ Qúy Ly's death at the hands of a neighboring country's army was just, since the Vietnamese had already attempted to kill him many times. He asserted that subjects who rebel against their rulers should not be allowed to live even a single day.[63] If a neighboring country had not killed Hồ Qúy Ly, the barbarians should have murdered him, Ngô Sĩ Liên declared. These comments reveal Ngô Sĩ Liên's strong belief in the importance of extreme loyalty to one's rulers. The reason he condemned Hồ Qúy Ly as a usurper of the Trần throne was not simply a matter of Confucian ethics; he was probably concerned about the apparent weakening of the throne when Lê Lợi's death heralded a succession of young rulers. No doubt Ngô Sĩ Liên was also mindful of the coup d'état staged by the former crown prince Nghi Dân in 1459. In other words, it seems Ngô Sĩ Liên was attempting to stabilize the throne by encouraging court officials to follow the Confucian principle of loyalty to the emperor.

Just as it was for Lê Văn Hưu, the safety of the dynasty from Chinese attack must have been a major concern for Ngô Sĩ Liên, even though a Ming invasion was not an immediate threat. Despite Lê Lợi's success in restoring Việt Nam's independence by defeating the Ming after the twenty-year occupation, Ngô Sĩ Liên was worried that internal instability could prompt another Chinese invasion. Perhaps this is why he inserted Nguyễn Trãi's *Bình Ngô đại cáo* (Great Proclamation on the Pacification of the Wu), commissioned by Lê Lợi, in its entirety into the *Toàn thư*. The *Bình Ngô đại cáo* essentially asserts that Việt Nam is an independent civilized country differing from China in culture and natural environment.[64] Unlike Lê Văn Hưu, Ngô Sĩ Liên sets the beginning of Vietnamese history all the way back to the times of the mythical Chinese ruler Shen Nong. Thus Vietnamese history becomes at least as long as Chinese history. Ngô Sĩ Liên implies that in some respects Việt Nam even surpasses China. For example, the legendary first ruler of Việt Nam, Kinh Dương Vương, is described as superior to his half-brother, Đế Nghi.[65] Their father, Đế Minh, portrayed as the great-grandson of Shen Nong, wanted his talented younger son, Kinh Dương Vương, to succeed to the throne instead of his first son, Đế Nghi. However, since Kinh Dương Vương declined this offer, he was given control of the southern country, while Đế Nghi ruled the northern one (China).

Ngô Sĩ Liên's concern about the security of the Lê dynasty is reflected in his commentaries on the invasions of the Mongols and the

Chams during the Trần dynasty. For example, he applauded Trần Thánh-Tông's response to the Mongol invasion.[66] As senior emperor, Thánh-Tông performed several important tasks that contributed greatly to Vietnamese resistance to the Mongols. He summoned the elders from throughout the nation to gather at the Stair of Diên-Hồng and discuss countermeasures against the Mongols, enabling him to mobilize public support which greatly aided in the expulsion of the invaders. Ngô Sĩ Liên concludes that Thánh-Tông's actions helped deter future Mongol invasions.[67]

On the other hand, Ngô Sĩ Liên deplored the fact that rulers of the late Trần dynasty had not prepared for Champa's invasion of Việt Nam. According to him, ethics and order had become lax during the late Trần dynasty. This laxity included neglecting preparations for the defense of Việt Nam, even though it should have been clear to the Trần dynasty rulers that Champa posed a serious threat. Ngô Sĩ Liên criticized the senior emperor Dụ-Tông, who had become so accustomed to peace that he did nothing but "indulge in pleasure-seeking." Furthermore, the emperor Nghệ-Tông (r. 1370–72) was so concerned with art and literature that he ignored his military duties. Given such a state of deterioration, Ngô Sĩ Liên asserted, it was inevitable that the Trần dynasty's capital, Thăng Long, would fall in 1371 to Champa.[68] His comments about the occupation and pillage of Champa in 605 by the Sui dynasty general Liu Fang is quite telling. Instead of criticizing the attack, Ngô Sĩ Liên heralds it as just punishment for barbarian Champa, which had been encroaching on Việt Nam's territory.[69] He approves of the general's attack since it would discourage Cham invasions of Việt Nam. Here Ngô Sĩ Liên clearly reveals his concern for Việt Nam's security.

As a neo-Confucian living under the Confucian-dominated Lê dynasty, Ngô Sĩ Liên systematically denigrated the practice of Buddhism in previous dynasties. For example, he disapproved of the senior emperor who ordered that Buddha statues be installed throughout Việt Nam during the reign of Trần Thái-Tông, immediately after the establishment of the Trần dynasty. The Buddha statues were meant to be a tribute to a Buddhist monk who had predicted future greatness for the senior emperor when he was a mere child. Critical of such Buddhist-inspired excesses, Ngô Sĩ Liên sarcastically remarked that anyone with a reasonable amount of foresight could have uttered these prophetic words.[70] Ngô Sĩ Liên had praised Trần Nhân-Tông for his victory against the Mongol invasion but condemned him for becoming a Buddhist priest upon abdicating the throne. He had violated the "way of moderation" (đạo trung dung) by becoming a monk, living in a Buddhist temple, and founding the Zen Buddhist sect called the Trúc Lâm.[71]

As an adamant opponent of Buddhism, Ngô Sĩ Liên could not resist criticizing Lý Thái-Tông for his decision to change the title of his reign when sarira-dhatu (Buddha's corporal relics) were discovered among the cremated remains of two monks in 1034.[72] He skeptically remarked that discovery of sarira-dhatu should not have impressed the emperor since sarira-dhatu is simply a natural product of concentrated "essences" (tinh khí). Moreover, Ngô Sĩ Liên claimed that Thái-Tông's decision to change the title of the reign inspired the mischief of fame seekers and set a bad precedent. He also strongly disapproved of Lý Nhân-Tông's pardoning of criminals after Buddhist dharma talks.[73] Nhân-Tông's decision to pardon criminals and ignore legal standards in the name of the Buddhist dharma would, according to Ngô Sĩ Liên, result in the arbitrary dispensation of justice and benefit the undeserving. In addition, it was improper that Nhân-Tông cremated the empress dowager upon her death and buried her lady-in-waiting alive with the empress dowager's ashes.[74] Cremation was a Buddhist practice, and it is likely that the empress dowager's cremation was in accordance with her wishes. Although Ngô Sĩ Liên recognized this, he still asserted that Nhân-Tông had to take responsibility for the "unjust" cremation because he ordered it himself. Here, Ngô Sĩ Liên's criticisms are quite anachronistic; it is difficult to imagine how Nhân-Tông could have refused the empress dowager's wish to be cremated, especially during a time when Buddhism was the dominant religion. This clearly shows that Ngô Sĩ Liên evaluated historical figures and events from the Confucian point of view of his times.

Two Historians Compared

The historical perspectives of Lê Văn Hưu and Ngô Sĩ Liên are products of their times. For Lê Văn Hưu the most pressing concern was how to preserve the independence of the Trần dynasty amid the threat of constant Mongol invasion. For Ngô Sĩ Liên, who lived during the Lê dynasty, when Confucianism was the ruling ideology, promoting Confucian ethics and morality was of utmost concern. Of course, since Ngô Sĩ Liên had witnessed the Ming invasion of Việt

Nam, he was also keenly aware that the Chinese might invade Việt Nam if the country became weakened. Thus he was also concerned with preventing internal instability to protect Việt Nam's autonomy.

The divergent perspectives of Lê Văn Hưu and Ngô Sĩ Liên become clear when we analyze the fifteen incidents on which both historians commented. While Lê Văn Hưu focuses on issues of national security and Việt Nam's equality with China in ten of these, Ngô Sĩ Liên addresses the same concerns in only four of the common incidents. On the other hand, while Ngô Sĩ Liên focuses on Confucian ethics in eleven of the fifteen, Lê Văn Hưu makes only five comments relating to Confucianism. The two different perspectives will become clear as we consider their evaluations of Ngô Quyền, Đinh Bộ Lĩnh, Lê Hoàn, Lý Bổn, and Shi Xie.

Lê Văn Hưu believed that Ngô Quyền failed to restore fully the independence Việt Nam had enjoyed prior to the invasion of Wu Di of the Han dynasty. Even though he gave Ngô Quyền credit for repelling the invading southern Han army and deterring further Chinese attacks, Lê Văn Hưu complained that full independence was not obtained since Ngô Quyền failed to designate himself as emperor. In contrast Ngô Sĩ Liên praised Ngô Quyền not only for his military feats but also for establishing government offices and ritual codes for various dynastic institutions. He concluded that these accomplishments gave Ngô Quyền the "stature worthy of an emperor."[75]

Lê Văn Hưu maintained that Đinh Bộ Lĩnh was able to restore Việt Nam's independence (to the previous glory of the Nam Việt era) by establishing various dynastic institutions and designating himself as emperor. Ngô Sĩ Liên did not comment on Đinh Bộ Lĩnh's decision to designate himself as emperor and rename the country. Perhaps Ngô Sĩ Liên believed these acts were relatively insignificant since Ngô Quyền had already restored the complete independence of Việt Nam. He did, however, criticize the "anti-Confucian" acts of Đinh Bộ Lĩnh and his son, Đinh Liễn. According to Ngô Sĩ Liên, it was improper for Đinh Bộ Lĩnh to overlook his eldest son, Đinh Liễn, and choose a younger son as successor to the throne. Đinh Bộ Lĩnh's transgression eventually resulted in Đinh Liễn's murder of his younger brother, another grave ethical violation. Ngô Sĩ Liên's criticism may also have been related to his concern about potential succession disputes in the Lê court. As we know, Đinh Bộ Lĩnh's mistake led to the fall of his dynasty.

The two historians' evaluations of Lê Hoàn differ drastically. Lê Văn Hưu praised Lê Hoàn's prompt suppression of the rebellion that Nguyễn Bặc and Đinh Điền instigated. These timely measures to quell internal instability had prevented China's Song dynasty from invading Việt Nam.[76] In contrast Ngô Sĩ Liên believes that the rebellion against Lê Hoàn was necessary and just. As loyal subjects, Nguyễn Bặc and Đinh Điền had acted to preserve the sovereignty of the young ruler that Lê Hoàn had threatened in an attempt to gain power. In Ngô Sĩ Liên's view, Lê Hoàn deserved severe punishment.[77] Once again Lê Văn Hưu was primarily concerned with foreign aggression, while Ngô Sĩ Liên focuses on Confucian ethics.

Differences can also be seen in their comments on Lý Bổn. Lê Văn Hưu simply regarded Lý Bổn as an ordinary general, while Ngô Sĩ Liên attributed his failure to the will of heaven.[78] Ngô Sĩ Liên believes that Lý Bổn's having to fight against a formidable general like Chen Ba Xian was the result of heaven's will; heaven had decided it was not yet time for Việt Nam to achieve independence. Here Ngô Sĩ Liên, unlike Lê Văn Hưu, interpreted Lý Bổn's defeat from a Confucian perspective.

It is no surprise that they diverge again regarding Shi Xie. Lê Văn Hưu emphasized Shi Xie's achievement in preserving the territorial integrity of Việt Nam even though he had become a vassal of China. Ngô Sĩ Liên extolled Shi Xie's virtues for having introduced Chinese civilization into Việt Nam. By encouraging the spread of literature, proprieties, and music, Shi Xie was instrumental in turning Việt Nam into "a civilized country."[79]

Nevertheless, in some areas Lê Văn Hưu and Ngô Sĩ Liên share the same opinion. For example, both criticize Buddhism and oppose Chinese intervention in Việt Nam. Both historians also praise the Trưng sisters' struggle against Chinese rule. In contrast with the glory of these women, both deplore the way even men subjected themselves to servitude rather than resisting the Chinese.[80] It is safe to conjecture that underlying this comment is the Confucian attitude that reserves a low social position for women.

Although both Lê Văn Hưu and Ngô Sĩ Liên attack Buddhism, the criticisms of the former are much more indirect. During Lê Văn Hưu's time Confucian scholar-officials had very little political power even though they held some bureaucratic posts. As previously mentioned, during the Trần dynasty Buddhism was strongly supported by the ruling class and overpowered Confucian elements. According to the *Toàn thư*, the first instance of a Confucian formally criticizing Buddhism did not occur until nearly one hundred years after the compilation of the *Đại Việt sử ký*. In this first formal attack in 1370, a Confucian official named Lê Quát attempted, without much success, to brand Buddhism as heretical and to promote Confucianism.[81] Times had drastically changed by Ngô Sĩ Liên's Lê dynasty. Since Confucianism had been adopted by the Lê dynasty as the official ideology of government, adamantly supported by Emperor Thánh-Tông, Ngô Sĩ Liên could afford to criticize Buddhism openly and without reservation. He believed that the adoption of Confucian ethics was the only viable way of bringing stability to both the court and society in general.

The concept of "Việt Nam's equality with China" and the related "spirit of resistance" against the Chinese dynasties can be traced back to Đinh Bộ Lĩnh's time. Thereafter, all the Vietnamese rulers of successive dynasties used the title "emperor" and a reign title. A further indication of this idea of equality with China can be seen in the way Vietnamese writers called China the "northern country" while referring to Việt Nam as the "southern country." Chinese were called the "men of the Tang" or the "northern people," while Vietnamese referred to themselves as the *hoa dân* (civilized people), or the "southern people."[82] The idea of "Việt Nam's equality with China" and the "spirit of resistance" against foreign intervention have continued unaltered up to the twentieth century.

Confucianism began to penetrate deeply into Việt Nam with the Mongol invasion in the second half of the thirteenth century. It expanded its influence by the fourteenth century and eventually established itself as the ruling ideology of the Lê dynasty after the period of the Hồ regime and the Ming occupation. However, the Confucian ethics of loyalty and filial piety, which Ngô Sĩ Liên advocates so emphatically, failed to gain enough support to prevent the usurpation of the Lê dynasty throne by the Mạc family in the early sixteenth century. Following this, the movement for restoration of the Lê dynasty and the subsequent antagonism between the two families, the Trịnh in the North and the Nguyễn in the South, which continued up until the seventeenth and eighteenth centuries, made traditional Confucian ethical concerns less conspicuous. Nevertheless, Confucianism remained the ruling ideology of the state, and examinations based on the Confucian classics continued to be held for the selection and promotion of government officials. As a result Confucianism was able to penetrate, albeit slowly, into Vietnamese society. It was still the ruling ideology when the Nguyễn dynasty was established in the early nineteenth century. Although the abolition of the examination system in 1918 dealt a heavy blow to Confucian power, Confucian ethics continue to significantly influence Vietnamese society today.

Notes

1. Wolters, "Le Van Huu's Treatment of Ly Than Tong's Reign (1127–1137)"; idem, "Historians and Emperors in Vietnam and China"; idem, "What Else May Ngo Si Lien Mean?"

2. Phan Đại Doãn, Ngô Sĩ Liên và Đại Việt sử ký toàn thư.

3. Ngô Sĩ Liên, Đại Việt sử ký toàn thư (cited hereafter as TT), 55, 348.

4. Yamamoto Tatsuro suggests that the Đại Việt sử ký may have been a thirteen-volume or perhaps three-volume work ("Etsshiryaku to Taietsshiki," 62–63).

5. The "Ngoại Kỷ" covers Vietnamese history from the Hồng Bàng dynasty up to Ngô Quyền's victory over the Nam Hán in 938. The "Bản Kỷ" begins with Ngô Quyền's seizure of power and ends with the collapse of the movement for the Trần restoration in 1413. Last but not least, the "Lê Thái Tổ Kỷ" covers the period when Việt Nam was fully brought under the rule of Ming China in 1413 up until Thái-Tổ's accession to the throne in 1428. See TT, 55, 57–58; Chen Chingho, "Taietsshikizensho no henshu to tembon" [The Compilation of the Đại Việt sử ký toàn thư and Its Various Editions], in TT, 8. Other scholars still believe that Ngô Sĩ Liên compiled the Toàn thư by the order of Lê Thánh-Tông. See Wolters, "What Else?" 94; Phan Huy Lê, "Đại Việt sử ký toàn thư—tác giả, văn bản, tác phẩm," [Đại Việt sử ký toàn Thư—compiler, editions, work], in Đại Việt sử ký toàn thư, 22–23.

6. Wolters says that the compilation of history books by the two historians was closely related to the political and ideological situations in which they lived ("Historians and Emperors in Vietnam and China," 69–89; idem, "What Else?" 94–114).

7. Si Ma Qian, Shi Ji, 97:2689; TT, 108.

8. Wolters, "Historians and Emperors in Vietnam and China," 76–77.

9. TT, 113–14.

10. TT, 180. According to the Toàn thư, Đinh Bộ Lĩnh ascended to the throne in 968. However, Kawahara Masahiro has proven that Đinh Bộ Lĩnh's ascension to the throne was in 966, not in 968 ("Teiburyo no sokui nendai ni tsuite") Cf. Taylor, Birth of Vietnam, 281.

11. TT, 172. Cf. Taylor, Birth of Vietnam, 270. Modern Vietnamese scholars praise Ngô Quyền's accomplishments more highly than Lê Văn Hưu did. See Nguyễn Quang Ngọc, Tiến trình lịch sử Việt Nam, 61–63.

12. The division of the "Ngoại Kỷ" and the "Bản Kỷ" in the present day *Toàn thư* was made by Vũ Quỳnh, who followed the idea of Lê Văn Hưu in his *Đại Việt Thông Giám* written in 1511. See *TT*, 59, 83.

13. *TT*, 120.

14. Nguyễn Quang Ngọc, *Tiến trình lịch sử Việt Nam*, 47.

15. *TT*, 150.

16. *TT*, 126.

17. *TT*, 188–89.

18. *TT*, 198.

19. *TT*, 217.

20. Wolters, "Le Van Huu's Treatment of Ly Than Tong's Reign (1127–1137)," 207–9.

21. *TT*, 180. Cf. Wolters, "Le Van Huu's Treatment of Ly Than Tong's Reign (1127–1137)," 208.

22. Taylor, *Birth of Vietnam*, 284; Yu Insun, "Bilateral Social Pattern and the Status of Women in Traditional Vietnam," 226.

23. Wolters, "Le Van Huu's Treatment of Ly Than Tong's Reign (1127–1137)," 208–9, 225.

24. *TT*, 203.

25. *TT*, 175.

26. *TT*, 233.

27. Ibid.; Wolters, "Historians and Emperors in Vietnam and China," 75.

28. *TT*, 294.

29. *TT*, 132.

30. *TT*, 130, 167.

31. *TT*, 208–9.

32. Wolters, "Assertions of Cultural Well-Being in Fourteenth-Century Vietnam (Part One)," 436.

33. *TT*, 271.

34. *TT*, 224.

35. When an emperor died, he was called Đại Hành Hoàng Đế until his posthumous name was determined.

36. *TT*, 197, 268. See also the *TT*, 220, 272, 228–29.

37. *TT*, 272.

38. *TT*, 273.

39. Phan Huy Lê, "Ngô Sĩ Liên và Đại Việt sử ký toàn thư," in *Đại Việt sử ký toàn thư*, 11.

40. Ngô Sĩ Liên became a *tiến sĩ* around the age of forty mainly because the first national examination in the Lê dynasty was held in 1442. Cf. Đỗ Đức Hùng, "Góp phần tìm hiểu tiểu sử và hành trang của Ngô Sĩ Liên," 127–28.

41. Wolters, "What Else?" 112–13. Cf. *TT*, 57.

42. Ngô Sĩ Liên harshly criticized Hồ Qúy Ly for calling Zhou Gong an ancient sage and Confucius an ancient teacher, not following Zhu Xi's interpretation of Confucianism. *TT*, 467–68, 471–72. Hồ Qúy Ly, who was a subject of the Trần dynasty, took the throne by forcing Thiệu Đế (1398–1400) to abdicate. This is most likely why Hồ Qúy Ly rejected neo-Confucianism, which

demanded strict loyalty to one's ruler. His decision to rename the country as Đại Ngu can also be understood in this context.

43. *TT*, 401; Wolters, "What Else?" 97–98.

44. *TT*, 401; Wolters, "What Else?" 98.

45. *TT*, 327–28, 335, 340; Wolters, "What Else?" 110.

46. *TT*, 407; Wolters, "What Else?" 99.

47. *TT*, 282.

48. *TT*, 174.

49. *TT*, 182–83.

50. A so-called imperial attendant named Đô Thích killed them later. *TT*, 182–83.

51. *TT*, 315.

52. *TT*, 340.

53. *TT*, 335.

54. Koo Bum-Jin, "Betunam jinjo (1225–1400) mollak ui il yoin."

55. *TT*, 341.

56. *TT*, 189.

57. *TT*, 234. See also *TT*, 374–75, 495.

58. *TT*, 360–61.

59. *TT*, 453. When Champa invaded in 1383, Nghệ-Tông was afraid and started to run away. Nguyễn Mộng Hoa, a Confucian scholar, tried to dissuade the emperor by taking hold of his escape boat. Referring to this incident, Ngô Sĩ Liên quipped, "Shouldn't the military men be ashamed since a mere Confucian scholar was so brave?" (*TT*, 457).

60. *TT*, 248.

61. *TT*, 184, 189; Đặng Văn Tu, "Danh nhân Ngô Sĩ Liên," 49–50.

62. *TT*, 322.

63. *TT*, 497; Nguyễn Danh Phiệt, "Ý thức hệ tư tưởng chính thống và tính khách quan lịch sử trong Đại Việt sử ký toàn thư," 177.

64. *TT*, 546.

65. *TT*, 97; Hoàng Hồng, "Tư tưởng sử học của Ngô Sĩ Liên," 103.

66. *TT*, 357, 368.

67. *TT*, 339.

68. *TT*, 442.

69. *TT*, 157–58.

70. *TT*, 325.

71. *TT*, 390; Wolters, "What else?" 98. Ngô Sĩ Liên praised the talent of Lý Công Uẩn as a founding father of the Lý dynasty. However, he judged that Lý Công Uẩn erred by respecting Buddhism and Daoism (*TT*, 220); Phan Đại Doãn, "Mấy khía cạnh triết lịch sử của Ngô Sĩ Liên," 29.

72. *TT*, 224.

73. *TT*, 272–73.

74. *TT*, 258–59.

75. This is why Ngô Sĩ Liên started the "Bản Kỷ" from Ngô Quyền's seizure of power in 939. See note 5. *TT*, 172; Hoàng Hồng, "Tư tưởng sử học của Ngô Sĩ Liên," 95.

76. *TT*, 188; Nguyễn Danh Phiệt, "Ý thức hệ tư tưởng chính thống và tính khách quan lịch sử," 171.

77. *TT*, 188–89; Nguyện Danh Phiệt, "Ý thức hệ tư tưởng chính thống và tính Kkhách quan lịch sử," 172.

78. *TT*, 150.

79. *TT*, 132–33.

80. *TT*, 126–27.

81. *TT*, 441.

82. O'Harrow, "Nguyen Trai's *Binh Ngo Dai Cao* of 1428," 165–66.

3

Chinese Gunpowder Technology and Đại Việt, ca. 1390–1497

SUN LAICHEN

Military technology tends to be the first to be borrowed, since the penalties for not doing so are immediate and fatal.
    —Anthony Reid, *Europe and Southeast Asia.*

Any big change in weapons and military organization affects politics and society by helping some people attain ends more easily than before, while putting new, perhaps insuperable, obstacles in the way of others. The advent of guns was such a change.
    —William H. McNeill, *The Age of Gunpowder Empires,*
    1450–1800.

There is a large lacunae in Asian military history on the transfer of Chinese gunpowder technology to Southeast Asia before the sack of Melaka by the Portuguese in 1511. Elsewhere I have shown how the gunpowder technology of early Ming China (ca. 1368–1450) disseminated to all of northern mainland Southeast Asia (defined as including southern Yunnan, Northeast India, and northern parts of modern mainland Southeast Asia) and discussed its implications.[1] This

research focuses on two issues in Sino-Vietnamese relations and Vietnamese history with respect to the spread of Chinese firearms.

The first issue between China and Việt Nam is who borrowed
gunpowder technology from whom. This involves the well-known
but highly puzzling passage in the *Ming shi* (History of the Ming
dynasty): "When it came to [the time] of Ming Chengzu [Yongle,
1403–24] Jiaozhi (Đại Việt) was pacified, the techniques of magic
gun and cannon (*shenji qiangpao fa*) were obtained; a firearms battalion (*shenji ying*) was especially established to drill [firearms]."[2] This
has led to the popular belief that the Chinese, through their invasion
of Đại Việt in 1406–7, acquired firearms technology from the Vietnamese.[3] Though this view has been challenged in many ways, it is
far from discredited.[4] In particular no efforts have been made to
demonstrate convincingly that Việt Nam acquired gunpowder technology from China rather than the other way around. More than one
Chinese source express a similar view in the passage in the *Ming shi*
quoted here, indicating that the subject merits closer attention. This
study examines the issues in detail by making full use of Chinese
and Vietnamese sources. On the one hand, it stresses the Chinese
origins of gunpowder technology; on the other hand, it also ac-
knowledges Vietnamese innovations in some aspects of gunpowder
technology.

The second issue involves the driving forces behind the external
expansion of Đại Việt during the fifteenth century, including both the
well-known episode of the fall of the Cham capital, Vijaya, in 1471
and the little-known "long march" of Đại Việt troops to the Irrawaddy River between 1479 and 1484. The main question here is
why, after having confronted Champa for more than one thousand
(or five hundred) years, Đại Việt was able to defeat Champa deci-
sively at this time.[5] To date available views can be summarized as
follows.

First, the agricultural and demographic theory: This view holds
that the population increase of Đại Việt both drove and provided an
edge for the southward march (*nam tiến*) of the Vietnamese.[6] Earlier
views tend to stress population growth as a result of the agricultural
development in the Red River delta but without giving much
thought to the latter.[7] But in a more recent article explaining the ethnic succession of the Pyu, the Mon, the Khmer, and the Cham by the
Burmese, the Thai, and the Vietnamese in mainland Southeast Asia,

Richard A. O'Connor attributes it to the replacement of "lowland agriculture" ("garden farmers") by "wet rice specialists" who could produce more rice to foster "the trade, population growth, and resource concentration that promote state power and societal expansion."[8] Li Tana's research on the demographic trend in northern and central Việt Nam lends more credence to this theory.[9]

Second, the Confucian transformation interpretation: This construal argues that the Ming invasion of Đại Việt in 1406–7 finally led to the adoption of the Ming Chinese model by the Vietnamese, especially under the rule of Lê Thánh-tông (r. 1460–97). As a result, the Vietnamese state was transformed. In particular Đại Việt embraced the Chinese "civilized versus barbarian" ideology and applied it to its relations with Champa. In the words of John K. Whitmore, "Now the moral question became central and marked the difference between the 'civilized' and the 'barbarian.' No longer did cultural relativity reign, nor were the attacks mere looting raids after which another local prince would be put on the throne. The goal instead became to bring 'civilization' to the uncivilized." In other words, only when the Vietnamese occupied Champa permanently could they civilize its people.[10]

Third, the institutional interpretation: While the previous view accounts for the institutional strength of Đại Việt, this view explains the institutional weakness of Champa. According to Kenneth R. Hall, Champa, rather than being a centralized state, was "a weakly institutionalized state system that depended upon personal alliance networks to integrate a fragmented population." With a very limited agricultural base and maritime trade, Champa was operated primarily on a "plunder-based political economy," which fluctuated according to the availability of resources and especially the success or failure of external plundering expeditions. Thus, "[t]he inherent institutional weakness in the Cham state ultimately sealed its fate."[11]

Each of these views has merit, but the questions have not yet been comprehensively answered. This research approaches the issue from a technological perspective by taking military technology into account. It argues that Chinese-derived gunpowder technology played an important role in Đại Việt southward and westward expansion in the late fifteenth century.

Transfers of Gunpowder Technology from Ming China to Đại Việt, ca. 1390–1427

1. THE EARLIEST FIREARMS IN ĐẠI VIỆT AND THE DEFEAT OF CHAMPA

Although the transfer of military technology from China to modern Việt Nam can be traced to the time before the Common Era, a signi ficant transfer took place during the early Ming period. In 1390 the powerful Cham king Chế Bông Nga was killed by a volley of *huochong* in a naval battle.[12] This weapon has long been widely under-stood as a cannon, but it was more plausibly a handgun (figure 1).[13] It was, as pointed out by Momoki Shiro, a new weapon.[14] The firing of these handguns and especially the death of Chế Bông Nga caused psychological chaos among the Cham soldiers, who were conse-quently routed. Đại Việt was thus saved from a "total collapse" or "one of the major crises in the history of Dai Viet."[15]

A brief review of Đại Việt's situation in the second half of the four-teenth century can help us better understand the significance of Đại Việt's victory in 1390. For three decades (1361–90) Chế Bông Nga launched about ten invasions, large and small, of Đại Việt (in 1361, 1362, 1364, 1365, 1368, 1371, 1377, 1380, 1382, and 1383), and the capi-tal of Đại Việt fell three times (in 1371, 1377, and 1383). In 1389 a series of domestic revolts preceded another full-scale Cham invasion. Hồ Quý Ly led Đại Việt troops to confront the enemy but was defeated on the Luong River. Hồ Quý Ly fled to the capital, followed by his

Figure 3.1.   The handguns would have been like the ones held in the History Museum in Hà Nội (probably from the fifteenth to sixteenth centuries). Photo by author.

generals, one of whom commented: "The enemy is stronger than we are, and resistance is impossible." Then the most dramatic episode took place (in the words of Georges Maspéro):

Continuing his advance, he (Che Bong Nga) reached the Hoang River. Terror once again reigned in the capital. The order was given to Tran Khac-chon to march and meet him. The fear inspired by the Cham king and his armies was so great that when this general presented himself before the old emperor, he could not contain his tears despite his courage, and his sovereign also wept. Nevertheless, he advanced to the Hoang River. Finding the Cham there in too great force to enter into combat, he pulled back to the Hai-trieu River. The situation appeared hopeless; everything seemed to indicate a prompt occupation of the country by Cham troops. The emperor's younger brother, Nguyễn Dieu, then crossed over with all his men to the camp of Che Bong Nga, hoping no doubt that the latter, master of Annam, would entrust him with its government. At the same time, a monk, Pham Su-on, occupied the capital at the head of a group of partisans. The two emperors had to flee and call back General Huynh The Phuong.[16]

At this crucial moment when "Vietnamese civilization was badly shaken," as Whitmore put it, a low-ranking Cham officer defected and helped the Vietnamese identify Chế Bông Nga's warship among several hundred. A concentration of firepower from the Vietnamese took the life of the Cham king, and the Cham troops retreated. When the Vietnamese king, Trần Thuận-tông, (r. 1388–98) was roused from his sleep and saw the head of Chế Bông Nga, he was startled and thought the enemy was already at his camp. Upon learning about the death of Chế Bông Nga, the jubilant Vietnamese king commented with great relief: "Bông Nga and I have been confronting for long but we did not get to see each other until today. Is not this like that Han Gaozu saw the head of Xiang Yu![17] [Now] the country is pacified."[18]

Maspéro maintained that it was the Cham officer's betrayal that "stopped the victorious march of the Cham and saved Annam from an invasion in which its independence would perhaps have been lost." However, without the newly acquired gunpowder technology, Đại Việt's victory in this naval battle and the subsequent fate of the Vietnamese state would have been extremely uncertain. Thus the year 1390, as many scholars have observed, signaled a shift in the balance of power between Đại Việt and Champa.[19] From this time on, Đại Việt seemed to have gained the upper hand. Apparently, the effectiveness of Đại Việt's new military technology played a part in this shift of the balance of power in general and a determining role in the 1390 victory of the Đại Việt navy in particular.

Though the origin of the Vietnamese handgun is not specified, it is reasonable to speculate that it had been obtained from either Ming traders or military deserters prior to 1390. Wang Ji, the minister of war and commander-in-chief of the campaigns against the Maw Shans (Luchuan) in modern southwestern Yunnan, memorialized in 1444: "In the past Luchuan rebelled primarily because profit-seekers on the frontier, illegally carrying weapons and other goods, sneaked into Mubang (Hsenwi), Miandian (Ava), Cheli (Sipson Panna), Babai (Lan Na), and so on, and communicated with the aboriginal chieftains and exchanged goods. There were also those who taught them to make weapons, liked [their] women, and remained there."[20] Though not specifically mentioned here, Đại Việt should have been on the list.

It seems that the adoption of firearms in Đại Việt increased the need for gunmetal, because in 1396 the late Trần dynasty, under the control of Hồ Quý Ly, issued paper money and required people to exchange their copper cash, possibly with the purpose of collecting more copper for manufacturing firearms.[21]

2. THE EMPLOYMENT OF FIREARMS BY MING TROOPS IN ĐẠI VIỆT (1406–21)

The Ming invasion and occupation of Đại Việt between 1406 and 1427 greatly furthered the transfer of military technology from China to Đại Việt. As a military superpower determined to subdue Đại Việt, Ming China mobilized its best generals and troops for that purpose. The Yongle emperor was highly concerned with this campaign and paid much attention to every detail in the preparation. To withstand Đại Việt's firearms (huoqi), he ordered the Ministry of Works to manufacture large, thick, and durable shields.[22] He ordered that the technology of making firearms, including the "magic handgun/cannon" (shenji chong), should not be leaked to the enemy. Particularly, the "firearm generals" (shenji jiangjun) were ordered to make sure that when their troops withdrew, firearms would "be counted each to its original number and not a single piece be allowed to go."[23] Among the 215,000 invading soldiers of the Ming army were some troops armed with firearms. They were headed by at least four firearm generals: Cheng Kuan, Zhu Gui, Luo Wen, and Zhang Sheng.[24] If we accept the estimate that 10 percent of the early Ming army was equipped with firearms, then around 21,500 soldiers should have served under these generals.[25] They must have formed the backbone of the Firearms Battalion, a special and separate type of troops specializing in firearms that was established soon after the invasion of 1406–7 (discussed later). One Chinese source sheds light on the composition of firearms in one battalion (*ying*) by the mid-sixteenth century. It consisted of forty batteries or units (*dui*) and was equipped with 3,600 "thunderbolt shells" (*pili pao*), 160 "wine-cup muzzle general cannon" (*zhankou jiangjun pao*), 200 large and 328 small "continuous bullet cannon" (*lianzhu pao*), 624 handguns (*shouba chong*), 300 small grenades (*xiao feipao*), about 6.97 tons of gunpowder, and 1,051,600 or more bullets of approximately 0.8 ounce each. The total weight of the weaponry was 29.4 tons.[26]

On November 19, 1406, Ming troops led by Zhang Fu entered Đại Việt from Guangxi, while those under Mu Sheng marched from Yunnan.[27] Soon afterward, Đại Việt troops—twenty thousand at the Ai-luu Pass and thirty thousand at the Ke-lang Pass—tried to block Zhang Fu's armies with *huochong* and other weapons, but they were routed easily.[28] Earlier the Ming court had worried about the lack of a navy for the campaign.[29] But in either December 1406 or January 1407, when the Ming troops arrived in the Tam-doi prefecture on the north bank of the modern Red River, they started to "build ships and set cannon (*chong*) on them."[30] This was the beginning of the Ming navy in Đại Việt. On January 19, 1407, Vietnamese soldiers crossing the river fired *chong* on the Chinese but were routed by the latter.[31]

The capture of Do-bang by the Ming armies demonstrates the crucial role played by Ming firearms. Do-bang was the most important strategic point in Đại Việt's defense against the Ming. The Ming commanders told their soldiers, "This city is what the enemy relies on."[32] Đại Việt must have counted on Do-bang's defense to prevent the Ming troops from penetrating farther south. Therefore, Đại Việt deployed heavy troops and its best weapons to defend it. The city wall was high, and significant quantities of *chong*, arrows, wooden, and stone obstacles were deployed. To defend the city, two deep moats were constructed with bamboo sticks inside. Outside the moats pits for trapping horses were dug, with pointed bamboo and wooden sticks on and beneath them. In brief, Đại Việt's defense was well prepared. Before the attack, troops under Zhang Fu prepared weapons and other equipment.[33] The Ming armies' general offensive took place on January 19–20, 1407. The Ming troops attacked the city from all directions, employing scaling ladders (*yunti*; see figure 2), *xianren dong*, and gunpowder signal lights (*yemingguang huoyao*).[34] According to the *Đại Việt sử ký toàn thư* (Complete book of the historical record of Đại Việt), "the dead bodies [of the Ming soldiers] piled up as high as the city wall, but [the Ming troops] still kept climbing and fighting; nobody dared to stop."[35] When the Ming troops climbed onto the city wall, the alarmed and bewildered Vietnamese defenders could only shoot a few arrows and *chong*. After having successfully entered the city, the Ming soldiers were confronted by Đại Việt elephants and numerous infantry. The Ming troops covered their horses with lion masks to scare the elephants.[36] In particular, soldiers led by the fire-arm generals Luo Wen and Cheng Kuan played a crucial role in the victory of the Ming. The magic handguns or cannons (*shenji chong*) were set up along the sides of the horses, and both *chong* and rocket arrows (*huojian*) were shot to rout the elephants.[37] This was significant because the Southeast Asian elephant corps had been a formidable force against the Chinese over the centuries; but with the advent and especially heavy employment of firearms, "the elephants stood no chance."[38] While the Vietnamese troops were in chaos, the Ming advanced their horses and foot soldiers and shot a large number of arrows, handguns, and cannons (*pao*). As a result countless Vietnamese soldiers died.[39] The *Đại Việt sử ký toàn thư* informs us that the elephants turned back, and the Ming soldiers proceeded into the city. The city fell, and the defense line along the river collapsed.[40] The *Ming shi* states that Do-bang "fell, [the Vietnamese] disheartened" (literally "their gallbladder cracked").[41] With the fall of Do-bang, the Đại Việt troops could no longer prevent the Ming armies' march forward to the east and the south. On January 20 the eastern capital (Đông-đô, Thăng-long, or modern Hà Nội) fell. Six days later, on January 26, the western capital (Tây- đô, in Thanh-hoá province) fell as well.[42]

In all the subsequent battles Ming firearms also proved to be very effective. In early February 1407, Ming troops killed at least 37,390 Đại Việt soldiers.[43] On February 21, on the Lục-giang, the Ming mobilized their navy and foot soldiers. They employed "magic handgun/cannon" and "bowl-sized muzzle cannon" (*wankou chong*; see figure 3) to attack over five hundred Vietnamese ships led by Hồ Nguyên Trừng, son of

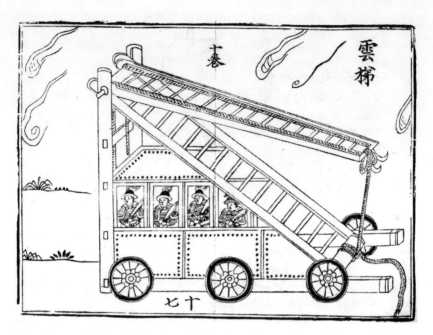

Figure 3.2.   Scaling ladder (*yunti*). Reprinted from Cheng Dong and Zhong
Shaoyi, *Zhongguo gudai bingqi tuji,* 219.

Hồ Quý Ly, and killed more than ten thousand Vietnamese soldiers.[44]
One Chinese source describes the scene as one in which the firing of
"firearms [was] like flying stars and lightning."[45] Retreating to
Mường-hải, Hồ Nguyên Trừng manufactured firearms and warships
that could withstand the enemy.[46] On March 18, 1407, in the Phung-
hoa prefecture, Ming troops used "great general cannon" (*da jiangjun
chong*; see figure 4) to smash many enemy ships.[47] On May 4, 1407, a
major battle took place at the Hàm-tư Pass. The Vietnamese employed
a sizable number of soldiers (seventy thousand) and numerous warships and riverboats, which extended to more than ten *li*.[48] Vietnamese soldiers loaded *chong* to fire at the Ming soldiers. Though the
sources are silent regarding this issue, the Ming side no doubt employed heavy firearms, especially considering that the firearms generals Zhang Sheng, Ding Neng, and Zhu Gui were involved.[49] The Ming
troops won a significant victory, killing over ten thousand Vietnamese soldiers and capturing more than one thousand warships.[50]
On May 30, the Ming soldiers killed another ten thousand Vietnamese

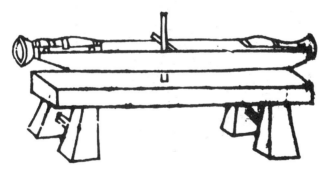

碗口銃

碗口銃用鹭為架上
加活盤以銃嵌入兩
頭打過一銃又打一
銃放時以銃口內衝
大石彈照準賊船底
艙平水面打去、以碎
其船家為便利、

Figure 3.3. "Bowl-sized muzzle cannon" (*wankou chong*). The Chinese text says: "The 'double bowl-mouthed gun' consists of (two) guns set on a movable support pivoted (so that it can rotate horizontally) on a (wooden) bench. Thus there were two heads (muzzles) pointing away from one another. Immediately after the firing [of] the first gun, the second is (rotated into position) and fired, each one being muzzle-loaded with a large stone projectile. If the gun is aimed at the hull of an enemy ship below the water-line, the cannon-balls shoot along the surface and smash its side into splinters (so that it sinks). It is a very handy weapon." Translation by Joseph Needham. Reprinted by permission from Joseph Needham, *Science and Civilisation in China,* vol. 5, *Chemistry and Chemical Technology,* pt. 7, "Military Technology: The Gunpowder Epic," 321, 324.

大將軍銃

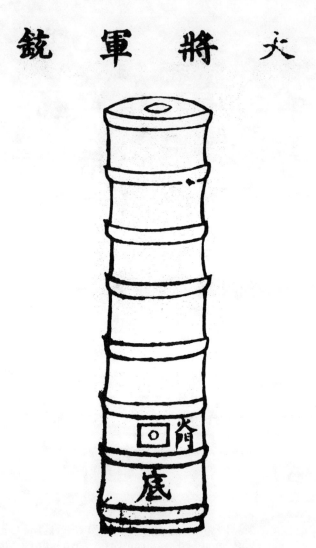

Figure 3.4. The "great general cannon" (*da jiangjun chong*). It originally weighed 150 *jin* (1 *jin* = 0.5 kg) with a length 3 *chi* (1 *chi* = 0.3 meter), but in the late fifteenth century the weight was increased to 250 *jin* and the length doubled to 6 *chi*, with a shooting range of 800 paces. Reprinted by permission from Joseph Needham, *Science and Civilisation in China*, vol. 5, *Chemistry and Chemical Technology*, pt. 7, "Military Technology: The Gunpowder Epic," 336–337, 338.

soldiers in Thanh-hoá.[51] Among the Ming troops chasing Hồ Quý Ly and his followers to the south were those led by the firearm generals Luo Wen, Cheng Kuan, Zhang Sheng, and Ding Neng.[52] On June 16–17, 1407, Ming troops finally ended their invasion of Đại Việt by capturing Hồ Quý Ly and his sons.[53] The quick Ming victory was noted by Huang Fu, who was in charge of military supplies during the war and later served as administration and surveillance commissioner of the annexed Jiaozhi province: "The speedy success was never known in the past."[54]

From February 1409 to February 1421, in suppressing a series of Vietnamese rebellions, especially those led by Trần Quí Khoách and Trần Gian Đinh (or Gian Đinh Đế), Ming troops again employed firearms. The Ming troops were commanded mainly by Zhang Fu, who was sent to Đại Việt on February 11, 1409, for the second time, and on February 10, 1411, for the third.[55] On July 3, Zhang Fu had more warships built because he realized that the Vietnamese took advantage of rivers and the sea to resist the Chinese.[56] On September 29, 1409, at the Ham-tu Pass, Zhang Fu's troops fought with twenty thousand Đại Việt soldiers, who had more than six hundred ships; "the [firepower] of the firearms [was] intense while the arrows were shot like raindrops." As a result over three thousand Vietnamese soldiers were killed, and "countless" drowned, and the Ming captured more than four hundred ships.[57] On September 6, 1412, a fierce naval battle took place at the Than-dau estuary. Although the Vietnamese had more than four hundred ships and were in high spirits, they could not withstand the Ming's firearms and fled.[58] On February 7, 1421, Ming troops chased a Vietnamese rebel to the Ngoc-ma prefecture and were confronted by the Tais. The latter employed elephants to charge at their enemies, but the Ming soldiers "shot the elephant riders, and then used firearms to attack them; the elephants turned back, the rebels were routed."[59]

In some battles the use of firearms is not mentioned, but there is no reason for the Ming troops not to have employed them. For instance, on February 12, 1410, in the Dong-ho prefecture, Ming troops under Zhang Fu fought twenty thousand Vietnamese, killed over forty-five hundred, and captured more than two thousand.[60] On August 6, 1411, in a battle that took place in Cuu-chan prefecture, the Vietnamese had more than 300 boats, but the Ming army and navy killed over four hundred soldiers and captured over 120 boats. We know that Zhang Sheng, one of the firearms generals, was among the leading Ming generals in this battle.[61]

Most Ming firearms were manufactured in China in 1409, 1414, 1415, 1421, and 1426. Without question, these manufacturing dates are connected to Yongle's five campaigns against the Mongols in the north, but the campaigns in Đại Việt may well have been another factor.[62] The establishment of the Firearms Battalion, discussed later in this study, may have been the result of the effectiveness in Đại Việt of Ming firearms, which were employed there for the first time on a large scale in Ming foreign military campaigns.

Although the Vietnamese were familiar with gunpowder technology and had employed firearms since 1390, this weaponry must have been inferior in both quality (with one to two exceptions, examined later in the discussion) and especially quantity vis-à-vis Chinese weapons. Because China's attempts to conquer Đại Việt ever since the latter's independence in the tenth century failed both before and after the Ming, the Yongle emperor himself could proudly point out that the Ming achievements exceeded that of the Song and the Yuan, and Vietnamese chroniclers, when referring to the Ming conquest of Đại Việt, commented that "the disaster caused by the Ming people was unprecedented."[63] We know that the Qing suffered also in its invasion of Đại Việt in the late eighteenth century. Thus the Ming indeed stands out for its success in conquering Đại Việt and occupying it for twenty years. Đại Việt under Hồ Quý Ly prepared early (from 1401 on) and well for the Ming invasion, mobilizing an unprecedented number of soldiers and civilians.[64] Nonetheless, the Ho regime collapsed rather quickly. The reason, besides factors such as resentment against Hồ Quý Ly's reforms, low morale, strategic mistakes, and the bad military leadership of the Hồ, lies in Ming China's military superiority, including firearms.[65]

3. THE EMPLOYMENT OF FIREARMS BY ĐẠI VIỆT TROOPS (CA. 1426–1427)

The Ming troops gradually lost this technological superiority as their Vietnamese counterpart under Lê Lợi captured more and more Ming weapons and other military supplies in several major battles in 1418, 1420, 1421, 1424, and 1425. Thus Lê Lợi's troops were able to arm themselves quickly.[66] Though Vietnamese records do not specify the

types of weapons, they doubtless included a large number of firearms, something attested by the battle of Ninh-kiều (or Chuc-dong-
Tat-dong) on December 4, 1426.[67] Earlier the Ming troops in Jiaozhi
city (Dông-quan, modern Hà Nội) employed firearms (*huochong* and
rockets) to repel Đại Việt armies. The latter retreated, and the Chinese
decided to pursue them.[68] About 100,000 Ming soldiers led by Wang
Tong and other generals were ambushed and defeated. It is important
for our purpose to mention that among these Ming troops were 510
soldiers led by the regional military commander of the Firearms Battalion, Xie Rong; they had been sent on May 8, 1426, by the Ming emperor to follow Wang Tong to Đại Việt.[69] Three thousand crack Đại
Việt soldiers armed with the best weapons played a decisive role in
this victory. According to Vietnamese accounts, over 50,000 Ming soldiers were killed (Chinese records state 20,000 to 30,000), "countless"
drowned, and over 10,000 were captured, while "countless" horses,
supplies, weapons, and so on fell into Vietnamese hands.[70] As a result
these Ming troops lost almost all their weapons. After retreating to
Dong-quan, they thus had to manufacture firearms and ammunitions
using bronze obtained by destroying the famous giant bell Quy-dien
and urns at the Pho-minh temple.[71]

   This great victory was decisive for the Vietnamese for two reasons.
First, they captured the largest number of firearms and other military
supplies ever from the Ming. As a result, the Vietnamese troops'
weaponry must have been enhanced to an unprecedented degree.

   Second, this battle was a turning point in Đại Việt's anti-Ming
movement. Encouraged by this victory, the troops led by Lê Lợi
marched north from Thanh-hoá (or Nghệ-an according to the *Ming
shilu*).[72] Soon afterward, on December 8, 1426, Lê Lợi and his troops
besieged Đông-quận and "obtained . . . many enemy ships, weapons
and equipment; tens of thousands of army provisions all fell to us."[73]

   In addition Ming captives and defectors also provided the Vietnamese with military technology. Around February 1427, some Ming
captives provided the Vietnamese with techniques for attacking city
walls, models for protective shelters (*zhanpeng*, or *xupeng*), primitive
tanks (*fenwen che*; see figure 5), "flying horse carts" (*feimache*), and
Muslim (counterweighted) catapults (*Xiangyang pao* or *Huihui pao*; see
figure 6).[74] Le Loi ordered the manufacture of weapons and equipment based on these models and distributed them to different
places.[75] Just before the final attack of Xuong-giang, city-siege carts

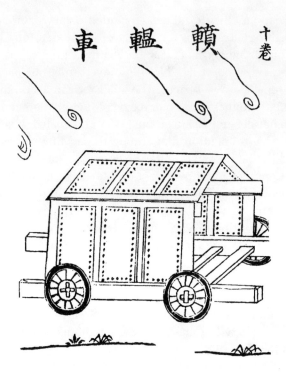

Figure 3.5.   Primitive tank (*fenwen che*). Reprinted from Mao Yuanyi, *Wu bei zhi*, 5:4540.

(probably *Lügong che;* see the discussion later in this study) were also constructed on the order of Lê Lợi.[76] Among the Ming captives, one by the name Cai Fu, probably the highest-ranking (commander-in-chief, *dudu,* rank 1a), had played an important role in the fall of Do-bang in 1407; around January 1427, however, he and other Ming officers surrendered to the Vietnamese and taught them how to make city-siege devices to take Xương-giang and Đông-quận.[77]

All these captured or newly manufactured weapons helped Đại Việt troops defeat and drive out the Ming invaders, something reflected in the siege of the city of Xuong-giang, the most strategic point for the Ming armies in early 1427 insofar as they depended on Đông-quan while awaiting reinforcements from China.[78] Vietnamese troops were determined to take it before the arrival of sizable Chinese reinforcements from Yunnan. Đại Việt troops had besieged the city

Figure 3.6. Muslim (counterweighted) catapult (*Xiangyang pao*). Reprinted from Wang Zhaochun, *Zhongguo huoqi shi,* 66.

for over six (or nine according to the *Ming shilu*) months but could not take it. About two thousand Ming defenders employed *chong* and presumably catapults hurling huge stones (*jiangjun shi* or *jiangjun shizi*) to defend the city. Eventually the eighty thousand Vietnamese succeeded in taking the city using the technology they had learned from the Chinese. They built earth hills around the city from which they then shot their weapons into the city. They dug tunnels into the city and employed turtle-colored "Duke Lü's overlook and assault carts" (*Lügong che*), fire lances (*feiqiang*; literally "flying lances"), rocket arrows (*huojian*), cannon (*huopao*), scaling ladders, and so on.[79] The *Đại Việt sử ký toàn thư* describes the siege thus: "[The Vietnamese employed] hooks, halberds, rocket arrows, cannon, and attacked from the four directions; thus the city fell."[80] This occurred on April 28, 1427. Just as the taking of Do-bang by Ming troops in early 1407 signaled the collapse of Đại Việt's defense, the fall of Xương-giang destroyed the Ming's. According to the "Lâm sơn thực lục": "The enemy relied on Xuong-giang's defense; upon learning that Xương-giang had been taken [they] lost their hope."[81] As modern Vietnamese historians have pointed out, the taking of Xương-giang paved the way for the final Vietnamese victory and was also significant from a military point of view, confirming that Vietnamese troops could besiege and take strong fortifications as well as fight guerrilla wars.[82] Without heavy firearms, the Vietnamese victories would have been extremely difficult if not impossible. One of the differences between the siege of Do-bang and that of Xương-giang was that after twenty years, the Đại Việt troops had more advanced firearms, especially handguns and cannons, and other equipment, most of which had been captured from the Ming armies.

The Vietnamese captured more weapons and military supplies when they took Xương-giang, and from September to November 1427 they obtained even more when they defeated the reinforcing units from Guangxi and Yunnan, which totaled over 150,000 soldiers. One Vietnamese source provides detailed information on the battle at the Chi-lang Pass. Several hundred brave Vietnamese soldiers and two hundred crack troops armed with "sufficient cannon, arrows, [and] gunpowder" were hiding at the two sides of the pass. Liu Sheng and his soldiers were surprised by the shot of a signal gun, while "from the two sides arrows were shot like raindrops, the sound of cannon was like thunder . . . [and] countless [enemies] died."[83] According to Vietnamese accounts, more than ninety thousand Chinese troops perished in the fighting, and "countless" weapons were captured.[84] The *Đại Việt sử ký toàn thư* specifically points out that the number of weapons and military supplies the Vietnamese troops captured from the Ming reinforcing armies from Yunnan doubled those obtained from the battle of Xuong-giang.[85] The more than one hundred thousand troops from Guangxi, led initially by Liu Sheng, must have carried a considerable number of firearms. Liu Sheng had been in charge of the Firearms Battalion and had fought against the Mongols many times on the northern frontier of the Ming between 1410 and 1423, and heavy firearms played a crucial role in those northern campaigns.[86] Liu Sheng's soldiers demonstrably included ten thousand crack troops who had followed Zheng He on his expeditions and were sent to Đại Việt on March 29, 1427.[87] They were undoubtedly armed with the best weapons. In January 1428, about 86,640 Ming military personnel and civilians withdrew from Đại Việt, all of whom were all certainly disarmed.[88]

It is thus not surprising that Lê Lợi himself pointed out "many enemies joined our side and fought against [the Ming army], [thus] all the bows, arrows, lances, and shields they had became our weapons."[89] Ngô Sĩ Liên, one of the compilers of the *Đại Việt sử ký toàn thư*, commented, "Most weapons, equipment, and grains were obtained from the enemy."[90]

The large number of Ming people and weapons remaining in Đại Việt after the withdrawal was understandably a major concern of the Ming court, and the court repeatedly requested that Đại Việt return the Ming officials, soldiers, and weapons. Some Chinese sources claim that "countless" Ming subjects still remained in Đại Việt, while a Vietnamese source states that the number was closer to several tens of thousands.[91] Despite its claim of having done so, Đại Việt did not return a single piece of weaponry, and the Ming court eventually ceased its demands.[92]

Vietnamese Contributions to Chinese Gunpowder Technology

It should be noted that Đại Việt not only imported military technology from but also exported better techniques to Ming China.[93] After the conquest of Đại Việt in 1407, the Ming acquired from the Vietnamese a weapon called *shen qiang, shen qiang jian,* or *shenji huoqiang,* meaning literally "magic fire-lance arrow."[94] This fire lance was better than its Chinese counterpart because of one unique feature: it had a heavy wooden wad (*mu ma zi* in Chinese) made of ironwood behind the arrow to increase pressure within the barrel. The arrow could, therefore, be shot as far as three hundred paces (see figure 7). Indeed, Chinese sources inform us that the fire lances made in Đại Việt were the best.[95] Many Chinese soldiers were probably killed by

神鎗

此即平安南所得者也箭下有木送子并置鉛彈
等物其妙處在用鐵力木重而有力一發可以三
百步、

Figure 3.7.   Fire lance (*shen qiang, shen qiang jian,* or *shenji huoqiang*). The Chinese text says: "This was acquired during the conquest of Annam. There is a
wooden wad (*mu song zi*) behind the arrow; some lead bullets and such are
also placed with it. Its ingenious part is that [the wooden wad] is made of
ironwood (*tieli mu*), [hence it is] heavy and forceful. It can shoot three
hundred paces" (my translation). Reprinted from Mao Yuanyi, *Wu bei zhi,*
6:5362–63.

this Vietnamese weapon during the Chinese invasion. Since ironwood was readily available in Đại Việt as well as Guangdong, Guangxi, and Yunnan, it is possible that the Vietnamese employed this indigenous resource to invent the wooden wad to increase the shooting range of the fire lance. This technique was adopted in China for handguns by 1415; a Ming handgun made in this year had a wooden wad between gunpowder and "bullets" (iron grits), while the handguns prior to this time did not yet have this salient feature (see figures 8a–b).

Moreover, from at least 1410 onward the igniting device of the handguns was improved by replacing the small hole where a fuse was inserted with a rectangular, lidded slot on the rear of the barrel. This feature made it easier to ignite the gunpowder, because the slot and the lid prevented the gunpowder and the fuse from getting wet when it rained. Evidence suggests that the Vietnamese may have invented this device. First, no handgun with this improved igniting device existed until after the Ming invasion of Đại Việt in 1410; second, the tropical climate in Đại Việt, with great humidity and the long rainy season, may have encouraged this invention.[96] Interestingly, among the six Vietnamese handguns at the Việt Nam History Museum, three of them have such an ignition device (see figure 9a–b; see also figure 1).[97]

On the order of the Yongle emperor, Vietnamese captives skilled at making firearms such as handguns or cannons (*huochong*), short lances (*duanqian*), fire lances (*shenjian*), and gunpowder were sent to the Chinese capital, Nanjing, with many other kinds of craftsmen. Altogether about seventeen thousand Vietnamese captives were taken to China, among them Hồ Nguyên Trừng ("Li Cheng" in Chinese). The Vietnamese chronicle specifically mentions that in 1407 Nguyễn Trung made firearms and warships to combat the invading Chinese.[98] The fact that Nguyễn Trung, as the Left Grand Councilor (*zuo xiangguo* in Chinese), was skilled in making firearms shows the importance Đại Việt attached to gunpowder technology and the intense competition between Đại Việt and its neighbors, primarily China and Champa.[99] This expertise changed Nguyễn Trung's fate in China. While in Nanjing Nguyễn Trung's father, Hồ Quý Ly, and brother Hồ Hán Thương, the two kings of the Hồ regime, were jailed after their capture by the Chinese, but Nguyễn Trung was pardoned and allowed to serve in the Ministry of Works.[100] He took charge of manufacturing firearms (*chong* and *jian*) and gunpowder at the

Figure 3.8a. Chinese handgun of 1372 without wooden wad. Reprinted from Cheng Dong and Zhong Shaoyi, *Zhongguo gudai bingqi tuji*, 231.

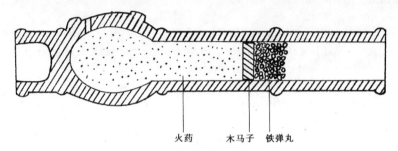

火药   木马子 铁弹丸

Figure 3.8b. Chinese handgun of 1415 (length 42.6 cm, muzzle bore diameter 4.4 cm, weight 8.9 kg) with wooden wad. The Chinese words mean (from left to right) "gunpowder," "wooden wad," and "iron bullets." When unearthed they were still in the barrel of the gun. Reprinted from Cheng Dong and Zhong Shaoyi, *Zhongguo gudai bingqi tuji*, 231.

weapon-manufacturing bureau (*Bingzhang ju*) and was eventually promoted to Minister of Works. He probably played an important role in establishing the Firearms Battalion in Ming China. According to one unofficial Chinese account, after receiving the order to accompany the Yongle emperor to attack the Mongols on the north frontier, three Vietnamese, including Nguyễn Trung, set up the Firearms Battalion prior to 1412. At least one of them (other than Nguyễn Trung) participated in the campaign and died soon afterward on June 9, 1412.[101] Some alley (*hutong*) names in Ming Beijing (lasting to the Qing and even today) such as "Annan Battalion (*Annan ying*)," "Jiaozhi," "Greater Annan Battalion (*Da Annan ying*)," and "Lesser Annan Battalion (*Xiao Annan ying*)" were probably derived from the settlement of Vietnamese soldiers.[102]

According to other Chinese records, when the Ming court held a memorial ceremony for the God of Firearms, it also offered a sacrifice to Hồ Nguyên Trừng.[103] Upon the death of Hồ Nguyên Trừng at the age seventy-three, his son replaced him and continued to manufacture firearms for the Ming until he retired at age seventy in 1470.[104]

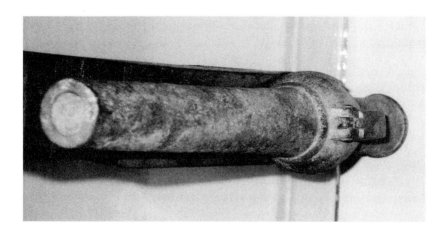

Figure 3.9a.   One of the three Vietnamese handguns (see figure 3.1) with the ignition device or protector.

Figure 3.9b.   Chinese handgun of 1415 with this device (length 44 cm, muzzle bore diameter 5.2 cm). Reprinted from Cheng Dong and Zhong Shaoyi, *Zhongguo gudai bingqi tuji*, 231.

Up to 1489, the descendents of these Vietnamese craftsmen were still in the service of the Ming.[105]

The Vietnamese techniques discussed here were used widely and had implications for the Ming military. During the early Hongzhi reign (1488–1505), thirty thousand linden and ninety thousand sandalwood wads were manufactured. Another kind of hardwood was sent from Guangxi to the capital as tribute for the manufacture of fire lances (*shen qiang*). The wooden wad technique was still used even after the arrival of Portuguese firearms in China in the late sixteenth century, as was the new ignition device.[106] The establishment of the

Firearms Battalion, to which the Vietnamese contributed at least some personnel and techniques, proved effective and sometimes crucial in Ming China's fighting with the Mongols. In 1414, when Yongle and his armies were surrounded by the Mongols, firearms with presumably Vietnamese technical features helped Ming troops break the siege. The effectiveness of the firearms in this event even impressed the Koreans; they recorded it in their record of the Yi (Choson) dynasty.[107]

The Vietnamese fire lance was also put to good use. One Chinese source states that when the Yongle emperor fought the Mongols, "[they had] just got the fire lance (*shen qiang*) from Annam; one barbarian (*lu*) marched straight forward, and two followed; [they were] all hit by the fire lance and died."[108] Teng Zhao, the vice minister of the Ministry of War during the reign of Chenghua (1465–87) commented: "[We] basically rely on the fire lance (*shen qiang*) to defeat enemies and win victories. From Yongle (1403–24) to Xuangde (1426–35), [the fire lance] was properly drilled and was most feared by the barbarians (*luzei*, or the Mongols)."[109] In 1449, after the Ming suffered the Tumu debacle, more than 28,000 handguns (*shen chong*) and 440,000 fire lances (*shen jian*) were collected from the battle scene.[110] The point that concerns us here is that these handguns and fire lances must have had Vietnamese techniques.

We now have a better understanding of the puzzling and often misunderstood passage in the *Ming shi* quoted at the beginning of this study. Despite the mistaken inference by later scholars, the passage means that China acquired only some new techniques, not gunpowder technology, from Đại Việt. This was first suggested by Arima Seiho and recently further supported by Li Bin's research.[111] Othersources also shed new light on the issue. The *Ming shi,* which was completed in 1739, seems to have derived its information from earlier works, including Shen Defu's. According to Shen, "Our dynasty employed firearms to combat the northern barbarians, [which] are number-one weapons from ancient times to the present. However, the ingenious (*qing miao,* meaning literally "light" and "wonderful") techniques of these firearms were not obtained until Emperor Wen (Yongle) pacified Jiaozhi. Hence, [our dynasty] hired its false Grand Councillor . . . to work in the Ministry of Works, [to be] solely in charge of manufacturing [Vietnamese-style firearms], and all the techniques were truly grasped."

This shows clearly that the Chinese obtained from the Vietnamese "the ingenious techniques of these firearms."[112]

The Increased Use of Firearms during the Early Lê (1428–1497)

On September 18, 1428, soon after the withdrawal of the Ming, Đại Việt started to strengthen its navy. Each main general was to command, inter alia, ten big warships, two small sentry boats, one super-sized *huotong* (*hoả dong* in Vietnamese), ten large *huotong*, ten medium-sized *huotong*, and eighty small *huotong*.[113] This demonstrates that from this time on the ĐạiViệt navy was equipped with more and heavier firearms. Also it seems that soldiers using *huotong* were organized into a unit headed by the Associate Administrator of Strong Crossbows and *Huotong*, and in 1449 the names of the two units of the *huotong* were changed to "magic thunder" and "magic lightning."[114] Between January 26 and October 4, 1429, unspecified weapons and warships were built.[115] According to the Thiên nam dư hạ tập (Collection of Works Written during Leisure Time in the South), which was written in December 1483, the Ministry of Works of Đại Việt manufactured powerful handguns (*chong*) and cannon (*pao*).[116] Though the numbers produced are not specified, firearms seem to have been used extensively. For example, soldiers in some *ve* (*wei* is a Chinese military unit) specialized in firearms; their titles included "firearms specialist," "handgun shooting specialist," and "cannon shooting specialists," while in many *ve* across the country only one out of five or six *so* (*suo* is a Chinese military unit) employed handguns and crossbows. These data suggest that such firearms units comprised around 20 percent of the military.[117] In 1467 Lê Thánh-tông (r. 1460–97) ordered the manufacture of new types of weapons.[118] In 1469 an edict was issued regarding the drill of the different military units, including those employing *chong* and crossbows.[119] In 1479 a firearm arsenal, where sharp weapons, guns, gunpowder, sulfur, and so on were stored, was burned down when Lê Thánh-tông was on his way to invade Ai-lao.[120] On January 11, 1493, a firearm arsenal was added to each arsenal.[121]

Soon after the withdrawal of the Ming from Đại Việt in 1428, the acquisition of gunpowder- and firearm-making materials accelerated in Đại

Việt. On September 18, 1428, the government urged acquisition of copper, iron, saltpeter, and so on.[122] In 1467 the use of saltpeter for fireworks was prohibited.[123] All these governmental actions imply that a greater amount of saltpeter was needed for military use than in the past. At the Ministry of Works, special units were in charge of saltpeter manufacturing.[124]

Not coincidently, 1429 witnessed the beginning of the exportation of a large quantity of copper from Yunnan into Đại Việt for making fire-arms. Around the fifteenth century, there were altogether nineteen copper-producing sites in prefectures such as Chuxiong, Lin'an, Chengjiang, Yunnan, Luliang, Yongning, and Yongchang, and several located in eastern and southeastern Yunnan were close to the Yunnan–Đại Việt border.[125] According to a memorial in 1429, silver, copper, and so forth were illegally mined by both military personnel and civilians in Dongchuan and Huili in northeastern Yunnan. But because these places were close to foreign countries (probably Đại

Figure 3.10a.   Vietnamese flamer-throwers (*huo pentong* in Chinese; *hoa phun dong* in Vietnamese) on one of the nine tripods (*cuu dinh*) in the Hue palace (cast in 1835). It is not clear what material was used for the tube. Photo by Phan Thanh Hai.

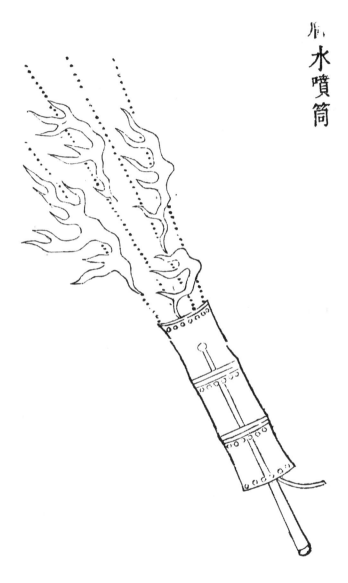

Figure 3.10b. Chinese flamethrower (*shenshui[huo] pentong*) with bamboo tube. Reprinted from Mao Yuanyi, *Wu bei zhi*, 6:5465, 5466.

Việt), the mining was ordered to stop lest soldiers and civilians create trouble.[126] However, the mining did not stop; instead the scale increased. Because the profit was enormous, a substantial number of people became involved in the mining and smuggling of copper, a considerable amount of which was smuggled into Đại Việt.[127]

In 1477 Đại Việt purchased copper from Mengzi for manufacturing weapons.[128] A Chinese source clearly states that the Đại Việt people purchased copper and iron from Lianhuatan for making handguns.[129] Prior to 1481 merchants transported goods to Lianhuatan to trade with the Vietnamese.[130] In 1481 the Ministry of Revenue of Ming China reported that a copper mine in Lu'nan of Yunnan was mined illegally for Đại Việt to manufacture weapons, and it stipulated that those who illegally traded copper out of Yunnan be executed and their families exiled to the malarial regions.[131] In 1484 the illegal trade of copper to Đại Việt occurred in another county.[132] Not only did the border officials in Yunnan not prohibit these activities; they abetted them.[133] The military use of copper is also recorded in Vietnamese sources. In 1497 the Đại Việt government ordered that the number of copper-extracting households be increased to fulfill military needs.[134] The practice of importing copper from Yunnan for manufacturing cannon in Đại Việt continued into the seventeenth century, though the scale seems to have dwindled.[135]

Gunpowder technology also spread from Đại Việt westward to the Phuan region and Chiang Mai. In most of the fifteenth century, Đại Việt waged military campaigns against Muong Phuan, eventually annexing the land and making it the Tran-ninh prefecture in 1479.[136] As a result the Phuan people were heavily influenced by the Vietnamese, particularly in military technology. By the eighteenth century the capital of Muong Phuan was fortified better than Do-bang in the fifteenth century. In particular the Phuans had in their possession, and probably manufactured themselves, "countless" saltpeter, sulfur, and firearms including handguns and rockets.[137] Vietnamese gunpowder technology traveled further westward. In 1443, when Chiang Mai was invading Nan, it was a Vietnamese by the name of Pan Songkram who helped operate the cannon. As a result, Nan eventually surrendered.[138]

Based on this discussion, one can speculate that after 1390, especially as a result of the Ming invasion and occupation, the proportion of firearms in the military weaponry of Đại Việt increased. To some extent, we may say that a military revolution had taken place, and Đại Việt had become a "gunpowder state," if not a "gunpowder empire."

Southward and Westward Expansion of Đại Việt (c. 1430s–1480s)

During the reign of Lê Thánh-tông (r. 1460–97), Đại Việt reached its golden age, witnessing rapid, stunning, and unprecedented internal consolidation and external expansion. In the words of John K. Whitmore, it was "a Vietnam more peaceful, prosperous, and powerful than any before the nineteenth century, and perhaps after."[139] Internally, following the Ming model the state of Đại Việt was transformed ideologically, bureaucratically, and militarily.[140] The latter point refers not only to Đại Việt's establishment of a large and well-organized military force, but also to its extensive employment of firearms as demonstrated in the earlier discussion.[141] These factors must have increased the authority and power of the Vietnamese state domestically and facilitated the external expansion of Đại Việt.[142] This expansion is best reflected in Đại Việt's sack of Champa to the south and march westward to the Irrawaddy River in the kingdom of Ava.

Beginning in the 1430s Đại Việt intensified its military activities on its western frontier, where different Thai peoples dwelled in the Sip Song Chu Tai (Xip xong chau Thai), Ai-lao, and Muong Phuan (modern Xiang Khuang in Laos). The result was greater stability.[143] Following this development, Đại Việt's attention turned to its age-old foe, Champa. From 1370 to 1390 Đại Việt faced repeated depredations from Champa but offered no effective resistance.[144] After the naval victory in 1390, however, Đại Việt seems to have gotten the upper hand. In 1396 Đại Việt troops under the leadership of a general invaded Champa and captured a Cham general. From 1400 to 1403, Đại Việt invaded Champa every year, sometimes successfully. The invasion in 1402 was massive and the most effective in terrifying the Cham king, who agreed to cede territory to Đại Việt in exchange for peace. Thus the northern Cham territory of Amaravati fell into Vietnamese hands and was divided into four subprefectures (*châu*): Thang, Hoa, Tu, and Nghia. In 1403 Đại Việt mobilized two hundred thousand troops to invade Champa. Vijaya was besieged but did not fall, Đại Việt troops having withdrawn because of poor leadership and insufficient grain supplies. This unsuccessful invasion lasted nine months. Although the Ming court sent nine warships at Champa's request, they seem to have encountered only the withdrawing Vietnamese navy at sea, and no fighting occurred.[145] In 1407 Champa, taking advantage of Đại Việt's subjugation by the Ming, won a victory by regaining the four subprefectures previously lost to Đại Việt.[146]

From the mid-1440s, according to Vietnamese sources, Đại Việt intensified its attacks on Champa because of the latter's repeated encroachments on its territory. In 1446 Đại Việt troops (allegedly over six hundred thousand) sacked the capital of Champa and took the Cham king and 33,500 captives to the Vietnamese capital.[147] But the Cham apparently remained strong since in 1470 the Cham king led over one hundred thousand Cham troops to invade Hóa Châu. Lê Thánh-tông decided to invade Champa again. The 100,000-strong Vietnamese naval expedition set out on November 28, 1470, followed by another 150,000 Vietnamese forces on December 8. Lê Thánh-tông also marched in person on the same day and composed a poem with the sentence: "The boom of the thunder-cannon shakes the earth," implying that the Đại Việt navy was heavily armed with firearms, as suggested by the preceding discussion. Fighting started on February 24, 1471, when five hundred Đại Việt warships and 30,000 troops were ordered to block the way of 5,000 Cham troops and elephants. Then one thousand warships and 70,000 troops followed under the leadership of Lê Thánh-tông.[148] On March 18, Thi-nai was taken and more than 400 Chams killed. On March 22 the Cham capital Cha-ban (Vijaya) collapsed after a four-day siege. According to the Vietnamese chronicle, more than 30,000 Chams were captured, including King Tra Toan and his family members, and over 40,000 killed. During the siege signal-guns were fired by the Đại Việt side. Although other forms of firearms must also have been employed, the sources are silent on this point.[149]

According to the *Ming shilu*, the Annam (Đại Việt) troops arrived in Champa during the second month of the seventh year of Chenghua (February 20–March 21, 1471), sacked its capital and captured its king and over fifty family members, took the seal of the Cham king, set fire to and destroyed houses, and killed and captured "countless" military personnel and civilians.[150] The Malay annals, *Sejarah Melayu*, also record this war: "The Raja of Kuchi (Đại Việt) accordingly invaded Champa: and the men of Kuchi fought a fierce battle with the men of Champa. One day the Raja of Kuchi sent messengers to the Treasurer of Champa to win him over to his side. The Treasurer of Champa acquiesced (and undertook to) open the gate. Accordingly when day dawned he opened the gate and the men of Kuchi entered the city and fought the men of Champa, some of whom resisted, while the others concerned themselves with saving their families. And Yak (Vijaya) fell and the Raja of Champa was killed."[151]

As a result Đại Việt annexed two Cham regions, Avaravati and Vijaya, or about four-fifths of Champa's total territory, a defeat from which Champa never recovered.[152] The fate of Champa was thus sealed, and the balance of power that had lasted more than a millennium (ca. 192–1471) between Đại Việt and Champa was finally broken, partially because of the utilization of firearms by Đại Việt.[153]

No evidence suggests that Champa ever acquired firearms. In 1410 Cham soldiers seem to have possessed no firearms.[154] A Chinese envoy who arrived in Champa in 1441 observed: "Its people [read: army] is very weak; [their] guards on the city walls in its country all hold [only] *bamboo spears*" (emphasis added).[155] The fact that the terms for weapons in a fifteenth-century Cham-Chinese dictionary all refer to conventional weapons (spear, lance, etc.) offers more support to the Chinese observation.[156] It is at least suggestive that an early-twentieth-century source states that Champa employed strong crossbows to fight against the Lý, the Trần, and the Lê dynasties.[157] More importantly, the fact that not a single firearm of Champa has been found (despite the numerous artifacts of Champa available today) supports the proposition that Champa, at least by the end of the fifteenth century, did not have access to firearms.[158]

This contrasts sharply with the contemporary Vietnamese, who were actively procuring copper and iron from Yunnan to manufacture firearms. According to a Portuguese observation made in the 1590s, the people of Champa were "weak and with no courage, their weapons are of bad quality and they are clumsy in using them and very disorganized during the battle." The common weapons they used were still lances and crossbows. They did possess some pieces of artillery and nearly one thousand arquebuses, which were, however, "badly adjusted and with a very bad quality [gun]powder." In particular the people of Champa could not handle the weaponry themselves and had to hire mercenaries. Therefore, "it is foreign slaves who deploy them, *for they themselves have little taste for that and they use them more to terrify than to have an effect*" (emphasis added).[159] As such, it is clear that Champa lagged behind Đại Việt technologically from the 1390s. We also have reason to believe Lê Thánh-tông's claim in his war proclamation to the king of Champa

that Đại Việt possessed more troops and better weapons than
Champa.[160]

In early 1471, sensing the change in the balance of power in the region, Thai principalities such as Ai-lao sent tributes to the Vietnamese
capital while Đại Việt troops were marching toward Champa, even
before the fighting started. After Đại Việt crushed Champa, more of
its western neighbors came to pay tribute, apparently feeling the
shockwave of Đại Việt's unprecedented feat.[161] In the fall of 1479 Đại
Việt, with a force of 180,000 according to Vietnamese sources,
launched more fierce invasions into Ai-lao, Muong Phuan, Lan Sang,
and further west.[162] Of these, Lan Sang was subdued easily.[163] Afterward, in 1480, Đại Việt troops went on to invade Nan, which was then
under Lan Na, and then threaten Sipsong Panna, which, under great
pressure, was reportedly going to submit to Đại Việt.[164] Finally, Đại
Việt troops even reached as far as the Irrawaddy (Kim-sa or Jinsha)
River in the Ava kingdom.[165]

The details of Đại Việt's incursion into Ava are not available, but
one can speculate that Đại Việt troops probably marched through the
region around Keng Tung and reached the territory of Ava, because
Keng Tung was later advised by the Ming court to be on alert.[166] In
1482 Mong Mit planned to borrow troops from Đại Việt to invade
Hsenwi and Lan Na. The intrusion itself is confirmed by several Chinese and Vietnamese sources. According to the *Ming shi*, in 1488 Ava
sent a mission to the Ming, complaining about Đại Việt's incursion
into its territory. In the next year (1489) the Ming court sent envoys to
admonish Đại Việt to stop.[167] Other sources, both Vietnamese and
Chinese, state that Ming envoys were sent in 1488 to Đại Việt to an-
nounce the ascension to the throne of the new Ming emperor. The
Chinese source also mentions Đại Việt's disturbance in the Burmese
territory.[168]

The Ming regime was very concerned with Đại Việt's expansionist
activities. In July 1480 the Yunnan authorities, upon learning that Lan
Sang had been attacked by Đại Việt, sent spies to reconnoiter the latter. The spies, who returned via Sipsong Panna by September 10 of
the same year, reported that Đại Việt had taken more than twenty
stockades from Lan Sang, killed over twenty thousand people, and
attempted to invade Lan Na. They also said that Sipsong Panna had
received a "false edict" from Đại Việt dated in 1479. As a result the
Ming sent envoys to Đại Việt to reprimand it for its actions.[169] On

December 7, 1480, the Ming court learned that Đại Việt had already
subdued Lan Sang and was drilling for the invasion of Lan Na. On
July 5, 1481, the Ming, after having learned more about Đại Việt's invasions of Lan Sang, warned Đại Việt not to encroach on its neighbors
on the strength of its armed forces and prosperity and ordered
Sipsong Panna, Yuanjiang, Mubang (Hsenwi), Guangnan, Keng Tung,
and other states to protect one another.[170] On June 30, 1482, Lan Na
reported to the Ming that it had helped Lan Sang to repel the troops
of Đại Việt and had destroyed the edict of Đại Việt.[171] It was reported
on January 8, 1484, that in 1483 Đại Việt, allegedly with 1,060,000
troops (a grossly exaggerated figure), had perhaps approached the
territory of Sipsong Panna along four routes to demand that this state
pay a tribute of gold and assist Đại Việt in invading Chiang Mai and
Lan Sang. Đại Việt denied the accusation in a letter to the Yunnan authorities.[172] On October 31, 1484, Lan Sang and Lan Na each reported
to the Ming that Đại Việt had withdrawn its troops.[173] Thus Đại Việt's
"long march" throughout mainland Southeast Asia, which had lasted
about five years, came to an end.

Although the sources say little about the sorts of firearms used by
the parties involved during Đại Việt's "long march," without doubt
they employed the best firearms. As mentioned earlier, in 1479, when
Đại Việt troops were on their way to invade Ai-lao, a firearm arsenal
was burned down accidentally. The incident was recorded, probably
because of the urgency of firearms for the campaign.[174] *The Chiang Mai
Chronicle* records that "blunderbusses" were made and used by Lan
Na to repel the Đại Việt forces. The original Thai Yuan word for
"blunderbuss" is *puun yai,* or "big gun" whose muzzle was around
ten centimeters.[175] Hence, this "blunderbuss" could have been a
Chinese-style handgun or cannon.

Not only mainland but also maritime Southeast Asia felt the reper-
cussions of Đại Việt's expansionist activities. In 1481 envoys from Melaka complained to the Ming that in 1469 Đại Việt had plundered its
envoys to the Ming court when they were forced by strong wind to
the shore of Đại Việt. "Annam had occupied the cities of Champa and
wanted to annex Melaka's territory," but Melaka "dared not raise
troops to engage war with them." The Ming emperor's edict admon-
ished Đại Việt for these actions and informed the Melakan envoys: "If
Annam is again aggressive or oppresses you, you should train soldiers and horses to defend against them."[176] The details of Đại Việt's

attempted invasion of Melaka cannot be substantiated, but it seems
that Melaka may have been directly threatened in some way.[177] According to one Chinese source, Lê Thánh-tông led ninety thousand
troops to invade Lan Sang but was chased by the troops of Melaka,
who killed thirty thousand Vietnamese soldiers.[178] Although intriguing, this Đại Việt–Melaka connection is not supported by hard
evidence. In 1485 Đại Việt included Melaka on the list of tributary
countries together with Champa, Lang Sang, Ayudhya, and Java.[179]

The immediate impact of Đại Việt's southward expansion and sack
of the Cham capital, Vijaya, was the diaspora of the Cham to different
places, such as Hainan, Cambodia, Thailand, Melaka, Aceh, and Java.
For example, over one thousand Chams fled to Hainan with a Cham
prince, who later became king of the remnant Champa under Ming
patronage. According to the *Sejarah Melayu*, after Vijaya fell, "the
children of the Raja of Champa together with the ministers scattered
and fled in all directions. Two sons of the Raja, one of them named
Indra Berma Shah and the other Shah Palembang, escaped by ship,
Shah Palembang to Acheh and Shah Indra Berma to Malaka. . . . That
was the origin of the Chams of Malaka, all of whom are sprung from
Shah Indra Berma and his descendents." This exodus of the people of
Champa resulted in the modern linguistic distribution of Chamic dialects.[180]

Through the Cham emigration other countries or regions in maritime Southeast Asia may have felt the shock wave of Đại Việt's aggression and expansion. According to a Vietnamese source, Đại Việt
during the late Hồng-đức reign (1470–97) also subdued Ryukyu (Liu-
qiu).[181] However, this is so far not supported by other sources. The
records on the Ryukyu side, such as the *Rekidai hoan* (The Precious
Records of the Consecutive Dynasties), are completely silent on Ryukyu–Đại Việt relations until 1509, when the king of Ryukyu sent a
mission to Đại Việt.[182] The so-called subjugation of Ryukyu may refer
to the fight that occurred when a Ryukyuan ship was cast onto the
Đại Việt shore in 1480.[183]

Different countries and peoples perceived the expansion of Đại
Việt differently. The Vietnamese were jubilant and content with Lê
Thánh-tông's reign: "Thánh-tông . . . revitalized all the professions,
set up *phu* and *ve*, fixed official ranks, promoted rite and music, chose
clean and able officials, sent expeditions to the four directions, expanded the territories; Tra Toan was captured, Lao-qua (Lan Sang)

collapsed, Ryukyu was defeated, Cam Cong fled and died, the barbarians in the four directions surrendered, wind blew from the eight directions. [During his] thirty-eight-year rule, the country was peaceful and well governed. How spectacular was this!"[184]

In the eyes of the Chinese, the Vietnamese were extremely troublesome: "In the seventeenth year of Chenghua (1481), Laowo (Lan Sang) [sent envoys to the Ming court] for emergency help. The Ministry of War memorialized: 'Annam annexed Champa on the east, took Laowo on the west, dilapidated Babai (Lan Na), issued a false edict to the Cheli (Sipsong Panna) Pacification Commission, killed the envoys of Melaka. [We] heard that its country will send three thousand warships to attack the Hainan [island].'"[185]

However, for other Southeast Asians, such as the Chams, the Thai/Shan from the western frontier of Đại Việt to modern Burma, the Burmans of Ava, and even the Melakans (and perhaps the Ryukyuans), Đại Việt of the second half of the fifteenth century was a formidable enemy and a great potential threat. This study suggests that the borrowed gunpowder technology contributed to the golden age of Đại Việt, a factor that may or may not have been acknowledged by the contemporaries of China and Southeast Asia.

The Legacy of Chinese-Style Firearms in Post-1497 Đại Việt

The Vietnamese continued to employ firearms after Lê Thánh-tông's reign. As Đại Việt's territory extended to the south, its military forces and technology followed. In 1471, immediately after the victory over Champa, one *ve* was set up in the conquered Cham land Quang-nam. In 1498 a *"chong* and crossbow" unit (*so*) was added, and two more *ve* were set up, each with a *"chong* and crossbow" unit.[186] From the early sixteenth century onward, handguns, signal guns, cannons, and rockets were regularly used, though mostly in the domestic fighting of Đại Việt rather than against external enemies. In 1508 King Lê Uy Mục's body was blown to pieces by a big cannon (*pao*).[187] In 1511 and 1522 signal guns (and probably other firearms) were fired by Đại Việt government troops in fighting against rebels.[188] After the usurpation of the Mạc in 1527, firearms, including signal guns, cannons, and handguns, were more frequently employed by both the Mạc and the Trịnh forces in 1530, 1555, 1557, 1578, 1589, 1591, 1592, and 1593.[189]

Vietnamese records attest the effectiveness of these firearms. For instance, in 1555 almost all of the several tens of thousands of Mạc troops were killed. In 1578 the Trịnh soldiers "fired [their] *chong* together at them, [killing] countless Mạc soldiers." In 1593 the troops under Nguyễn Hoàng, who was sent to Thuận-hoá as a military commander, came back with heavy firearms, including cannons, to fight the Mạc forces. As a result the fortification of the Mạc was broken, and about ten thousand Mạc soldiers were killed.[190] It is also noteworthy that in the decisive battle between the Mạc and the Trịnh in 1592 in Thăng-long, Mạc troops employed heavy firearms (*dachong baizi huoqi* in Chinese, literally meaning "big *chong* and hundred-*son* [bullet] firearms"); a description of the fighting scene notes that "the [sound] of handguns and cannons shook the sky," showing the intensity of the use of firearms.[191] In 1597, 1619, and 1623, big *chong* (presumably cannons) and *chong* were fired in suppressing rebellions or in connection with royal intrigues.[192]

Especially from the fifteenth century onward, firearms became an increasingly significant part of the political life of the Đại Việt state and of individual Vietnamese people of different levels of society. First, the institutionalization of gunpowder technology is clearly indicated by the fact that, at least by the eighteenth century, skills in operating handguns and cannon were tested in the triennial military examination, and the examinees of the first three levels were rewarded with copper coins based on the accuracy of their shooting. Second, at some state ceremonies for worshipping firearms, after firearms were fired cannons carried by carriages and different kinds of firearms shooters paraded following a certain order. Eventually the firearms were sent back to the arsenals.[193] Third, the Đại Việt state had to regulate the manufacture, use, repair, and trade of firearms and gunpowder because of their penetration into the ordinary lives of people, especially soldiers and craftsmen. Đại Việt laws and statutes prohibited trading firearms with foreign countries, privately storing and manufacturing firearms, and stealing firearms from government arsenals. Violators of these laws and statutes were severely punished.[194] Fourth, gunpowder and firearms-manufacturing materials, including iron (cannon) balls, lead, saltpeter, and sulfur, were increasingly required by the Vietnamese state. Consequently the mining of these materials was intensified. For example, an edict issued in 1740 ordered ethnic minorities to turn in lead, saltpeter, and sulfur for ammunition in lieu of taxes and corvée.[195]

From the first half of the seventeenth to the early nineteenth century—in the nearly half-century (1627–72) confrontation and war between the Trịnh and the Nguyễn, in the Tây Sơn rebellion and their war against the Qing troops in the late eighteen century, and even in the Nguyễn's fight against the Tây Sơn —though the Vietnamese still retained the Chinese terminology (*chong* and *pao*) for most of their firearms, Chinese-style firearms yielded more and more to European ones and decreased in importance. Since they did not disappear completely, however, more research needs to be done to discern these developments. The use of Chinese-style rockets for both war and entertainment purposes continued and was even widespread.[196]

European and Korean records shed much light on the unique mastery of firearms by the Vietnamese. Among the many countries and regions in Southeast Asia, modern Việt Nam (first the north and then the south) stood out for its impressive number and skillful use of firearms. Đại Việt, rather than Champa, Burma, Siam, or other countries, impressed Tomé Pires at the very beginning of the sixteenth century (prior to the arrival of European firearms in Đại Việt) with its large-scale production of firearms. He observed: "[H]e (the king of Cochin China) has countless musketeers, and small bombards. A very great deal of [gun]powder is used in his country, both in war and in all his feasts and amusements by day and night. All the lords and important people in his kingdom employ it like this. Powder is used everyday in rockets and all other pleasurable exercises." He also reports that a great quantity of sulfur and saltpeter was imported from both China and the Solor islands beyond Java via Melaka: "The island of Solor . . . has a great deal of sulphur, and it is better known for this product than for any other. . . . There is so much of this sulphur that they take it as merchandise from Malacca to Cochin China, because it is the chief merchandise that goes there from Malacca."[197] Pires clearly suggests that a sizeable amount of sulfur was imported into Việt Nam.

A personal observation by a Korean merchant provides unique insight into the matter. Cho Wan-byok ("Zhao Wanbi" in Chinese) was captured and taken to Japan during the Japanese invasion of Korea in 1597. Between 1603 and 1607 he sailed on merchant ships three times from Japan to the Hung-nguyễn county in Nghệ-an. Among many things in the northern realm during the early seventeenth century, the skillful use of firearms by the Vietnamese greatly impressed Cho Wan-byok: "[The Vietnamese] also liked to drill handguns (chong); even children were able to fire them."[198]

In 1653 Alexander de Rhodes said that the weapons of the soldiers in Tonkin included muskets that "they handle[d] with great dexterity."[199] Samuel Baron wrote in 1683 that the Tonqueen (Tonkin) soldiers were "good marksmen, and in that . . . inferior to few, and surpassing most nations in dexterity of handling and quickness of firing their muskets."[200] He also said Tonqueen possessed "guns and cannons of all sorts, as also calibres, some of them of their own fabric, but the greatest part bought of the Portuguese, Dutch, and English, and stored with other ammunition suitable to their occasions."[201] In 1688 William Dampier said that the king of Tonkin purchased cannons and had seventy thousand professional soldiers armed with handguns under him.[202] This purchase of foreign firearms by the Trịnh in the north is also confirmed by a Vietnamese source. In 1670 an edict was issued to ban this practice, probably conducted by private parties.[203] In 1633 Cristoforo Borri observed: "The Cochin-Chinois being now become so expert in the managing of them [artillery], . . . they surpasse our Europeans."[204] By contrast, the Chams' aloof attitude toward firearms is perfectly illustrated in the source cited earlier. Modern historians have pointed out that other Southeast Asian peoples, including the Malays, the Javanese, the Achinese, the Siamese, and the Burmese, though they may have been familiar with firearms before 1511, never "developed their artillery into a very effective arm."[205]

These highly praised skills in firearms can only be explained by Đại Việt's profound knowledge and long experience with firearms ever since 1390. The point to be stressed here is that superior European military technology did not arrive in Đại Việt in a vacuum in the seventeenth century; rather it built on an earlier Sino-Vietnamese layer.[206] It is also noteworthy that the Vietnamese, unlike the Burmese, had a tendency not to hire mercenaries, relying instead on their own native armies.[207] The expertise of the Vietnamese in firearms may have rendered recruiting mercenaries unnecessary.

Several conclusions may be drawn from our discussion. First, this research has shown that Chinese firearms reached Đại Việt by 1390, over 120 years before 1511, when Melaka fell to the Portuguese. This transfer of military technology was greatly furthered by Ming China's invasion and occupation of Đại Việt during 1406–27. The Ming troops, relying in part on their superior firearms, had conquered Đại Việt, a feat which other Chinese dynasties had envied but unsuccessfully attempted. Contrary to the Ming wish, however, the Vietnamese acquired its advanced military technology and numerous firearms during the later period of the Ming occupation, an acquisition ultimately contributing to the expulsion of Ming forces from Đại Việt.

Cultural exchange is a two-way process, and this was also true of the spread of gunpowder technology between China and Đại Việt. Though Đại Việt first acquired gunpowder technology from China, it later exported better techniques such as the wooden wad and possibly a new ignition device to China. On the one hand, it is thus time to rectify once and for all the misunderstanding of the *Ming shi,* or the belief that China learned to make firearms from Việt Nam. On the other hand, it is also time to recognize Việt Nam's contributions to Chinese gunpowder technology.

Second, to quote O'Connor, "States and peoples rise and fall for reasons."[208] The fall of Vijaya in 1471 is a complex issue requiring an equally complex answer. A single explanation is too simplistic. Following Victor Lieberman's multivariable scheme explaining political, socioeconomic, and cultural changes during early modern Southeast Asia and other parts of Eurasia, I propose that gunpowder technology should be considered as one of the variables that caused the downfall of Champa and facilitated Đại Việt's "long march" as far as the Irrawaddy River in modern Burma.[209]

The second half of the fifteenth century witnessed Đại Việt's golden age, especially its external expansion. To the south Đại Việt subdued Champa in 1471 after more than one thousand years of confrontation, with Champa subsequently ceasing to be a viable competing power. Thus the political geography of the eastern part of mainland Southeast Asia dramatically changed. One may even claim that to some extent it was gunpowder technology that paved the way for the *nam tiến,* or Việt Nam's march to the south, and that it was thus responsible for the creation of a new kind of Vietnamese state (Cochin China) and identity, as delineated by Li Tana. To the west Đại Việt not only stabilized its border region with the different Tai peoples but also marched all the way to the Irrawaddy River in Burma in the late 1470s and early 1480s. As a result kingdoms in northern mainland Southeast Asia, including Lan Sang, Chiang Mai, Sipsong Panna, and Burma, were terrified, and even Ming China was alarmed. Parts of maritime Southeast Asia such as Melaka felt the threat of Đại Việt as well.

Although many other factors contributed to these developments in fifteenth century northern mainland Southeast Asia, gunpowder technology was one of the most crucial. To paraphrase the epigraphs at the beginning of this essay, Đại Việt borrowed, digested, and internalized Chinese gunpowder technology and employed it to achieve its ends more easily than before, while Champa, for reasons still unclear to us, failed to grasp this technology and was penalized fatally. Lan Sang, Lan Na, and other Tai peoples, though obtaining gunpowder technology, incorporated it less effectively than Đại Việt in terms of quality and quantity.

Notes

This article is derived from my dissertation, "Ming–Southeast Asian Overland Interactions, c. 1368–1644" (University of Michigan, 2000), with substantial revision and enlargement. My thanks go to Dai Kelai, under whom I studied Sino-Vietnamese relations and whose translation of Vietnamese works was extremely useful for this research; to John K. Whitmore, whose research was crucial for my understanding Vietnamese history and for lending me sources; to Li Tana for her valuable suggestions; to Geoff Wade for suggesting and lending numerous sources and commenting on some points; to Bruce Lockhart for sharing his unpublished papers and his comments; to Aroonrut Wichienkeeo for checking the original text of the *Chiang Mai Chronicle;* to Trần Kỳ Phương for his comments on the paper and Vietnamese firearms; to Đinh Văn Minh for his important help with my research at the Institute for Hán-Nôm Studies in Hà Nội; to Phan Thanh Hải and Sujira Meesanga (Noi) for sending me illustrations; and to Kennon Breazeale and Volker Grabowsky for helping me with a Thai source. I am especially indebted to Victor Lieberman for his critical and constructive comments on the content and style of this paper; to Anthony Reid and Nhung Tuyet Tran for their valuable suggestions, patience, and numerous efforts in editing the paper; and to the Asia Research Institute, National University of Singapore for funding my trip to Việt Nam, which allowed me to have access to more Vietnamese historical records and Vietnamese firearms. I also thank two anonymous referees for their comments and suggestions.

1. Sun Laichen, "Transfers of Military Technology from Ming China to Northern Mainland Southeast Asia."

2. *Ming shi,* 92:2264. See also 89:2176–77. Here and elsewhere in the essay the translations are mine unless otherwise noted.

3. Needham, *Science and Civilisation in China,* 311 (pointing out that both Chinese and Western scholars have followed this belief); Phan Huy Lê et al., *Một số trận quyết chiến chiến lược trong lịch sử dân tộc,* 142 n 3.

4. Arima Seiho, *Kaho no kigen to sono denryu,* 166–71; Needham, *Science and Civilisation,* 311–12; Wang Zhaochun, *Zhongguo huoqi shi,* 106–7; Li Tana, *Nguyễn Cochinchina,* 43–44. See also Zheng Yongchang, *Zhengzhan yu qishou,* 39 n 65; Liu Zhenren, "Mingdai weisuo zhidu yanjiu," 309. One participant at the conference on Việt Nam at UCLA, where this study was originally presented, informed me that she had been teaching the old view.

5. The time spans are based on 192–1471 or 939–1471, with 192 as the beginning date of Champa and 939 the start of Việt Nam independent of Chinese control.

6. For discussion of the divergent views on the *nam tiến* in modern Vietnamese historiography (1954–75), see Lockhart, "Competing Narratives of the *Nam tien.*"

7. For example, "the Vietnamese march southward at the expense of Champa was, to a large extent, a demographic pressure. The Vietnamese victory was above all a victory of number;" and "the fourteenth century . . . witnessed the demographic explosion in Vietnam that brought about the imbalance of forces that existed between the two kingdoms. . . . Champa . . . was defeated by sheer number." See Quách-Langlet, "Geographical Setting of Ancient Champa," and Lafont, "New Patterns on the Ethnic Composition of Champa," 41–42, 69. See also Maspéro, *Champa Kingdom,* 112; Trần Trọng Kim, *Yuenan tongshi,* 10.

8. O'Connor, "Agricultural Change and Ethnic Succession in Southeast Asian States," 986.

9. Li Tana, *Nguyễn Cochinchina,* 159–72.

10. Whitmore, "Transforming Dai Viet, Politics and Confucianism in the Fifteenth Century," chap. 5; idem, "Two Great Campaigns of the Hong-Duc Era (1470–1497) in Dai Viet," 3; Momoki Shiro, "Dai Viet and the South China Sea Trade," 18–23.

11. Hall, *Maritime Trade and State Development in Early Southeast Asia,* 178–93; idem, "Economic History of Early Southeast Asia," 1:252–60. The French colonial image of Champa as a mono-ethnic Cham and centralized state has been challenged in recent years. In addition to Hall's works, see Hickey, *Sons of the Mountains,* 78–120; Taylor, "Early Kingdoms," 153–57; Li Tana, *Nguyễn Cochinchina,* 31–33; Reid, "Chams in the Southeast Asian Maritime System," 49–53. For a detailed overview of the debate on the nature of "Champa" in Vietnamese historiography, see Lockhart, "Colonial and Post-colonial Constructions of 'Champa,'" 1.

12. Chen Chingho (Chen Jinghe), *Đại Việt sử ký toàn thư* (cited henceforth as *Toàn thư*), 1:464. *Kham dinh Viet su thong giam cuong muc* (cited henceforth as *Cương mục*), 11:12a, says *huopao* (cannon), which was a nineteenth-century alteration. For consistency and simplicity, I use Chinese terminology for all the weapons that appear throughout this study. The Vietnamese borrowed

terms from the Chinese for all the firearms as well as other types of weapons. For example, *hoa tiên* for *huojian, phao* for *pao,* and *súng* for *chong.*

13. Trần Trọng Kim, *Yuenan tongshi,* 128; Li Tana, *Nguyễn Cochinchina,* 43. The word *chong* in the early Ming period could mean either "handgun" or "cannon." When it is not clear whether it refers to a handgun or a cannon, the original term is kept instead.

14. Momoki Shiro, "10–15 seiki Betonamu kokka no minami to nishi," 166.

15. Momoki Shiro, "Was Champa a Pure Maritime Polity?" 7; Whitmore, "Two Great Campaigns," 2.

16. Maspéro, *Champa Kingdom,* 64. See also 92–94, 107–9.

17. Defeating his rival Xiang Yu, Han Gaozu, or Liu Bang, founded the Former Han dynasty (206 BCE–25 CE).

18. *Toàn thư,* 462–64; Whitmore, *Vietnam, Ho Quy Ly, and the Ming,* 29–30; idem, "Two Great Campaigns," 2; Li Tana, *Nguyễn Cochinchina,* 21.

19. Lo Jung-pang, "Intervention in Vietnam," 159; Whitmore, *Vietnam,* 30–32; Momoki Shiro, "10–15," 166.

20. *Ming shilu youguan Yunnan lishi ziliao zhaichao,* 2:642.

21. *Toàn thư,* 471; Zheng Yongchang, *Zhengzhan,* 48; Whitmore, *Vietnam,* 43–44.

22. Li Wenfeng, *Yue qiao shu,* 2:17b.

23. Ibid., 2:18b, 23a.

24. *Ming shilu,* 1:215, 228; Qiu Jun, *Pingding Jiaonan lu,* 47:1–12; *Toàn thư,* 1:495; Li Wenfeng, *Yue qiao shu,* 2:23a–b, 30a; 6:4b; 10:8a, 12a, 16a.

25. Regarding the estimated percentage, see Wang Zhaochun, *Zhongguo huoqi shi,* 103.

26. Cited in Needham, *Science and Civilisation,* 339.

27. All the dates were converted by following Hazelton, *Synchronic Chinese-Western Daily Calendar.* Regarding the military operation, see *Ming shilu,* 1:223, 225.

28. *Ming shilu,* 1:225; Li Wenfeng, *Yue qiao shu,* 10:4b–5a. Some figures for troops and war casualties in both Chinese and Vietnamese sources seem to have been exaggerated, but this cannot be verified. Wei Yuan challenged the figures of armies in Ming records. See his *Shengwu ji,* 2:492. For a battle between the Ming and the Shan in 1388, the actual number of troops is doubled in the *Ming shilu.* See Zhang Hong, "Nanyi shu," bk. 255, p. 199; *Ming shilu,* 1:98, 110–11, 130. On the Vietnamese side, at least on one occasion we know the figure is inflated due to scribal error (see note 148).

29. *Ming shilu,* 1:222; Li Wenfeng, *Yue qiao shu,* 2:22a.

30. Li Wenfeng, *Yue qiao shu,* 6:6b; 10:6b.

31. Ibid., 6:7a; 10:7a.

32. Ibid., 10:7b, 16a; *Ming shilu,* 1:228.

33. Li Wenfeng, *Yue qiao shu,* 10:15b.

34. In the accounts *xianren dong* are not identified.

35. *Toàn thư,* 1:490.

36. As early as 445, the Chinese armies had already employed the effigies of lions to rout the elephantry of Champa. See *Gudai Zhong Yue guanxi shi*

ziliao xuanbian, 1:94. Similarly, in 1592, during the Japanese invasion of Korea, the Japanese soldiers wore hats with a "ghost head and lion face" (*guitou shimian*) on them to scare Chinese horses, and the technique was very successful. See Zheng Liangsheng, *Mingdai Zhong Ri guanxi yanjiu*, 587.

37. Here *shenji chong* seems to refer to heavy cannon.

38. Whitmore, "Two Great Campaigns," 8.

39. Li Wenfeng, *Yue qiao shu*, 6:7a; idem, 10:7b–8a, 16a; *Ming shilu*, 1:228.; Wang Shizhen, *Annan zhuan*, 48:14a.

40. *Toàn thư*, 1:490. See also Li Wenfeng, *Yue qiao shu*, 6:7a and 10:8b.

41. *Ming shi*, 321:8315.

42. *Ming shilu*, 1:228–29; *Toàn thư*, 1:490; Li, *Yue qiao shu*, 6:7b; 10:8a–b, 16a–b.

43. *Ming shilu*, 1:229. See also Li Wenfeng, *Yue qiao shu*, 10:9a.

44. *Ming shilu*, 1:230; Li Wenfeng, *Yue qiao shu*, 10:9b; *Toàn thư*, 1:493.

45. Li Wenfeng, *Yue qiao shu*, 10:17a.

46. *Toàn thư*, 1:493.

47. Li Wenfeng, *Yue qiao shu*, 10:10a.

48. One *li* = 0.5 kilometers = 500 meters.

49. *Annan zhiyuan*, 229.

50. *Ming shilu*, 1: 231–32; Li Wenfeng, *Yue qiao shu*, 10:10a–11a.

51. Li Wenfeng, *Yue qiao shu*, 10:11b; *Toàn thư*, 1:493–94.

52. Li Wenfeng, *Yue qiao shu*, 10:12a; *Annan zhiyuan*, 231.

53. Li Wenfeng, *Yue qiao shu*, 6:8b; *Toàn thư*, 1:494.

54. Huang Fu, *Huang Zhongxuangong wenji*, 2:15.

55. *Ming shilu*, 1:277, 278, 295. Both Chinese and Vietnamese sources overwhelmingly attest Zhang Fu's extraordinary military leadership, but only one Chinese record reveals the cruel side of this Ming general. According to Gu Yingtai (*Mingshi jishi benmo*, 22:249), during the first month of the eighth year of Yongle (February 4–March 5, 1410), Zheng Fu in the battle at Dong-trieu chau killed five thousand Vietnamese rebels and captured two thousand, who were "all buried alive [first and then dug out] and piled up for display in the [Vietnamese] capital." The Yongle emperor, who had been bothered by Zhang Fu's continuous cruelty in battles, recalled him. This account, however, is not corroborated by other sources.

56. *Ming shilu*, 1:280; *Ming shi*, 321:8317; Li Wenfeng, *Yue qiao shu*, 6:9b.

57. *Ming shilu*, 1:283–84; Yamamoto Tatsuro, *Annan shi kenkyu*, 435. The *Ming shi* (321:8317) describes the assault from the firearms of the Ming side as "cannon [balls] and arrows burst[ing] out."

58. *Ming shilu*, 1:308–9;

59. Ibid., 1:370–71.

60. Ibid., 1:287.

61. Ibid., 1:301.

62. Regarding the connection to the campaigns against the Mongols, see Wang Zhaochun, *Zhongguo huoqi shi*, 102.

63. Regarding the Yongle emperor's boast, see *Ming shilu*, 1:236. A late Ming scholar commented that Ming Chengzu "stands out among the hun-

dred kings" (Zhang Jingxin, *Yu Jiao ji*, bk. 104, p. 487). For the Vietnamese chronicle, see *Toàn thư*, 2:835.

64. *Toàn thư*, 1:479, 484–87; *Ming shilu*, 1:226, 235; Li Wenfeng, *Yue qiao shu*, 6:6a; 10:6a; Lo Jung-pang, "Intervention in Vietnam," 171.

65. *Toàn thư*, 1:487, 489; Lê Thành Khôi, *Histoire du Viet Nam, des origins à 1858* (1987), 200–201; Gaspardone, "Le Quy-ly," 1:798; Zheng Yongchang, *Zhengzhan yu qishou*, 46, 49–50. For example, when facing the Mongol invasion in 1284, the Vietnamese king invited the elderly wise men from across the country to his court for advice; they unanimously said "fight": "Ten thousand people said the same word, which was just like coming from one mouth." While facing the Ming invasion in 1405 when King Hồ Hán Thương consulted officials in the capital, some said fight and some said peace. His brother Hồ Nguyên Trừng replied: "I am not afraid of fighting but afraid that people will not follow" (*Toàn thư*, 357, 487). Although Ming military superiority (including the Ming navy) has been partially acknowledged, the role of firearms has not been addressed. See Lo Jung-pang Lo, "Emergence of China as a Sea Power during the Late Song and Early Yüng Periods," 493; idem, "Decline of the Early Ming Navy," 150–51; Zheng Yongchang, *Zhengzhan yu qishou*, 38.

66. "Lam sơn thực lục," 1:8b–10a, 13a, 15a–16a; Yamamoto Tatsuro, *Annan shi kenkyu*, 622, 653, 657, 658, 671; "Thiên nam dư hạ tập," "poetry section," 102a; *Toàn thư*, 2:516, 519, 523, 525; Lê Quý Đôn. *Đại Việt thông sư*, 12b, 15b, 16a, 21a, 26b, 27b, 40b.

67. *Toàn thư*, 2:528–29; *Ming shilu*, 1:431; Phan Huy Lê et al., *Một số trận quyết*, 86–130.

68. *Ming shilu*, 1:431.

69. Ibid., 1:420.

70. Regarding the casualties, see "Lam sơn thực lục," 2:6a; "Thiên nam," "poetry section," 109b; *Toàn thư*, 2:529; Phan Huy Lê et al., *Một số trận quyết*, 124–25; *Ming shi*, 154:4240.

71. *Toàn thư*, 2:529; *Cuong muc*, 13:31b; Lê Thành Khôi, *Histoire du Viet Nam* (1987), 211. According to the latter, the bell and the urns were two of the four wonders in ancient Việt Nam.

72. *Ming shilu*, 1:431; *Toàn thư*, 2:529; Phan Huy Lê et al., *Một số trận quyết*, 89, 126–27.

73. *Lam-on*, in "Thiên nam," "poetry section," 111a; *Toàn thư*, 2:530.

74. Unidentified.

75. *Toàn thư*, 2:532–33; Lê Quý Đôn. *Đại Việt thông sư*, 30a; "Viêm bang niên biểu," 64a; "Đại Việt sử ký tục biên," 1:13b, states that Le Loi ordered an iron plant to be opened at Tan-phuc (modern Da-phuc county in the Bac-giang province) to make *Xiangyang pao*.

76. *Toàn thư*, 2:540.

77. *Ming shilu*, 1:228, 456, 465, 472; *Toàn thư*, 2:531.

78. "Thiên nam," "poetry section," 115b; *Ming shilu*, 1:469; Phan Huy Lê et al., *Một số trận quyết*, 141.

79. *Ming shilu*, 1:441, 469–70; *Toàn thư*, 2:541. Regarding *Lügong che*, see Needham, *Science and Civilisation*, vol. 5, pt. 6, p. 439.

80. *Toàn thư*, 2:541.

81. "Lam sơn thực lục," 2:10b. Also in "Thiên nam," "poetry section," 115b.

82. Phan Huy Lê et al., *Một số trận quyết*, 141, 143.

83. "Lam sơn thực lục tục biên," 16b, 17b.

84. "Lam sơn thực lục," 2:11a; "Thiên nam," "poetry section," 114a–15b, 116b–17a; *Toàn thư*, 2:541–43; *Ming shilu*, 1:434–35, 445, 447–48, 449–50; Phan Huy Lê et al., *Một số trận quyết*, 144–75. The "Lam sơn thực lục" puts the number of the Ming reinforcing troops at two hundred thousand.

85. *Toàn thư*, 2:543.

86. Wang Zhaochun, *Zhongguo huoqi shi*, 104–5, 110.

87. *Ming shilu*, 1:438.

88. Ibid., 1:453 (see also 456–57); "Lam sơn thực lục," in "Thiên nam," "poetry section," 117b; *Toàn thư*, 2:545–46. The "Lam sơn thực lục" claims that over two hundred thousand Ming troops, old and new, returned to China.

89. More importantly, in one of his letters to Wang Tong, the Ming commander-in-chief, Lê Lợi, stated: "In the past, [we had] few weapons, now [our] warships line up like clouds, armors shine against the sun, firearms (*chong jian*) pile up, gunpowder is stored full. Comparing the past to the present, [the change] from weak to strong is apparent." See Nguyễn Trãi, *Uc Trai tap*, E36a (CCLXXV), 551, "Tai du Vuong Thong thu" [Another Letter to Wang Tong].

90. "Lam sơn thực lục," 3:8a; *Toàn thư*, 2:549. Although no firearms are specified, they were doubtless included.

91. Gu Yingtai, *Mingshi jishi benmo*, 22:257; *Ming shi*, 321:8325; Ngô Thị Sĩ, "Đại Việt sử ký tiền biên," 10:52b. See also Yan Congjian, *Shuyu zhouzi lu*, 198.

92. *Ming shilu*, 1:453, 460, 469, 479, 489, 491; *Toàn thư*, 2:515, 550, 554, 555, 556, 562, 569, 602; *Ming shi*, 321:8325.

93. This section benefited from the following works: Li Bin, "Yongle chao he Annan de huoqi jishu jiaoliu"; Arima Seiho, *Kaho*, 169; Needham, *Science and Civilisation*, 311–13.

94. Qiu Jun, *Daxue yanyi bu*, 122:11b–12a; Yan Congjian, *Shuyu zhouzi lu*, 183, 243; Hui Lu, *Pingpi baijin fang*, 4:32b; Zhang Xiumin, "Mingdai Jiaozhi ren zai Zhongguo zhi gongxian," 55–57.

95. Hui Lu, *Pingpi baijin fang*, 4:32b; Needham, *Science and Civilisation*, 240, 311–13, 488 n b; Qiu Jun, *Daxue yanyi bu*, 122:11b–12a.

96. Li Bin, "Yongle che ha Annan," 151–54.

97. The Lamphun handgun (see note 174) also has this device, though it is missing.

98. *Toàn thư*, 1:493.

99. Ibid.

100. Regarding the fate of Hồ Quý Ly and Hồ Hán Thương, see *Ming shilu*, 1:247. Yan Congjian (*Shuyu zhouzi lu*, 183) says that they were executed, but Gu Yingtai in the *Mingshi jishi benmo* (22:248) states that Hồ Quý Ly was

released from prison later and sent to Guangxi as a soldier. Accounts on the Vietnamese side also differ on this point. Two state that Quý Ly, Hàn Thường, and others were executed, while the third says that Quý Ly was released from prison and died a natural death after his son Nguyễn Trung became the Minister of Rites (sic) and petitioned on behalf of him. See Ngô Thị Sĩ, "Đại Việt sử ký tiền biên," "Bản kỉ," 8:24b.

101. Li Xu, Jiean Laoren manbi, 220. Other Vietnamese also participated in Yongle's expeditions against the Mongols. It is noteworthy that in 1449 after the capture of the Yingzong emperor, when the Mongols were besieging Bei-jing, a Vietnamese officer trained and led elephants to rout the horses of the Mongols (Ming shilu leizuan—Shewai shiliao juan, 745; Zhang Xiumin, "Ming-dai Jiaozhi ren zai," 62; idem, "Mingdai Jiaozhi ren yiru neidi kao," in Zhang Xiumin, Zhong Yue, 80). Meanwhile, at the highest level a Vietnamese eunuch named Xing An (1389–1459), a descendent of an aristocratic Vietnamese fam-ily, and others, including the minister of war Yu Qian, commanded the troops of the Capital Battalions (jing ying bing) defending Beijing. This was the be-ginning of eunuchs being in charge of the Capital Battalions. See Chan Hok-lam (Chen Xuelin), "Mingdai Annan ji huanguan shishi kaoshu," 209, 228, 230–31, 233–34.

102. Zhang Jue, Jingshi wucheng fangxiang hutong ji, 15, 18; Chen Zongfan, Yandu congkao, 322, 522.

103. Wang Hongxu, Ming shigao [Draft history of the Ming dynasty] (Tian-jin: Tianjin Guji Chubanshe, 1998), cited in Li Bin, "Yongle chao he Annan," 155; Li Xu, Jiean Laoren manbi, 219.

104. Ming shi, 89:2176–77; 92:2264; Li Wenfeng, Yue qiao shu, 2:32a; Zhang Xiumin, "Mingdai Jiaozhi ren zai," 54–62; idem, "Mingdai Jiaozhi ren yiru," 78; Wang Zhaochun, Zhongguo huoqi shi, 104–7; Li Bin, "Yongle chao he An-nan," 154–56; Ming shilu, 1:455; Ming shilu leizuan—Shewai shiliao juan, 757, 758.

105. Li Bin, "Yongle chao he Annan," 156.

106. Ibid., 152; Wang Ji, Junjitang rixun shoujing, 28; Cheng and Zhong, Zhongguo gudai bingqi tuji, 232–33.

107. Ming shilu leizuan—Junshi shiliao juan, 88–186; Wada Sei, Ming dai Menggu shi lun ji, 1:66, 68.

108. Wang Ao, Zhenze jiwen, 1:15a.

109. Ming shilu, "Xianzong," vol. 168, quoted in Zhang Xiumin, "Mingdai Jiaozhi ren zai," 57.

110. Ming shilu leizuan—Junshi shiliao juan, 1078. For a discussion of the Tumu incident, see Frederick W. Mote, "T'u-mu Incident of 1449," 243–72.

111. See note 93.

112. Shen Defu, Wangli yehuo bian, 2:433. Many similar accounts of the Ming and Qing times discovered by this author will be discussed elsewhere. The original source must have been the one in the Daixue yanyi bu (122:1058), written by Qiu Jun in 1487: "Recently there are magical-mechanism firelances (shenji huoqiang) whose arrows are made of iron and are propelled with [gun-powder] fire. It can shoot more than one hundred paces. They are very fast

and wonderful, when the sound is heard the arrow reaches [its target]. During the reign of Yongle, Nanjiao (Đại Việt) was pacified, and the kind made by the Jiao people (Vietnamese) was especially wonderful. Eunuchs were ordered to manufacture [it] following the technique."

113. *Toàn thư*, 2:555. It is hard to know what kind of firearm *huotong* or *hoa dong* refers to here. Li Tana (*Nguyễn Cochinchina*, 41) contends it was a (wooden-barreled) cannon, while Nguyễn Ngọc Huy and Tạ Văn Tài, in *The Lê Code*, interpret it as "brass tube used as weapon to throw flame" (1:129; 3:134). It certainly could have been a handgun as well. If it was a flamer-thrower, it would have been like the ones in figure 10a–b. Indeed, this kind of flamethrower was still widely employed on Chinese (and Korean) warships during the late sixteenth century. See Qi Jiguang, *Jixiao xinshu*, 280–81.

114. *Toàn thư*, 2:599, 625.

115. Ibid., 2:557.

116. Regarding the date, see *Toàn thư*, 2:718. Regarding the "governmental organization," see "Thiên nam," 26b, 86a, 87a–b, 88a. See also "Quốc triều quan chế điển lệ," vols. 2 and 4.

117. "Thiên nam," 32a–49b; "Quốc triều quan chế điển lệ," vol. 5; *Cuong muc*, 20:31b–35b; 34:31a–b; Yan Congjian, *Shuyu zhouzi lu*, 239. At least two of the six Vietnamese handguns at the Vietnamese History Museum in Hà Nội carry inscriptions saying they belong to certain *ve* or *so*.

118. *Toàn thư*, 2:664.

119. Ibid., 2:676.

120. *Tay nam bien tai luc*, 31a; *Toàn thư*, 2:710; "Thiên nam," "governmental organization," 17a, 73a; Nguyễn and Tạ, *Lê Code*, 2:161.

121. *Toàn thư*, 2:740.

122. Ibid., 2:555.

123. Ibid., 2:658.

124. "Thiên nam," "governmental organization," 86b–87a, 89a.

125. He Mengchun, *He Wenjian shuyi*, 8:26b–35b, especially 27a, 29b, 32a; Xie Zhaozhe, *Dian lue*, 3:22a; Bai Shouyi, "Mingdai kuangye de fazhan," 100, 104.

126. *Ming shilu*, 1:478.

127. He Mengchun, *He Wenjian shuyi*, 8:26b–35b.

128. *Ming shilu*, 2:802; Zhang Xuan, *Xiyuan wenjian lu*, 68:17b.

129. Zhang Xuan, *Xiyuan wenjian lu*, 68:17b.

130. *Ming shilu*, 2:819; He Mengchun, *He Wenjian shuyi*, 4:17a–b, 18a, 26b, 30a.

131. *Ming shilu*, 2:822; Ni Tui, *Dian Yun linian zhuan*, 7:33a; Liu Kun, *Nanzhong zashuo*, 18a.

132. Wu Xingnan, *Yunnan duiwai maoyi*, 62.

133. *Ming shilu*, 2:802.

134. *Toàn thư*, 2:749.

135. Liu Kun, *Nanzhong zashuo*, 18a.

136. *Toàn thư*, 2:685, 706–11; Đào Duy Anh, *Việt Nam Văn hóa Sử cương*, 253, 329–30.

137. Phan Huy Chú, "Lịch triều hiến chương loài chí," 1:143, 149.

138. Wyatt and Wichienkeeo, *Chiang Mai Chronicle*, 80–81.

139. Whitmore, "Development of Le Government in Fifteenth-Century Vietnam," ix. See also Trần Trọng Kim, *Yuenan tongshi*, 173, 180.

140. Whitmore, "Development."

141. "Thiên nam," "governmental organization," 32a–49b; *Cương mục*, bk. 5, 2015–22.

142. Whitmore suggested to me that throughout the early Lê not a single domestic rebellion had occurred.

143. *Toàn thư*, 2:590, 604, 605, 607–8, 613, 616, 630, 631, 659, 661–62, 663; Gaspardone, "Annamites et Thai au xve siècle"; Whitmore, "Colliding Peoples," 8–12; Yamamoto Tatsuro, *Betonamu Chugoku kankeishi*, map.

144. *Toàn thư*, 403–4.

145. Ibid., 1:471, 479–83; Whitmore, *Vietnam*, 72–76; Chen Chingho, *Historical Notes on Hoi-An (Faifo)*, 1–5.

146. *Ming shilu*, 1:244, 332.

147. *Toàn thư*, 2:611; *Ming shilu*, 2:709–10.

148. *Toàn thư* says seven hundred thousand, but *Tay nam* states seventy thousand. The former must be a scribal error.

149. The fighting lasted nearly a month, but the sketchy Vietnamese chronicle devotes only one page to it.

150. *Ming shilu*, 2:89. Yan Congjian (*Shuyu zhouzi lu*, 256) states that the Vietnamese killed more than three hundred people. This does not seem correct.

151. *Sejarah Melayu*, 102. For the etymology of the word "Kuchi," see Li Tana and Reid, *Southern Vietnam under the Nguyễn*, 2–3.

152. *Tây nam*, 9b–22b; "Thiên nam," "Champa section," 28a; *Toàn thư*, 2:679–84; Whitmore, "Development," 207–15; Maspéro, *Champa Kingdom*, 118.

153. Although the Cham kingdom did not disappear completely, it stopped being a viable force competing with Đại Việt.

154. Yan Congjian, *Shuyu zhouzi lu*, 250.

155. Quotation from Wang Ao, *Zhenze jiwen*, 1:26b. See also *Ming shilu*, 2:599; Yan Congjian, *Shuyu zhouzi lu*, 253.

156. Blagden and Edwards, "Chinese Vocabulary of Cham Words and Phrases."

157. Hoàng Côn, "Chiêm Thành khảo," 1a.

158. I thank Trần Kỳ Phương, former curator of the Đà Nẵng Museum of Champa Sculpture, for informing me about the absence of firearms among Champa artifacts.

159. Gonçalez, "Relation des affaires du Campā"; Reid, *Southeast Asia in the Age of Commerce*, 2:226. The first quote is translated for me by Pholsena Vatthana while the second one is from Reid. I thank Vatthana Pholsena also for reading the French translation of Gonçalez.

160. "Thiên nam," "Champa section," 2b; Maspéro, *Champa Kingdom*, 117.

161. *Tay nam*, 20b–21b; *Toàn thư*, 2:683, 685.

162. Muong Phuan appears as "Bon man" in Vietnamese and "Meng Ban" in Chinese records (*Ming shilu*, 2:828).

163. *Tây nam*, 23a–33a; *Toàn thư*, 2:705–10; Stuart-Fox, *Lao Kingdom of Lan Xang*, 65–66.

164. Wyatt, *Nan Chronicle*, 57; Wyatt and Aroonrut, *Chiang Mai Chronicle*, 98–99; Cannsu Kamani Sankram, *Jan May rajavan*, pp. ka–gi; *Ming shilu*, 2:813, 818, 828.

165. *Tay nam*, 31a; *Toàn thư*, 2:710.

166. Keng Tung here and Mong Mit and Hsenwi later in the discussion were all independent (though under nominal Ming control) Shan principalities in modern northern Burma.

167. *Ming shi*, 315:8132.

168. Yan Congjian, *Shuyu zhouzi lu*, 201–2; *Toàn thư*, 2:733.

169. *Ming shilu*, 2:812–13; *Tay nam*, 33a–b; *Toàn thư*, 2:712–13.

170. *Ming shilu*, 2:814, 818. Both Yuanjiang and Guangnan were in southeastern Yunnan.

171. Ibid., 2:825.

172. Li Wenfeng, *Yue qiao shu*, 11:18a–b.

173. *Ming shilu*, 2:837.

174. The hard evidence for the employment of firearms by the Đại Việt troops is a Vietnamese handgun held in the Lamphun Museum in northern Thailand. Limited knowledge of Vietnamese firearms led this piece to be wrongly identified as a Chinese handgun (Samran Wangsapha, "Pu'n san samai boran thi lamphun"). Based on the Vietnamese-style inscription (which is clearly different from the Chinese ones) on the gun, plus the historical context of Vietnamese invasion of Nan, one can confidently assign a Vietnamese origin to the gun. Otherwise, it would be hard to explain how a (fifteenth-century) Vietnamese gun appeared in northern Thailand. This gun is probably the only artifact of the Vietnamese invasion. I thank Kennon Breazeale for bringing this article to my attention and Volker Grabowsky for translating it.

175. *The Chiang Mai Chronicle* says that an archer named Mun Thum knew how to make "three-fathom arrows and blunderbusses" (99), while the Burmese *Jan May rajavan*, which is a translation of *The Chiang Mai Chronicle*, records "big bows and big machines" (*le kri yantara cet kri*) (p. ga), no doubt from the Thai Yuan words. Aroonrut in a personal communication informed me of the original Thai Yuan word and the size of the muzzle.

176. *Ming shilu*, 2:820, 822; Wade, "Melaka in Ming Dynasty Texts," 43. The translation is from Wade.

177. For example, Đại Việt may have used the harboring of a Cham prince by Melaka as a casus belli against Melaka, or Melaka's complaint to the Ming court against Đại Việt was perhaps made on behalf of these Cham refugees (see the following discussion).

178. Mao Qiling, *Mansi hezhi*, 10:1b.

179. *Toàn thư*, 2:726; Momoki Shiro, "Dai Viet," 21–22 and n 29.

180. Thurgood, *From Ancient Cham to Modern Dialects*, especially 22–23; *Ming shilu*, 2: 842; *Sejarah Melayu*, 102–3; al-Ahmadi, "Champa in Malay Literature," 104; Marrison, "Chams of Malaka."

181. *Toàn thư*, 2:762, 835.

182. Kobata Atsushi and Matsuda Mitsugu, *Ryukyuan Relations with Korea and South Sea Countries*, 183–86.

183. Ibid., 119.

184. *Toàn thư*, 2:835.

185. Wan Sitong, "Ming shi," "shibu, baishi lei," 413:598. See also the *Ming shilu*, 2: 817–18, 820–23.

186. *Toàn thư*, 2:686; *Cương mục*, 24:31a–b.

187. *Toàn thư*, 2:789.

188. Ibid., 2:801, 829.

189. Ibid., 2:839, 853, 854, 877, 886–90, 893, 895.

190. Ibid., 3:899; Quốc Sử Quán Triều Nguyễn, *Đại Nam thực lục*, 1:25.

191. Mao Yuanyi, *Wu bei zhi*, 6:5187–88.

192. *Toàn thư*, 2:911, 935.

193. "Lê triều hội điển," vol. 3; Phan Huy Chú, "Lịch triều hiến chương loài chí," 41:122–23, 126–27, 133–36.

194. "Quốc triều hình luật mục lục," 1:16b–17a; 2:46a; "Lê triều hội điển," vol. 3; Phan Huy Chú, "Lịch triều hiến chương loài chí," 35:12; 40:85–88; idem, *Lịch triều hiến chương loài chí*, 13:138, 140, 142.

195. "Lê triều hội điển," vol. 1; Phan Huy Chú, *Lịch triều hiến chương loài chí*, 13:118; 31:471–72; Nguyễn Ngọc Huy and Tạ Văn Tài, *Lê Code*, 2:83.

196. Pires, *Suma Oriental*, 1:115; *Toàn thư*, 3:1095.

197. Pires, *Suma Oriental*, 1:115, 203. "Solor" includes not only the Solor Islands but also the island of Flores in modern Indonesia.

198. Iwao Seiichi, "Annan koku tokou Chosenjin Cho Wan-byok ni tsuite," 11.

199. Rhodes, *Rhodes of Viet Nam*, 57.

200. Baron, "Description of the Kingdom of Tonqueen," 6:686.

201. Ibid., 6:665.

202. Cited in Reid, *Southeast Asia in the Age of Commerce*, 2:226.

203. *Toàn thư*, 3:991.

204. Borri, *Cochin-China: Containing Many Admirable Rarities and Singularities of that Country*, chap. 7; Boxer, "Asian Potentates," 166.

205. Boxer, "Asian Potentates," 162, 165–66; Li Tana, *Nguyễn Cochinchina*, 44–45.

206. "Sino-Vietnamese" here means "Chinese" by origin and "Vietnamese" in application.

207. Reid, *Southeast Asia in the Age of Commerce*, 2:226; Frédéric Mantienne, "Le recours des états de la péninsule indochinoise," 59.

208. O'Connor, "Agricultural Change," 987.

209. Lieberman, "Local Integration and Eurasian Analogies" and "Transcending East-West Dichotomies."

4

Beyond the Myth of Equality
Daughters' Inheritance Rights in the Lê Code

NHUNG TUYET TRAN

In the historiography on Việt Nam, women emerge as a distinct sign of that country's cultural heritage. Women mark "tradition" and appear in three reified forms: as signs of Confucian oppression; of Vietnamese uniqueness; or of Southeast Asian autonomy. As signs of Confucian oppression, women have been represented by Vietnamese feminists and Western scholars as bound by "a whole system of moral principles that preached moral submission."[1] In the historiography on Southeast Asia, Vietnamese women symbolize a cultural commonality binding the various states into a cohesive unit.[2] Between the two cultural traditions of the Southeast Asian and the Sinic world, another model of Vietnamese womanhood emerged, one emphasizing Vietnamese uniqueness insofar as "Woman" embodies an indigenous cultural tradition predating Chinese influence.[3] Outstanding female figures in Vietnamese history, such as the nation's mythical fairy mother, Âu Cơ; the Trưng sisters and Triệu Thị Trinh, who led successful military assaults against the Chinese invaders; and poetesses such as Princess Ngọc Hân and Hồ Xuân Hương mark an ostensibly unified national culture that predates and outlasts Chinese cultural influence.[4]

In the historical literature on Việt Nam, scholars have argued that the penal code of the Lê dynasty (1428–1788), the Quốc Triều Hình Luật (hereinafter, Lê Code), granted women equal inheritance rights, displaying a remarkable resistance to Chinese patriarchal influences.[5] Departing from that interpretive framework, this essay argues that the "myth of equality" distorts the letter and logic of the law with respect to women's property claims. New local sources and a review of the available evidence suggest that the Lê Code never guaranteed women equal property rights. Rather, the law and legal practice guaranteed the property claims of sons over daughters. Although women did enjoy a number of limited property claims, these claims were conditional and appear to reflect Chinese inheritance norms in the Tang, Song, and early Ming dynasties.[6] Although the logic of the law emphasized the transmission of property along the agnatic line, in practice the property regime was more nuanced. Local power dynamics, familial relationships, and a woman's sexual fidelity determined the extent to which a woman could lay claim on household property. Sons, however, enjoyed an equal claim to household property because of their gender.

Much of the scholarship that alludes to Vietnamese gender relations relies on a binary construction between Chinese and Vietnamese custom in which Chinese women's bound feet signify the hegemonic oppressiveness of Confucianism. These reified constructs of Chinese women, however, have been explicitly challenged and undermined by research during the last two decades.[7] Empirical research on Chinese women's history reveals that their experiences belie such a simple characterization.[8] Recent scholarship on Chinese women's property rights suggests that their claims varied across class boundaries and changed with the socioeconomic and cultural agendas of each ensuing dynasty. Kathryn Bernhardt's and Bettine Birge's studies on Chinese women's property rights demonstrate that in the Tang through the Ming periods, women enjoyed customary and legal sanction of their property claims with male heirs.[9] The complexity of Chinese women's experiences emerging from these works serves as a cautionary warning against representing Vietnamese women's experiences against ahistorical notions of Chinese womanhood.

Drawing on these insights in Chinese women's history, this essay locates the property claims of women in the Lê period within the discourses on gender in early modern society. It takes two prevailing paradigms of Vietnamese nationalist historiography, women and the village, and demonstrates that these narratives obscure the dynamics of local power in Vietnamese society. After a brief overview of the existing scholarship, I explore the village codes' representation of community and authority, examine the Lê dynasty's prescriptions on women's property rights, and test these statutes against testamentary records available from the later Lê period. The local sources describe a nuanced property regime that officially legitimated men's authority over most familial property, though women could sometimes negotiate these boundaries and exercise limited control over familial property. Unlike men's, however, women's property claims were closely linked to their sexuality. In short, Vietnamese women enjoyed property claims in spite of codified law, not because of it.

The arguments made in this study derive from local and state documents that prescribe the property regime. At the state level the Penal Code of the [Lê] dynasty (Quốc Triều Hình Luật) and the [Book] of Good Government (Hồng Đức Thiện Chính) present the major penal and civil regulations during the dynasty.[10] The former, commonly known as the Lê Code, has served as the major evidence base for much of what has been written on Vietnamese law.[11] The various statutes and legal cases compiled in the Book of Good Government demonstrate how district officials applied legal rules during the Lê dynasty.[12] Although judgments included in the compilation were specifically chosen by the state, by no means is it a simple replication of the Lê Code. At the very least, this document offers clues to local judgments that the state sanctioned and in doing so provides evidence for how many disputes were adjudicated.

Preliminary findings from local records—including village regulations, magistrates' manuals, and testamentary documents—balance the property regime described in the prescriptive legal sources. Village conventions (hương ước), represented as a covenant among all members of a community, offer a local perspective on expectations placed on women and their legitimated authority in local communities. These conventions allow a limited test against the oft-cited supremacy of village custom over state law (phép vua thua lệ làng). Although village conventions provide insight into local expectations concerning women's property claims, testamentary records demonstrate more directly how women fared within the particular power dynamics of each family. Few pre-nineteenth-century testamentary records remain, but one important source, a collection of contracts from a village in Kiến Xương district, northern Việt Nam, available under the title *Chúc thư văn khế cửu chỉ*, contains originals of testaments from the eighteenth century.[13]

Past Scholarship

Discourses on Vietnamese womanhood emerged out of turn-of-the-twentieth-century colonial discourses on legal reform. These discourses were subsequently appropriated by nationalist scholars, and women emerged as symbols of national uniqueness.[14] In the early years of the twentieth century, scholar-officials from the École Française d'Extrême-Orient (EFEO), charged with realizing the civilizing mission in French Indochina, engaged in vociferous debates on the essence of the "Annamite," his institutions, and readiness for modernity.[15] Under pressure to demonstrate the colony's readiness for Western civilization, these new orientalists wrote Vietnamese women into an ancient, tolerant culture on its way to modernity and created the foundations of the current "Vietnamese woman as unique" paradigm.

The EFEO's publication of Raymond Déloustal's translation of the Lê Code from 1908 triggered debates on the links between Vietnamese women's status in the Lê code and Vietnamese culture writ large. Déloustal's translation made the laws of the Lê dynasty available to Western readers for the first time.[16] In a 1908 introduction to the translation, then director of the EFEO and legal jurist Claude Maitre equated the Lê code with Vietnamese tradition, questioning the appropriateness of applying the Nguyễn dynasty's (1802–1945) legal code as a template for colonial rule.[17] Characterizing the Nguyễn dynasty's legal code as a copy of the Qing Code, Maitre argued that the Lê Code exemplified Vietnamese custom, proclaiming that "the study of justice under the Lê is not only important for the study of history [but] also important for understanding the Annamite mentality." Linking the law directly to indigenous culture, Maitre continued, "The only way in which the Annamites have demonstrated their incontestable superiority over the other peoples of the Far East [is] in the roles that they have given to women, roles [which] were almost equal to men's roles."[18] Although

Déloustal's translation suggested greater ambiguity, Maitre's proc-lamations created a new role that Vietnamese women would play in the history: they would mark the colony's readiness for French civi-lization. Not surprisingly, Vietnamese reformists and nationalists, trained in French legal theory, appropriated this discourse to define the new national character.[19]

NATIONALIST WRITERS AND THE EMERGENCE OF WOMAN AS A NATIONAL SYMBOL

In the first few decades of the twentieth century, French-trained Vietnamese legal scholars equated Vietnamese women's property rights with the emergent national identity.[20] In the few decades before the Second World War, the proliferation of doctoral theses and stud-ies linking "traditional" Vietnamese law as exemplified in the Lê Code, the family, and women attests to the hold that this particular paradigm had on nationalist legal scholars.[21] In the postwar period, Vietnamese and Western scholars rearticulated these claims to exem-plify national greatness. In Hà Nội scholars charged with writing women's history traced the country's history from its matrilineal origins to a transition to patriarchy to the socialist revolution that lib-erated them from feudal society.[22] Evidence of the high status of women in Vietnamese culture and history, they argued, could be found in the Lê Code's guarantee of "equal property rights for a wife and husband [and] daughters' rights to succession."[23]

Scholars from the Republic of Việt Nam, the majority of whom were Sài Gòn law school professors trained by the French, became key transitional figures in exporting the "Vietnamese woman as unique" paradigm to the Western academy. In 1987 Nguyễn Ngọc Huy and Tạ Văn Tài published a three-volume English translation of the Lê Code. In their introduction Nguyễn and Tạ argue that "despite the legal ramifications of Confucian patriarchal thought, a more feminist tradition of indigenous Vietnamese customs persisted and was incor-porated into the Lê Code."[24] In a series of articles detailing his argu-ment, Tạ Văn Tài articulates clearly the connection that subsequent scholars have made between the Lê Code, women's status, and Viet-namese tradition: "The Le Code, unlike the Nguyen Code which was a copy of the Ch'ing code, represented genuine Vietnamese custom with its idiosyncrasies and incorporated original provisions unknown

in any Chinese code . . . to give equal rights to Vietnamese women."[25]
By defining Vietnamese women against ahistorical Chinese women,
Tạ contributes to and perpetuates the paradigm of Vietnamese
women's uniqueness.[26]

Owing much of their framework to French and Vietnamese research on the Lê Code, Western scholars linked women's property
claims in the fifteenth-century code with wider debates on
Vietnamese historical identity. Depending on their own interpretation of Vietnamese historical identity, scholars imputed a protofeminist agenda to the Lê lawmakers' provisions for women's property
rights or saw remnants of a bilateral tradition implicit in the code.
Those trained in the Southeast Asian regional studies tradition
tended to make the latter interpretation, while scholars sympathetic
to the Vietnamese national struggle emphasized the uniqueness of
the endeavor.[27] Reliance on these two models to represent Vietnamese identity has obscured the nuances in women's property claims in
the law and legal practice. This study seeks to challenge the exisiting
paradigms of Vietnamese womanhood by reexamining their property claims in state law, local custom, and legal practice.

Women in the Village Codes

In the contemporary historiography and popular discourse, the
Vietnamese village (*làng*) represents the indigenous rural institution
that protected local custom.[28] The oft-quoted proverb "the laws of the
emperor bow to the custom of the village" (*phép vua thua lệ làng*) ex-
emplifies to some scholars the importance of the village in preserving
an indigenous culture. Vietnamese and Western scholars alike have
used the image of the inward-looking, bamboo-fenced village as yet
another sign of Vietnamese uniqueness.[29] Because Vietnamese villages
have long represented indigenous uniqueness, the village conventions
provide rare insight into customary law. If, as previous scholarship
asserts, Vietnamese women embody indigenous culture and the
village the institution that protects it, then customary law should provide special protection for women's property claims. However, if the
village regulations do not afford women any greater role than does
state law, then a closer look at the Lê Code and its regulations on
women and property is in order.

VILLAGE STRUCTURE:
AUTHORITY AND OWNERSHIP

As one of the most important signs of Vietnamese cultural identity, the village (*làng,* or *thôn*) is often described as a timeless, enclosed, autonomous community surrounded by a bamboo hedge that preserves Vietnamese culture.[30] Evidence from village conventions, land registries, and family genealogies suggests that in contrast to a closed community, villages in the Red River Delta were porous communities based on social obligations discernable in other parts of Southeast Asia.[31] Anthony Reid observes that in many early modern Southeast Asian settings, social relations were held together by "vertical and horizontal bonds of obligation between people" reflected in speech and practical obligations owed one another.[32] Likewise, Vietnamese villages were structured vertically and horizontally, with worthy elder males representing all adults within the village and "outsiders" and women relegated to the bottom of the scale. Members of the village community formed horizontal bonds of obligation through the collective activities of work and worship. The gendered character of the work and religious domains created social, religious, and trade networks that facilitated spheres of action for women. For women of all social classes, Reid's model of vertical and horizontal bonds of patronage clarifies how women could create spheres of influence in a male-oriented hierarchical village structure.

Local power in Vietnamese villages was highly asymmetrical, with older men enjoying the preponderance of power. Village regulations (*hương ước,* or *lệ làng*) allow a rare glimpse into how local customary rules established the gender system.[33] These regulations set forth the regulations for local governance, economic activities, collective work duties, religious practice, and community well-being. Although represented as an agreement among all members of the village community (*bản thôn/làng thượng hạ,* "this village's top and bottom sectors"), the system described within the conventions suggest that the village head (*xã trưởng*), village elders (*hương lão*), and village council (*hội đồng kỳ mục*) established and agreed on those rules.

Within the village, power and position were linked to a complex system of patronage usually determined through the principles of patrilineal succession. The village authority was structured vertically with a council of (male) elders (*hội đồng hương lão*) sitting at the top of this structure. Below the council of elders, the village headman (*thôn trưởng*) and village council (*hội đồng kỳ mục*) oversaw all matters of relevance to the community at large and served as the representative body to the local magistrate.[34] It was in those with village councils and meetings, where males convened and defined the local structures, that ordered community life.[35]

The village-wide meetings functioned as the major space in which community cultural, social, and economic plans were structured. Among other duties, the council, headmen, and elders drafted and voted on the regulations and resolved disputes between villagers and with other villages.[36] The conventions outlined procedures for preventive maintenance during natural disasters, specified punishments for infractions, and established local restrictions with regard to marriage rites, local taxation, and the conscription of able-bodied men (*đinh*) for communal labor.[37] The number of able-bodied men in each village determined the amount of labor owed the state. Moreover, only able-bodied men could participate in deciding who could be elected as a village headman or member of the council of elders. In addition to establishing the conventions, the village council, headmen, and elders also decided on matters of immediate concern to the community as a whole. Evidence from stèle inscriptions of the period indicates that village elders and headmen made decisions on the sale of community cultural performances, the adjudication of minor property disputes between villages, and the election of members of the village community to patron "saints" (*bầu hậu*).[38] Although most documents from the village represent decisions as emerging from consensus among all members of a village community, extant inscriptions demonstrate that those who were required to give their approval were men. Participation in the village power structure was thus strictly limited to male representatives of their lineages.

For purposes of tax collection and local governance, able-bodied men formed the locus of registration.[39] Beneath the elders, headmen, councilmen, and able-bodied men who formed the upper echelons of the village community stood the "outsiders," who wielded little authority within the political structure but could purchase property within the village.[40] Women, too, had no official role in village administrative matters: because they were not registered as members of a lineage, they could not participate in community voting and thus were unrepresented productive members of village society. That they were not recognized officially by the village structure did not disenfranchise them, however, for the economic and demographic realities of early modern Vietnamese life triggered land-holding patterns that enabled women to wield de facto influence in village politics.[41] More specifically, women could accumulate capital, and demographic trends required that they engage in such activity as a survival mechanism; these factors enabled them to exert political influence through economics, particularly in the endowment of public spaces. Thus, although women were likened to "outsiders" in the village system, state mobilization of labor and local agricultural demands wove a complex system in which women performed the majority of economic labor, accumulated capital, and enjoyed spaces of autonomy. However, village regulations suggest that women did not enjoy special protection from customary law. Rather, customary law served to complement (and often reinforce) state law, which emphasized the equal inheritance of sons and legitimized authority for male members of the lineage. Because local regulations offer little support for the proclaimed customary elevation of women in local society, a reexamination of the legal statutes that appear to accord these rights is in order.

Daughters and Inheritance in the Lê Dynasty

Conventional wisdom holds that the Lê lawmakers, guided by proto-feminist or bilateral traditions, codified these values in several statutes to protect women's property claims.[42] That these rights did not exist in the Chinese codes allegedly shows that Vietnamese women were unique and that they enjoyed equal civil rights under the law.[43] Such an interpretation of the statutes that provide for daughters' inheritance and succession rights distorts the logic of the state code.

Inheritance can be separated into two distinct but related processes: household division and succession.[44] Household division refers to the parceling of family property among family members following the parents' death. In the Chinese context household division was governed by the principles of equal inheritance for sons. Daughters generally received a dowry upon marriage, which included landed and moveable property.[45] Succession refers to the assumption of the role of the head of household with the concomitant ceremonial duties following a father's death. Birge argues that through the Song period, law and custom guaranteed a daughter a portion of household property in the form of a dowry, which was never absorbed into her husband's estate. Bernhardt, on the other hand, argues that in the absence of sons, daughters generally inherited landed property through the process of succession.[46] During the Ming period, Bernhardt argues, the rights of daughters and wives were severely limited when lawmakers implemented mandatory nephew succession, a process whereby nephews automatically succeeded their dead uncle.[47]

In the Vietnamese context conventional scholarship argues that daughters shared the same rights over household property, that is, "family property was distributed equally among all children, regardless of sex."[48] The claim that daughters enjoyed such rights over household property relies on a specific reading of Article 388 of the Lê Code. In particular scholars argue that this provision guaranteed daughters equal rights over household division in the form of a dowry, a phenomenon distinct from Chinese inheritance patterns. However, in the Chinese context, as Bernhardt and Birge demonstrate, daughters did inherit household property in the form of dowries.[49]

HOUSEHOLD DIVISION:
AN EQUAL SHARE FOR DAUGHTERS?

The inheritance rights of daughters lie at the crux of the debate on inheritance and succession in the Lê period. That the Lê state, a centralizing, neo-Confucian state, would decree equal inheritance for children regardless of sex certainly deviated from contemporary conceptions of the East Asian model, prompting many scholars to conclude that this law, along with others involving the possibility of female succession, reflected the state's attempt to protect indigenous Vietnamese/Southeast Asian values that celebrated women's status in society. However, an examination of household division and succession as two separate processes in the code reveals that the law never guaranteed daughters an equal right over household division. Rather, the language of the law specifically invested parents with the duty to bequest property equally among their sons, and their male offspring with the duty to respect their parents' will. The logic implicit in these regulations is one of maintenance of the male line, while daughters inherit household property subject to the will of the parents and the power dynamics in the family.

Article 388 of the Lê Code serves as the basis for the interpretation that daughters enjoyed equal claim over household property, but a careful examination of the statute in the original Chinese reveals a more ambiguous regulation. Rather than specifically regulating household division, Article 388 sets the standard for succession and only incidentally refers to household division. The statute reads: "If, at the mother and father's death, they have landed property but did not promulgate a testament in time, then the brothers (huynh đệ) and the sisters (tỉ muội) shall divide it among themselves (tương phân), reserving the first one-twentieth [of the property] for the ancestral duties; to be entrusted in the hands of the eldest son. If, however, the father and mother have left a testament (chúc thư), then their will shall be followed."[50]

Nowhere in the text is there evidence that the daughters had an equal right to the family property in case of household division. The law decrees that *only in the absence of a will and testament* will the brothers and sisters divide the remaining property among themselves. Furthermore, in mentioning division among brothers and sisters, the statute uses the phrase "to divide among" (tương phân), not "to divide equally" (quân phân), a difference with enormous implications. If the law decreed equal inheritance for daughters and sons, then the characters for "equal division" (quân phân) would have been used.[51] At the very least we can say that the substatute so often used as evidence for equal inheritance rights for daughters does not, in fact, decree it. That the strongest evidence pointing to equal inheritance for daughters is at best ambiguous requires supporting evidence for this argument from other sources.

The various statutes and cases in the Book of Good Government do not support the claim that the Lê Code guaranteed equal shares of household property for daughters but rather suggest that the state specifically invested brothers with the power to ensure their share of the general estate. In a statute proscribing household division disputes, the Book of Good Government decrees: "[With regard to] the power of the parents to promulgate a testament, or that of the brothers (huynh-đệ) to draw up a contract (văn khế) to divide [it], the state has laws so that the sons and grandsons (tử-tôn) can inherit for generations without extinction. . . . This is the king's law to be left for future generations."⁵² Here we see a specific reference to the state's position on household division. In this particular case the law clearly indicates that parents and brothers have the power to divide household property equitably. At the risk of stating the obvious, daughters did not enjoy the right to participate in the division process.

In a different statute proscribing feuds over household division, the limitations placed on sons' quarrelling over household division reveal to whom equal division of parents' property applied: "[If, according to] the will and testaments and various documents (*chúc thư văn khê*) the brothers (*huynh-đệ*) have already divided [the property] equally (*quân phân*) and seek to redivide [it], then whoever does so shall carry the crime of impiety (*bột đạo*), and shall be punished with eighty strokes of the cane and be sent to hard labor; [he] shall be required to forfeit his share."⁵³ A daughter's absence of duty in this provision suggests that the law did not grant her that right to equal division of household property. Other statutes in this section reinforce this interpretation. In clarifying how household property should be divided, another statute specifically places the responsibility of overseeing the division on the eldest son. In instances in which parents passed away before dividing the family property, the law decreed "the will and testament (*chúc thư văn khê*) shall be entrusted to the eldest son (*trưởng nam*) [to administer]; his portion [of the property] must be equal to that of the rest of the sons' (*chúng tử*)."⁵⁴ Here, again, the statute specifies that sons enjoyed the right to equal division of household property.⁵⁵ A corollary statute specified that parents were obliged to divide the property fairly among their sons. In this instance, should the parents pass away and "the sons and grandsons' (*tử tôn*) shares of the landed property are not equal (*bất quân*), with one having much and another having little; then [one] may use that reason to establish a new will and testament."⁵⁶ Here, the law specifies that the sons and grandsons have a right to equal division of household property, without mention of daughters' rights.

In only one instance did the law guarantee a daughter a share of the inheritance equal to that of her brothers. The same statute, however, served to limit a daughter's property claims severely. This particular statute regulated widows' remarriage and instances in which a mother conceived a son in the first marriage and a daughter in the second. Here, the law stated that "upon the latter husband's death, the *hương hỏa* property shall be returned to his daughter, with respect to the husband's rights, and cannot be returned to the first husband's son to succeed."[57] The logic behind this provision is clear, that the child of another man (the first husband) cannot succeed the second husband. Thus, in this scenario the daughter may succeed her father. More telling, however, is the provision that seemingly guarantees the daughter an equal share: "As for the mother's property, [it] shall be divided in two, the first husband's son to receive one portion and the latter husband's daughter to receive one portion."[58] Here is the only instance in which a daughter is specifically given the same claim to her mother's property as her brother. However, this provision should not be read in isolation; if the provision is read with the first part of the statute, it becomes evident that the logic behind this particular was to *restrict* a daughter's claim to household property. The first provision in the statute states: "In instances in which the mother has a son with the first husband [and] he prematurely passes away; she remarries and has a son with the second husband, who passes away; and she passes away without remarrying, then the mother's ancestral property and share of the newly created property shall be regarded in the will as the *hương hỏa* property and given to the latter husband's son so that he can maintain the ancestral rites."[59] The first portion of the regulation clearly states that the mother's property would be given to the son of the second husband; the logic behind this provision is clear: upon remarriage, the mother became a stranger to her deceased husband's family, and it would thus be the responsibility of the latter husband's son to maintain her ancestral rites. However, if the child in the second union were a daughter, the law provided that the daughter had to split that portion of the mother's property with her half brother: the son of the first husband. Thus, the law explicitly limited a daughter's claim to her mother's property *because of her gender.*

DAUGHTER'S INHERITANCE RIGHTS IN PRACTICE

We have seen that the law did not decree that daughters were entitled to the same property rights sons enjoyed. In fact, the law is ambiguous and at best allows daughters to inherit some property. The article could be applied only if the parents did not leave a will and testament. Thus the testaments themselves reveal more about inheritance practices than the prescriptive legal sources. Examples from wills and testaments demonstrate that in practice daughters did not enjoy equal inheritance and that the portion of their share of the household property depended on the power dynamics within each family.

Example 1: Vũ Văn Bân and Principal Wife

Vũ Văn Bân and his principal wife, Trương Thị Loan, issued a testament in the eighth year of the Cảnh Hưng reign (1748) to clarify their wishes for the distribution of their property to three children.[60] The eldest son, Vũ Đức Thắng, was their biological son, while the second son, Vũ Văn Liễn, and daughter, Vũ Thị Hợp, were the children of a concubine, though it is unclear whether the two were born of the same woman. In their testament the couple carefully designated the source of the property: the couple's property could be divided into that earmarked for the maintenance of ancestral rites (hương hỏa điền sản); that originating from the father (phụ điền sản) and the mother (mẫu điền sản); and the portion of the property the couple acquired together (tân mại điền sản).[61] In this family the principal wife, Trương Thị Loan, brought an unusually large amount of property to the marriage.

Table 4.1 details the amount of property that each of the children received from the parents. As the chart details, the eldest son, Vũ Đức Thắng, received four times the amount of property that the daughter received, while the second son, Vũ Văn Liễn, received three times as much property. In fact, if we subtract the amount of property earmarked for the hương hỏa property (6 sào, 9 khẩu) and the dowry granted to the eldest son (7 sào), then the two sons were promised roughly equal amounts of property (6.4 mẫu, 9 khẩu and 5.9 mẫu, 9 khẩu, respectively). However, the daughter's share is remarkably less than that of either of the sons.

This example clearly demonstrates that the daughter in the family did not enjoy claim to the division of household property. From the text of the testament, one can also tentatively infer several features of the power dynamics within this family. First, though neither the second son nor the daughter were the natural children of the principal wife, the second son was treated as if he were her son (reference to their relationship is mẫu-tử), while the daughter was treated as the daughter of a concubine (reference to their relationship is đích-mẫu, nữ

Table 4.1.   Will and testament of Vũ Văn Bân and Trương Thị Loan

Child's name	"Fire and incense" property	Father's property	Principle wife / "mother"	Newly acquired property	Other	Total
Vũ Đức Thắng (eldest son)	0.69	1.61	3.5	1.22	.86	7.88
Vũ Văn Liễn (next son)	0	1.3	3.16	1.1	0.39	5.95
Vũ Thị Hợp (daughter)	0	0.9	0.6	0.27	0.06	1.83
Total	0.69	3.81	7.26	2.59	1.31	15.66

Source: Chúc thư văn khế Vũ Văn Bân & Trương Thị Lan.

Note: All figures are calculated in mẫu. One mẫu was equal to 3,600 square meters. "Other" property includes parcels of "ponds and waters" distributed to children.

tử). In this family a son's standing was related to his gender, while the daughter's standing was related to her mother's status as a concubine. Second, on the last page of the testament, the parents, witnesses, and children acknowledged the validity of the document with a signature or a fingerprint. Although the two sons signed for themselves, the daughter's husband placed his acknowledgment of the validity of the document before her own fingerprint, suggesting that the family and the local authorities involved viewed the son-in-law as the one with authority over the daughter's inheritance. Finally, although conventional wisdom tells us that Vietnamese women enjoyed complete autonomy over the property they brought into the marriage, the way in which the principal wife's property was allocated suggests that she might not have had that much authority over the testament, an issue that will be revisited later.

Example 2: Trương Thị Khanh

Vũ Văn Liễn, the second son of Vũ Văn Bân, passed away within the next ten years and his mother, the concubine Trương Thị Khanh, promulgated a testament in his name in the twenty-second year of the Cảnh Hưng reign (1762). In this case, Trương Thị Khanh, in her

Table 4.2.   Testament of Trương Thị Khanh

Child's name	Fire and incense property	General property	Other property	Total
Vũ Văn Huân (natural son)	0.38	2.63	0.7	3.71
Vũ Thị Sơ (natural daughter)	0	1.83	0.04	1.87
Vũ Xuân Đồng (adopted son)	0	1.86	0.04	1.9
Total	.38	6.32	0.78	7.48

Source: Chúc thư Trương Thị Khanh

Note: All figures are calculated in mẫu. One mẫu was equal to 3,600 square meters.

capacity as Vũ Văn Liễn's natural mother, promulgated a will and testament to divide his property between his natural son and daughter and adoptive son. In this family Vũ Văn Huân, Vũ Văn Liễn's eldest son, received almost twice as much property as his sister (3.8 *mẫu* vs. 1.8 *mẫu*). Although the daughter in this family did receive a far greater percentage of the family property than in the previous family, the adopted son, Vũ Xuân Đông, received slightly more property than she did. The specifications made in the will are detailed in table 4.2.

In the case of Trương Thị Khanh and her heirs, we see again that the daughter did not inherit as much property as the son. In fact, in this case she even inherited slightly less property than the adopted son. Although Trương Thị Khanh's distribution of her son's property seems a little more equitable than in the previous example, it still suggests that a daughter did not enjoy the same property rights as either her natural brother or her adopted brother.

Example 3: Vũ Xuân Dương

In the sixth year of the Cảnh Thịnh reign (1798), Vũ Xuân Dương and his principal wife, Bùi Thị (character illegible), promulgated their will and testament, decreeing that their four children adhere to their

Table 4.3.   Testament of Vũ Xuân Dương

Child's name	Fire and incense property	General property	Other property	Total
Vu Xuân	0.79	2.16	0.14	3.09
Vu Xuân Hoàn	0	1.94	0.11	2.05
Daughter 1	0	0	0	0
Daughter 2	0	0	0	0
Vu Xuân Ban (grandson)	0	0.1	0	0.1
Vu Xuân Lien (grandson)	0	0.1	0	0.1
Total	0.79	4.3	0.25	5.34

Source: Chúc thư Vũ Xuân Dương
Note: All figures are calculated in mẫu. One mẫu was equal to 3,600 square meters.

wishes under penalty of unfilial behavior. This is perhaps an extreme circumstance, since the brothers received roughly equal amounts of property while the two daughters received nothing.

In this family the principal wife brought little or no property to the marriage (there was no distinction). Furthermore, after detailing what the parents promised the two sons and their sons, the testament ends without any mention of the daughters' names or shares. We simply see that the Vũ Xuân Dương signed the document to verify its validity, along with the village head's signature and those of the witnesses.

These examples suggest that in practice as in the law, daughters were not guaranteed equal inheritance rights. Evidence tentatively suggests instead that their rights varied among families, and that even when daughters were allowed to inherit from the family estate, this claim was not absolute: the statutes clearly stated that the division of the family estate was subject to the will of the parents and the power dynamics within each family. As the examples show, daughters might or might not inherit, depending on the parents' mandate. Moreover, although additional evidence is needed, these examples suggest that a daughter's ability to inherit property was related to her mother's status. Third, the law's statement that the parents' property should be divided among brothers and sisters may simply have meant that daughters should receive a dowry, a phenomenon not unlike that in Chinese law.[62] Article 388 of the Lê Code, oft cited for its preservation of a daughter's equal rights in Việt Nam, is unusually vague about who gets to decide on the division of that property. Statutes from the Book of Good Government reveal that the state was interested in protecting the rights of sons and grandsons to an equal share of family property but make little mention of daughters with regard to the division of household property. These statutes support Samuel Baron's observations of inheritance practices in Đàng Ngoài in the seventeenth century: "Everyone enjoys what he gets by his own industry, and may leave his estate to his heirs and successors. . . . The eldest son's portion is much larger than the rest of the children of the deceased; the daughters have some small matter allow'd them, yet can claim but little by law, if there be an heir male."[63]

Finally, a daughter's right to family property was conditional. The power to decide who could inherit a family's property lay in the hands of her parents. As in the third example, sometimes a daughter did not receive *any* portion of the family's property. The law did not guarantee equal division for daughters, nor did it grant daughters an absolute right over the division of household property; it only allowed daughters to inherit property, subject to the parents' wishes. Because the law is so ambiguous, the appropriateness of using this statute to signify Vietnamese cultural uniqueness should be reassessed. As the examples illustrate, the Lê Code did not decree an equal division law for brothers and sisters and can thus no longer be considered evidence of Vietnamese lawmakers attempting to protect women's rights in an increasingly patriarchal legal system. Furthermore, in light of the absence of guarantees of equal property rights in the laws regulating the inheritance rights of daughters, other claims about daughters' succession rights and their relationship to bilateral kinship practices need to be reexamined.

This study has traced the foundations of the discourse on Vietnamese womanhood that adduce the Lê Code as the champion of indigenous protofeminist values and has suggested an alternative interpretation of the statutes. The reification of Vietnamese womanhood and its relationship to the Lê Code emerged out of a debate among French colonial scholar-officials about legal reform. To demonstrate the colony's readiness for French civilization, these scholars equated the Lê precepts with an indigenous, almost noble-savage tradition that did not distinguish between males and females. Nationalist scholars adopted this construction to demonstrate Viêt Nam's readiness for modernity, and Western academics perpetuated it to support their claims about its historical identity, whether uniquely national or re-flective of regional cohesiveness. The empirical evidence suggests that daughters did not enjoy equal inheritance rights under the law, and that in practice household division varied among families. Prelimi-nary evidence from testaments suggests that women may not have had complete autonomy over the property they brought to marriages.

My interpretation of the statutes, substatutes, and edicts collected in the Lê Code and in the Book of Good Government and of the tes-tamentary documents differs from that of previous scholarship, even if my translations do not. This alternative interpretation disentangles women's property claims from narratives of Vietnamese historical identities and places the logic of the property regime at the center of inquiry. In the last two decades challenges to the national narrative have profoundly changed the way scholars think of Vietnamese his-tory, shifting the conception from that of one grand narrative to one of multiple versions of Vietnamese history. Writing about gender in Viêt Nam, however, seems to have survived these innovations as scholars continue to accept a hundred-year-old construction of Vietnamese womanhood as historical fact. Images of Vietnamese women who defy Confucian standards and symbolize a national essence have maintained a tenacious hold on the contemporary imagi-nation. Forcing Vietnamese women to conform to intellectual and political agendas, whether imperialist, nationalist, postcolonial, feminist, or postfeminist, does an injustice to their experiences. Given the importance that historical constructions of Vietnamese women's social status have had in the triangular relationship between China, Southeast Asia, and Viêt Nam, the time has come for concerted efforts to write Vietnamese women's history from the perspective of their experiences.

Notes

1. For Vietnamese feminist interpretations, see Mai Thị Tú, "Vietnamese Woman, Yesterday and Today"; and Mai Thị Tú and Lê Thị Nhâm Tuyết, *La femme au Vietnam*. Regarding the representation by Western scholars, see

Công Huyền Tôn Nữ Nha Trang, "Traditional Roles of Women as Reflected in Oral and Written Vietnamese Literature"; and Marr, "1920s Debate on Women's Rights." Quotation is from Mai Thị Tú, "Vietnamese Woman, Yesterday and Today," 9.

2. See, for example, Coedès, *Indianized States of Southeast Asia;* Wolters, *History, Culture and Region in Southeast Asian Perspectives;* and Reid, *Southeast Asia in the Age of Commerce.*

3. For example, Woodside has noted that the "rights of women had always been more the mark of Vietnamese social conventions than Chinese" (*Vietnam and the Chinese Model,* 45). See also, Taylor, *Birth of Vietnam,* 77.

4. Although Woodside devoted a sizeable portion of the introduction to a discussion of Hồ Xuân Hương's poetry in his classic *Vietnam and the Chinese Model,* only recently have the Western academy and popular readers become captivated by her writing as a sign of Vietnamese uniqueness. That Hồ Xuân Hương wrote her poetry in the demotic script (*chữ nôm*) as a concubine (a symbol of Confucian, read Chinese, oppression) reinforces her image as an embodiment of Vietnamese identity to Vietnamese and Western scholars alike. See, for example, *Spring Essence: The Poetry of Hồ Xuân Hương,* trans. John Balaban (Port Townsend, WA: Copper Canyon Press, 2000). Regarding the role of these female figures, see Trần Quốc Vượng, *Truyền Thống Phụ Nữ Việt Nam,* 9; and Taylor, *Birth of Vietnam,* chap. 2. Though their works focus on the exploitation of women, Mai Thị Tú ("Vietnamese Woman, Yesterday and Today"), Lê Thị Nhậm Tuyết (*Le femme au Vietnam,* with Mai Thị Tú), and Công Huyền Tôn Nữ Nha Trang ("Traditional Roles of Women") also point to these unique women as model Vietnamese women.

5. Taylor, *Birth of Vietnam,* 77; Tạ Văn Tài, "Status of Women in Traditional Vietnam," 123; Trần Mỹ Vân, "The Status of Women in Traditional Việt Nam"; Yu Insun, "Bilateral Social Pattern[s] and the Status of Women in Traditional Vietnam"; O'Harrow, "Vietnamese Women and Confucianism," 175.

6. Readers familiar with the Lê Code will remember that the code was based on that of the Tang dynasty. Johnson has provided the first Western-language translation of the code in *The Tang Code.* Although they differ in their conclusions about catalysts for changes in the Chinese property regime in the Song period, Bernhardt's and Birge's recent works demonstrate that in the Tang and Song periods, daughters typically inherited landed property earmarked as a dowry. Bernhardt demonstrates that in the Song period, daughters inherited household property through the process of succession, but the dowries bestowed by parents were standard. Birge in particular argues that the dowry was never absorbed into the husband's household property, and its special legal status encouraged families to transfer property to their daughters as a form of insurance. See Bernhardt, *Women and Property in China;* and Birge, *Women, Property and Confucian Reaction in Sung and Yuan China.*

7. Holmgren demonstrates that (then) contemporary images of Chinese women relied on scholarship that privileged the transition of Chinese society from a relatively egalitarian Taoist-based society to that of a patriarchal

Confucian system. Moreover, Holmgren argues, feminist and/or development agendas skewed emphasis on a patriarchal system's oppression of women and its subsequent demise, thereby obscuring women's experiences ("Myth, Fantasy or Scholarship," 153). See also Ko, *Teachers of the Inner Chambers*. In her study on women and culture spanning the Ming-Qing transition, Ko demonstrates how commercialization in the Jiangnan region and the rise of print culture enabled women to enter the historical record through their own writings, allowing them to travel beyond the inner quarters figuratively. Ko also demonstrates that contemporary conceptions of an oppressed Chinese womanhood emerged out of May Fourth discourses, when young revolutionaries appropriated Chinese women's status and Confucianism to signal the backwardness of "Chinese civilization."

8. For example, see Bernhardt, *Women and Property in China*; Ebrey, *Inner Quarters*; Ko, *Teachers of the Inner Chambers*; and Mann, *Precious Records*.

9. Bernhardt, *Women and Property in China*; and Birge, *Women, Property and Confucian Reaction*.

10. The version of the Lê Code used in this essay can be found at the Institute of Hán-Nôm Studies. Raymond Déloustal translated the legal section of the *Lịch triều hiến chương* into French, and Nguyễn Ngọc Huy and Tạ Văn Tài translated the code into English. See Déloustal, "La justice en ancien Annam"; and Nguyễn Ngọc Huy and Tạ Văn Tài, *Lê Code*.

11. Currently two versions of the legal code are extant. Western language translations and earlier scholarship on the Lê Code rely on a hand copy of the code that Charles Maitre, director of the École Française d'Extrême-Orient, retrieved from the Huế Imperial Archives in 1898, from which Déloustal made his French translation (Maitre, "Introduction à l'ouvrage du M. Deloustal"; and Nguyễn Huy Lai, *Les Régimes Matrimoniaux en droit annamite,* 20). According to Cadière and Pelloit, this complete copy of the code was promulgated in 1777 and reproduced by Phan Huy Chú in 1800 ("Premiere étude des sources d'histoire annamite"). A woodblock printing of the code is preserved at the Institute of Hán-Nôm Studies and thought to date to the seventeenth century.

12. Although the Book of Good Government can be dated to the sixteenth century, only two nineteenth-century hand copies of the document are extant. Both of these copies are available at the Institute of Hán-Nôm Studies, and one is reproduced in Nguyễn Sĩ Giắc's *quốc ngữ* translation of the document. Copy of A.330 and A.331 are reproduced in *Hồng Đức thiện chính thư*. See also Đình Khắc Thuân's analysis of Mặc dynasty reforms in "Contribution a l'histoire de la dynastie du Mặc au Việt Nam." Using clues from reign names included in the document, Vũ Văn Mẫu dates the compilation of the Book of Good Government to between 1541 and 1561, during the Mặc reign (introduction to *Hồng Đức thiện chính thư*, xvii).

13. Nguyễn Ngọc Huy and Tạ Văn Tài cite two Nguyễn dynasty documents from the selection (a loan contract and a land sales contract) but make no mention of the testamentary records included in this group of documents

See Nguyễn Ngọc Huy and Tạ Văn Tài, *Lê Code*, 3:50–51; and *Chúc thư văn khế cửu chỉ*.

14. For an in-depth discussion of the emergence of these discourses, see Tran, "Vietnamese Women at the Crossroads."

15. See, for example, Schreiner, *Étude sur la constitution de la propriété foncière en Cochinchine*; Briffaut, *Études sur les biens cultuels familiaux en pays d'Annam*; Maitre, "Critique sur M. Briffaut."

16. Déloustal, "La justice dans l'ancien Annam." Déloustal and Maitre both specify that the translation was based on the legal portion of Phan Huy Chú's *Lịch triều hiến chương loài chí*, which Paul Pelloit found in the Imperial Archives in Huế several years earlier. For more on these sources, see Cadière and Pelloit, "Première étude sur des sources annamites de l'histoire d' Annam."

17. Maitre, "Introduction à l'ouvrage du M. Deloustal," 177.

18. Maitre, "Critique sur M. Briffaut," 245.

19. Trần Văn Chương, *Essai sur l'esprit du droit sino-annamite*.

20. See Hồ Đặc Diễm, *La puissance paternelle en droit annamite*; Bui Quang Chieu, *La polygamie dans le droit annamite*; Nguyễn Huy Lai, *Les régimes matrimoniaux en droit annamite*; Nguyễn Mạnh Tường, *l'individu dans la vielle cité annamite*.

21. Bùi Văn Thịnh, *L'usfruit familial et la veuve en droit vietnamien*; Hồ Đặc Diễm, *La puissance en droit vietnamien*; Lê Văn Hồ, "La mère de famille annamite"; Nguyễn Huy Lai, *Les régimes matrimoniaux en droit annamite*; Nguyễn Phú Đức, *La veuve en droit vietnamien*.

22. Mai Thị Tú and Lê Thị Nhậm Tuyết, *La femme au Vietnam*; Trần Quốc Vượng, *Truyền thống phụ nữ Việt Nam*.

23. Trân Quốc Vượng, *Truyền thống phụ nữ*, 25.

24. Nguyễn Ngọc Huy and Tạ Văn Tài, *Lê Code*, 1:81.

25. Tạ Văn Tài, "Women and the Law in Traditional Vietnam," 23.

26. Taylor refers to the special roles that women likely played in Văn Lang society in his description of how Vietnamese society might have transitioned from a matriarchal to a bilateral society (*Birth of Vietnam*, 73). Trần Mỹ Vân cites the widely accepted argument that Vietnamese women were guaranteed equal property rights to emphasize the high status that women enjoyed in traditional Vietnam ("Traditional Status of Women in Vietnamese Nam"). Contemporary French scholars also allude to this alleged high status of women in traditional Vietnamese society by citing the Lê regulations. See Đỗ Chi Lan, *La mère et l'enfant au Vietnam et d'autrefois*.

27. See, for example, Yu Insun, *Law and Society in Seventeenth and Eighteenth Century Vietnam*; and Taylor, *Birth of Vietnam*.

28. I deliberately use the term *làng* for village because it is an indigenous term, contrasted with the *xã*, an administrative term. For more on this topic, see Yu Insun, "Cấu trúc của làng xã Việt Nam ở Vùng Đông Bắc Bé và mối quan hệ của nã víi nhà nước thời Lê." See also Phan Huy Lê's discussion of the regional variations of the term in "Research on the Vietnamese Village" in this volume.

29. Marr, *Vietnamese Anticolonialism;* Bùi Xuân Đính, *Hương ước và quản lý làng xã.*

30. The "village" (*thôn*) can be distinguished from a "commune" (*xã*), which served as an administrative unit from the tenth century. As defined by Phan Huy Lê, the village, as the term is used here, was a naturally forming communal network sharing common local animist and cultural practices in community spaces. Regarding the description of the village, see Yu Insun, *Law and Society in Seventeenth and Eighteenth Century Vietnam,* 23.

31. Reid, "Slavery and Bondage in Southeast Asian History."

32. Ibid., 183, 188.

33. *Hương ước:* literally, "rural convention"; *lệ làng:* "village regulations." The word *làng* (village) is generally found in folk songs, proverbs, and vernacular literature but is not used in official papers. The phrase *lệ làng* is a vernacular term used to indicate village custom and is found in various folk sources. This vernacular term was written in the demotic script, borrowing characters from the Chinese.

34. *Hội đồng kỳ mục:* literally, "the council that leads." Regarding this structure, see Phan Huy Lê, "Research on the Vietnamese Village," this volume.

35. Regarding the absence of a single lineage, see Yu Insun, "Cấu trúc của làng xã Việt Nam ở Vùng Đông Bắc Bé và mối quan hệ của nã víi nhà nước thời Lê," 29.

36. See, for example, "Đông Khê Thôn Khoán Ước," where the preface lists the names of all the members of the village community who have agreed on the aforementioned regulations. All these members were men.

37. Mathews's *Chinese Dictionary,* the *Thiếu Chữu Dictionary,* Đào Duy Anh, and Trần Văn Kiệm all define *đinh* as able-bodied men, leaving little ambiguity as to whether the character can possibly refer to females.

38. Regarding property disputes, see, for example, Tạo Văn Khê Bi Ký, no. 6683; Tạo Văn Khế Bi Ký, no. 15652; Đình môn thạch bi ký, no. 15419, Institute of Hán-Nôm Studies, Hanoi. These inscriptions record contracts and/or disputes between villages resolved through mediation and commemorated for posterity.

39. Ory, *La commune annamite.*

40. Phan Huy Lê, "Research on the Vietnamese Village."

41. For more on women, property, and local politics, see Nhung Tuyet Tran, "Vietnamese Women at the Crossroads."

42. Tạ Văn Tài, "The Status of Women in Traditional Vietnam" and "Women and the Law in Traditional Vietnam"; and Yu Insun, *Law and Society in Seventeenth- and Eighteenth-Century Vietnam* and "Bilateral Social Pattern and the Status of Women in Traditional Vietnam."

43. Tạ Văn Tài, "Women and the Law in Traditional Vietnam."

44. The discussion here of inheritance as dual processes of household division and succession is paraphrased from Bernhardt, *Women and Property in China.*

45. Ebrey, *Inner Quarters;* Bernhardt, *Women and Property in China;* and Birge, *Women, Property and Confucian Reaction.*

46. Citing a demographic study, Bernhardt, *Women and Property in China,* reports that daughters stood a 20 percent chance of being born into a household without male heirs.

47. Bernhardt, *Women and Property in China.*

48. Yu Insun, *Law and Society in Seventeenth and Eighteenth Century Vietnam,* 17. Tạ Văn Tài, referring to Art. 388, claims that "brothers and sisters would share equally in their parents' general estate" under the Lê Code. Tạ Văn Tài, "Status of Women in Traditional Vietnam," 123.

49. Bernhardt, *Women and Property in China;* and Birge, *Women, Property and Confucian Reaction.*

50. "Quốc triều hình luật," Art. 388.

51. Vietnamese and Chinese legal conventions as well as a careful examination of the way in which "equal division" is used in this text and other supporting documents lead me to this conclusion. In Tạ Văn Tài's own translation, there is no indication of the "equality clause," but he and others make the conceptual leap from one to the other: "When the father and mother have died intestate and left landed property, the brothers and sisters who divide this property among themselves shall reserve one-twentieth for this property to constitute the *hương hỏa* property which shall be entrusted to the eldest brother—the remainder of the property shall be divided among them" (Nguyễn Ngọc Huy and Tạ Văn Tài, *Lê Code*). Déloustal's translation is equally ambiguous: "Lorsqu'un père et une mère seront tous les deux décédés en laissant des rizières et des terres pour la disposition desquelles ils n'auront pas eu le temps de transmettre leurs dernières volontés par un testament, et que les frères et les sœurs procéderont au partage entre eux, ils devront réserver la vingtième partie de ces biens à la constitution du huong hoa destiné à assurer le culte de leurs parents. Cette part sera attribuée au fils aîné qui en aura l'administration et la garde. Ils se partageront le surplus" ("La justice dans l'ancien Annam," 500).

52. "Hồng Đức thiện chính [thư]," Art. 2, chapter on landed property.

53. Ibid., 40.

54. Ibid., 38.

55. The term *chúng tử* can only refer to sons. In this text regulations on mourning also refer to *chúng tử* and their wives, making it clear that this text only uses the term to refer to sons (ibid., 30).

56. Ibid., p. 40.

57. Ibid., 55.

58. Ibid.

59. Ibid., 54.

60. "Chúc thư văn khế cửu chỉ": Chúc thư Vũ Văn Bân.

61. During the later Lê period, the character for "new" was taboo. The character in this text was written with the two radicals switched.

62. Bernhardt, *Women and Property in China;* and Birge, *Women, Property and Confucian Reaction.*

63. Baron, "Description of the Kingdom of Tonqueen," 10.

Southern Pluralities

5

The Eighteenth-Century Mekong Delta and Its World of Water Frontier

LI TANA

Water is the most important feature of the Mekong Delta. It is present in hundreds of place names in the delta itself as well as in the names of the kingdoms arising in the area. It was no accident that the area was called Water Chenla in eighth-century Chinese records, nor was it by chance that, a millennium later, the two rulers of seventeenth-century Cambodia were called the Mountain King (based in Oudong) and the Water King (based in Sài Gòn).[1] The pervasive nature of its water is so essential a part of the Mekong Delta landscape that the very boundary between land and water is often indistinct, as pointed out by Pierre Brocheux.[2]

Equally indistinct were the ethnic elements that interacted in this region, especially among the minor ports dotted along the coast of the Mekong Delta, the Gulf of Siam, and the northern Malay Peninsula. In this coastal region of mixed ethnicities and fluid settlements, water-borne commerce was an essential component of local life. It can even be argued that the whole coastal region from the Mekong Delta in modern Việt Nam to the sultanates and later British colonies of the

Malay Peninsula formed a single economic region, an extended water
frontier knit together by the itineraries of Chinese and other
merchants and small traders. This water frontier in turn formed a major component in the wider web of Chinese commercial networks
throughout Asia.

Colonial historians, whose main focus has been the colonial cities
of Batavia, Manila, Melaka, Penang, and later Singapore, are understandably little interested in this murky area. Twentieth-century
nationalist historians have shared this attitude of indifference. For a
variety of reasons, they have had little interest in lines of inquiry that
do not fit with the national myth and the focus on the current capital
city and dominant ethnic configuration. Because their view of the past
ends at their present territorial borders, the region this study surveys
is fragmented and is never seen as a whole with a historical integrity
of its own.[3]

The effects of this bias are particularly serious in regard to Việt
Nam. The nationalist ideology in the last few decades has effectively
fossilized the interpretation of Vietnamese histories and restricted
research to the use of a few classical sources. As a result many historians focusing on Việt Nam find it hard to resist an essentialized
version of "a unified Việt Nam, a village Việt Nam, a Confucian Việt
Nam, and a revolutionary Việt Nam."[4] This encapsulation of Vietnamese history is particularly damaging to our understanding of the
history of southern Việt Nam. A critical part of our knowledge about
Việt Nam is missing, one bearing on the most complex and vigorous
part of the nation. This essay places the Mekong Delta back in
Southeast Asia's water frontier where it belongs and traces the connections linking the eighteenth-century Mekong Delta to Cambodia,
Siam, and the Malay Peninsula.

A Period of Intensive Trade and Human Movement

Canton was the only port in China open to foreign trade after 1757,
but because of a lack of consistent trade records for Canton, the picture has never been clear. Some newly discovered European records
on Canton trade, however, make it possible to reconstruct the previously obscure Canton trade of the 1760s.[5] One of the most important
findings drawn from this new information is that the focus of Canton
junk trade of this period was the coastal area of the Mekong Delta,

Cancao, and Cambodia.[6] Among the thirty-seven Canton junks sailing annually between Canton and Southeast Asia, 85 to 90 percent of them came to trade in this area, particularly to Bassac (today's Sóc Trang in the Mekong Delta), Cancao, and Cochin China.[7] This finding contradicts conventional scholarship, which saw Melaka, Batavia, and Ayutthaya as the centers of trade and that of the Mekong Delta as negligible. These new data also throw light on existing but fragmented sources such as the English records on the Canton-Southeast Asia trade, one of which recorded that of thirty-two junks returning to Canton in 1767, nine were from Pa-chuck (Bassac), nine from Cochin China, two from Cambodia, seven from Kang-kow (Cancao or Hà Tiên), four from Palembang, and one from Batavia.[8] These figures are consistent with Danish and Dutch trade records throughout the 1760s.

A further examination of the data reveals that trade among these minor ports was quite well integrated. Evidence indicates that export items from one port often did not correspond to their original producing area. For example, in 1761 2,539 piculs of sappanwood, a substantial amount, were exported from Cochin China, an area producing no sappanwood, while only 563 piculs left Siam, the chief producing locale of the item.[9] The list of 1768 reveals the wide scope of interregional trade on the water frontier. Siam, after its devastating war with Burma, exported only 200 piculs of tin, while 2,700 piculs were exported by Cancao and 1,000 piculs by Bassac and Cambodia, the purely tin importing areas. Adjustments were surely made among the minor ports of the water-frontier region to suit supply and markets.

Perhaps the most intriguing aspect of these Canton trade records of the 1760s is that export items included no rice, the chief product of both the Mekong Delta and Siam. This was also the case with the Canton trade of the early nineteenth century.[10] In part because of the lack of consistent data, the question of why is never asked, and this study cannot presume to answer it conclusively. Among the short answers, however, is that the nature of the eighteenth-century Canton and Amoy trade changed. According to Ng Chin-keong, despite the Qing government's incentive scheme to encourage the rice trade, by the eighteenth century the sophisticated Fukienese merchants had lost interest in the direct rice trade because of its high freight costs and bulky, low-value cargo.[11] This was also reflected in the Canton trade, the leading merchants of which were all Fukienese. They rediverted their energies toward the "Straits produce" of Southeast Asia and there developed sophisticated smuggling networks at both ends of the South China Sea.[12] Both factors affected Southeast Asia markets profoundly.

Barbara Watson Andaya's work provides a key for understanding the Southeast Asia end of the trade. According to Andaya, the Chinese in Cancao and Cambodia traded rice for tin with Bangka. Royal junks under the command of Palembang Chinese also took cargoes of tin to Cancao to be exchanged for rice and other goods.[13] Sappanwood from Siam was perhaps exchanged in the same fashion. It was as a nexus of local trade, collecting "Straits produce," that Cancao prospered. The stories of Canton and the Southeast Asian ports reveal a fascinating aspect of the native interregional trade of the eighteenth century. Even though rice was a crucial trade item, it was often not directly shipped to China, suggesting that while China was the driving force of the eighteenth-century Nanyang trade, it was neither the beginning nor the end of this lucrative trade. In other words, China was the major stop, no more, no less, on this string of terminals in the Southeast Asian trade. Goods changed hands many times before arriving at the Chinese ports, and the same cycle of exchanges started again right after the ships left China. Behind the China market, therefore, there was a developed port complex well integrated into the interior of the Mekong Delta, Cambodia, southern Siam, and the Malay Peninsula—this was the water frontier of Southeast Asia.

The legacy of colonial and nationalist historiography in Southeast Asia has obscured the history of the ports of the Mekong Delta, Cambodia, and Siam. Since the trade data cited here indicates the importance of Bassac, today's Sóc Trang, it is useful to look at the evidence from there.[14] Although as a town it has become insignificant in contemporary Việt Nam, it was crucial in the regional entrepôt complex of the 1760s. English, Dutch, and Danish records of the 1760s all mention "Passack" or "Pa-Chunk," as did eighteenth-century Cambodian and Siamese chronicles. There might be two major reasons that Bassac rose rapidly in the 1760s. First, the years between the 1750s and early 1770s seemed to be a golden era for the Chinese junk trade and saw one of the first waves of immigration to Southeast Asia. Perhaps an equally, if not more important factor for the flourishing of Bassac was its connection with Cambodia's hinterland.

Salt was one of the most important trade items between Cambodia and the Mekong Delta. Bassac produces a special kind of red salt said to be particularly tasty for making salt fish. The trade of salt boiling could be traced back to the Angkor period or earlier, as described by the Chinese traveler Zhou Da Guan (Chou Ta-kuan) in the thirteenth century.[15] This trade was a specialty of the Chinese. They "pack the salt into bags, each bag contains 5–6 cân [2.5–3 kg] of salt, forty bags would make one Khmer 'xe' [a measure of about 100–120 kg]. This trade is very profitable when the salt is sold in Cambodia."[16] Bassac was also well known for its good quality rice. "Miếu ông Ba Thắc linh thiên cổ, Gạo xứ Ba Xuyên để nhất danh" (The deity of Ba Thắc is efficacious for thousands of years, and the rice of Ba Xuyên is the most famous in the country).[17] This should not be surprising, as Bassac lies in one of the two major agricultural areas of the old Khmer Empire, the corridor from Angkor to the river mouth of Bassac (Ba Thắc, or Cửa Tranh Đề).[18] Ba Xuyên and Châu Đốc were on the main shipping routes to Phnom Penh in the eighteenth century, and Bassac seemed to be the main gateway linking Cambodia to the outside world. In 1795, for example, "the Khmer king asked those foreign ships trading to Nam Vang (Phnom Penh) to pass Bassac. The king [Nguyễn Ánh] gave his permission."[19] It was natural that Bassac should have occupied such a place in the history of the Mekong Delta, being strategically connected to the hinterland of Cambodia, a rice- and red-salt-producing area itself, and at the same time a port open to trade with China and Southeast Asia.

Its location at the crossroads of several different trade currents would not necessarily make the Bassac area the focus of the Canton–Southeast Asia trade, since dozens of such minor ports existed in the eighteenth-century world of the water frontier. Something more had to make Bassac attractive. It seems significant that Bassac lived a short but glorious life in the 1760s. Although it came under Nguyễn control in 1757 on paper, until the end of the eighteenth century its political status was extremely ambiguous.[20] Control of the Bassac region was shared by at least four forces: Nguyễn Ánh, the Khmer "ruler of Bassac" Luat, and the Khmer king Nac An, and through him, the Siamese king.[21] None could claim complete dominance throughout most of the eighteenth century.

Bassac's greatest asset, however, was the ambivalence or ambiguity of its political status. This ambiguity of political identity was in fact a characteristic of all the minor ports of the water frontier. This pre-nation-state world of shifting and multiple alliances was the necessary condition for the flourishing trade of the water frontier.[22] Compared with the more established and more strictly controlled area of Biên Hòa, in the 1760s Bassac was a new frontier and a new political and economic space open to all the contesting forces. The most important advantage it offered merchants was duty-free trade. Along with Cancao, Bassac became a trading center midway between the Malay Peninsula and southern Siam and Cambodia, reexporting the items that later became known as "Straits produce."[23] The tin and sappanwood exported from it exemplified this position. By 1768 the Cambodia-Bassac trade doubled that of Cochin China in volume, and was taking business from Cochin China. Three thousand piculs of betel nuts were exported from the Cambodia-Bassac region, compared to the one thousand piculs from Cochin China, most likely from the Biên Hòa area, which was famous for betel nuts.[24]

This condition seems to be what the Canton junks were looking for and explains why they were coming to the region. The booming Canton trade with the region in the 1760s must have considerably activated the subregional markets of the Mekong Delta and the Gulf of Siam region, including Kampot. From the perspective of the eighteenth-century world of minor ports, Cambodia was not yet sealed off from maritime access but was open to the intensive trade carried out by its neighboring ports. John Crawfurd, for example, describes a distinct trading network along the Gulf of Siam in the early nineteenth century. On the western coast of Bangkok were Champon, Chaiya, Ligor, Singora [Songkla], and on the east were Bang Plasoi, Rayong, Chanthaburi, Kampong Som, and Kampot of Cambodia, and Ha Tiên, Rạch Giá, Cà Mau, and Sài Gòn in Việt Nam.[25] These names also appear frequently in late eighteenth-century Nguyễn chronicles, and some of them, like Chanthaburi and Rayong, played important roles in Nguyễn Ánh's restoration, unlike during the late nineteenth century, when the paramouncy of Sài Gòn and Bangkok marginalized these centers.

There was another economic link connecting the eighteenth-century Mekong Delta and Cambodia. We know that early nineteenth-century Sài Gòn was the present-day Chợ Lớn, and Bến Nghé was today's Sài Gòn.[26] In its written form Bến Nghé was also called Bến Trâu or Ngưu Chử.[27] All are Vietnamese translations from one Khmer name, "Kompong Krabei," which means "ferry for young buffaloes."[28] Does this name hint at economic interchange between Vietnamese and Khmers in the eighteenth century?[29] I find the location of this "ferry of young buffaloes" significant because buffaloes were crucial for rice cultivation in the Gia Định and Biên Hòa area. According to Trịnh Hoài Đức of the early nineteenth century, "land in the Phiên An and Biên Hòa areas requires buffaloes to cultivate. Such land could yield one hundred *hộc* of rice when one *hộc* of seeds were planted." Land in the Bassac area, however, did not "require the usage of buffalo."[30] The old placename for today's Sài Gòn may conceal a reference to a trading practice critical to the opening of the Mekong Delta. Only in this context might we understand why some rich Vietnamese could possess three hundred to four hundred oxen and buffaloes in a single family in the mid-eighteenth century.[31] One family's ownership of such a striking number of draft animals would have been unimaginable to anyone residing in the old territories of Vietnamese-speaking people except in the Mekong Delta. Even if the hypothesis that Sài Gòn was the old port of buffalo trade is wrong, we still have to find such links in other places in the Mekong Delta. That the buffalo-oxen link between Việt Nam and Cambodia definitely existed is attested by Cambodia remaining the major source for oxen and buffaloes for the Mekong Delta in later centuries. This trade must have been fairly regular and profitable, since some Vietnamese became specialized in this trade to Takeo in their heavier vessels.[32] The large number of farming animals was crucial for the mass production of rice, on which large-scale commercialization of rice cultivation was founded. This was achieved by trade with the Khmers and the uplanders in the region. In other words, the opening of the Mekong Delta was facilitated by this regional system in which Vietnamese interacted with other peoples in the region and from which the region drew its vitality.

This discussion illuminates the position of the lower Mekong Delta and the northern Malay Peninsula and their role in shaping the modern nation states of Việt Nam and Siam. Although both were important at the time, both faded in the nineteenth century, ultimately becoming marginal and insignificant. Yet from this marginal, insignificant, and mobile frontier rose three major political powers (Taksin, Rama I, and Nguyễn Ánh) in mainland Southeast Asia. Based on the strength of the former frontiers, these powers ultimately came to

dominate the north, pushing it into political and economic backwa-
ters. This seems to concur with what Sakurai Yumio described as the
traditionally "empty centre" of Southeast Asia in the late eighteenth
century.

There is yet another important dimension to the story of the
Mekong Delta and its water frontier. Although scholars have long
recognized that the Chinese presence was a primary factor enabling
Việt Nam and Siam to recover rapidly from the wars in each country
in the late eighteenth century, they have always regarded the peoples
as two separate populations rather than as a single population center.
This essay argues that the Chinese of the water frontier were a highly
mobile group and are more appropriately seen as a common resource
pool from which Taksin and his Chakri successor in Siam, and later
Nguyễn Ánh in Việt Nam, could all draw strength. It was against this
broad background of the water frontier that Sài Gòn and Bangkok
came into existence. Never before were two major economic and
political centers of mainland Southeast Asia built so close to each
other in space and time. Yet this phenomenon has been taken for
granted. The births of Sài Gòn and Bangkok have been chronicled and
celebrated as local inventions and significant only within national histories. Such discourse separates Sài Gòn and Bangkok from the
broader background of the water frontier, and downplays the role of
the Chinese. The histories of the two nations are now being
researched as separate entities and in isolation from each other. To
escape this straightjacket of nationalism, we need a full review of the
trading patterns that were common in the eighteenth- and early
nineteenth-century world of Southeast Asia.

"Smuggling" Revisited

The newly published Nguyễn Archives gives the numbers of ships
and junks visiting Việt Nam in 1825 and 1826. According to the table,
forty Chinese junks came to trade in the two ports of Nam Định and
Hà Nội in 1825, while only nine came to Sài Gòn and Cần Giờ. The
trade in the south in 1826 seems to have been even more dismal.
There were twenty-five Chinese junks visiting the north, while in the
south there were merely four Chinese junks and one British ship.[33] If
no other sources existed, we would be inclined to accept the idea that
commerce was negligible in Việt Nam, particularly in southern Việt

Nam. From John Crawfurd, however, we learn that from Siam alone forty to fifty junks visited the ports of southern Việt Nam annually.[34] Chaigneau, a French officer who lived in Cochin China at the time, gave a more complete picture of trade in the early nineteenth century, maintaining that "there enter the ports of Cochin China yearly about 300 Chinese junks, great and small, varying in size from 100 to 600 tons."[35]

The implication of this cross-checking of sources is significant since it suggests that the government was able to tax only 5 percent or less of the maritime trade carried out along the coastal area of Cochin China in the early nineteenth century. A French officer in the 1880s gave a list of items being smuggled between the two minor ports of Cà Mau and Kampot. Cà Mau traded mats and honey wax with Kampot for lime, oil (for painting boats), planks (for shipbuilding), water melon, sweet potatoes, sugar, tobacco, whetstones, rushes, fish sauce, and betel nuts. Imports of Cà Mau from Hainan Island included peanuts, jars, chinaware, tables and chairs, and suckling pigs. These suckling pigs from Hainan would be fed in Cà Mau until they were big enough to be exported to Singapore. Cà Mau seems to have relied on Singapore for obtaining cotton fabric as well as for securing ironware, silk, and opium. The chief trade items from Cà Mau were rice and dry fish.[36]

Although this document describes the Cà Mau trade in 1880, it may well reflect the trade carried out in west of the Mekong Delta during the previous one or two centuries as well. The list of trade items reveals that virtually every necessity of life in the Cà Mau area was imported to supplement the major local products of rice and dry fish. This is similar to what a Western observer described in the Archipelago: "This one product wherewith they abound must furnish them with everything else; this is to say all kinds of food are very dear, save their own product, which is cheap. And why these people are constrained to keep up continual intercourse with one another, the one supplying what the other wants."[37] In these minor ports dotting the water frontier, even Sài Gòn was too far way for Cà Mau. The tobacco from Cambodia was cheaper to transport than was that imported from Gò Váp near Sài Gòn.[38] Likewise, rice transported from the Menam basin of Siam to Cancao (Hà Tiên) cost much less than rice carried from the Mekong Delta.

This was the context for the rice trade in the Mekong Delta. Although on paper it was always forbidden to export rice from Cochin China, it was the single staple product that the Mekong Delta produced and was the main source of cash with which the ordinary people paid for necessities. The answer to this seeming contradiction was simple and straightforward, as Crawfurd observes, according to whom the prohibition on rice was "rather nominal than real." He states: "Except in times of apprehended scarcity, [it] is sent out of the country in abundance."[39] "Smuggling" simply means that rice was sold in the vicinity to passing traders or brought to other ports of the region rather than being shipped to central and northern Việt Nam.

This frequent and intensive trade between the minor ports of the water frontier area saved both Nguyễn Ánh and Taksin. In 1782 Ánh and his followers were on the edge of starvation on an island when a Chinese junk saved them. According to the Siamese chronicles, this junk was owned by a Chinese man married to a Vietnamese woman from Chanthaburi. They were carrying rice to sell to Cà Mau and the Rạch Giá region, but the junk was driven off course to Kut Island, where Ánh was seeking refuge.[40] A similar event was observed a decade earlier in Siam with Taksin and his followers. When more people died of starvation than in the war, in 1768 Taksin "bought rice from ships coming from Pontameas (Cancao or Hà Tiên) at the high cost of 3 to 5 *baht* per *thang* to distribute to the people."[41]

It is interesting in this context to examine a Vietnamese text of the early nineteenth century: *Xiêm la quốc lộ trình tập lục* (A collection of routes to the Kingdom of Siam).[42] Compiled in 1810, it gives two land routes, three sea routes, and one mixed route by land and sea between the Mekong Delta and the ports of the Gulf of Siam. Although it was compiled for official use for traffic between Siam and Cochin China, the capital of Siam is curiously mentioned briefly only twice. By contrast, a string of minor ports on the water frontier such as Chanthaburi, Chaiya, Ligor (Nakhon Si Thammarat for Siam), Songkhla, Pattani, Trengganu, and Ujung Salang (Phuket) are repeatedly mentioned. It pays great attention to detailed information about minor ports, such as routes leading to them, the landscape and local products, the location of fresh water, and the distances between stops. Interestingly Hà Tiên is also mentioned only twice. It seems that the minor rather than the major ports in the region were the main concern of this collection.

This is significant because the coasts between the Mekong Delta and the Malay Peninsula, the water frontier to which this study refers, had become the centers of growth in Southeast Asia by the mid-eighteenth century, and the key feature of this center was this string of minor ports. Among the various reasons for this growth were the Siamese and Vietnamese population movements to the two major deltas (Menam [Chao Phraya] and the Mekong) and their corresponding practice of intensive wet rice farming in the areas, techniques of which were characteristic of the two peoples.[43] Parallel to this were the sizeable communities of Chinese laborers settling in the pockets of Southeast Asia's thinly populated coasts or islands, mining or producing cash crops.[44] Because these colonies had to be provisioned from outside sources on a more or less permanent basis, they remained tied to the outside for continuing flows of supplies and immigrants and for the purpose of exporting their produce.[45] Hence a permanent Chinese market emerged outside China itself, or rather, a string of minor markets. The main form of exchange between these minor ports was invariably seen as smuggling by the larger nearby states. Barbara Andaya observes: "It was more profitable for miners in isolated settlements to sell tin to passing ships, like those of the English and Bugis. The Chinese thus became ever more prominent as 'smugglers,' private traders who bypassed the ruler's monopoly."[46]

It is illuminating, to reexamine the text *Xiêm la quốc lộ trình tập lục* and to reconsider the text's intensive interest in the minor ports and their natural products. This Vietnamese list of routes and ports coincides strikingly with the route taken by the British country traders of the eighteenth century as discussed by Andaya. She describes how English country traders bartered opium for tin and spices in Malay waters and then sailed for China: "Anyone who followed the normal route to China through Ujung Salang, Kedah, Selangor, Melaka, Linggi, Palembang, and Batavia, could be assured of a ready market."[47] Putting the Vietnamese text back into the context of the water frontier, the haven of smugglers, it reveals itself as a map for smugglers. This knowledge was accumulated throughout the decades of the eighteenth century and through contacts with diverse peoples. As such it attests the importance of the minor ports to the economy of the region of the eighteenth and early nineteenth centuries, before Sài Gòn and Bangkok became predominant cities.

It is engaging to see the role played by Penang, Melaka, and later Singapore in this context. The goal of these ports against the Dutch East India Company monopoly was free trade, the princes of which were the "country traders." Breaking this monopoly was particularly important for tin. According to Mary Heidhues, in the 1770s as much as one-half of Banka tin was "smuggled," a large amount of it being carried by the English.[48] Despite the Dutch East India Company monopoly on tin, in 1778 Melaka obtained only 394,511 pounds of tin, while the English shipped 501,250 pounds.[49] Anthony Reid points out that the major increase in trade for Singapore in the first twenty years came from independent states such as Siam, Việt Nam, Aceh, Siak, Trengganu, and the Balinese states rather than from European-controlled Java and the Philippines.[50] These two pictures combine to tell one major story of trade in late eighteenth- and early nineteenth-century Southeast Asia, namely, that the driving force of trade in this region between the coast of China and Batavia was private traders, whether English, Chinese, Portuguese, or Bugis. This lucrative trade of rice, tin, pepper, cloth, opium, and firearms could be described with one word—smuggling.

Smuggling and the Nguyễn Government Sanction

The question is, how were the government's revenues affected; losing about 90 percent of taxes from the maritime trade carried out among the minor ports on its territories.

A slightly different perspective might clarify how relationships were worked out between the Nguyễn court and the irregular trade. According to scholars in Hồ Chí Minh City, in just six years, between 1817 and 1822, the Nguyễn cast five hundred copper canons, each weighing between 364 and 387 kilograms.[51] Casting these cannons would require a minimum of 182 tons of copper, a striking amount considering that although northern Việt Nam produced copper, not much was mentioned in the Nguyễn chronicles about transporting large amounts of copper to Sài Gòn. The sources of this copper might have been Chinese copper coins, but it likely also came from Java and Luzon, where the Nguyễn envoys visited occasionally.[52]

The most important source for copper, however, must have been private traders, particularly the Chinese. The newly discovered Minh Hương material in Vĩnh Long has proven invaluable in identifying the specific functions of the Chinese in the Nguyễn economy and state building. One of the documents lists the names of thirty-one heads of this Chinese community from 1783 to 1847 and describes certain tasks carried out by each of them. Among the duties of the Chinese were tailoring robes for the officers and repairing and building ships. Their more important duties, however, were purchasing rice, copper, tin, zinc, and gunpowder and then submitting them to the Nguyễn tax collectors. Although there might have been bad years when the Chinese were expected to purchase rice from Cambodia and Siam, rice that the Chinese purchased would more likely have come from the Mekong Delta in exchange for copper, tin, zinc, and gunpowder from overseas.

This evidence suggests that the rice export, although illegal in theory, was a government-sanctioned activity in practice, particularly during the Gia Long era and early Minh Mạng period. The Nguyễn court viewed "illegal" rice export as a necessary and important supplement for their political economy. In other words, the Nguyễn revenue from the trade of local Chinese came not from import and export duties but from the exchange of commodities, especially for the strategic items for which the Chinese paid taxes. In this fashion the Nguyễn regulated trade to their advantage, channeling local Chinese trade into the Nguyễn economy. This agreement meant that trade could be carried out by the Chinese as long as they paid taxes for strategic items as required by the government. This arrangement became the most effective means for ensuring social control of the Chinese in an area where government rule could hardly reach anyone—Vietnamese, Khmers, or Chinese. It enabled the government to extract money and commodities relatively painlessly from trade along the infinitely complex coastal areas that would otherwise have been hard to patrol. As such the Nguyễn policy toward the Chinese parallels and even pioneers those of the colonial governments of the nineteenth century.

In the eighteenth century, although several trade networks operated between various ports of China and Southeast Asia, the most dynamic passed through the regions around the Mekong Delta, the Gulf of Siam, and the Malay Peninsula. This water frontier of Southeast Asia was comprised of dozens of minor ports busily exchanging goods and at the same time collecting products from other ports for China markets. These ports were operating at a similar level and had similar capacities before a clear port hierarchy in the region appeared. Cancao (Hà Tiên) and Bassac emerged favorably against this background and became the focus of the Canton trade in the 1760s. Their strength lay in their autonomous status and in their connections with the hinterlands as well as with other ports of the water frontier. The crucial point that emerges from this study is the advantage that a port possessed over local trade and over other ports. This seems to be the difference between Bangkok and Sài Gòn, one that had become clear by the late 1820s, when Bangkok's central position as the major entrepôt of the China trade was firmly established. Thus, instead of collecting local products and shipping them back to China directly from the minor ports, in Ligor "the Chinese were in complete control of the transfer of goods to Bangkok for re-export to China." In Trang and Pattani "the Chinese also exported elephant's teeth, tin and birds' nests to the capital for the junk trade."[53] A question remains for further investigation: While these minor ports declined in favor of Bangkok, did the same occur between Cancao, Bassac, and Sài Gòn?

Notes

1. Ishii Yoneo, *Junk Trade from Southeast Asia,* 90–98.

2. Brocheux, *Mekong Delta,* 2.

3. I owe this insight to Carl Trocki, who also helped me extensively in forming and substantiating the idea of the Water Frontier.

4. Taylor, "Viêtnamese Studies in North America," 7.

5. Van Dyke, "Canton-Việt Nam Junk Trade in the 1760s and 1770s."

6. In this period the local Amoy trade veered toward Luzon and Batavia (Viraphol, *Tribute and Profit,* 129).

7. Van Dyke, "Canton-Việt Nam Junk," chart 5.

8. Dalrymple, *Oriental Reportory,* 282.

9. Van Dyke, "Canton-Việt Nam Junk," 13.

10. Cushman, *Fields from the Sea,* appendix B, "The Cargo Manifests of Four Siamese State Trading Vessels," 160–69.

11. Ng Chin-keong, *Trade and Society,* 60.

12. "The Lintin anchorage was not, however, only an opium station. All vessels bound to Whampoa were loaded with general cargo, or with rice only, and were subject to what were called Cumsa and Measurement charges. These were very heavy in the case of the former, but moderate in the latter. It was therefore an object for a vessel entering the river with only part of a general cargo to fill up with any freight that might be offered, and thus reduce the heavy charges, or to send up what she had on board, if of

moderate quantity, in another ship, then load with tea for her return voyage" (Hunter, *"Fan kwae" at Canton before Treaty Days*, 12).

13. Andaya, *To Live as Brothers*, 191, 291.

14. I thank Nola Cooke for her information on and analysis of the late-seventeenth-century French missionaries' reports on the location of Bassac.

15. Zhou Da Guan said that salt was obtained by boiling sea water, and that the producing areas were from Chen-pu (today's Baria area) to Ba-jian, today's Sóc Trang area, according to Aymonier. See Zhou Daguan, *Zhen la feng tu ji*, 29 n 161.

16. Trinh Hoài Đức, *Gia Định thành thông chí*, 3:7b. Here and elsewhere in the essay the translations are mine unless otherwise noted.

17. Đinh Thái Sơn, *Nam kỳ phong tục nhơn vật diễn ca*, 79.

18. R. C. Ng, "Geographical habitat of historical settlement in mainland Southeast Asia," 271. See also Mabbett and Chandler, *Khmers*, 30–31.

19. Quốc Sử Quán Triều Nguyễn, *Đại Nam thực lục tiền biên. Chính Biên*, I, 7:411.

20. Quốc Sử Quán Triều Nguyễn, *Đại Nam thực lục Tiền Biên*, 10: 147–48; Li Tana, *Nguyễn Cochinchina*, 143.

21. *Chính Biên* said that in 1790 a Khmer *okya* was appointed as the governor of Bassac, in charge of collecting gambling taxes from the Chinese (*Chính Biên*, I, 4:361); the arrangement changed in 1791 when Anh appointed *okya* La to oversee Khmer affairs, and a Chinese for Chinese affairs (5: 372); this "La" was very likely the "Luat" whom Siamese chronicles record as the "ruler of Bassack." See Ford and Ford, *Dynastic Chronicles*, 28, and 32. "[In 1792] Granting Bassac (Ba Thắc) prefecture to Khmer, the Oyas Duhoan sa, Oya Phi miet hoan sa and Oya Lien Song lan came to present a letter from the Siamese [king?] and asked for the land of Ba Thắc so that the taxes from this area could support the king Nac An. The king (Nguyễn Ánh) gave permission" (*Chính Biên*, I, 6: 385).

22. My thanks to Anthony Reid for the descriptive phrase "pre-nation-state world of shifting and multiple alliances" and for his encouragement in developing my ideas in this direction.

23. Cushman, *Fields from the Sea*, 65.

24. Van Dyke, "Canton-Việt Nam Junk," 13.

25. Crawfurd, *Journal of an Embassy*, 413–14. For an excellent discussion on the Trans-Mekong trading networks of the early nineteenth century, see Puangthong Rungswasdisab, "Siam and the Control of the Trans-Mekong Trading Networks."

26. Crawfurd, *Journal of an Embassy*, 223.

27. "Gia Định thất thủ vinh" (The song on Gia Định being lost [to the French]), in Trương Vĩnh Ký, *Gia Định phong cảnh vịnh*, 47 n 1.

28. Trương Vĩnh Ký, *Petit cours de géographie de la basse Cochinchine*, quoted from Nguyễn Đình Đầu, "Địa lý lịch sử thành phố Hochiminh" (A history of geography of Hochiminh City), in Trần Văn Giàu, Trần Bạch Đằng, and Nguyễn Công Bình, *Điia chí văn hóa Thành phố Hochiminh*, 223.

29. "Bến Nghé" (Ngưu Chử) first appeared in the Nguyễn Chronicles in 1775. This is later than many place names in the Mekong Delta, such as Sài Gòn and Đồng Nai. See Quốc Sử Quán Triều Nguyễn, *Đai Nam thực lục Tiền Biên*, 12:165.

30. Trịnh Hoài Đức, *Gia Định thành thông chí*, 5:3b.

31. Lê Quý Đôn, *Phủ biên tạp lục*, 243a.

32. See Sơn Nam, *Đồng bằng sông Cửu Long*, 38.

33. *Mục lục châu bản Triều Nguyễn*, 32–33.

34. Crawfurd, *Journal of an Embassy*, 414.

35. "MS of M. Chaigneau," quoted by Crawfurd, *Journal of an Embassy*, 519–20.

36. Report of M. Moreau, *Excursion et reconaissance*, vol. 3 (1881), quoted from Sơn Nam, *Đồng bằng Sông Cửu Long*, 37–39.

37. Quoted from Reid, *Southeast Asia in the Age of Commerce*, 2:32.

38. Sơn Nam, *Đồng bằng Sông Cửu Long*, 38.

39. Crawfurd, *Journal of an Embassy*, 519.

40. The Chinese let Ánh have the rice on credit in view of Ánh's plan for reconquering Sài Gòn (Ford and Ford, *Dynastic Chronicles*, 135–37). *Chính Biên* says it was a woman from Hà Tiên who came to Ánh to "donate" rice to him; see I, 2:323.

41. L. Hong, *Thailand in the Nineteenth Century*, 40.

42. Tống Phúc Ngoan, Dương Văn Châu, and Nhâm Văn, *Xiêm la quốc lộ trình tập lục*.

43. O'Connor, "Agricultural Change and Ethnic Succession in Southeast Asian States."

44. Trocki, "Chinese Pioneering in Eighteenth-Century Southeast Asia."

45. Ibid., 89.

46. Andaya, *To Live as Brothers*, 219.

47. Andaya, *Perak*, 327.

48. Heidhues, *Bangka Tin and Mentok Pepper*, 30.

49. Andaya, *Perak*, 325.

50. Anthony Reid, "A New Phase of Commercial Expansion," in Reid, *Last Stand of Asian Autonomies*, 67.

51. Phạm Hữu Công, "Mười một khẩu đài bác bằng đồng thời Nguyễn tại Bảo tàng lịch sử Việt Nam TP. Hồ Chí Minh," 228–30.

52. Reid, "Southeast Asia before the Nation-State," chap. 2, p. 3. The latter is a real possibility if we consider that thirteen Nguyễn envoys were sent to Batavia, two to Semarang, two to Luzon, one to Johor, and one to Goa and Melaka. See Chen Chingho, "Les missions officielles dans les Ha châu ou 'contrées meridionales' de la première periode des Nguyên," 119.

53. Viraphol, *Tribute and Profit*, 215. The Trans-Mekong areas was also largely under the control of Bangkok, as shown by Puangthong Rungswasdisab's "Siam and the Control of the Trans-Mekong Trading Networks."

6

One Region, Two Histories
Cham Precedents in the History of the Hội An Region

CHARLES WHEELER

While researching the long-term history of a Vietnamese port and its hinterland, I found myself faced with two separate bodies of scholarship, one Vietnamese, the other Cham. At some indistinguishable point, Vietnamese history ended, and Cham history began. In this Cham history, I discovered a narrative about another world manifested within the very same space yet divorced from its Vietnamese counterpart. The more I tried to resolve these overlapping histories, Vietnamese and Cham, the more their differences blurred, and the more their artifice became clear to me. Even within a regional history, I had been led by nationalist prejudices that limited agency to figures in Vietnamese dress, admitting others only when their presence reaffirmed claims to Vietnamese destiny within the region.

Yet Vietnamese migrants who settled this former land of Champa during early modern times, fashioning "new ways of being Vietnamese, did so "enclosed in a destiny" inscribed by Cham predecessors.[1] Not that all Chams had disappeared either: many remained and adapted to a new Vietnamese order. Through various forms of interaction and assimilation, Chams themselves contributed to the collective vocabulary of being or doing Vietnamese. Thus the history of this region proved far more complex than the conventional ethno-centered thesis would allow.

The segregation of Cham and Vietnamese histories upholds a false and misleading dichotomy in the Hội An region. Once local history has been liberated from these nationalist discriminations, contradictions between Cham and Vietnamese pasts resolve, and we can begin to discern the patterns of long-term processes that underlie the structuring of a self-consciously Vietnamese society, its relations of power, economic functions, and cultural expressions. These patterns display Cham precedents that have endured from deep past to immediate present and shaped the development of trade in Hội An and its hinterland. From this expanded vista we can begin to appreciate "the infinite perspective of the longue durée," and its effects on the riverside seaport of Hội An.[2]

This study is divided into three parts. The first part describes the key elements of the Hội An region, its significance to the Asian sea trade and the expansion of Vietnamese power and settlement southward across southeastern Indochina, sketching previous explanations for the region's development in the seventeenth century. The search for the beginnings of the region's trade and settlement in this literature quickly exhausts itself. The second and third parts show why this is so. Limiting attention to monarchs and merchants means the critical role that local inhabitants played in the development of Hội An's overseas trade has been overlooked. Attempts to identify this local society, however, have been frustrated by a division between two scholarly traditions, one Vietnamese, the other Cham, both of which assume a temporal demarcation between Cham and Vietnamese histories in the Hội An region, a demarcation that is artificial. Once the artifice has been shed, however, the importance of Cham people and perspective to Hội An's history cannot be overstated. Hội An's system of trade and the society that operated it were defined in fundamental ways by Cham precedents. Within the strata of these precedents we can begin to look for signs of functions and forms that, by about 1600, developed into a city known as Hội An. In conclusion I argue that, in approaching regional histories within modern-day Việt Nam, culturally distinct eras such as that of the Chams must not be segregated from Vietnamese experience.

Hội An, Port and Hinterland

The Hội An region centers around the long-silted seaport of Hội An. Just south of Đà Nẵng in present-day Quảng Nam province, Hội An sits at the mouth of the Thu Bồn River, about three kilometers upriver from the Eastern Sea (V: *Biển đông*), also known as the South China Sea (see map 6.1).[3] Known to Europeans as *Faifo*, the city in its heyday throughout the seventeenth and eighteenth centuries served as a major export and transshipment site serving Asia's sea trade, the primary commercial nexus within the Nguyễn state of Cochinchina (a.k.a. Đàng Trong). Most notably, Hội An's merchants exploited the port's strategic position in overseas shipping networks to compete successfully against other Asian port cities, especially Macao, in capturing the covert triangular trade between China and Japan, diplomatically divorced but still interacting on an informal basis, through sea merchants who exchanged silks, silver, copper, and other manufactures from both countries at clandestine offshore markets such as Hội An. The town's merchants, predominantly Hokkien Chinese (and Japanese before 1639), collected local goods transported by porter, beast, and boat from the mountains, the alluvial plains, and the seacoast for export abroad. As the monsoon winds of August arrived, mariners transported native metals, stones, flora, fauna, and manufactures to markets in China, Japan, and Southeast Asia. With the lunar new year, ships returned to Hội An laden with manufactures always in high demand, for they satisfied a range of practical and luxury demands for uses in medicine, ritual, cuisine, dress, and so on. As the central market for Cochinchina, Hội An served as a collection and distribution point for its regional neighbors, including a string of rivermouth seaports situated along the coast of Cochinchina. It also provided a key station in the clandestine overland and coastal trade between northern Trịnh and southern Nguyễn realms within the theoretical Lê empire, which were separated from each other throughout the seventeenth and eighteenth centuries by political rivalry.[4] The development of Hội An played an important role in Asia's early modern trade but more importantly influenced the establishment of the Nguyễn state and the development of Vietnamese societies in formerly Cham territories.

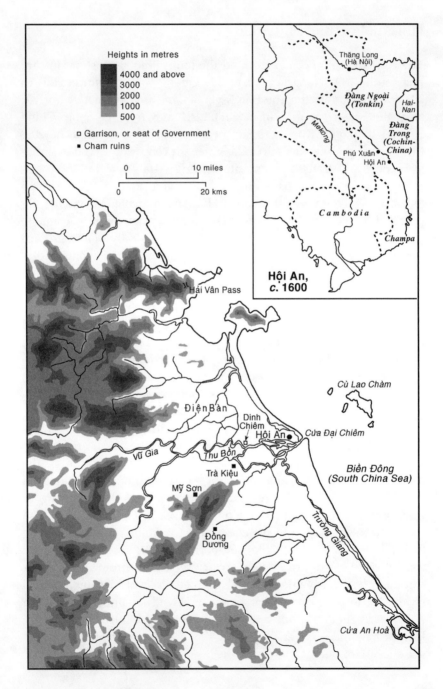

Map 6.1. Map of heights.

HỘI AN IN VIETNAMESE HISTORIOGRAPHY

In the early twentieth century historians of Việt Nam collected and analyzed placenames in hopes of deciphering Hội An's genesis and evolution. Although no evidence authoritatively pinpointing the town's earliest foundations has yet emerged, these studies agree that the earliest known references to the Sino-Vietnamese name Hội An phố or its Western form, Faifo, date from the 1630s.[5] These and other texts hint that Hội An was a prosperous international entrepôt decades before Nguyễn Hoàng, the first of the Nguyễn lords, established direct rule over Quảng Nam in 1602. From there theories proliferate. The broadest interpretations of historical placenames, drawn from Portuguese and Vietnamese descriptions of the region, have deduced that Hội An began operating as a trading port early in the sixteenth century, perhaps as early as 1525.[6] If so, the town does not appear to have gained its size, name, or status until after the turn of the seventeenth century. This approach to the port through its names leads to a quick and frustrating dead end.

Hội An's rise to international trade status appears to have been contemporaneous with two other early modern events: the beginning of Southeast Asia's "age of commerce" and the Nguyễn clan's creation of a Vietnamese-ruled state in the southeastern portion of mainland Southeast Asia.[7] Foreign trade played a key role in the Nguyễn clan's strategy for survival against the rival Trịnh clan ever since Nguyễn Hoàng first turned down the path of autonomy after 1600. Through its mercantile links, the Nguyễn court could obtain revenues, weaponry, and information about their adversary's activities.[8] In return the court guaranteed merchants a "haven" (V: phố) where they could "safely gather"—the literal meaning of the term "Hội An"—and seek their material gain.[9] The mutual interest of monarch and merchant ensured Hội An's rise to major status within the Asian sea-trading world, an arrangement that accords with descriptions of other Southeast Asian seaports.

Historians cite one administrative act to illustrate the importance of foreign trade to Nguyễn strategy. According to the nineteenth century Đại Nam thực lục (Veritable Records of Đại Nam), sponsored by his imperial descendents in the nineteenth century, one of Lord Hoàng's first acts of defiance against his northern Trịnh rival was to establish,

on his own authority, an administrative garrison (*dinh trấn*) for Quảng
Nam Territory (*xứ* Quảng Nam) several kilometers upriver from Hội
An, next to the village (*xã*) of Cần Húc, then on the banks of the Thu
Bồn River. Court records refer to it as Quảng Nam Garrison (Quảng
Nam Dinh). However, natives and foreigners alike knew the palace
colloquially as Cham Garrison, or Dinh Chiêm.[10] The *Đại Nam thực lục*
notes that the garrison's surrounding territory—which Vietnamese
colloquially referred to as "Cham Country," or Kẻ Chiêm—was "fertile and well populated, material goods were abundant, and tax revenue greatly exceeded what could be collected in Thuận Hoá [site of
the Nguyễn capital]."[11]

To signal the post's importance, Lord Hoàng appointed his son and
heir, Nguyễn Phúc Nguyên, to govern it. Once the garrison was established and Nguyễn order prevailed, "the market did not have two
prices [i.e., there was one fixed price], people did not become bandits,
[and] the boats of merchants from all kingdoms gathered." Lord
Nguyễn could tap the wealth of foreign trade at arm's length, a comfortable distance from his capital near Ái Tử far to the north. This
satisfied both the lord and the foreign merchants. "Consequently, a
large city was established."[12]

Vietnamese had migrated into this historically Cham territory
south of the Hải Vân Pass since the fourteenth century, both inde-
pendently and in conscripted colonies, but their numbers had been
few and concentrated in a stretch of plain north of the Thu Bồn
River, close to the sea.[13] Prior Cham occupants had been decimated,
dispersed, or displaced, and the alluvial plain upriver from Vietnamese settlements remained "wild and uncultivated," according to
Vietnamese historians. But Nguyễn Hoàng and Hội An changed all
that. In the southern frontier territories of Thuận Hoá and Quảng
Nam, the Nguyễn created a new Vietnamese state with "its fundamental basis in foreign trade."[14] Responding to the newly stabilized
political order and economic prosperity created within the region,
greater numbers of foreign merchants frequented Hội An's "guest
quarter" (*phố khách*), which increased the size and pace of trade.
Commercial possibilities expanded too. Waves of Vietnamese immigrants from impoverished Tonkin (Đang Ngoài) flowed into Quảng
Nam Territory and transformed it with unleashed industry. Allegedly as a result, a new, commercially oriented society grew among
Vietnamese who pioneered the southern frontier.

According to this scenario, Hội An grew as a result of the demands of Asia's early modern commercial boom and the imperatives of Nguyễn lords to ensure a reliable influx of state revenue. Foreign trade and domestic politics conspired to build a wealthy port of trade in a territory on the southern pale of Vietnamese settlement and in doing so funded a viable Vietnamese state in the still-undeveloped lands of the southern "frontier." Moreover, they attracted Vietnamese migrants who developed local production and transformed the region into its now recognizably Vietnamese form. Hội An brought them all together.

Although largely convincing, this narrative overlooks the role that local society also plays in generating foreign trade. Monarchs and foreign merchants were indispensable to the prosperity of Hội An, but a sufficiently thriving local economy equally predicated Hội An's functions in commerce and trade. The seaborne, coastal, and riverine trade that made up Hội An's trading network, for example, depended on sufficient resources of human labor to serve its various and indispensable needs. Hội An's warehouses depended on a hierarchy of constellate market networks whose agents calculated their itineraries in accord with a complex of local factors as diverse as seasonal migrations, harvest timetables, village customs, or monsoon rhythms. Women and men, beasts and boats wended their ways up- and downstream, along the coast and through parallel inland lagoons, and in so doing set the tempo of trade in the hinterland. Services such as piloting and refitting, or the labors of mining, hunting, and harvesting were performed not by foreign sojourners or settlers but by local inhabitants of the coast, the plains, and the hills. Even village and town services such as lodging, board, and brokerage fell largely within the operative domain of local inhabitants, usually through the negotiations of the ubiquitous native "wife"; although such negotiations did sometimes constitute a merely temporary bond, it was one "without which one [could not] do business."[15] In other words, no port could have developed without a prior local population to build and support it.

Indirect evidence for this local population is the substantial portion of export goods that made up Hội An's trade. The business of transshipping goods filled only one stream in Hội An's commercial traffic. Export goods also helped to fill the court's coffers, and its share of Hội An's trade grew steadily into the eighteenth century, long after entrepôt trade declined. The large inventory of local products, already "abundant" when first recorded in the first two decades of the seventeenth century, offers evidence that both the state and the local population were deeply invested in the extraction of natural resources to attract foreign exchange. Vietnamese court and Jesuit mission inventories between 1617 and 1633 list products from mining industries that extracted gold and iron; from forest tribes who harvested cinnamon, areca, pepper, incense and construction woods, or hunted for ivory, rhino horn, and deerskins; from lowland households that processed fragrant oils and manufactured silk for export or crafted ceramics and woodworks to support shipping; from plantations that grew tobacco and sugar cane; and from littoral and island communities that harvested the sea.[16] Local goods, produced for export, formed a significant portion of Hội An's trade, especially with China and Japan, as evidenced in the archives of Japanese customs and letters between the Nguyễn and the Tokugawa courts.[17] In predictable fashion, in the seventeenth century the new Nguyễn overlord appropriated the most precious of these goods as monopolies for his new royal clan.[18] Such an act suggests the takeover, rather than wholesale creation, of such enterprises. Even mining, operated by Chinese from the seventeenth century on, may represent the reform of a long-existing industry rather than the creation of a new one. The execution of these enterprises demanded complex processes and a good deal of knowledge, organization, and labor from the diverse groups participating in this commerce. Export enterprises required a base labor force to guarantee a reliable flow of goods downriver and a spectrum of necessary services to maintain ships and markets before commerce of this kind could even begin or could enrich the Vietnamese court.

Hội An required a local workforce to facilitate production and exchange and to otherwise serve the merchants and mariners from overseas who paid for their labor, for the itinerant soldiers who provided security, and for the bureaucrats who fixed prices. As the economy grew, these roles were increasingly filled by the Vietnamese and Chinese who migrated in augmenting waves of southern advance, but the labor to fuel Nguyễn Hoàng's scheme came from those already settled in the region. To ensure a regular volume of large receipts, the Nguyễn court had to secure the local population that filled Hội An's warehouses for the trading season. Thanks to a well-populated hinterland, coffers were filled and ambitions were satiated in merchant quarters and the royal halls.

There was more to the merchant-monarch network than guarantee of protection exchanged for wealth; the monarch's guarantees of a steady supply of labor were important as well. To attract and keep the foreign merchants in Hội An, Lord Nguyễn had to politically secure the hinterland, that is, the mountains, valleys, deltaic plain, coast, and islands, the flesh of Hội An's alluvial arteries.

LOOKING AT THE RIVER, THINKING OF THE SEA

A reexamination of Nguyễn administrative geography for the Hội An region supports this view. Nguyễn Hoàng considered the sea trade paramount when he created Cham Garrison and placed his son Nguyễn Phúc Nguyên in power there as governor of Quảng Nam Territory in 1602. However, his political strategy centered on the river rather than on the sea. According to Vietnamese historiography, Hội An was not yet part of Quảng Nam Territory when Nguyễn Phúc Nguyên was given rule over it. Since the beginning of the Lê dynasty in the fifteenth century, the town had been under the jurisdiction of the district (*huyện*) of Điện Bàn, in the prefecture (*phủ*) of Triệu Phong, governed by Thuận Hoá Military Territory (*trấn*) centered north of the Hải Vân Pass. Two years later, in 1604, the Nguyễn court elevated Điện Bàn from district to prefectural status (*phủ*) and transferred it to Quảng Nam Territory, bringing Hội An under the Quảng Nam governor's control and setting the boundary between Thuận Hoá and Quảng Nam territories at Hải Vân.[19] In other words, Nguyễn Hoàng's political strategy behind establishing Cham Garrison had more to do with the local population and less to do with the foreign merchants.

If Nguyễn Hoàng and his son did not regard Hội An's foreign merchants of paramount importance, it was not because they lacked appreciation for the preeminent value of Hội An's sea-trading network in their state-building enterprise. Rather, they appreciated it quite fully, for they tried to control the region's export trade at its hub. Cham Garrison was strategically set at the confluence of the Thu Bồn's major tributaries before the river again fanned out across the deltaic plain. It overlooked a "riverside market" (*sông thị*) called Sài Giang (named after the now-silted river that served it), the central

market for the Hội An hinterland. Under Cham Garrison's watchful
eye, the Sài Giang market was visited by most of the region's local
inhabitants, who preferred (or were allowed only) to barter here with
local Vietnamese merchants, who then moved goods on to the larger
market of Hội An. Traffic flowed upriver and down, between Sài
Giang and subsidiary markets, to integrate the highland and lowland
economies of Hội An's hinterland along a riverine axis. Once collected
in the Sài Giang market, goods funneled downriver to Hội An.[20] Hội
An functioned as the catchment for three ecological zones—highland
hunter-gatherers of the Trường Sơn (ancestors of Katu), lowland
agriculturalists of the Thu Bồn Basin, and littoral aquaculturalists of
the South China Sea coast—and channeled their products into the
long-distance networks of the Asian sea trade. To keep these channels
open and prevent the loss of trade to subordinate (but potentially
rival) rivermouth ports along Cochinchina's coast, Hội An depended
on Cham Garrison and its subordinate hinterland markets, that is, on
both the ruler and his laboring subjects. If Cham Garrison's market
lost its hinterland sources, Hội An's export market would vanish, and
most likely so would Hội An. To ensure control and continuity in Hội
An, the Nguyễn had to first control the port's source of wealth by
placing its most powerful instrument of control adjacent to the Sài
Giang market.

Nguyễn religious patronage reflects this upriver political and
economic nexus too. In the same year he founded the garrison, 1602,
Lord Hoàng sponsored the foundation of Long Hưng Monastery, set
to the east of Cham Garrison. To the west, about two kilometers upriver from Cham Garrison, he founded another temple on Bửu Châu
Hill in Trà Kiệu village.[21] He named this pagoda Chùa Bửu Châu.
Perhaps Nguyễn Hoàng was trying to mollify possible residual resentment among former Mạc soldiers who had settled in the area after
surrendering in 1558, though fifty years is a long time for resentment
to simmer without either boiling over or dissipating. The lord's atten-
tions likely held a more local focus. Trà Kiệu lies amid a cluster of
Cham ruins, all of them associated with the city called Simhapura that
Cham inscriptions identify as the first royal capital of the Indic rulers
of Nagara Campa. Upriver, about fifteen kilometers from Simhapura's ruins in Trà Kiệu, sits Mỹ Sơn, a massive temple complex
often referred to as the "religious heart" of the old Cham kingdoms.
At the top of Bửu Châu Hill, in Trà Kiệu, a Cham temple allegedly

once stood. This hill still enjoys a reputation as a spiritually powerful site, just as it did in 1602.[22] In contrast, although the Nguyễn court frequently patronized temples in Hội An, they never sponsored the creation of new temples in the city itself.[23]

All this evidence suggests that Hội An's hinterland was already well populated enough to support large-scale, export-oriented trade even before Nguyễn Hoàng involved his court in the affairs of such trade. It also means that, when he established Cham Garrison in 1602, Nguyễn Hoàng first considered subjugating the inhabitants living in Hội An's hinterland, that is, the deltaic plain, the foothills, and the highlands integrated by the Thu Bồn watershed. Foreign traders could be controlled with relative ease compared to this complex, hard-to-categorize population, diffused throughout a maze of waterways, mountains, and valleys difficult to perceive through the thick foliage blanketing all but the coastal plain. In other words, the labor and basic patterns of trade were already set before the establishment of Nguyễn power and large-scale Vietnamese immigration. Hội An needed new settlers to augment existing commerce, not to create it anew. It was this productive antecedent population that Nguyễn Hoàng had in mind when he first imposed his rule over the lands south of the Hải Vân Pass. But who were they?

Hinterland Historiography: One Region, Two Histories

If the hinterland is so important to the central port, then a wider regional perspective is necessary. Historians of Việt Nam who have described the greater Hội An region depend on a body of Nguyễn historiography written in the nineteenth century in analyzing the history of present-day Quảng Nam province, a territorial unit whose political boundaries are roughly congruent with the Thu Bồn rivershed that fed Hội An's markets. The history of this region in the years prior to Hội An's emergence in historical records is vague, despite the fact that this territory once comprised the religious and political center of the historical kingdom of Champa (Chiêm Thành) until the tenth century CE and retained its spiritual gravity long afterward. According to this view, the Chams abandoned the region altogether in 1306, when the Cham king Jaya Simhavarman III ceded the northern provinces of Lý and Ô to the Trần king Trần Nhân Tông in exchange for marriage with his sister, the princess Huyền Trân. The

Đại Việt government eventually renamed this territory Thuận Hoá, including northern Quảng Nam, which was part of Hoá Châu. Despite Cham cessions and Vietnamese conquests, the region passed back and forth between Vietnamese and Cham hands until its final absorption into the Vietnamese empire by Đại Việt emperor Lê Lợi in the 1470s. Included in Lê spoils was the Hội An region's southern half, which they alternately dubbed Đại Chiêm Châu, "Great Cham Province," and Chiêm Động Châu, "Province of the Cham Grottoes."[24] With each defeat, Cham leaders allegedly removed their subjects wholesale to within their diminishing boundaries. From this point on, Vietnamese political control over the territory was lasting.

What happened to the demography of the region before Nguyễn Hoàng embarked on building a new state in 1602 is unclear. The societal transition from Cham to Vietnamese is generally summed up as the combination of military conquest, penal and military colonies of Vietnamese, and "the peaceful infiltration of an 'avant-garde' of [Vietnamese] colonists who established themselves on soil abandoned by Cham."[25] Based on this literature, we can at best speculate that a kind of dark age descended over the region for hundreds of years. A pall descended over the region with Cham death and departure, suggesting activity ceased altogether until Vietnamese settlers introduced a new way of life. In this portrait, if settlers assumed Cham behaviors, they did so indirectly through abandoned gods, temples, and other inanimate objects. Although neither trade nor any other sort of exchange receives consideration, one would conclude by inference that Hội An developed from this wave of Vietnamese "pioneers" that repopulated the region.

Cham scholars tend to support this view, which is not surprising since much of their data for this transitional period derives from the same batch of Vietnamese historiography. Cham scholars identify the Hội An region as the heart of Amaravati, one of the five regions of historical Champa. The crumbled citadels and temple complexes at Trà Kiệu, Đồng Dương, and Mỹ Sơn—all upriver from Hội An—are prominent among Amaravati's remains and once served as the political and religious heart of the federation of regional chiefdoms known as *nagara Champa*. Simhapura formed the mandalic center of Amaravati and, in changing degrees, of the entire federation and greater Cham society as well. According to this view, the Cham period in

Amaravati began with the establishment of what Chinese court chronicles called the kingdom of Lâm Ap, sometime between the second and the fourth century BCE, then reached its peak as the kingdoms of Hoàn Vương and Chiêm Thành during the seventh through tenth centuries. An abundance of inscriptional artifacts and the tendency to associate Amaravati with general descriptions of the royal capitals in Chinese and Arab sources mean that historical data for the Hội An region abounds, relatively speaking. Archaeology continues to amass a solid case supporting historiographical hints of a thriving Cham sea trade centered in the lower Thu Bồn. Unfortunately, after the destruction of the second capital at Đồng Dương in the tenth century, and a new Chiêm Thành resurrected farther south, in Vijaya (a.k.a. Chà Bàn, in today's Bình Định province). The Cham center shifted south; center became periphery, and the Hội An region disappeared from historiography. For centuries thereafter Vietnamese and Cham rivals volleyed the land back and forth in a struggle for supremacy. Here, sometime between the eleventh and the fifteenth century, depending on which history one reads, Cham inhabitants vanished in the face of Vietnamese political expansion. The narrative of Cham scholarship neatly ends, yet the data supporting this finale is extremely vague: the Cham were there, then simply disappeared, sometime.[26]

In these ethnocentric narratives there is a set beginning, middle, and end to Cham society in the Hội An region.[27] Like the Vietnamese literature, Cham scholarship tells of decimation, displacement, and decline, reversed only with the arrival of Vietnamese colonies. Some Chams were pushed to the mountains, while others are said to have assimilated, but no evidence is provided. As political history, this division between Cham and Việt Nam epochs perhaps has veracity; as social history, however, we are left with only presumption and habit to support such views.

Yet the Cham perspective provides insights that question many of the assumptions underlying the Vietnamese experts' approach to the Hội An region's history. Geography and its influence demonstrate a fundamental difference. Where the Vietnamese perspectives emphasize the limiting effects of terrain, the Cham alternative describes a region operating according to a maritime logic, a model as fitting to post-Cham Hội An as it is to the Cham era.

SEEING LIKE THE CHAM: HỘI AN AS A MARITIME
REGION

How incredible that this region lay dormant for so many centuries,
given its geography. Hội An lies near the exact center of a strand of
small, parallel river plains that snakes around a north-south axis
between the great deltas of the Red and the Mekong rivers. Mountains and sea are the dominant features of this territory commonly
identified today as central Việt Nam. To the west, mountains hug Việt
Nam's coastline, which undulates as it progresses south. This
phenomenon is most dramatic in the region of Hội An. There, the
north-south range called Trường Sơn veers closest to the sea. Mountain and sea pin "[Vietnamese] towns . . . back into the mountains
facing the sea," a seventeenth-century visitor recorded.[28] From these
north-south ranges of worn sandstone plateaus and weathered mountains, high spurs of granite and limestone peaks extend transversally
into the sea and create offshore islands. Mountains, then, effectively
boxed the inhabitants of central Việt Nam into "islands" of small
alluvial plains fed by short, steep riversheds. To historians this mountainous characteristic supports the standardized view of Việt Nam as
"the least coherent territory in the world," to quote the oft-repeated
words of Pierre Gourou.[29] In addition to this geographical confusion,
historians have overlooked central Việt Nam as nothing more than "a
thin band of coastal plains" connecting Việt Nam's "two cores," the
Red and the Mekong river deltas, illustrated best by the metaphor of
metageography ubiquitous to Vietnamese, the idea of Việt Nam as
composed of two rice baskets held together by a pole. In this concept
what good is the center, other than to connect the important, relevant,
and history-making "cores" of Việt Nam? It is as if this now-poor
region mattered nothing to the first Vietnamese conquerors other than
as a way station to Sài Gòn.

But what mountains divide, waters unite. Although the influence
of the maritime on economic development has been given scant attention by barrier-conscious historians of Việt Nam, it has received careful consideration by historians of the Chams. In their analyses of
geography, scholars of both Champa and maritime Southeast Asia
have generally emphasized a basic similarity between central Việt
Nam and the lands inhabited by Malay groups in island Southeast
Asia. In much of the Malayan world, we find the same geography,

producing the same results: diverse, small river sheds flowing at steep grades, separated by mountains, their populations concentrated on the alluvial plains near the river mouths. This model, first described by Bennet Bronson, emphasizes the ecological determination of trade and polity formation in island Southeast Asia (see map 6.2). Cham scholars have incorporated this archipelagic model into a number of studies and have used it to explain and theorize a broad range of topics, suggesting that environment and ecology had a profound impact on the political, cultural, and social patterns that shape the region's commerce and trade. For example, this regional dynamic even explains the Cham custom of plunder—or piracy, depending on where one stands—as a central function in Cham economy and politics. With this realization, regions such as Hội An, no longer a mainland anomaly but an "island," have been usefully compared with similar places in, say, Sumatra, the Malay Peninsula, Borneo, or the Philippines.[30]

Scholars of Champa and island Southeast Asia have emphasized the unifying role played by waterways. Recalling his 1695 visit to Cochinchina, the Chinese monk Shilian Dashan recognized this phenomenon as well: "There is no way to go between two prefectures [via land]. When one goes to one seaport, that is one prefecture. If you want to go to another prefecture you must leave the port by sail onto the sea and, following the mountains, and proceed to the other port."[31]

The boat was the principal mode of conveyance in this region threading the regional strands of central Việt Nam together. (The monk's statement is not entirely true. Roads did exist, paralleling the coastline, though their travelers faced steep obstacles.) Offshore, coastal traffic configured the trunk that linked the river regions along the coast together, creating the slender matrix within which the politically willful would configure their various Cham polities, then Cochinchina, and eventually Việt Nam. This maritime logic is reflected in early Đại Việt administrative geography, in which provincial units from Thành-Nghệ south conform nicely to Bronson's Southeast Asian scheme. A number of movements in Vietnamese history followed maritime streams as well, from the legendary conquests of Lê Thánh Tông to Nguyễn Hoàng's departure for the southern frontier in 1600.[32] Most came by boat, along the coastal corridor. Into this

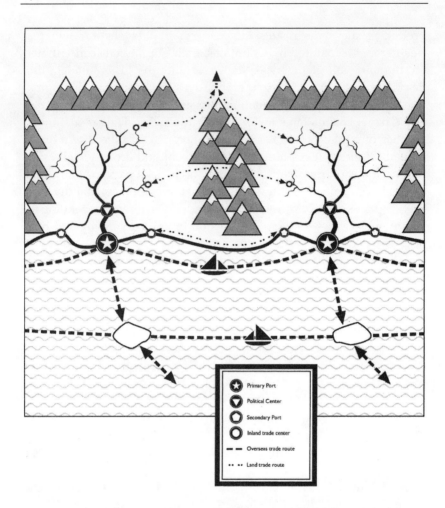

Map 6.2. Bronson's scheme. The river unifies port and hinterland; the coastal routes unify parallel regions; the overseas routes link ports to markets abroad.

north-south conduit flowed not only goods but also migrants, most importantly to the history of Hội An (and Việt Nam at large) Vietnamese from their historic territory surrounding the Red River delta, who transformed the face of historically Cham and Khmer domains.

Interestingly, these geographical similarities are not confined to Southeast Asia. As they reached their new, strange land, central Việt Nam must have looked quite familiar to the Chinese migrants who settled in Hội An, especially the Fujianese. The isolating influences of this Chinese regional geography drew the attention of a number of Chinese economic-historians and anthropologists. In its fundamental aspects, descriptions of central Việt Nam's geography differ little from those of most maritime regions of southern China, in particular those of Fujian, the source of most of Hội An's merchants.[33] In fact, with the exceptions of the Pearl, the Red, the Mekong, and the Chao Praya rivers, the mainland Asian coastline from the Yangtze to the Melakan Straits conforms to Bronson's Malayic model. Hội An, then, not only typifies a Malayic region; it represents the common South China Sea subregion. A series of parallel rivers separated by rocky promontories create small alluvial plains as they empty into the sea. Similarly bays and inlets tuck into this coastline, and numerous coastal islands pepper the waters offshore, offering safe passage from one coastal region to the next. Of course, in such a wide comparative context, the similarities soon break down under the weight of particulars such as climate, habitat, and so on. Southern shores are much sandier, and northern coasts more rugged with many more islands. But the fundamental geographical similarities are real. Dendritic waterways integrated into the permeable sea mitigated isolation in this world of crested valleys along a jagged littoral.

Where scholars of mainland Southeast Asia might see dissolution in the region's lack of a unifying river like the Mekong or the Irrawaddy, or mutual isolation in its transversal mountains, scholars of island Southeast Asia perceive a unity made possible by coastal vessels. The seacoast served a vital role as a unifying thoroughfare in the economic lives of central Vietnamese inhabitants, performing a function essentially the same as the great rivers of the mainland. Although this feature does not rule out the divisions created by mountains, it does counterpoise against them. This dynamic between mountain and sea, and the structure of the coastal circuit, is fundamental to the task of comprehending the historical development of economies in central Việt Nam, and crucial to understanding the commercial world of Hội An.

The more we come to understand this region, the more difficult it is to accept the notion that it lay completely dormant for centuries before Nguyễn Hoàng reintroduced it to the current of history.

The Productive People of Cham Country

Logic dictates that Cham Country was indeed well populated in 1602—but by whom? Vietnamese are known to have settled south of the Hải Vân Pass as early as the Trần period (1225–1400), but their numbers remained very small compared to settlements north of the pass.[34] By the mid-sixteenth century evidence of permanent Vietnamese settlement on the Thu Bồn plain at a significant scale emerges in historiography and archaeology. Excavations have produced a number of ceramic artifacts of Vietnamese production dated to the sixteenth century, and several villages listed south of the Hải Vân in a sixteenth-century Vietnamese historical geography of Thuận Hoá, *Ô Châu cận lục* (A Record of Ô Châu and Environs), are of Vietnamese origin. For example, Võng Nhị claimed to be the oldest extant village in the vicinity of Hội An, founded in the 1470s.[35] In Cẩm Thanh village near Hội An, one grave is dated 1498. Archaeological data from this era is beginning to amass and shows signs of large-scale Vietnamese settlement dating possibly to the first half of the sixteenth century, but no earlier.[36] Apparently a wave of Vietnamese came south in the footsteps of Lord Hoàng, after 1558 and again after 1600, according to official records as well as local epitaphs and genealogies.[37] This epigraphical collection presents a number of problems— verity the first of them, but also the absence of Vietnamese women in this settlement record. Again, however, the numbers implied are too small to attest a Vietnamese population in the Hội An region sufficient to support the thriving trade that Nguyễn Hoàng encountered.

Although earlier datings and additional settlements may emerge from future analyses, scattered or sporadic Vietnamese settlement in Hoá Châu does not mean Cham dispersal. Scant evidence documents Cham abandonment of their ancestral lands in the Thu Bồn Basin. Evidence to the contrary also exists. A nineteenth-century Chinese geography of Việt Nam says that "although the Lý and Trần dynasties [1010 to 1400] took Hoá Châu, the land extending south of the Hải Vân was still the soil of Champa."[38] The Chams seized the region repeatedly during the fourteenth century without lasting success until an army under the Hồ dynasty (1400–1407) took Hoá Châu again in 1402, and it thereafter became a permanent Vietnamese possession. The *Nhất thông chí* records that the armies under the Hồ family forcibly relocated Chamic lowland dwellers in the wake of their 1402 conquest of the region. After the Hồ conquered the Cham provinces (*châu*) of Chiêm Động and Cổ Luỹ (roughly the southern part of Quảng Nam [Chiêm Động] as well as Quảng Ngãi [Cổ Luỹ] today), they "moved the people to the river headwaters and established the fort (*trấn*) of Tân Ninh for the purpose of control."[39] However, it is doubtful that this forced relocation, even if successful, emptied the lower plain of its Cham habitation, because the Hồ were soon after defeated by the invading armies of Ming China. Moreover, in the face of this invasion, the Hồ gave control of Hoá Châu to Chê Ma Nô Đà Nan "in order to keep the multitudes of Champa peaceful," according to the *Yueqiao shu*.[40] Territory south of the Hải Vân, from Hoá Châu south, "continued to be occupied by the people of Chiêm Thành [Champa]."[41] The Thu Bồn Basin passed into Lê hands after victory over the Ming in 1427, but the *Đại Việt sử ký toàn thư* includes the land among Cham territories conquered in the 1470s as well.[42]

Vietnamese records refer numerous times to Cham raids and rebellions in the region, from the fourteenth to the early sixteenth century, another sign of continued Cham presence in the lowlands of the Hội An region.[43] Bands of Chams occasionally launched raids on Hoá Châu, in the north of the region, while local rebellions occasionally flared in the south, then administered as part of Quảng Nam. In one example, in 1508 a Cham royal descendent named Chà Phúc led a rebellion comprised mostly of local Cham inhabitants of Quảng Nam, allegedly the "slaves of powerful families and officials inhabit[ing] fields and villages" who had "escaped and returned [their loyalty] to their realm," according to the *Toán thư*. The Đại Việt emperor ordered the military to "kill the Cham completely." Đại Việt forces soon crushed the rebellion, though Chà Phúc and "inestimable numbers of trouble-making Cham took to the seas after the policy was announced."[44] Seventy years later, under Nguyễn Hoàng's early administration, the people of Quảng Nam "still stirred rebellion."[45] Whether inhabitants in the Hội An region still included Chams, one can still only guess; further archaeological work could provide some answers.

Although the Hội An region nearly vanished from Vietnamese historiography, it attracted some attention from Chinese authors. Instead of the names that appear in Đại Việt records, Chinese texts now and again refer to the region only as Jiuzhou (V: Cụ Châu), "Old Province," with brief mention of a port, called Jiugang (V: Cụ Cảng), "Old

Harbor." These two names, Jiugang and Jiuzhou, first appear in Vietnamese histories dating from the thirteenth century, which nearly
conforms to the beginning of Đại Việt rule and settlement or rather
the beginning of a Cham-Việt period in the Hội An region. The names
appear in texts written as late as the Ming period, that is, into the
sixteenth century. The place is sometimes complained about as a
pirate's lair and appears to have fallen into stages of disarray depending on the state of ongoing Việt-Cham struggles between the tenth
and the fifteenth centuries.[46] Whether or not the region was a pirate's
lair, its estuaries apparently did provide safe haven to Chinese and
Japanese smugglers, collectively known as Wako, during China's
prohibition against foreign trade during the fifteenth and sixteenth
centuries. Even after the ban was rescinded in 1567, it appears smuggling continued. About this time Chinese and Japanese authors begin
to refer to the southern region of Đại Việt as Jiaozhi (V: Giao Chỉ; J:
Kochi), the ancient name for the Red River Delta region when it was a
province of the Han Empire. One Chinese literatus, in about 1600,
complained that these smugglers circumvented the continuing
Chinese boycott against Japan: "The kingdom's laws prohibit trade
with Japan. Nevertheless, merchants recklessly send out goods to
Jiaozhi [central Việt Nam] . . . and other places where Japanese come
to trade with them."[47] Whatever the case, archaeological evidence
indicates that exchange of some kind continued, albeit on a much
reduced scale, during this period. Digs have produced ceramics dated
to the Song, Yuan, and early Ming periods, though surprisingly little
Đại Việt ware.[48]

In the fertile alluvial plains between the Thu Bồn and the mountains of Hải Vân, Vietnamese migration was underway, and a cultural
realignment had begun as well. Dương Văn An, a Mạc official, compiled a survey of Thuận Hoá Territory in 1555 and recorded 133
villages in the lands of Hoá Châu. Contrary to assumptions, these
settlers were not necessarily Vietnamese. Even in the fertile lower
plains of Điện Bàn district, the site of Hội An, "a land rich with rice
paddy, where people peacefully drive carts for crossings and travel
the rivers by boat," Dương Văn An wrote that "the women wear
Cham clothing; the men use the customary umbrellas of the North."[49]

Even to the north, in Tư Vinh district (near modern-day Huế),
"some Hoá [Châu people] [spoke] a relic of Cham."[50] Clearly the
women were Cham; the men, Vietnamese, perhaps Chinese even or

Cham assimilating to Sinitic norms, no different than twentieth-century Vietnamese men who shunned all traditional clothing for a sweaty Western suit and tie (dress change in response to a changing political economy). By 1555 a new way of doing everything was developing in a new, multiethnic society in the Hội An region. Dương Văn An recorded a number of settlements in the area of present-day Đa Nẵng and Hội An, which then comprised Điện Bàn, the south-ernmost district in Thuận Hoá, bordering Quảng Nam.[51] These new settlements remained concentrated in the coastal plain between today's Đa Nẵng Bay and the Thu Bồn's north bank. Only seventeen years later, in 1572, after "Lord [Hoàng] had been in the territory over ten years" and only one year after the latest rebellion in Quảng Nam, Vietnamese chroniclers would describe Thuận Hoá Territory, which included the district of Điện Bàn, as a rich and peaceful world, a place where "the boats of merchants from all kingdoms gathered."[52] Even where the Vietnamese politically dominated, ostensibly Cham people constituted a key component, if not a majority, of the population in the Hội An region.

South of the Thu Bồn River, the lands continued to be settled by Chams. The numbers of Vietnamese settlers were not yet adequate to support trade; others had to be there as well, and these were Chams.

Even in the seventeenth century the process of transformation from Cham to Vietnamese identity was incomplete. The *Đại Nam thực lục*, for the year 1644, stated: "At this time, [the land] from Thăng Điện [Thăng Bình and Điện Bàn *phủ*, i.e., which covered the Hội An region] into the South is all settled by Chams [while] the immigrant [Vietnam-ese] settlers are still sparse."[53] Not that these inhabitants were not seek-ing Vietnamese ways: the Thiên master Hương Hải sojourned twice on the island of Cù Lao Chàm in the 1680s, recruited by the Cham chief to instruct his people in the civilized norms of the right path.[54] As late as 1695 we still find evidence of Cham settlers on the island. Recording his stopover on Cù Lao Chàm, Shilian Dashan remarks on the local inhabitants whom he calls "Man" to distinguish them from the "Yue" (Việt) living on shore: "From above [aboard his ship] I looked down at these people, naked and hair disheveled, with only a cloth for their fronts. Among [them] there are those who speak a pygmy tongue and blacken their teeth [C: *zhuli heichi*].[55] . . . A boat approached with an official who also has disheveled hair and goes barefoot."[56] Shilian Dashan used the term *zhuli* specifically in reference to the language

of "Southern Man" (C: Nan Man), that is, the non-Sinicized people of
Southeast Asia. We can only assume that these are a Cham people who
had yet to vacate Cù Lao Chàm or assimilate to Vietnamese norms.

The Cham Legacy

Evidence of Cham culture in the Thu Bồn Basin must have seemed
ubiquitous to anyone who settled or sojourned in the Hội An region
as late as the twentieth century, both in material form and in cultural
practice. Remnants of buildings, façades, statuary, and stelae populated Quảng Nam before French archaeologists cleared away most of
the moveable relics and American bombs blew up much of the rest.
Cham statuary still appear in the courtyards of churches and inhabit
sacred space on sea goddess altars in village temples. Architectural
vestiges still punctuate modern urban spaces, interrupt rice fields,
and hide in mountain forests. The remains of Cham citadels and temple complexes lie within a forty-mile arc radiating from west to south
of Hội An—An Bàng, Trà Kiệu, Đồng Dương, and Khương Mỹ, and
most important among them the famous temples of Mỹ Sơn—up the
Thu Bồn River at the foot of the Trường Sơn range. In addition to the
great Cham Museum in Đà Nẵng, local districts and even private
homes throughout Quảng Nam keep and display their own collections of Cham relics.[57] Vietnamese who settled in the region were
quick to appropriate them.[58] This cultural influence is most conspicuous within the religious realm. As late as the 1920s French scholars
described the local use of abandoned Siva temples, though they
misunderstood the innovations of "the Annamites [who] completely
ignore[d] the Saivite representation of the linga."[59] One can still find
Hindu-deity statues enshrined in several local village temples, in addition to temples dedicated to Thiên Y A Na, the local version of the
sea goddess Avalokitesvara, whom the Vietnamese adapted directly
from the Cham version named Po Nagar.

We are left mostly with topographical relics until archeologists and
historians pursue the question in earnest. In addition to the many
Vietnamese placenames that incorporate words used to denote
"Cham" such as Chiêm, Chàm, Chăm, and Trà/Chà (e.g., Thành
Chiêm [Cham Citadel], Cù Lao Chàm [Cham Island], Bến Cồn Chăm
[Cham Islet Landing], Trà Quế [Cham Cinammon], and Sơn Trà
[Cham Mountain]), there are also etymological connections to Cham

trade activities and practices.[60] The Thu Bồn River's outlet to the sea is commonly called Của Đại, short for Của Đại Môn Chiêm, "Great Cham Rivermouth," as it was known in Nguyễn times, a reference to the old province of Đại Chiêm. Vietnamese locals colloquially referred to Hội An as Hổ bi xứ, "Tiger-Skin Place," well into the twentieth century. (Hổ was alternately used with Hời, a variation of Mọi or Hời, Vietnamese terms for ethnic Chams.)[61] The name perhaps refers to its role as a collection center for the village-level tiger-trapping enterprises that foreigners observed in Hội An as late as 1819–20.[62] The name for the village (làng) of Chiên Đàn is the Sino-Vietnamese transliteration of Chamal, a Chamic word drawn from the Sanskrit candana, which means "scented wood." Commerce in the aromatic aquilaria wood of Quảng Nam's mountains was the village's mainstay for centuries.[63] The name Thi Lai, a village south of Hội An on the Thu Bồn River, was derived from Thị Nại, short for Thi Lị Bì Nại, a Sino-Vietnamese transcription of the Sanskritic name Sri Bonay, which the Cham commonly used to signify seaports.[64] Cù Lao Chàm is rich with such suggestive toponyms.[65] These names, preserved through transliteration into Vietnamese vernacular, suggest common economic activities during the province's Cham era.

The process of cultural transformation from Cham to Vietnamese in the Thu Bồn Basin was thus more complex than simply "the peaceful infiltration of an 'avant-garde' of colonists who established themselves on soil abandoned by Cham."[66] Displacement indeed occurred, either in massive convulsions or in fits and starts. Impressive new linguistic evidence persuasively demonstrates that "much of the disappearance of the Cham [Mon-Khmer] speakers along the coastal plain must be attributed not to their being killed or even displaced but to their absorption into the emerging [Vietnamese] lowland civilization," according to Graham Thurgood.[67] He quotes Charles Keyes, who theorized that "once the various territories had been conquered, Vietnamese migrants would move into and settle these areas. Here, they often intermarried with Chams and Khmers, and, even when they did not, they were exposed to the different social and cultural patterns of these Indianized peoples. These contacts tended to result in some compromising of the dominant Chinese-derived tradition, at least among the peasantry."[68]

The compromises went beyond the "high cultures" of China and India, or even Việt-Cham categories, involving a number of linguistic and cultural communities inhabiting the hinterland of the Hội An region from Cham to the Mon-Khmer-speaking ancestors of the Katu peoples who now inhabit the high ground of western Quảng Nam. Wherever they settled and in whatever they endeavored, Vietnamese immigrants encountered the well-established patterns of behavior of the peoples who preceded them and very likely continued to live alongside them. At cross-cultural junctions old ideas came together from disparate sources and intermingled, producing new modes of behavior. These compromises, or rather cultural realignments, are important, for the Hội An case suggests a "new way of being Vietnamese" fashioned collectively from Vietnamese and Cham cultural vocabularies but in the end given a Vietnamese stamp in ways reflecting the changing realities of power in the region. A number of these cultural realignments probably occurred from within, as intermarriage brought Cham practices into the everyday lives of Vietnamese and Vietnamese practices to the Cham. This process of cultural synthesis was well underway when Dương Văn An wrote *Ô Châu cận lục* in 1558, yet was incomplete for the Thu Bồn Basin as late as 1644 and for the island of Cù Lao Chàm as late as 1695, long after Hội An's emergence as an Asian entrepôt.

   Clearly too much emphasis is still placed on the vision of pioneering, ethnically pristine Vietnamese immigrants without considering the impact of inhabitants with a long legacy in the region. Narratives describing cultural change along the coastal plains of southern Indochina generally assume Vietnamese agency. Vietnamese adopted local Cham deities such as Po Nagar and took up a form of Siva worship. Most of Cochinchina's Vietnamese lived in Malayic-style stilt houses, traveled in Cham-style boats, tilled with Cham plows, and even buried their dead in Cham-style graves. Immigrant Vietnamese "adopted" piracy and barter in slaves.[69] Were these phenomena wholly the agency of immigrant Vietnamese? Is Vietnamese ethnohistory somehow especially immune to the hybridization accepted as a given in similar ethnic expansions in world history? We must also reflect on the agency of local Cham, who must have been involved in the act of disseminating such complex religious, technological, and cultural knowledge. In other words, does Vietnamization reflect the displacement of a people or the displacement of a category? Why is it easier to believe that Vietnamese "pioneers" moved into Cochinchina and assumed the complex cultural programming of a vanishing (or vanished) ethnic group than it is to imagine a population of Cham, stable in their cultural practices, maintaining their longstanding economic and societal functions while yet assuming the public norms and language of a new Vietnamese state apparatus and local elite? Could we not as easily say we are looking at a new way of being Cham? For that matter, can we even assume Cham rather than Katu or other ethnicities?[70]

Cham culture had not disappeared from the Hội An region when Nguyễn Hoàng began to assert his control over it. The land was suffused with the relics of a vanished kingdom and with the remnant people who had yet to transform their sociopolitical identity. During this gradual cultural transition, as people vacated their ancestral homes or merged with the politically dominant Vietnamese society, Cham identification passed, and Cham, Vietnamese, and no doubt other cultural practices blended to create a new Vietnamese choreography in the lands of Hội An. Each new region that emerged in Vietnamese history expressed itself anew over the long span of the sixteenth, seventeenth, eighteenth, and nineteenth centuries. The unique story of this early modern seaport and its hinterland cannot be told divorced from the Cham precedents that prescribed it.

As for Hội An's origins, it seems likely that Chinese and Japanese privateers established themselves in a place known to Chinese as Jiugang and pursued their clandestine trade between China and Japan, as many other privateers had done throughout the South China Sea during the sixteenth century. As they settled into the Thu Bồn River's central port, they developed exchange relationships with the local Viet-Cham inhabitants. But the boundaries of legal trade shifted as first China, then Japan, and then the Nguyễn clan "opened" doors to trade or rather extended their political influence over it, introducing regulation where none had existed. As law shifted its barriers and thereby tweaked the formulas by which the risk, the price, and the profits of overseas trade were calculated, incentives changed for the most daring entrepreneurs and most desperate people of maritime society. It certainly must have changed things for the privateers of Jiugang. Just as trade had become smuggling, smuggling once again became trade, and Jiugang became Hội An.

Thus only by moving out of the habit of segregating Cham and Vietnamese histories when discussing the regions of what we now call Việt Nam could I begin to sort out questions about Hội An's emergence on the world stage. In functional terms the port never ceased to exist: names may change, specific locations may shift, but the downriver port endures (as it does today, in the form of Đà Nẵng).

Notes

1. First quotation from Li Tana, *Nguyễn Cochinchina*, 118. Second quotation from Braudel, *Mediterranean and the Mediterranean World*, 2:1244.

2. Braudel, Mediterranean and the Mediterranean World, 2:1244.

3. For clarity's sake—and clarity's sake only—I will stick to the term best known to most English-language readers, the "South China Sea," rather than the Vietnamese *Biển đông*, "Eastern Sea." Following the same rationale, I will refer to the southern realm of Đàng Trong as Cochinchina, and the northern realm of Đang Ngoài as Tonkin.

4. The itineraries of monks, merchants, and officials—mainly from Europe or China—suggest a good deal of informal coastal interaction between Tonkin and Cochinchina; unfortunately little study has been done on the subject. Đỗ Bang is the sole exception; see "Relations between the Port Cities in Dang Trong and Pho Hiên in the Seventeenth 1/N Eighteenth Centuries." As for overland connections, sources describe routes linking Hội An's with Nghệ An in Tonkin. For example, Wuysthoff noted that merchant subjects of both Cochinchina and Tonkin visited the same markets on the Middle Mekong. See Lejosne, *Le journal de voyage de Gerrit can Wuysthoff et de ses assistants au Laos*, 74, 95, 181, 211. Shilian Dashan visited Hội An in 1695 and described the overland routes leading from Hội An to the "Kingdom of Aí Lào," Cambodia, Thailand, and the inland Chinese province of Yunnan and Guangxi (*Haiwai jishi* 4:107). This is also reflected in a number of Vietnamese maps, albeit of nineteenth-century provenance.

5. Cristoforo Borri was the first to write at length about the city known to Europeans as "Faifo." See Robert Ashley's translation, titled *Cochin-China*, p. B1. In this book Borri describes his observations of Cochinchina, where he lived from 1618 to 1622, as part of an early Jesuit mission there. For more on the life and work of Father Borri, see Léopold Cadière, "Les Européens qui ont vu le Vieux Hué: Cristoforo Borri." Hội An also appears on editions of a Vietnamese map titled "Thiên Nam Tứ Chí Lộ Đồ Thư" [Atlas of the quadrants of the celestial South], dated between 1630 and 1653, reprinted in Trương Bưu Lâm and Bửu Cầm, *Hồng Đức bản đồ*, 94–95. The earliest local reference to Hội An is the Phô Đà Sơn stele, which was inscribed ca. 1640 (Institute of Hán-Nôm Studies, Hà Nội).

6. Pierre Manguin claims it may have been as early as 1525–30, citing early Portuguese accounts, though there is no evidence of Portuguese-Vietnamese trade until the 1550s, at the same time Macao was established (*Les Portugais sur les côtes du Vietnam et du Campa*, 186). The *Ô Châu cận lục*, completed in 1555, lists the village of Hoài Phô, which many have identified

as an alternate name for Hội An; see Dương Văn An, *Ô Châu cận lục* [A record of Ô Châu and environs] (1961), 41; (1997), 48. For a summary of the various theories about Hội An's origins based on historical names, see Nguyễn Sinh Duy, "Danh xưng Hội An xưa," 20.

7. This idea was expressed by both Li Tana, *Nguyễn Cochinchina,* and Đỗ Bang, *Phố cảng Thuận-Quảng thế kỷ 17 va 18,* 44. See also Reid, *Southeast Asia in the Age of Commerce,* vols. 1 and 2.

8. Nguyễn reliance on Portuguese and Chinese merchants and Jesuit missionaries for weaponry has been well documented. Nguyễn use of merchants for intelligence is not as well understood. For example, in 1776 in his description of the recently conquered Cochinchinese royal archive, Tonkinese governor Lê Quý Đôn reported that in 1713 "[t]he Lord [Nguyễn] Phước Châu [r. 1694–1725] ordered Fujianese merchants trading [t]here, named Bình and Quý, to go from Guangxi through the Southern [Chinese] Customs in Lạng Sơn [a key Sino-Vietnamese border garrison], to ask about the situation in the capital as well as all the *trấn* under control of the Trịnh clan." From Lạng Sơn, the merchant Bình traveled to the capital Thăng Long. Through the city's merchants, he obtained an audience with the Diên khánh Quận công, a member of the military under Trịnh Cương (a.k.a. An Đo Vương, r. 1709–29). After two months he traveled south as far as Nghệ An, then reversed his course, stopping at the capital before heading overland to Guangdong, where he caught a boat headed for the Nguyễn capital of Phú Xuân near Huế. For more on Bình's grand adventure, see Lê Quý Đon, *Phủ biên tạp lục,* 104–5. Thanks to George Dutton for helping to light my way through the *tạp lục.*

9. A definition of "haven" aptly describes the meaning of the Sino-Vietnamese term *phố*: "A recess or inlet of the sea, or the mouth of a river, affording good anchorage and a safe station for ships; a harbour, port" (*Oxford English Dictionary*).

10. Quốc Sử Quán Triều Nguyễn, *Đại Nam thực lục tiền biên*(1962), 42 (hereafter cited as *Thực lục*). Early Jesuit missionaries such as Alexandre de Rhodes called the citadel Dinh Ciam. Quảng Nam Garrison (Dinh Quảng Nam) and Quảng Nam Territory (*xứ* Quảng Nam) refer to different territories. Dinh Quảng Nam refers both to the garrison established by Lord Hoàng in 1602 and to the territory it supervised, and it conformed to the Thu Bồn watershed. In 1806 this became the province (*tỉnh*) of Quảng Nam. The realm of Cochinchina comprised two territories (*xứ*), Thuận Hoá and Quảng Nam (hence the name Thuận- Quảng), divided at or just south of the Thu Bồn until 1604 and thereafter at Hải Vân Pass north of Đà Nẵng.

11. *Thực lục* (EFEO microfilm, no. A.2714), q. 1: p. 24a, quoted in Taylor, "Nguyễn Hoàng and the Beginning of Vietnam's Southern Expansion," 63. Taylor uses a Hán version; for the standard *quốc ngữ* translation, see *Thực lục* (1962), 42. The modern Vietnamese translation differs greatly from the Hán edition.

12. *Thực lục* (EFEO microfilm), q. 1: p. 24a, quoted in Taylor, "Nguyễn Hoàng," 49. The capital eventually migrated south to the vicinity of present-day Huế, first to Kim Long in 1636, then to Phú Xuân in 1687.

13. See note 34.

14. Li Tana, *Nguyễn Cochinchina,* 12, 71.

15. Shilian Dashan, *Haiwai jishi,* 3:80, 81. All translations are my own unless otherwise noted.

16. *Thực lục* (1962), 48 (for the year 1617); Borri, *Cochin-China,* pp. C3, D2. Other goods included silks, ship and other construction woods, beeswax, rattan, minerals, *lac* wood, honey, lacquer, fruits, and caulking resin.

17. "Minh Đô sử," q. 53. Japanese demand was especially high for *kỳ nam hương* and *trầm hương* (aloeswood and eagleswood, respectively), grades of fermented *aquilaria* wood that upper-class Japanese used for aromatics, incenses, and hair oil. For more on this and other Vietnamese-Japanese exchanges, see Innes, "Trade between Japan and Central Vietnam in the Seventeenth Century," 10 (courtesy of the author).

18. Nguyễn Hoàng had developed mining colonies in, for example, the mountains of Thuận Hoá and Quảng Nam, called "harvest households" (V: *liêm hộ;* C: *lianhu*). These collectives provided annual supplies of gold, to which he reserved the exclusive right to sell or barter. *Thực lục* (1962), 48. Gold was not the only commodity that the Nguyễn monopolized. All of the most valuable commodities in Cochinchina were monopolized, including *aquilaria* wood, cinnamon, pepper, bird's nest, and salvage from wrecked ships. Some commodities the lord controlled himself, such as the white and black pepper that grew in the mountains of Thuận Hoá, which he farmed out to local merchants. Other products he handed over to his kin, such as the cinnamon trade centered in Trà Bông, southwest of Hội An. On Trà Bông, see Nguyễn On Khe, *"Phu man tap luc* ou notes diverses sur la pacification de la région des Mọi,"* 447.

19. The elevation and transfer of Điện Bàn is recorded in *Thực lục* (1962), 43. The *Đại Nam nhất thông chí* reports: "In the time of the Lê, [the court] established Điện Bàn *huyện,* in the *phủ* of Triệu Phong, Thuận Hoá" Cao Xuân Dục, *Đại Nam nhất thông chí* (1964), 7 [*quốc ngữ*]; 2 [Hán]; hereafter cited as *Nhất thông chí.* The sixteenth-century *Ô Châu cận lục* lists Điện Bàn district (*huyện*) under Triệu Phong prefecture (*phủ*), Thuận Hoá circuit (*lộ*); see Dương Văn An, *Ô Châu cận lục* (1977), 43 (*quốc ngữ*), 232–33 (Hán). The *Nhất thông chí* says that Duy Xuyên (southern Hội An region, today's southern Quảng Nam province) became a part of Điện Bàn prefecture under Gia Long; *Nhất thông chí* (1964), 9 (*quốc ngữ*), 4 (Hán); (1997), 333–34. The location of the governor's residence and garrison is also revealing. Many mistake this first garrison with the site of the Quảng Nam provincial office under the Nguyễn emperors, in the village of Thành Chiêm. This provincial office was built in 1835. The location of the seventeenth-century garrison has yet to be found. The best conjecture, based on local lore, places the Cochinchina-era citadel ten kilometers upriver from Hội An in the vicinity of Phước Kiệm village (*xã*) and three or four kilometers downriver from Trà Kiệu. See *Nhất thông chí* (1964), 16 (*quốc ngữ*), 9 (Hán).

20. Phan Du, *Quảng Nam qua các thờ dài,* 53; *Nhất thông chí* (1964), 13, 59, 96 (*quốc ngữ*); 13, 18 (Hán); (1997), 5:376. Since at least the nineteenth century, the

market has been known as *Chợ Củi, sông thị Sài Giang*, or *chợ Thành Chiêm*. See Phạm Đình Khiêm, "Đi tìm địa-điểm và di-tích hai thành cổ Quảng-nam và Phú-yên đầu thế-kỷ XVII," 78.

21. *Thực lục* (1962), 43. The 1962 Viện Sử học edition calls this temple "Chùa Bảo Châu." The character for *bảo* can alternately be pronounced *bửu*, as local residents do. See Gouin, *Dictionnaire vietnamien-chinois-français*, 53a.

22. According to people in Trà Kiệu, the French destroyed the Vietnamese temple atop Bửu Châu Hill in the 1880s and replaced it with a Catholic church. Sometime during the rule of South Việt Nam by Ngô Đình Diệm (1954–63), the French church was destroyed, and a monstrous white complex was built in its place, which remains there today. Curiously, no museum of the revolution has replaced it. Cham bricks and sculptural fragments literally stick out of the hill ground like landfill refuse.

23. The only visit by a Nguyễn lord to Hội An was Nguyễn Phúc Châu's visit in 1712. *Thực lục* (1962), 186.

24. *Nhất thông chí* (1964), 6 (*quốc ngữ*), 2 (Hán); Ngô Sĩ Liên, *Đại Việt sử kỷ toán thư*, vol. 3, *Bản kỷ* 12:684.

25. Nguyễn Thế Anh, "Le Nam Tien dans les textes vietnamiens," 121–22. This is a good summary of the *Nam tiến* thesis.

26. This scholarship is summarized in Lafont, *Proceedings of the Seminar on Champa*. The standard work is still Maspéro, *Royaume de Champa*.

27. The term "ethnocentrism" is unfortunately a politically loaded and often jargonistic term. However, I mean it in its most literal sense. I am arguing that Cham historians focus solely on a single ethnic group, overlooking or effacing cohabitants and the interethnic exchanges and fusions that must have occurred. The same applies to Vietnamese historiography.

28. Shilian Dashan, *Haiwai jishi*, 3:31b–32a.

29. Pierre Gourou, quoted in Li Tana, *Nguyễn Cochinchina*, 18.

30. Bronson, "Exchange at the Upstream and Downstream Ends." Examples of works influenced by Bronson include Hall, *Maritime Trade and State Development in Early Southeast Asia*, 12–20; and Wicks, *Money, Markets and Trade in Early Southeast Asia*. Hall also shows the environmental effects of the water world on Cham political and economic practices (practices that no doubt gave them their feared reputation throughout the seas) in "The Politics of Plunder in the Cham Realm of Early Vietnam."

31. Shilian Dashan, *Haiwai jishi*, 3:31b–32a.

32. See, for example, Lord Hoang's campaigns during the 1550s as well as his final voyage south; *Thực lục* (1962), 33–41.

33. See Hurlbut, "Fukienese"; Clark, *Community, Trade and Networks*, 3–10; Bielenstein, "Chinese Colonization of Fukien until the End of the Tang," 98–122. Paralleling Vietnamese scholarship, anthropologist Maurice Friedman emphasized the limiting effects of mountains to describe Fujian.

34. Huỳnh Công Bá provides four examples from local materials for Vietnamese settlement in northern Quảng Nam during the Trần period. But these materials, genealogies, and local inscriptions speak only about individual, rather than large-scale, settlement. See his "Tìm hiểu cộng cuộc khai khẩn

vùng bắc Quảng Nam dưới thời Trần." If state-sponsored colonization actually was the primary engine of Vietnamese settlement, as alleged, there is no evidence that these colonists and their descendents remained or retained Vietnamese cultural practices during periods when Vietnamese rule faded in the southern frontier, if indeed such rule was ever effective south of the Thu Bồn River before Lord Hoàng imposed his own.

35. Đỗ Bang, "Phố cảng Thuận-Quảng," 44.

36. Personal notes, Hội An Ceramics Museum, 1998, 1999. Most attention has been paid to periods either before or after this difficult transitional period; thus these data remain largely unpublished.

37. Among the few local genealogies and temple inscriptions of Vietnamese families that I have read, all claim their ancestor as someone who followed in Lord Hoàng's footsteps. Taylor notes in a recent article that a family in Đa Nẵng possesses a genealogy that records their Cham descent. See his "Surface Orientations in Vietnam," 961. See also Dăng Thu, *Di dân của người Việt từ thế kỷ X đến giữa thế kỷ XIX*, 74–81, 86–89.

38. Shen Qingfu, *Yuenan diyu tushuo* [Illustrated geography of Vietnam], quoted in Chen Chingho, *Historical Notes on Hội An*, 4.

39. *Nhất thông chí* (1964), q. 5 (Quảng Nam): p. 6 (*quốc ngữ*), p. 12 (Hán); (1997), 5:332.

40. Whitmore, *Vietnam, Ho Quy Ly, and the Ming (1371–1421)*, 173–74.

41. *Nhất thông chí* (1964), q. 5: p. 6 (*quốc ngữ*), p. 12 (Hán); (1997), 5:332.

42. "Đại Việt sử ký toán thư" (Hanoi ed.), Bản kỷ 12:237; (Tokyo ed.), vol. 3, Bản kỷ 12:685. Hereafter *Toán thư*.

43. For example, Cham settlers revolted during the reign of Lê Uy Mục (1504–9) (Hickey, *Sons of the Mountains*, 154–55).

44. *Toán thư* (Tokyo ed.), vol. 2, Bản kỷ 14:786.

45. In 1571 "there were still lands in Quảng Nam that stirred rebellion." Nguyễn Hoang dispatched Mai Đinh Dũng to quell these rebellions and bring Quảng Nam under greater administrative control. See *Thực lục* (EFEO microfilm), q. 1: p. 18a; (Hanoi, 1962), p. 34.

46. Chen Jiarong, *Gudai Nanhai diming huishi*, 271–73.

47. He Qiaoyuan (Ming), quoted in Innes, "Door Ajar," 55–56.

48. Personal notes, Hội An Ceramics Museum, 1998, 1999.

49. Dương Văn An, *Ô Châu cận lục* (1997), 48–49 (*quốc ngữ*), 38a (Hán). Bùi Lương translates the original Hán phrase—*bắc nhân*, or *běi rén* in Mandarin pronunciation—as "Chinese [*Tàu*]." See *Ô Châu cận lục* (1961), 42. The term was often used at this time to refer to Chinese. The custom of using Chinese umbrellas was prevalent in other countries of the South China Sea such as Java or Melaka.

50. *Ô Châu cận lục* (1997), 37a (Hán).

51. *Ô Châu cận lục* (1961), 24–26.

52. See notes 12 and 13 above.

53. *Thực lục* (1962), 78. See also *Thực lục* (EFEO microfilm), 3:50b–51a.

54. In Lê Quý Đôn, *Kiến văn tiểu lục*, 4:403–4.

55. Shilian Dashan uses the term *zhuli heichi* (*Haiwai jishi,* 19). The term *zhuli* originally referred explicitly to the music of the western barbarians but came to mean the music and language of both western and southern barbarians. See *Ciyuan,* 271b. The English translation "pygmy tongue" I have borrowed from Kelley's recent summary of the *Haiwai jishi;* in his master's thesis, "Vietnam through the Eyes of a Chinese Abbot," 52–53.

56. Shilian Dashan, *Haiwai jishi,* 19.

57. Such people I encountered in Đà Nẵng and Trà Kiệu, May–June 1999.

58. See Albert Sallet, "Les souvenirs Chams." See also Claeys, "Inspections et reconnaissances en Annam: Quang-nam," 596–98.

59. Sallet, "Les souvenirs Chams," 211.

60. Gouin says that *trà* is another term for *chiêm,* or Cham (*Dictionnaire,* 1424b).

61. Sallet, "Le vieux Faifo," 502–3.

62. Rey, "Voyage from France to Cochin-China," 122.

63. Trương Văn Ngọc, "Đình Chiên Đàn," 70. Ngọc translates Chiên Đàn as Chamal. In their Sanskrit-Chinese dictionary, Soothill and Hodous (p. 326a) translate Chiên Đàn as Candana (Chinese transliteration: Zhan da na). Moussay gives *gahlon* as the Cham word for *aquilaria,* obviously derived from the Malay *gharu,* though not to be confused with gharu wood, which the Chinese called *muxiang* (V: *mộc hương*); see Moussay, *Dictionnaire cam-vietnamien-français.* Chamal, then, must signify the Cham pronunciation of the Sanskrit word. Chiên Đàn is located in Tam Kỳ about forty kilometers south of Hội An on the Trường Giang, an arm of the Thu Bon that runs parallel to the coast and in its deeper days linked southern Quang Nam to Hội An by boat.

64. Another Thi Nại can be found, for example, near Qui Nhơn, in Bình Định province, which assumed the role of Champa's central port from the eleventh through fifteenth centuries. The phonetic evolutionary path from Sri Bonay to Thi Lai allegedly followed this trajectory: *Sriboney* (Sanskrit) > *Thi Lị Bì Nại* (Hán-Nôm) > *Thi Nại* > *Thi Lai.* Trần Kỳ Phương, "Của Đại Chiêm," in Nguyễn Đức Diệu, *Đô thị cổ Hội An,* 130. The Cham pronunciation of the Sanskrit *sri* is *thri',* a missing stage immediately revealing the Vietnamese logic behind their transcription (I have yet to find the Chamic word corresponding with *Bonay*). *Sri Bonay* is in fact the Sanskritic, not colloquial, Cham term.

65. Trần Quốc Vương, "Hội An-Đà Nẵng, Đà Nẵng và Hội An," 15–22.

66. Nguyễn Thế Anh, "Le Nam Tien," 121–22.

67. Thurgood, *From Ancient Cham to Modern Dialects,* 27. Thanks to Keith Taylor for pointing this book out to me.

68. Keyes, *Golden Peninsula,* 183–84, quoted in Thurgood, *From Ancient Cham,* 27.

69. Li Tana, *Nguyễn Cochinchina,* 99–116; idem, "Alternative Vietnam?" 114–19.

70. Trần Kỳ Phương made this last point to me, and I want to thank him for it.

7

Transnationalism and Multiethnicity in the Early Nguyễn Ánh Gia Long Period

WYNN WILCOX

During the war fought between the Tây Sơn dynasty and the Nguyễn dynasty for control of Việt Nam (1773–1802), both the Nguyễn emperor Nguyễn Ánh Gia Long (r. 1782–1820) in southern Việt Nam and the Tây Sơn emperor Quang Trung (r. 1788–92) in northern Việt Nam found it useful to seek technology, diplomatic support, and mercenaries from outside Việt Nam. For the Nguyễn, however, this task took on a particular urgency because of their dire situation in the early 1780s. Desperate to maintain a flicker of hope that they would again rule from Phú Xuân, the capital of their ancestors, in a part of modern-day Huế, the remnants of a once-proud Nguyễn scholar-elite forged rivers, avoided crocodiles, ate tubers and grasses to avoid malnutrition, and ran out of fresh water in their attempts to keep their dynasty alive.[1]

To alleviate their desperate supply situation, between 1777 and 1789 Nguyễn Ánh sent his officials on diplomatic missions to Cambodia,

Siam, India, France, and Melaka. Nguyễn officials were involved in attempting to negotiate direct assistance from the Dutch and the Portuguese. They did in fact successfully negotiate a treaty of assistance with the French monarch Louis XVI, even though this treaty did not come to fruition. Moreover, Nguyễn officials frequently purchased supplies, munitions, and ammunition from Spanish, Dutch, Chinese, and especially English outposts. Finally, during this period Nguyễn Ánh appeared to be willing to accept support from any person with ability, regardless of his education or nationality; as a result, Chinese pirates, Spanish mercenaries, and French missionaries, among others, not only assisted the Nguyễn regime but became integrated into Nguyễn official life. The best-known of these figures is the French-born Bishop of Adran, Pierre Pigneaux de Béhaine (1740–99), known in Vietnamese sources as Bá Đa Lộc. Many of these figures fought with distinction for the Nguyễn during the Tây Sơn war and were rewarded with special ranks and honors by Nguyễn Ánh Gia Long.

Thus, in the late eighteenth century, officials at the southern Vietnamese (Nguyễn) court came from all parts of the world, including Europe. However, since at least the 1860s, a decade which by no coincidence also inaugurated the French colonial era in Việt Nam, historians have understood those largely responsible for molding and forging history in Việt Nam in the late eighteenth century to be "the French," understood as a group of adventure- and power-seeking missionaries and military deserters, and "the Vietnamese," who usually are represented in two groups: Nguyễn Huệ Quang Trung, or the "northern" emperor and his officials, on the one hand, and Nguyễn Ánh Gia Long, or the "southern" emperor and his officials, on the other.

The first, characteristic of historians of the late nineteenth and early twentieth century who were supportive of French colonization, assign to "the French" the impetus for changing Vietnamese history. They do this to the disadvantage of Nguyễn Ánh Gia Long, who is regarded as an emperor enlightened by the influence of his French mercenaries and advisors but who failed to nominate a successor who would follow along the same path of progress, and also to Nguyễn Huệ Quang Trung, who is generally regarded as an uncivilized rebel.[2] The second approach, characteristic of Vietnamese nationalists, assumes that the eighteenth-century French in Việt Nam were colonizers and uses them to criticize Gia Long, who is viewed as a puppet, and to revitalize

Quang Trung, now viewed as a hero.[3] Finally, a third approach, most
notably taken by North American scholars of the last four decades,
emphasizes the insignificance of French actors in the late eighteenth
century and treats both Gia Long and Quang Trung as effective emperors. This approach, by constantly repeating the claim that the
French are insignificant, paradoxically gives their insignificance a kind
of significance.[4]

   All three of these narrative strategies have a single element in
common: they all read the politics of French colonialism back into the
late eighteenth-century situation.[5] Vietnamese history in this period
thus becomes an allegory for the colonial period. In this complex
moral tale, there are three important characters. First is the figure of
the French adventurer, who either represents the good civilizer (in the
colonial mode) or the bad colonizer (in the nationalist mode). He acts
as a foil for two types of Vietnamese, one who is either the wise person who requests assistance from the French (colonial) or the fool
who opens the door to colonialism (nationalist), and the other who is
either the uncivilized rebel (colonial) or the hero who fought against
imperialists and their Vietnamese collaborators (nationalist).

   Making the history of the late eighteenth century about these
distinctions allows historians to use it as a point of origin for their discussion of French imperialism, but it also ignores the more complex
ties at work at the early court of Nguyễn Ánh Gia Long. In fact, the
division between French and Vietnamese in the late eighteenth century is an artificial one, because alliances and divisions were made at
the Nguyễn court on the basis of personal relationships more than on
the basis of ethnic or national origin. Rather than relying on the a
priori legitimacy of the distinction between French and Vietnamese
groups at the court, this chapter will stress the diversity of backgrounds of officials from both within and outside Việt Nam. This
analysis will examine officials from other areas, such as China,
Cambodia, and Spain, and will emphasize the degree to which even
the "Vietnamese" at the court came from very different areas, to the
point at which it is difficult to identify a singular group of officials
from Việt Nam to which one can oppose "the French." Finally, this
chapter will examine some of the difficulties of assigning as a coherent French group those officials in Việt Nam who were born in
France. French-born missionaries, mercenaries, and officials often dis-
agreed. Moreover, many of the individuals identified as "French"

defy our expectations because they behave in a way that would not be recognizably "French" to us.

Diversity at Nguyễn Ánh Gia Long's Early Court

Those who make the distinction between French and Vietnamese the primary analytic framework for Vietnamese history marginalize the remarkable diversity of the court of Nguyễn Ánh Gia Long. Among those in Nguyễn Ánh's entourage or at his court at Gia Định during the time of the Tây Sơn wars were people of Cambodian, Thai, Portuguese, Spanish, and southern Chinese origin.

One of the more poorly understood figures of this era is the mercenary Vinh Ma Li (also known as Vinh Li Ma), who is depicted as Siamese in the *Đại Nam chính biên liệt truyện* and the *Đại Nam thực lục*, and as Malay in the *Gia Định thành thông chí*.[6] What can be established is that Vinh Ma Ly, along with several Siamese military officers such as Tôn Thất Cốc, came into contact with Nguyễn Ánh when he had taken refuge at Hà Tiên in 1783. Vinh Ma Ly provided the fugitive king with ten warships and an army regiment of more than two hundred people at a time when Nguyễn Ánh was perhaps in more desperate straits than at any other time during the Tây Sơn wars. Though little is known about Vinh Ma Ly, his ability to provide this quantity of gunships and troops for Nguyễn Ánh indicates the extent of his power, perhaps as a mercenary or a pirate. In that same year both he and Tôn Thất Cốc were killed in fierce fighting with Nguyễn Lữ's troops.[7]

In addition to Siamese and Malay officials, Nguyễn Ánh also employed several Cambodians in his court at the end of the eighteenth century, two of whom attained the status of officials, to be mentioned by the Quốc Sử Quán, or Board of History, in their compilation of Mandarin biographies half a century later. These two individuals are Nguyễn Văn Tồn and Diệp Mân.[8] Nguyễn Văn Tồn was given *cai đội* (commander) status by Nguyễn Ánh in the spring of 1786 when he followed the king on a trip to Bangkok and participated in the major surprise attack and defeat of Tây Sơn troops in the autumn of 1787. After the Nguyễn captured Huế in 1802, Tồn participated in several embassies to Siam for Gia Long until his death. His son, Vy, remained a force in southern Vietnamese politics through the 1830s, when he was accused of participating in the Lê Văn Khôi rebellion in

southern Việt Nam by sending secret information to Khôi. This affair
was dismissed because of Vy's death immediately thereafter.[9] Diệp
Mân is given only a short note at the end of Nguyễn Văn Tồn's entry
at the end of the imperial biographies; he was apparently a Cambodian official who aided Tồn and was made a provincial official at Trà
Vinh in 1805.[10]

Though many ethnically Chinese officials performed military and
civil services for Nguyễn, three officials who were actually born in
southern China appear in sources of the Nguyễn dynasty.[11] Not
surprisingly, all three are well-known southern Chinese pirates. The
leader and the most famous of these three is Hà Hỉ Văn, a member of
the White Lotus Society from the famed village of Tứ Xuyên in
Sichuan province.[12] This famed pirate first enters the Nguyễn annals
in 1785. While his ships were docked on Côn Lôn (Puolo Condore)
island, Văn heard that Nguyễn Ánh had fled again to Bangkok. Văn
decided that he had something to gain from assisting the expatriate
king. He ordered his disciples to draw up a letter to Nguyễn Ánh asking to serve him.[13] In 1787 the king returned to the Hà Tiên area,
where he met with Văn, who is described by the *Gia Định thành thông
chí* as the "leader of the sea bandits" (*tương hải phỉ*). Văn appeared
with his first officer Chu Viễn Quyền to formally offer their services
to Nguyễn Ánh in the tenth lunar month of 1787.[14] He was appointed
as a *tuần hải đô doanh* (admiral) and assumed the military command of
his group, while at the same time being nominated army commander
and division commander. In August 1787 Văn offered his protection
to the depleted Nguyễn troops and shuttled Nguyễn Ánh to Long
Xuyên.[15] Văn participated in several significant battles such as that at
Quy Nhơn in 1792 and died while serving on the Nguyễn march to
Phú Xuân in 1801.[16]

Portuguese traders and officials also played a significant role in
turning Nguyễn Ánh's fortunes in the 1780s and 1790s. One of the
most significant and enduring figures was An Tôn Vi Sản, or Antonio
Vicente Rosa. The Nguyễn had been quick to appeal to Portuguese
traders and to the Portuguese colonial government in Goa in the early
1770s, at the beginning of the Tây Sơn rebellion. Perhaps the Nguyễn
looked first to the Portuguese due to the historical presence of Portuguese traders and Portuguese Jesuit missionaries in southern
Việt Nam; but given the dissolution of the Jesuit order, the official ban
on missionaries by the Nguyễn after 1750, and the dwindling interest

of Portuguese traders in Đàng Trong by the late eighteenth century, turning to the Portuguese may have been simply an indication of the desperate need for help.[17] The relationship between Nguyễn Ánh and An Tôn Vi Sản became especially close in 1786 when the king fled again to Bangkok and became a virtual prisoner in the hands of the Siamese monarch Rama I. An Tôn Vi Sản met with the king on December 5, 1786, without the knowledge of Rama I and negotiated an agreement. This agreement was to give trading rights to the Portuguese, rights for Portuguese Christians in Việt Nam, and a fortress for the Portuguese at Vũng Tàu, in exchange for Portuguese military assistance to the Nguyễn.[18] These conditions bear a striking resemblance to the treaty signed at Versailles a year later between Bá Đa Lộc (Pigneau de Béhaine) acting on behalf of Nguyễn Ánh and the Count of Montmorin. Yet this Portuguese agreement, which like the French treaty did not come to fruition, has been overshadowed by that peculiar form of hindsight evinced by the eventual French colonization of Indochina.[19] Though there apparently were Portuguese mercenaries who served Nguyễn Ánh, none achieved any real notoriety.[20] Nevertheless, An Tôn Vi Sản made several commercial expeditions partially on Nguyễn Ánh's behalf, obtaining arms and munitions for him several times between 1787 and 1789.[21]

An Tôn Vi Sản was not the only Portuguese trader who worked for Nguyễn Ánh in the 1780s and 1790s. Perhaps even more significant in the long run was An Tôn Thù Di Cam Bô, or Antonio José Gamboa, a Portuguese captain who acted as a go-between for Nguyễn Ánh in his correspondence with the leaders of other countries and brought supplies to him throughout the 1790s.[22]

The Portuguese were joined by a number of Spaniards with close connection to the court at Gia Định. Few Spaniards served as officers in Nguyễn Ánh's army, and only one, the mercenary Man o ê (Manuel), was significant enough to warrant any extensive commentary in the Nguyễn imperial records.[23] Spanish missionaries were present at the court at Gia Định in the early 1790s thanks to the influence of Bishop Bá Đa Lộc. One Franciscan missionary in particular, Father Jacques, was appointed grand vicar along with Gia-cô-bê (Jacques Liot). Since they both served under the bishop of Adran during his tenure as Crown Prince Nguyễn Phúc Cảnh's regent and tutor, both were quite familiar with the bishop and the politics at the court.[24]

These brief sketches illustrate the diversity of officials serving Nguyễn Ánh in one capacity or another. It is not by any means an exhaustive list; traces remain of other functionaries, including those from England, Ireland, Portugal, Spain, Siam, Cambodia, Java, and China, in addition to those born in France and in Việt Nam.[25] Yet the mere fact of the international character of the entourage of Nguyễn Ánh Gia Long does not resolve the question of its significance. Those wishing to see Nguyễn Ánh Gia Long's entourage as being domi-nated by ethnic Việts acting autonomously from their European counterparts might point out that even these many figures are not significant in the grand scheme of mandarins at the court at Gia Định.[26] The contrary argument could be made as well: those wishing to see Nguyễn Ánh as a weak ruler who relied on foreigners, that is, those who view him as the king who "let the snake into the family henhouse," could claim that the presence of foreigners demonstrates Nguyễn Ánh's weakness and his inferiority as a hero in Vietnamese history relative to his rival Quang Trung.[27]

To the first interpretation it could be argued that numerical signifi-cance cannot be equated with military significance. Since those of for-eign birth supplied Nguyễn Ánh's other officials with ships, guns, and artillery, their importance during the crucial years of the 1780s and 1790s should not be underestimated. Even historically speaking, earlier Nguyễn courts included many influential non-Việts, from Japan and China and the West, including several European transla-tors, some of whom were missionaries. To the view that his reliance on foreigners made Nguyễn Ánh weak, it could be pointed out that the Tây Sơn courts also relied on a diverse mix of people.

But both arguments miss the central point, which briefly put is this: the structures of difference that drive the historiography of modern Việt Nam on the basis of the divisions of foreign/homegrown, East/West, and French/Vietnamese have little value in predicting the behavior of the figures in Gia Định at the end of the eighteenth cen-tury. Though the Gia Định court was flush with those born outside the Nguyễn realm, officials did not behave in a manner wholly consis-tent with their purported national identifications. In other words, not only were "the French" not the only foreigners at Gia Định, but "the French" did not behave predictably as a group. Rather, they associ-ated with others as individuals and did not constitute a comprehensi-ble faction at the court. In the next section I discuss the basis for

affiliations among figures at the court and the implications of reject-
ing the historiographical fallacy of giving primacy to the question of
"the role of the French" in the early Gia Long era.

Factionalism at the Early Gia Long Court

As K. W. Taylor and Li Tana have pointed out, Vietnamese historiography, both in North America and in Việt Nam, has overemphasized
the analysis of national and regional groups.[28] The primacy of
national and regional distinctions in behavior has recently most often
taken the shape of the strong historical claim that Vietnamese history
has been tainted by an overemphasis on Western sources and West-
erners in Việt Nam. In particular it has overemphasized the question,
What was the role of the French in aiding Nguyễn Ánh in winning the
Tây Sơn wars? This question, however, is essentially a parochial one
insofar as it assumes that "the French" behaved as a group at all.[29] In
fact, a closer analysis of those who were born in France and who were
present in Việt Nam during this period indicates a vast diversity of
values, attitudes, and behavior. It also indicated that national affinity,
if such a thing were indeed felt among French-born missionaries and
officials at the court in the period, was neither the only nor the most
important criterion determining the associations and factions in late
eighteenth-century Nguyễn court politics. A closer analysis also calls
into question in what way, other than by their birthplace, those born
in France were French at all.

Nationalist and colonial allegorical histories of this period, which
mirror each other by assessing the same events as significant but
reversing the moral implications of that significance, share several
conceptions about the role of national affinities in the history of the
period. The following discussion presents these assumptions and then
refutes them.

The first assumption that both nationalist and colonialist histories
make is that French missionaries and missions in Việt Nam were
united in their support for Nguyễn Ánh, who was viewed as sympathetic to Christians, and against the Tây Sơn, who were viewed as
xenophobic anti-Christian rebels.[30] Several historical details call this
interpretation into question. One fact that is reasonably well documented is that several French-born missionaries in northern Việt Nam
were vocal critics of Bá Đa Lộc's efforts on behalf of Nguyễn Ánh.

Father Lamothe, one of the most powerful missionaries in northern Việt Nam during the late eighteenth century, wrote several scathing letters to the directors of the Foreign Mission Seminary in Paris throughout the 1790s. His central argument was that the Tây Sơn knew that missionaries in southern Việt Nam were helping Nguyễn Ánh obtain military supplies. The Tây Sơn had good reason, therefore, to be suspicious of missionaries in northern Việt Nam. Thus Lamothe argued that the actions of southern missionaries were risking the lives of Christians in the Tây Sơn–controlled areas of Việt Nam.[31] The threat of persecution, Lamothe continues, was made much worse by "the occasion of the bishop of Adran, Mr. Olivier, and the other Europeans who are in [Nguyễn Ánh's] army in everyone's plain view."[32] Though it is unclear to what extent the threat was carried out, the Tây Sơn were well aware that missionaries such as Bá Đa Lộc were actively assisting Nguyễn Ánh in the war effort, and in one case they did (perhaps rather understandably) promulgate an anti-Christian edict as a result.[33]

These letters indicate the relatively good disposition of Lamothe and other missionaries in the north toward the Quang Trung emperor and his successor, his son Nguyễn Quang Toản (r. 1792–1802). In fact, the only Tây Sơn leader who was known to have actually persecuted Christians was Nguyễn Nhạc in central Việt Nam. One missionary, the prolific Lelabousse, even remarked that it was fitting that Quang Trung, having never persecuted Christians, died a peaceful and dignified death, and Nguyễn Nhạc, having persecuted Christians for nearly a decade from the middle 1780s to the early 1790s, died ignobly and painfully.[34] Several missionaries mentioned that a powerful mandarin at Quang Trung's court was in fact a Christian and provided protection for Christians throughout Quang Trung's reign as well as the reign of his son.[35]

Quang Trung and Nguyễn Quang Toản's relative tolerance of Christianity and Christian missionaries may be mild compared to the reported enthusiasm for Christianity of the youngest brother, Nguyễn Lữ. This brother, who had de facto control over the provinces of the far south for much of the late 1770s and early 1780s when the Tây Sơn had effective control over the area, even issued an explicitly pro-Christian edict from Sài Gòn in December 1783.[36] Some sources even claim that Nguyễn Lữ was a priest, though the reliability of this claim could certainly be called into question.[37]

There are two lesser known problems with the theory that missionaries supported the pro-Christian Nguyễn against the anti-Christian
Tây Sơn. The first is that Quang Trung, like Nguyễn Ánh, employed a
French Catholic missionary in his court. This missionary is the interesting Father Girard, a young priest who was normally stationed in
central Việt Nam. In late 1790 or early 1791, an apparently desperate
Quang Trung, concerned about the severe illness of his first wife, a
woman of the Phạm clan of Qui Nhơn, ordered his officials to search
for European missionaries. Quang Trung was under the impression
that the well-known scientific knowledge of certain missionaries
would give them medical expertise.

Girard, who had no medical training, was escorted to the capital,
where he was to take the title of the emperor's doctor and astronomer.
This befuddled missionary, who must have known that he would be
blamed for any harm that came to Quang Trung's wife, nevertheless
asked for a number of medical and astronomical books from the
Catholic procurer in Macao and did not refuse or resist in any way the
position that he was offered.[38] Though the queen was already dead
upon his arrival, Girard still served Quang Trung in the capacity of
encouraging the Portuguese and Spanish to trade with his regime; he
even made an expedition to Macao on orders of the emperor.[39] Moreover, other members of the French foreign mission society seemed
relatively unperturbed by Girard's position at Quang Trung's court.
His immediate superior, the bishop of Véren, noted that Girard was
being treated well and hoped for the best.[40] Thus we see that the idea
that the Nguyễn paved the way for French colonialism while the Tây
Sơn kept their regime free from the polluting influence of the French
cannot be sustained.

"The French" in Việt Nam during the Tây Sơn wars behaved as
individuals whose lives were in danger in wartime and who had to
respond to vastly different situations. Those in the areas controlled by
either of the Tây Sơn emperors could not afford to risk persecution by
being sympathetic to their southern colleagues, regardless of any perceptions held that they were all "French" or all Catholics.

The second assumption that both nationalist and colonial histories
tend to make is that "the French" were a group whose members acted
together and associated with one another, whether they were missionaries or officials working for Nguyễn Ánh. Yet a closer look
reveals that many of these French did not agree with one another or

act as a group. First, not all missionaries even in the south liked the famed Bishop Bá Đa Lộc or agreed with the actions that he and his other missionaries took. Father Boisserand, who accompanied Bá Đa Lộc and Nguyễn Ánh during the northern campaign in 1797, was one such dissenting missionary. Boisserand was known all over Việt Nam at the time for his electricity and hot-air-balloon demonstrations, which were so famous that Emperor Quang Trung wrote an edict about Boisserand's reputation as a great magician.[41] Father Boisserand complained bitterly about the accusations made about himself, the bishop, and the other missionaries who were close to the king. These accusations provide a window into the arguments that appear to have been made behind the scenes against Bá Đa Lộc. After summarizing the approval given to the bishop for taking time out to give baptisms under difficult circumstances, he summarized the unfair complaints made by the other missionaries against the supposed political actions of the bishop and the Sài Gòn missionaries with more than a hint of sarcasm: "But for the remainder of them, it seems that we have a very bad reputation. We follow neither the rules of justice nor those of the church; we are made lax with superstition; we are all soldiers. The monsignor, who sometimes does not see the king for two years and who on key days will flee to avoid him, the monsignor, I say, is too involved in temporal affairs. In truth we are schismatic, revolutionary, and soon heretical. Make it known, I ask of you, to these gentlemen to have the prudence to believe that we are a bit more careful."[42]

Conflicts between those born in France did not stop at mere disagreements over the bishop's actions. The more pious French missionaries were often disgusted by the impiety of the military mercenaries who became officials at the court. Especially bothersome to missionaries was the fact that some of these officials were Protestant. This appears at the time to have been an even greater obstacle to relationships between missionaries and court officials than the religious differences between Catholic missionaries and Buddhist officials.[43] More importantly, two of the French-born figures who were supposed to be the most significant, Bishop Bá Đa Lộc (Pierre Pigneaux) and Ô Ly Vi (Olivier de Puymanel, 1768–99, who engineered the campaign to retake Nha Trang in 1795 and designed the Vauban fortresses for many of the cities in southern Việt Nam, Sài Gòn included) strongly disliked each other. The missionary Bá Đa Lộc, in fact, was so disgusted by Ô Ly Vi's drinking and cavorting with prostitutes in Sài

Gòn that in one letter he refers to Ô Ly Vi as "the nasty piece of work" rather than using his name.[44]

The third assumption that is often made is that Nguyễn mandarins did not share Nguyễn Ánh and Prince Cảnh's enthusiasm for "the French." This is supposed to have created two implicit factions at the court: the Vietnamese mandarins, on the one hand, and the French, on the other. A closer examination shows that relations were much more complicated and personal. Certainly some mandarins at the court resented Bá Đa Lộc's position as crown prince Nguyễn Phúc Cảnh's regent and tutor, which must have given him great power at those times when Gia Long went to the battlefield and left Cảnh in control of Gia Định.[45] Thus, the bishop and other Catholics had to contend with various attempts by powerful mandarins, who unfortunately are not identified in the records, to spread rumors about unsavory Christian practices. One notable attempt claimed that the bishop encouraged a Catholic practice of prying the eyes out of live humans in their sleep and replacing them with cotton balls.[46]

Yet the bishop had close friends and supporters at the court as well. The most famous of these was the powerful mandarin Lê Văn Duyệt, who much later became the de facto ruler of the southern provinces. His respect for the bishop, and his long-standing tolerance and even defense of missionaries and Christians in general, is well known.[47] There were also Christian mandarins at the court who were close to the bishop. One such person was Tô Văn Đoái, a powerful mandarin known as Ông Giám ("Sir Commander") by the mission aries, who accompanied Prince Cảnh and Ô Ly Vi to Nha Trang in 1794 and was present for the entirety of the long siege of Nha Trang.[48] During the three months there, as several missionaries report, this mandarin, who was purportedly the most Confucian mandarin at the court, would come to the bishop and argue about religion and, to the surprise of all, decided at the end of this three-month period to convert to Catholicism. This relationship was only a brief one, though, because of Ông Giám's untimely early death.[49] Another Christian official, even less well identified as a "vice-admiral" and "ambassador" to the Siamese court, was buried with a procession of two hundred mandarins in July 1799 and with a grand speech by the king.[50] The implication of these relationships is that those born in France and those born in Việt Nam intermingled on the basis of their religious beliefs and on the basis of interpersonal relationships codified during sieges and battles. Those with Nguyễn Ánh during the Tây Sơn wars hardly segregated themselves on the basis of geographical origin.

The fourth and perhaps most prevalent assumption is that those born in France had an unquestionably French identity, regardless of how much time they spent elsewhere. The histories of the period tend not to state what they consider Frenchness to be, but all French-born officials and missionaries are presumed to have had it. This assumption is counterintuitive considering that the three officials Nguyễn Văn Thắng (Jean-Baptiste Chaigneau, 1769–1832; served the Nguyễn dynasty 1794–1819, 1821–26), Nguyễn Văn Chấn (Philippe Vannier, 1762–1842; served the Nguyễn 1789–1826), and Bá Đa Lộc (Pierre Pigneaux) all spent far more of their lives in Việt Nam than in the country of their birth. The dissonance seems even more significant when one considers the way in which these officials, and in particular Bá Đa Lộc, have become symbols of the French colonial mission in Việt Nam in several colonial histories and thus have come to symbolize the French presence in Việt Nam.

But to what extent were these figures French? To answer this question adequately would require a detailed examination of what, if anything, constitutes "Frenchness" or "Vietnameseness." However, one claim can clearly be made: these figures were consistently viewed as behaving in a way that was perceived as Vietnamese, and not as French, by their contemporaries. Perhaps most telling in this regard is the bishop's last will and testament, in which he gave most of his possessions to the king and the crown prince and requested that he be buried in his official mandarin's robes, in the fashion of a grand mandarin, and not in his vestments, in the fashion of a bishop.[51] Nguyễn Văn Thắng, despite being employed by both the Vietnamese and the French government at the end of his life, was not trusted by some of the traders and navy captains who visited the area late in his career, who considered him to be "an apostle of Cochinchinese etiquette."[52]

Most of these figures also possessed remarkable language proficiency. Thắng and Chấn both wrote letters and diplomatic correspondence to the emperor in Chinese. Several of these documents still exist in the Vermillion Records (Châu bản triều Nguyễn).[53] Bá Đa Lộc was fluent in speaking and writing nôm. In fact, his Latin-Vietnamese dictionary is still used as a reference and has recently been republished in Việt Nam. Moreover, later in life he even wrote his personal notes in a jumble of many different languages. Sometimes he wrote in

French; at other times he would write notes in *quốc ngữ, nôm,* or Hán.[54] This implies that those born in France did not necessarily retain unique "French" cultural and linguistic formations and attitudes. Rather, a process of transculturation occurred in which those born in France influenced and were influenced by those with whom they interacted. Those who spent time in Việt Nam were neither entirely French nor Vietnamese but hybrid figures influenced by the differences of both places.

Moreover, virtually all the nonmissionary figures who stayed at the court for any substantial period of time married into prominent Vietnamese Catholic mandarin families. The best known of these is Nguyễn Văn Thắng (Chaigneau), whose son Nguyễn Văn Đức, also known as Michel Đức Chaigneau, wrote an influential memoir about his youth in Huế and also served as a go-between for Phan Thành Giản's embassy to Paris in 1863.[55] But he was not the only such person: Nguyễn Văn Chấn (Vannier) also married a Vietnamese Catholic, as did Ba La Di (Laurent Barizy, 1769–1802). In the next section of this study, I will briefly discuss what is known about these and other multiethnic figures at the Gia Long and Minh Mạng courts in the early nineteenth century.

Multiethnicity in the Early Nguyễn Court

In his critical excursions into cultural studies, Homi K. Bhabha has discussed the moment of literary subversion caused by the existence of a cultural hybrid: something or someone who cannot be incorporated into either the category of self or that of other. For Bhabha this ambiguity subverts a presumed national authority over the production of textual and social categories and opens up the possibility of what he calls a "third space" that is neither self nor other and neither West nor East. Bhabha proposes that the mixing of cultures that produces a "third space" is liberating in its ambiguity, since those of mixed race and culture cannot easily be stereotyped. Thus, viewing history from the perspective of mixed identity would also liberate us from historical stereotypes because it "quite properly challenges our sense of the historical identity of culture as a homogenizing, unifying force, authenticated by the originary Part, kept alive in the national tradition of People."[56]

However, as I have pointed out elsewhere, the result of such a discursive reversal of colonialism and nationalism need not undermine all categories. Rather, a common historiographical response is to repress all indications that such a "third space" exists.[57] As Robert J. C. Young has pointed out, this repression often takes the form of a colonial taboo on intermarriage and cultural interaction.[58]

This colonial taboo is transformed in nationalist discourses into a desire to keep the nation pure of all polluting outside influences, which Ghassan Hage has called the "white nation fantasy."[59] In either case, national and colonial representations are not limited to the fields of literature or politics. Rather, the repression of representations of cultural hybridity occurs in historiography as well. Since in the past many histories have been written as histories of a national culture at a particular time, the history of intermarriage and the stories of those of mixed parentage have not gained prominence until recently. One simply cannot integrate those of mixed cultural parentage into Vietnamese history if prevalent and unquestioned methods of historical interpretation require a preinterpretive and a priori sorting of individuals into the analytical categories of "French" and "Vietnamese."

Many of the Portuguese, Spanish, Cambodian, Siamese, and Chinese officials at the early court of Nguyễn Ánh Gia Long must have married into Vietnamese families. In many cases the lives of their children are documented either in the *Đại Nam chính biên liệt truyện* or in the *Gia Định thành thông chí*. For example, the Cambodian Nguyễn Văn Tồn's son was a figure at the Minh Mạng court, but his mother is of course never mentioned. The lack of documentation on those of multiple ethnicities during this period should not be altogether surprising because there is no evidence that such intermarriage was really a concern. In other words, there is no evidence from the period that prohibitions on marriage prompted by concern for racial or national purity existed at all.

The records that do exist on intermarriage are the cases of intermarriage between French-born officials and Vietnamese Catholic court families. Here the records exist merely because the unions are Catholic ones. These marriages were usually performed by the bishop of Véren, Jean Labartette, who was perhaps one of the most prolific writers in Việt Nam in the early nineteenth century. For the Catholic community in Huê in the early nineteenth century, interracial marriages did not appear to cause controversy, since they were sanctioned and in some cases solemnized by the bishop of Véren. Considering the subsequent prohibitions of intermarriage during French colonial rule in Indochina, this fact is important because it indicates that while the difference between Christian and non-Christian was an important one for French-born officials and missionaries in Việt Nam, the distinction between French and Vietnamese was not.

Unfortunately, with the exception of Nguyễn Văn Thắng's family, which is well documented, relatively little is known about the other cases of intermarriage and mixed-heritage children. We know that Ba La Di married "a Cochinchinese," probably in Sài Gòn in 1798 or 1799, though we do not know her name. Their daughter, Hélène, who was born in 1800, became Nguyễn Văn Thắng's second wife after he was widowed in 1817 and moved with him back to Brittany in 1824. There is no indication that their son Jean Chaigneau was at all discriminated against because his mother was half Vietnamese: having received an education at the imperial schools, he became the secretary-general of the city of Rennes.[60] Others of their children stayed in Việt Nam, where most died in their youth, although one became a nun in the Saint Vincent de Paul Society in Naples.[61]

Similarly, relatively little is known also about Nguyễn Văn Chấn's marriage and children. Existing records primarily come from French sources dating from after Chấn's move back to Brittany in 1824. In 1811 he married Magdaleine Sen, identified in a marriage certificate signed by the bishop of Véren as the daughter of "Mr. Dõng, grand catechist, and Mrs. Dõng, his spouse." Magdaleine was from the Catholic village of Phủ Cam near Huế. Their daughters, Elizabeth and Marie, and their son, Michel, went to Brittany with their parents in 1824 and had no trouble attaining relatively prestigious positions in France, one as a navy purser and another as a preceptor. Magdaleine Sen enjoyed a long life in northern France after she became a widow in 1842 and was even visited by Phan Thanh Giản during his 1867 embassy to Paris. One of Chấn's children stayed in Huế after 1824 and married "a Vietnamese." Nothing is known about his life except that he died in 1835. Several of the children were photographed in the nineteenth century; and some are depicted proudly wearing Vietnamese clothing.[62]

Much more is known about Nguyễn Văn Thắng's family and his children in Việt Nam and in France. Thắng's first marriage was to Hồ Thị Huệ, from the Hồ Catholic mandarin family, also from Phủ Cam,

on August 10, 1802. Their first and most famous child was Nguyễn
Văn Đức (Michel Đức Chaigneau) (1803–94), who was educated and
spent his youth and early adult years in Huế before moving to Paris,
where he married a French woman and became a commissioner at the
French Ministry of Finances.[63] By the age of eight he was studying
Chinese language and literature with a mandarin "of great erudition,"
perhaps Trịnh Hoài Đức, and was known by the emperor to be studying to be a mandarin.[64] Đức recalls in *Souvenirs de Huế* that in an audience with Gia Long in his youth, the emperor told his father that he
had "given this boy a nose that [was] somewhat Vietnamese."[65] He is
known later in life for the publication of his books, some in French
and others in Hán and *quốc ngữ* with French translation.[66] Many of his
brothers and sisters died relatively young in Việt Nam; they are
buried with their mother in Phủ Cam. The others accompanied their
father back to Brittany in 1824, where they also assimilated with apparent ease into the local life.

Though these biographies say relatively little about the role of
mixed-race people in court politics, they do provide an important insight into the question of the historiographical division between
French and Vietnamese in the early history of the court of Nguyễn
Ánh Gia Long. The fact that officials at the court who were born in
France married the daughters of court officials demonstrates their
integration into court life and calls into question an easy division
between "French" and "Vietnamese" actors.

The Fallacy of Frenchness in Vietnamese History

The topic of the lives of foreign-born officials at Gia Long's court is
not a new one, particularly if those officials were born in Europe and
even more if they were originally from France. Research has been
done on those individuals because they have come to represent three
allegorical visions for the beginnings of modernity in Vietnamese history, each of which depends on an interaction between certain kinds
of French and certain kinds of Vietnamese. Colonial historiography
stakes its claim to legitimacy on the idea that French colonization assisted and protected the Vietnamese emperor and civilized the population as a whole. This claim at least partially rests on the idea that
French people were indispensable in winning the Tây Sơn wars, and

thus they are the catalysts of modern Vietnamese history. Nationalist historiography bases its interpretations of the beginnings of modern Việt Nam on the idea that the emperor Gia Long polluted Việt Nam by bringing in the French, paving the way for colonization. Finally, area studies historiography in North America over the past few decades, understandably written to reject the excesses of the claims of the preceding colonial history, has claimed that both of these interpretations are Eurocentric and has striven to expunge the Frenchness out of the Vietnamese historical narrative by constantly claiming that the French presence in Việt Nam in the eighteenth century was of only minor importance. While this effort may stem from an understandable desire to decouple Vietnamese historiography from its colonial past, it ironically reinforces the significance of the French by overemphasizing the importance of leaving them out.

Each of these approaches has the effect of making the late eighteenth century a struggle between Vietnamese and French actors. In fact, however, "Vietnamese" and "French" did not mark significant and coherent factions in Việt Nam during this period. Additionally, Gia Long's court contained officials of all sorts of other backgrounds. The contributions of these officials, who were born in places as various as Cambodia and Ireland, are reduced by the assumption that French and Vietnamese should be the essential categories of Vietnamese historical analysis.

Moreover, each of these approaches rests on the fundamental assumption that it is perfectly easy to tell who is Vietnamese and who is French in eighteenth- and nineteenth-century Việt Nam. In retrospect these methods for telling the story of eighteenth-century Việt Nam appear to assume too quickly the persistent importance of national affiliation in the behavior of individuals. These approaches lead to a mechanical application of "Frenchness" to those born in France and particular kinds of "Vietnameseness" to those from Việt Nam without proper regard for the degree to which these labels do (or do not) fit particular individuals. In part historians of Việt Nam hasten to generalize about eighteenth-century ethnicity because of the importance attributed to the "confrontation with the West" that "overwhelms" Vietnamese culture in the nineteenth and twentieth centuries, and the eighteenth century becomes fashioned according to the nationalist, colonial, or multiculturalist desires of historians in the nineteenth and twentieth centuries.[67]

In many ways creating metaphors or allegories of the present in the
past may not only be unavoidable but may even be a desirable way to
connect narratives of vastly different historical periods. Without such
devices, indeed, it would be very difficult to tell an interesting story
about the past. It is useful to note, however, that eighteenth-century
figures have a curious habit of not conforming to twentieth-century
labels. Perhaps getting beyond the idea of "French" and "Vietnamese" actors will allow us to see the unexpected and unpredictable
ways in which people manage to find connections with one another
and will force historians to examine more precisely the nature of precolonial contacts between Europeans and Vietnamese.

Notes

1. Quốc Sử Quán Triều Nguyễn, *Đại Nam thực lục chính biên đệ nhất kỷ*
(hereafter *ĐNTL*), 2:46–50; and Trương Sĩ Tải, *Bi Nhu quận công phương tích
lục*, esp. vii–xv.

2. For examples of this approach, see Gosselin, *l'empire d'Annam*, 99–117;
Septans, *Les commencements de l'Indochine Française*, 67–104.

3. Characteristic of this approach are Phan Bội Châu, "Việt Nam quốc sử
khảo," 466–74; Văn Tân, *Cách mạng Tây Sơn*, 184–233.

4. See especially McLeod, *Vietnamese Response to French Intervention*,
1–40; and Woodside, *Vietnam and the Chinese Model: A Study of Nguyễn and
Qing Civil Government in the First Half of the Nineteenth Century*.

5. For an examination of how French colonial politics affected earlier
Vietnamese historiography, see Nola Jean Cooke, "Colonial Political Myth
and the Problem of the Other."

6. In *Đại Nam liệt truyện tiền biên* he is a "Xiêm La Nhân" (Siamese), while
Đại Nam thực lục chinh biên đệ nhất kỷ and *Gia Định thành thông chí* describe
him as a "Chà Và Nhân" (Javanese). Quốc Sử Quán Triều Nguyễn, *Đại Nam
liệt truyện tiền biên* (hereafter *ĐNLT*), 477; Trịnh Hoài Đức, *Gia Định thành
thông chí* (hereafter *GĐTTC*).

7. *ĐNLT*, 2:478; *GĐTTC*, 131, 78a.

8. The rendering of his name as "Diệp Mâu" by the 1993 edition of the
ĐNLT appears to be a misprint.

9. *ĐNLT*, 2:473–74. Vy's alleged participation in Khôi's rebellion lends
support to the argument that the rebellion might have been looked on favor
ably both by ethnic Chinese and by those sympathetic to the vast majority of
Gia Long officials who were cast aside in the early years of the emperor Minh
Mạng. For more information on the role of ethnic Chinese in creating and
maintaining a southern Vietnamese regional identity, see Choi Byung Wook,
Southern Vietnam under the Reign of Minh Mạng, 77–80.

10. *ĐNLT*, 2:473–74.

11. I have limited this section to those officials actually born outside Việt Nam; obviously this approach has the drawback of marginalizing the very large number of scholars of Chinese origin (the Minh Hương) who were working for the Nguyễn in this period. These included the Mạc and their descendents in Hà Tiên as well as Trịnh Hoài Đức himself. For more information on this subject, see Zottoli, "Roots of Nineteenth-Century Vietnamese Confucianism."

12. "White Lotus Society" is a name used to describe a number of synchretic millenarian sects dedicated to the worship of an Eternal Mother and prophesied the imminent arrival of the Buddha Maitreya. Though usually referred to in the singular, connections between White Lotus sects over the centuries are loose. These sects typically blend features of Buddhism, Daoism, and Manicheanism. White Lotus Societies were responsible for several rebellions in the late eighteenth and nineteenth centuries. See Elizabeth J. Perry, "Worshipers and Warriors," 6–7.

13. ĐNLT, 471.

14. GĐTTC, 134. This event is not recorded clearly in the ĐNTL, which says that the first meeting was on Cô Cốt Island.

15. D. Murray, *Pirates on the South China Coast,* 187–88. Murray claims that the Nguyễn used Chinese pirates in a way that was "neither so extensive nor so significant as the Tây Sơns." Although this claim is more than reasonable, it should not be construed to imply that Hà Hỷ Văn and his cohort were insignificant for Nguyễn Ánh, considering Ánh's substantial need for the supplies, boats, and artillery that Văn provided in the mid-1780s.

16. ĐNLT, 472.

17. Li Tana, *Nguyễn Cochinchina,* 72–75; and Manguin, *Les Nguyễn, le Macao et le Portugal,* 29–34.

18. Manguin, *Les Nguyễn,* 61–67.

19. Mantienne argues that the Portuguese-Nguyễn agreement reflects An Tôn Vi Sản's commercial interests as a trader, and thus unlike the French treaty the Portuguese agreement is primarily a commercial one. He nevertheless notes that the two treaties share many similarities (*Mgr. Pierre Pigneaux,* 88–89).

20. The exception to this rule is Doãn Nói Vè, also known as Januario Phương Antonio de Rosa, a *cai đội* from Goa who is mentioned in the ĐNTL and in an edict issued by Nguyễn Ánh in 1793. ĐNTL, 2:183; Manguin, *Les Nguyễn,* 94–95. Other Portuguese-born people apparently worked in other capacities, such as carpenters, for the court throughout the 1780s and 1790s (Manguin, *Les Nguyễn,* 85).

21. Mantienne, *Mgr. Pierre Pigneaux,* 86–87; Langenois to Létondal, June 16, 1787, Archives des Missions Étrangères de Paris (hereafter AMEP), 801: 151–52. Direct commentary on An Tôn's role is given in the little original correspondence still existing that was sent between Nguyễn Ánh and Bá Đa Lộc. Cadière, "Les Français aux service de Gia-Long XI," 27–29.

22. Mantienne, *Mgr. Pierre Pigneaux,* 96.

23. He is not to be confused with the French-born Nguyễn regiment commander Mạn Hòe (Emmanuel), who was killed by Tây Sơn troops early in 1782 and long before most French-born officials came to Việt Nam. See GĐTTC, 130; Cadière, "Les Français au service de Gia Long III," 38–39.

24. Liot to Boiret and Descourvières, June 20, 1795, AMEP, 746:514.

25. On the interesting case of the Irish officer at the Gia Định court, see Cosserat, "Note au sujet de la mort de Ma no ê (Manuel) et de un officier Irlandais," 454–58.

26. Smail, "On an Autonomous History of Southeast Asia."

27. See Nguyễn Khắc Viên, Vietnam, 107.

28. Taylor, "Surface Orientations in Vietnam"; Li Tana, Nguyễn Cochinchina, esp. 99–116.

29. Thus the statements of colonial and nationalist historians that the French were significant in aiding Gia Long (statements that serve the respective ideological purposes either of reaffirming the mission civilisatrice or of branding the Nguyễn as colonial puppets) as well as the more recent claim by area specialists that "the French were not very important" in the period all fall into the heuristic trap of assuming the existence of a coherent group called "the French."

30. Septans, Les commencements, 67–104; Văn Tân, Cách Mạng Tây Sơn, 191–93.

31. Lamothe to Boiret and Descouvières, August 26, 1794, AMEP, 692:569–70; Mantienne, Mgr. Pierre Pigneaux, 167. For more information on northern Vietnamese missionaries and their attitudes toward the Tây Sơn, see Đăng Phương Nghi, "Triều Đại Vua Quang Trung dưới mắt các nhà truyền giáo Tây Phương."

32. Lamothe to Chaumont and Blandin, June, 28, 1797, AMEP, 692:850–52. Here and elsewhere in the essay, the translations are mine unless otherwise noted.

33. Lamothe to Létondal, Boiret, and Descouvières, March 21, 1795, AMEP, 692:629–30. It is significant that this edict was not carried out, apparently because of the relatively good relationship that Lamothe and the bishop of Gortyne had with an unidentified viceroy.

34. Lelabousse to Boiret and Descouvières, May 13, 1795, AMEP, 746:473–75.

35. It is unfortunate that none of the existing letters gives a better idea of this mandarin's actual identity. Girard to Boiret, November 25, 1792, AMEP, 692:397. Persecutions in the later days of the Tây Sơn were not unheard of, though some missionaries claimed that Christians were not singled out and these "persecutions" were part of the Tây Sơn's policies of exploitation in the waning years of the wars.

36. "Decret du Tây Sơn en faveur de Catholisme" (1783), AMEP, 746:1801. To my knowledge this document only exists in a Latin translation done by the Gia Định priest Father André Tôn. It is not absolutely clear that Nguyễn Lữ was the author of this edict, leaving the possibility that the future Quang Trung actually approved it.

37. Barrow, *Voyage to Cochinchina*, 250. The mysterious youngest brother of the Tây Sơn is also rumored to have been a Buddhist monk. Others claim that he was a Muslim cleric; it is even possible he may have been Manichean. See Tạ Chí Đại Trường, "Góp thêm về phổ hệ Tây Sơn" [An Additional Contribution to Tây Sơn Systems], 72–73.

38. Girard to Létondal, March 23, 1791, AMEP, 801:349–50.

39. Girard to Létondal, November 25, 1792, AMEP, 692:397.

40. Labartette to Létondal, July 9, 1791, AMEP, 801:390–91.

41. Boisserand to Mercier, February 20, 1792, AMEP, 746:343–45; "Manifeste de Quang Trung," AMEP, 746:457.

42. Boisserand to Létondal, June 7, 1796. AMEP, 801:660. Also in Launay, *Histoire de la mission de Cochinchine*, 3:308.

43. Lelabousse to Létondal, June 25, 1789, AMEP, 801:252–65.

44. Pigneaux to Létondal, June 12, 1796, AMEP, 801:661.

45. This apparently occurred at least once, if the missionary sources are to be believed, giving the bishop de facto interim control over the Nguyễn realm.

46. Boisserand to Létondal, May 24, 1791, AMEP, 801:385–87.

47. See Lê Đình Chân, *Cuộc đời oanh liệt của Tả Quân Lê Văn Duyệt*, esp. 34–35; and Choi Byung Wook, *Southern Vietnam under the Reign of Minh Mạng*, 60–66.

48. Tô Văn Đoái's title was *chánh giám thành sứ* (chief citadel commander). Đoái was one of the few people who could have accurately been "chief of the mandarins," as the missionary letters have known him. Moreover, it seems quite possible that he would have been designated by an abbreviated title as Sir Commander, or Ông Giám. He was the only official of such elevated military rank to have died during the sieges of Qui Nhơn and Nha Trang in 1794–95. See *ĐNLT* 2:250–51.

49. Lavoué to Létondal, April 27, 1795, AMEP, 801:574.

50. Lelabousse to Directors, June 1799, AMEP, 746:775; Launay, *Histoire de la mission de Cochinchine*, 3:364.

51. "Dernières Volontés de Mgr. d'Adran," AMEP, 801:786–87.

52. Taboulet, *La geste Française en Indochine*, 308–9.

53. Quốc Sử Quán Triều Nguyễn. *Mục lục châu bản triều Nguyễn.*, 1:194, 196–97.

54. Bá Đa Lộc Bi Nhu, *Tự vị Annam Latinh;* Pigneau, "Notes sur Chiêm Thành," AMEP, 746:797–816.

55. Chaigneau, *Souvenirs de Huế,* 116–20; Cadière, "Les Français aux service de Gia-Long III," 23–24.

56. Bhabha, "The Commitment to Theory," in *Location of Culture*, 37.

57. Wilcox, "Hybridity, Colonialism, and National Subjectivity in Vietnamese Historiography." See also Wilcox, "Allegories of Vietnam: Transculturation and the Origin Myths of Franco-Vietnamese Relations."

58. Young, *Colonial Desire*.

59. Hage, *White Nation*.

60. Cosserat, "Documents A. Salles IV: Laurent Barizy."

61. Ibid.
62. Cosserat, "Documents A. Salles III: Philippe Vannier."
63. Salles, *Jean-Baptiste Chaigneau et sa famille*, 105–12.
64. Chaigneau, *Souvenirs*, 112–13.
65. Chaigneau, *Souvenirs*, 111; Salles, *Jean-Baptiste Chaigneau*, 107.
66. Salles, *Jean-Baptiste Chaigneau*, 111.
67. Jamieson, *Understanding Vietnam*, 42–47.

Rediscovering
Vietnamese-European
Encounters

8

Crossing Oceans, Crossing Boundaries

The Remarkable Life of Philiphê Bỉnh (1759–1832)

GEORGE DUTTON

In late February 1796, a thirty-seven-year-old Vietnamese Jesuit priest named Philiphê Bỉnh boarded an English trading vessel in the waters near Macao and began a four-month journey to the Portuguese capital, Lisbon. With him traveled three other Vietnamese Catholics and the hopes of the substantial Vietnamese Jesuit–led community in northern Việt Nam. Bỉnh's life story is a dramatic one that spanned the oceans and continents from Việt Nam to the Iberian Peninsula, and that straddled the eighteenth and nineteenth centuries. It is a story that can be told only because Bỉnh left behind a remarkable body of writings providing insights into his life and experiences and more generally into the lives of Europeans and Vietnamese during the more than seventy years of his life.

The second half of the eighteenth century and the first three decades of the nineteenth, during which Philiphê Bỉnh lived, were times of enormous political and social upheaval both in Việt Nam and in Europe.[1] Among the dramatic events experienced in Việt Nam during this period were the Tây Sơn uprising (1771–1802), the subsequent collapse of the three-hundred-year-old Lê dynasty, the first Chinese invasion since the early fifteenth century (in 1789), the overthrow of the Tây Sơn regime, and the establishment of the Nguyễn dynasty (in 1802). These major political and military events were accompanied by innumerable droughts, floods, and famines, which further contributed to the social dislocations of this era.

It was a no less tumultuous time in Europe, an era that saw the Seven Years War (1756–63), the Pugachov rebellion in Russia (1773–74), the partitioning of Poland (1772–95), and the French Revolution. All this was followed by the Napoleonic wars, including the Iberian campaigns from 1807 to 1812, which directly involved the Portugal to which Binh would journey. These events served as a backdrop to Binh's life and experiences; as an observant traveler through his age, he often recorded the events taking place around him, for they frequently (if sometimes indirectly) affected his life.

In some ways Binh's story echoes that of an earlier traveler from Asia, "John Hu," the eponymous central figure of Jonathan Spence's fascinating study, *The Question of Hu*. Like Hu, Binh came from a modest background, was converted to Christianity by European Jesuits, and then traveled to Europe in the eighteenth century in the company of Jesuits. Despite these numerous parallels, closer examination reveals that the stories of the two men are only superficially alike. For the story of Hu's life we must rely almost exclusively on the writings of his companion, the Jesuit Jean-François Foucquet, supplemented by Hu's only known writing, a single letter. For the story of Binh's life, on the other hand, we have an enormous collection of his own writings supplemented by fragmentary evidence from the letters of European missionaries. Moreover, while Hu spent the majority of his sojourn in Europe in a mental hospital, Binh spent his time in Europe living in religious residences, fastidiously writing and performing religious duties. And finally, unlike Hu, who spent only three years in Europe before returning to China, Binh spent more than thirty years in Portugal, never managing to make the return trip to his native Việt Nam and finally dying in Lisbon in 1832.

This essay provides an introduction to Philiphê Binh's event-filled life and to his large literary output, both viewed against their historical backdrop. The study begins with a brief overview of the European Catholic missions in Việt Nam, specifically those of the Jesuits. Then follows a broadly sketched outline of Bình's life, travels, and travails, which places him in the political and intellectual context of his time. Finally, the essay considers his surviving body of writings and its significance as a source for understanding his life and for detailing early Vietnamese perceptions of Europe. This last point is an important one, for Bình's writings reveal much about these early connections between Europe and Việt Nam and about ways in which early Vietnamese travelers tried to make sense of "the West."

Background

In assessing Bình's life, we must first consider the arrival and impact of European Jesuit missionaries in his native Việt Nam. The factors linking Europe and Việt Nam in the early modern period were two of the oldest that have ever connected any parts of the world, namely, commerce and religion. Religions in particular have long been a central element in the diaspora of peoples and ideas across land and sea connecting Asia with lands to its west. Roman Catholicism, specifically that carried by the Catholic Jesuit missions, followed the earlier transmissions of Buddhism and Islam, leaving its own particular imprint on many parts of Asia.

The arrival of a Jesuit mission in Japan in 1549 was a landmark for Catholic proselytizing in Asia, paving the way for future generations of Christian missionaries. The mission to Japan, however, was a relatively short-lived one, for the Japanese shogun Tokugawa Ieyasu ordered the expulsion of the missionaries in 1614.[2] The Jesuit expulsion from Japan led the order to seek other territory for its mission, and the Jesuits turned their attention to, among other places, Việt Nam, which at the time was divided between two ruling families. The Nguyễn controlled the central and the southern territories (known to the Europeans as Cochin China and to the Vietnamese as Đàng Trong, the Inner Region), and the Trịnh governed the northern region (known to the Europeans as Tonkin and to the Vietnamese as Đàng Ngoài, the Outer Region).

The first Catholic mission in Việt Nam was established by the Genovese Busomi and the Portuguese Diego de Carvalho in 1615 at Faifo (Hội An) in what is today central Việt Nam. Cristoforo Borri soon joined them and recorded the first detailed European observations of Vietnamese life and civilization.[3] Although Borri's presence was important, even more significant was that of Alexandre de Rhodes (1593–1660), who was dispatched to the region in late 1624 after the mission's initial successes. With his facility for languages, Rhodes was preaching in the local vernacular in less than six months and at the same time baptizing large numbers of Vietnamese. His tenure in Việt Nam was brief, however. He was expelled from Nguyễn territory in 1626, after which he spent a few years in the Trịnh-controlled north, from which he was also expelled in 1630.[4]

Rhodes spent the next nineteen years in Macao, working on behalf of the mission. He reentered Việt Nam secretly several times between 1640 and 1645, before being definitively banished by both Trịnh and Nguyễn regimes. Rhodes finally returned to Rome in 1649, where he continued to lobby on behalf of the mission to Tonkin, arguing for the sending of several hundred missionaries to the region. When first the Portuguese rulers and then the pope showed little interest in the ambitious numbers that Rhodes was convinced were needed for such a potentially fruitful mission, he looked elsewhere for support. His efforts ultimately led to the establishment of the first major secular missionary society in 1659, the Société des Missions Étrangères de Paris (MEP). The MEP was to play a crucial role in the expansion of Catholicism in Việt Nam and, just as importantly for our story, would eventually compete with Rhodes's own Jesuits. Indeed, the pope's decision to open Việt Nam to the secular missions and their apostolic bishops provoked what has been described as "a hundred-year war between the Padroado and Propaganda [orders]."[5]

Despite the new competition, the Jesuit mission continued to prosper in Việt Nam. In fact, it made its most successful inroads to the Vietnamese centers of power only in the middle of the eighteenth century. Of these successes the most prominent came at the court of the mid-eighteenth-century Nguyễn lord Chúa Võ Vương (r. 1738–65). The first Jesuit to gain access to the Nguyễn court was Johannes Köffler, a German who arrived in Cochin China in 1741. He entered the service of the Chúa as a doctor and general source of scientific instruction in 1747. He remained at the court even through the 1750 expulsion of European Catholics from Nguyễn territories before eventually departing in 1755.[6] A second Jesuit, the Portuguese Joao de Loureiro, similarly traveled to Cochin China in 1741 and at some point in the 1740s entered the service of Võ Vương as mathematician and physicist at the court. In 1750 Loureiro, unlike Köffler, was expelled from the country. He did not, however, leave Asia, traveling instead around the region collecting botanical species, before eventually returning to Phú Xuân in 1752. He then remained at the Nguyễn political center for the next quarter century, finally leaving at the age of sixty-five in 1777, by which time the capital was in the hands of Trịnh forces that had invaded in the wake of the Tây Sơn uprising in Nguyễn territory.[7] Yet another Jesuit, Xavier de Monteiro, was also at the Nguyễn court at this time, like Loureiro serving as a mathematician. Monteiro similarly spent many years at the Nguyễn court, before dying at Hội An in 1776.[8]

At times the Jesuits in the north, like their counterparts in the Nguyễn realms, sought ways to gain entry to the political center of their region. An opportunity presented itself between 1747 and 1751, during the reign of the Trịnh lord Chúa Trịnh Doanh (1740–67). Doanh needed the assistance of Europeans to help him read the markings on some artillery pieces in his possession. He initially hoped to rely on the aid of a pair of Jesuits whom he had ordered jailed a few years earlier, only to discover to his chagrin that they had in the meantime been executed. When he learned of the presence of another group of Jesuits living near the capital, he ordered them brought in to help translate the inscriptions (describing the proper charge and powder to be used in the cannons). Having performed this service, these men promised that more and similarly useful Jesuits could be sent from Macao if the Chúa desired this. He assented to having more Jesuits sent to his court, but the order's overseers in Macao were unprepared to respond to this request, and it took several years to organize such a mission. By the time the next group of Jesuits arrived in Thăng Long in 1751, the Chúa had lost interest in their assistance.[9]

Despite these occasional successes, the Jesuits in Tonkin (Philiphê Bình's home region) faced a particularly complicated religious landscape. There were no less than three European religious orders (the Jesuits, the Dominicans, and the Franciscans) and one secular mission society (the MEP) active in that area. At times efforts were made to divide the region into territories for which different orders would have responsibility, but these boundaries were rarely observed and were, in any case, difficult to enforce. In 1753 the secular missionaries organized a synod to discuss precisely this question, but the Jesuits refused to attend, and nothing was resolved.[10]

A few years later, in 1759, the situation became even more complicated when the Jesuit order was abolished in Portugal. The Portuguese Jesuits who were found in Macao at that time were promptly arrested, and chaos beset the community of Portuguese Jesuits in Tonkin. It was suddenly unclear precisely where their allegiance now lay and whom they were to regard as their leader. In response to this crisis the Jesuits in Việt Nam decided in 1763 to elect their own leaders including a "vice-provincial" and a secretary, now ostensibly of the "Province of Japan." (This was apparently an attempt to circumvent issues relating to the disestablishment of the order.) But a schism soon broke out within the Tonkinese Jesuit community. Of the eight European Jesuits then active in Tonkin, five named themselves "superiors" of their mission, rendering any sort of a reconciliation with the seculars even less likely.[11]

Throughout this period, while the orders competed for converts, the Jesuits continued to hold a distinct and growing numerical advantage in terms of both Vietnamese adherents and European clergy. In 1744 there were only four Jesuit missionaries in the region, but nine years later the number had doubled, and by 1766 there were fourteen Jesuit clerics serving in Tonkin. Originally they had been restricted to Sơn Tây but over time had expanded their areas of influence to include other regions, most notably the more southerly provinces of Nghệ An and Sơn Nam. As for Vietnamese Catholics, of the estimated three hundred thousand living in Tonkin in 1766 (constituting perhaps 4 to 5 percent of the total population) 20 percent were followers of the secular missions of the MEP, while 40 percent or more were loyal to the Jesuit mission.[12] Thus even as their political footing became highly uncertain in the ongoing competition with the other European religious orders, Jesuits continued to thrive numerically. Into this complicated religious-political environment stepped the central figure of this tale, Philiphê Bỉnh, joining the small but expanding ranks of Vietnamese who had entered the Jesuit order since 1640.[13]

The Early Life of Philiphê Bỉnh

Philiphê Bỉnh, also known by his ordained name of Filipe do Rosário, was a meticulous chronicler of his own life, so let me allow him to introduce himself:

I am the priest Philiphê Bỉnh, of the region of Hải Dương, prefecture of Hải Hưng, district of Vĩnh Lại, village of Ngải Am, hamlet of Đại Linh, born in the year 1759, the same year that the king Jose of the country Portugal destroyed the Order of the Virtuous Lord Jesus in his realm. When I reached the age of seventeen in the year 1775, I entered the House of the Teachers, by which time the order had already been lost for two years in Rome, the Virtuous Pope Clemente XIV having disbanded the Order of the Virtuous Lord Jesus [i.e., the Jesuits] on the twenty-second of July in the year 1773. However, prior to disbanding the order and at the beginning of that year, eight members of the order had come to Annam: Master Tito along with Master Bảo Lộc had gone to Quảng [Nam], and the rest of the missionaries, Masters Ni, Thiện, Phan, Luis, and Cần, traveled to Đàng Ngoài. Thus in that year I went with Master Luis and left my home.[14]

Aside from this brief self-description, we have, unfortunately, relatively little detail about Bỉnh's early life, a period he apparently did not consider worth recording in any detail. From this text we at least learn where he came from, allowing us to place him in a particular geographical and historical context.

Bỉnh tells us that he is from the province of Hải Dương and more specifically the prefecture of Hải Hưng and the district of Vĩnh Lại. Hải Dương lies to the east of Thăng Long (present-day Hà Nội) and is part of the coastal region drained by the Red River and its tributaries. The prefecture of Hải Hưng lay in the southeastern part of Hải Dương, where it was transected by the Gia Lộc River, which widens as it flows through the area. Vĩnh Lại in particular was crossed by a network of canals and rivers. According to Phan Huy Chú, the prefecture of Hải Hưng was noted for its production of upright Confucian scholars.[15] Although Bỉnh's district of Vĩnh Lại does not stand out in Hải Dương for its particular contributions to the ranks of court literati, it was the home of one of the most famous Vietnamese scholar-officials of the premodern period, Nguyễn Bình Khiêm (1491–1585).

We know nothing further about Bỉnh's life until 1775, when he tells us that he entered a Jesuit seminary at the age of seventeen and began a course of study and apprenticeship that would occupy the next eighteen years of his life. Although the Jesuits had been banned by the pope two years earlier, as Bỉnh wrote in his introduction, the Vietnamese Jesuit mission had just been strengthened by the sending of eight Italians only one year before the ban was announced. These men were just becoming active at the time that Bỉnh was entering his training, with six of the Italians operating in his native Tonkin. From

Binh's writings we are also able to glean that his studies did not all take place in the same location, something that is hardly surprising given the turmoil of these years. Indeed, the years of his religious study were among the most dramatic of early modern Vietnamese history.

Among other things these years saw the death and bitterly disputed succession of the Chúa Trịnh Sâm (r. 1767–82) in the north. It was also a period during which this region was twice attacked by Tây Sơn forces—in 1786 and 1787—and then invaded by a huge Chinese army in late 1788. This was followed by a Tây Sơn counterattack that drove out the Chinese and simultaneously brought an end to the more than three-hundred-year reign of the Lê dynasty. Although this act served to unify the Vietnamese territories, it also created considerable rifts in northern society. The repeated invasions and subsequent political unrest only compounded an already difficult situation in Đàng Ngoài. Environmental disturbances of various types—floods, droughts, and related crop failures—had been a serious problem through much of the 1770s and had accelerated precipitously in the early 1780s, culminating in the famine of 1785–86, which may have killed more than one hundred thousand people.[16] Thereafter the situation improved, at least in parts of the north, though there continued to be sporadic crop failures and famines due to weather and the lingering effects of years of widespread population displacement.

Despite these social and economic upheavals during much of his training period, the final years of Binh's religious training, just prior to his departure for Europe, were ones of relative peace for Vietnamese Christians in the north. In the aftermath of the Tây Sơn defeat of the Qing armies in 1789, the new regime restored a semblance of order, and its rulers, Emperor Quang Trung (r. 1788–92) and his son and successor, the emperor Cảnh Thịnh (r. 1792–1802), were generally tolerant of Christianity in their realm, at least until 1795. Thus in the summer of 1791 a European missionary was able to report, "All our dear confederates in northern Cochin China are in good health, and our blessed religion is completely unpersecuted. I have been told that it is active and with a greater liberty than ever before."[17]

Similarly, in subsequent years European missionaries continued to comment on the considerable religious freedom they enjoyed. One letter of June 1793 reported that there was much greater religious freedom than had existed under the earlier Trịnh and Lê regimes, while another noted that "since Tonkin has been under the domination of the Cochin Chinese, there is no talk of persecuting the religion."[18] A year later a French missionary compared the religious situation in Tonkin favorably to that in his native France, then in the throes of the French Revolution. He wrote that the two situations of civil war were similar, with one distinction: "Our rebels [the Tây Sơn] do not touch the religion at all and on the contrary, they have given more freedom than it has ever had before."[19] Although it would be a distortion to suggest that the situation of Christians was entirely without difficulty in this period, it was certainly better than it had been.

It is only during this later period that we have more information about Binh's life and career, for it was at this time that he was ordained and began his ministry as a Catholic priest. This ordination took place on the fourth of August, 1793, with Binh noting that he was thirty-five years of age, having studied at "this" (unknown) location for six years.[20] He, along with five other students, was ordained by a pair of bishops, Jacobe and Phê, who were apparently not themselves Jesuits and hence not formally authorized to commission Binh and the others for the Jesuit mission.[21] Despite this, Binh remained a devoted Jesuit, often coming into open conflict with the secular (MEP) missionaries also active in Tonkin at this time.

In his writings he described his stubborn refusal to accede to the spiritual demands of the secular clergy in the period after the Jesuits had been formally banned.[22] In particular he found himself embroiled in the Vietnamese version of the "rites controversy" when, as a Jesuit, he continued to perform ritual offerings to his own ancestors even though he was aware of efforts by the other mission orders to ban such practices.[23] In retaliation religious leaders of these other orders, who were trying unsuccessfully to establish their own authority over the Vietnamese Jesuit community, sought to prevent Binh from saying masses. Despite these threats he apparently continued his defiance, upholding the more relaxed Jesuit interpretation of these rituals as civil rather than religious in nature. Indeed, Binh appears to have taken a certain pride in his acts of resistance in this regard, and in any case his defiant loyalty to the banned Jesuit order continued to be a thorn in the side of the secular missionaries even after his departure for Europe, as will be discussed later in more detail.

The Travels and Travails of Philiphê Bỉnh

Although Bỉnh began his career as a Catholic priest in Việt Nam, his
service in that location and capacity was of extremely short duration.
Not long after being ordained, he began a series of journeys that
would eventually bring him to Europe. Indeed, it was his travels and
most notably his eventual journey to and residence in Europe that
defined the trajectory of Bỉnh's life. It is important to note, however,
that Bỉnh was not the first Vietnamese Catholic to travel to Europe,
nor even the most famous Vietnamese visitor to Europe of his generation. We know from Bỉnh's comments and the testimony of European
missionaries that other Vietnamese Catholics had made the journey to
Europe, including several who traveled to Rome in the 1770s.[24] The
most famous Vietnamese visitor of the eighteenth century was surely
the young Nguyễn crown prince Cảnh, who traveled to France and
the court at Versailles in the years 1786–87 in the company of the MEP
bishop Pigneau de Béhaine. Cảnh had been sent with Pigneau by the
Nguyễn leader in the hopes of concluding an alliance with the French
court against the Tây Sơn. Cảnh became the darling of the court at
Versailles during his time in France, and Pigneau used him to great
effect in convincing the French monarch to accede to the Nguyễn
appeal. Bỉnh's claim to fame is thus not that he was a Vietnamese who
traveled to Europe at this relatively early point, but that he did so
without European companions, and that he remained in Europe
rather than returning home after his sojourn in the West.

What compelled Bỉnh to undertake this long and difficult trip to
Europe at this time, and why was his destination Portugal? Bỉnh's primary objective was a religious one—personally to request the appointment of another Jesuit bishop for the mission in Tonkin, or at least a
nonsecular religious leader, as the Vietnamese Jesuit community continued to resist the authority of the apostolic vicars of the MEP. In some
respects Bỉnh's efforts to engage Jesuit missionaries and particularly a
bishop to come to Tonkin did not constitute anything new. Literate
Vietnamese Catholics who had been baptized by members of the MEP
were making regular appeals to Europe at this time to send more missionaries. The letters of these Vietnamese Catholics, found interleaved
with the larger body of French missionary letters held in the MEP archives in Paris, are plaintive calls for assistance. They lament the fate of
seemingly forgotten communities of Vietnamese converts—often left

without a priest for many years—and beg the society to arrange for more priests to be sent.[25] What sets Bình apart from other Vietnamese pleading for more missionaries is that he traveled to Europe to make his plea in person; the Vietnamese Jesuit community, on whose behalf he was traveling, no doubt reasoned that a personal appeal would be far more effective than merely one more epistle.

The second question concerns his decision to go to Portugal. As Bình noted in his self-introduction, the Jesuit order had been formally abolished in 1773, perhaps a victim, as Jean Lacouture has argued, of growing nationalist sentiment in Europe that looked with suspicion on the transnational character of the Jesuit movement and its representatives.[26] The center of anti-Jesuit sentiment lay, in fact, in the very same Portugal to which Bình was to travel. Although the story of the Portuguese anti-Jesuit movement is a complex one, it revolved partly around tensions developing in South America, in Jesuit-led enclaves in Paraguay. Here Jesuit efforts to create small states around the indigenous Guaraní peoples ran into fierce opposition from Portuguese traders seeking to profit from their slave trade and the supposed wealth contained in the hinterland. The rise of the future Marques de Pombal (1699–1782), as the chief minister of the Portuguese king, Joseph I, further contributed to these tensions, for Pombal took the side of the Portuguese merchant community against the Jesuits. He actively attempted to discredit the Jesuit projects in the Americas, including overseeing the publication of scurrilous accounts of Jesuit depravities.[27]

Under these circumstances Bình's decision to travel to Lisbon might seem foolhardy, and yet a number of reasons dictated this destination. The most obvious was that the Portuguese monarch held a papally granted right of royal patronage of the faith, the Padroado Real. This was, as C. R. Boxer has described it, "a combination of the rights, privileges and duties granted by the Papacy to the Crown of Portugal as patron of the Roman Catholic missions and ecclesiastical establishments in vast regions of Africa, of Asia, and in Brazil."[28] The power of the Padroado meant that if he could be approached, the Portuguese ruler had the power to arrange for more missionaries to be sent.

Second, Portuguese Jesuit missionaries, through their connections at the Portuguese colony at Macao, had been closely involved in the Catholic missionary work in Việt Nam. P. Manuel Teixeira argues, in fact, that the Portuguese Jesuit Augustin Carneiro was involved in sending Binh to Portugal, though other sources suggest that the last European Jesuit in Tonkin died in 1783.[29] In any case, although the Padroado had been severely undermined by the pope's earlier decision to allow the secular mission societies to compete with the Jesuits, it still existed in principle and would allow the Portuguese rulers to act directly on Binh's request.

Finally, Binh's decision to journey to Lisbon was also dictated by the dearth of other options open to him at the time. France was in the midst of revolutionary upheaval, destroying churches rather than promoting them. The only other possibility would have been Rome, from which center the Jesuits had recently been abolished and which had not demonstrated much sympathy for the Jesuits in Việt Nam in any case. Moreover, as it turned out, Rome was soon to be attacked by Napoleon's forces, rendering it inaccessible and inhospitable to religious appeals, particularly when the pope himself was forced to flee the Vatican. Portugal was thus both a logical and a very practical destination for Binh.

The Early Journeys: Macao and Goa (1793–1795)

Although Binh ultimately traveled to Europe, he did not initially venture so far. He made several trips to Macao and one abortive effort to reach Europe in which Binh was again halted in Macao and his intended traveling companions blocked in Portuguese-held Goa. All these journeys took place at a time in which Vietnamese rulers forbade their subjects from traveling out of the country without imperial permission. Pierre Poivre, a French merchant, noted during his 1750 visit to the Nguyễn capital at Phú Xuân that on requesting permission to take some Cochin Chinese craftsmen with him, the Chúa Phúc Khoát "responded that the law prohibited his subjects from leaving the country and that the purpose of this law was to preserve for the prince the tributes that his subjects paid to him."[30] There is little doubt that this law existed more on paper than in practice, for Vietnamese moved in and out of neighboring states, and some ventured further afield by sea.[31] Indeed, two Vietnamese serving the very court of the Chúa in 1750 had journeyed as far as Goa, returning with some knowledge of European languages, which they then applied by serving the Chúa in his contacts with visiting Europeans.[32] Nonetheless, travel beyond Việt Nam's shores remained a rare undertaking only rarely carried out by among private individuals, making Binh's travels all the more remarkable.

Binh made his first overseas journey in 1793 when he sailed to Macao as part of a mission to help in arranging Jesuit financial matters at the Portuguese colony. The trip was a brief one, perhaps partly preparation for the longer journeys to follow. Binh's voyage to Macao on behalf of the order attests the degree to which he was trusted by the Jesuit community in Việt Nam and apparently also his ability to carry out such important assignments. It was to be only the first of numerous overseas journeys on behalf of his community.

It was late in the following year that Binh made his second trip out of Việt Nam and his first attempt to reach Europe. He left his home on September 25, 1794, and with two companions, Thomé Nhân and another man recorded only as Liên, traveled back to Macao, from which any trip to Europe at this time would have to begin. Once there the three men tried to find passage on a boat bound for Europe. Unfortunately, the best they could manage was a Macanese vessel willing to take them as far as Goa, for, as Binh wrote, "in that year, no western boats had come to Macao."[33] Then, however, their boat was delayed in its departure as the captain awaited good winds and the completion of onshore business.

The delay proved disastrous to Binh's plans, for it gave the French representative of the MEP time to conjure a means to prevent his departure. The representative managed to persuade the ship's captain not to transport the three clerics, and they were put off the ship on which they had booked passage.[34] They made their way back to the captain's house and demanded that he refund their fare. At this point the captain, in turn, demanded payment from the MEP overseer, who had promised a reward for the removal of the men from his ship. The MEP representative was not forthcoming with the money, leading the captain bitterly to denounce him as a thief and to declare that he would henceforth no longer transport that man's priests. Thereupon, he invited the three Vietnamese priests to return to the ship for the journey after all. Binh, however, was detained by the Bishop of Macao, and was forced to remain behind while his companions set sail on what proved to be a futile voyage. Turned back at Portuguese Goa by religious authorities and beset by French pirates on their return voyage to Macao, the two now destitute Vietnamese priests straggled back to Macao in March 1795.

Ever resilient and undaunted by these setbacks, Binh returned to his home and began efforts to secure supplies for another attempt to travel to Europe, as he reported in his later writings: "On the fourth day of the third month [April 22] in the year 1795, I returned to the city of An Lang and learned the news that Ông Đồng Lý [the young Tây Sơn ruler's regent, Bùi Đắc Tuyên] had banned the faith, and all the missionaries had had to go into hiding. The missionaries thus had to endure hardships, because officials had seized all the churches, and so I was greatly distressed, because I had had the intention of returning to Annam to request supplies, and now I had encountered this situation in which I did not know where to go or whom to ask."[35] This hardship did not last long, Binh notes, because the regent was arrested on May 24, 1795. His arrest promptly halted the persecution of Christians, for it was determined that although anti-Christian edicts bore the emperor's name, they had been the work of this senior official. After several more months of preparation and more than one year after his first ill-fated attempt to reach Portugal, Binh finally left his home again on November 15, 1795, in a second venture to reach the West (as Binh called it).[36]

The Final Departure: 1795–1796

After all these delays Binh set out again, only to encounter yet further difficulties almost immediately. His journey toward Macao coincided with a Chinese crackdown on piracy in the South China region (piracy that was being actively encouraged by the Tây Sơn regime). As a consequence his trip was further delayed, and he did not reach the Chinese coastal province of Guangdong until January 23, 1796. There he made arrangements to book passage on a European vessel, and with the permission of the local French clerical representative, Binh left Guangdong and arrived in Macao on the twenty-sixth of January. Once there he was reunited with Nhân and Liên, who had in the meantime returned from Goa. After a few weeks together in Macao, it was decided that Father Liên would remain behind in the Portuguese colony with instructions to send a letter back to Annam to seek another priest to join him in Macao, while Binh and Nhân, along with two other Vietnamese Jesuits, José Trung and Francisco Ngân, would attempt the journey to Europe.[37]

The four men then rented a small boat to sail them back toward Guangdong, where they hoped to meet with British ships visiting the area. Because of their earlier experiences with the French bishop in Macao (whom Bình referred to in his subsequent writings as an "enemy"), the men decided it would be better to make their travel arrangements surreptitiously.[38] They sailed among the coastal promontories and mountains for three days and nights, until the fifteenth of February, when they saw six European ships. The men set down with a small craft to row to each ship asking for passage to Europe. The first five ships were unable or unwilling to assist them, but the four men finally met with success on the last ship. Its captain apparently took pity on the men and agreed to transport them to the West.[39] Furthermore, he promised to provide food and drink for them and would not accept payment. Although the offer was one the men could not refuse, it did not quite accord with their original plan. Binh knew the risks involved in ocean crossings and accordingly had planned to divide his small party into two, each to travel on a separate ship. It was now clear that this would not be possible, and so the four men sailed together on the *Saint Anne.*

After traveling for more than a month, their vessel arrived on the Malay Peninsula (Binh is not more specific than that) in late March or early April, where it stopped for several days to take on drinking water. Soon thereafter the *Saint Anne* set sail across the Indian Ocean, during which passage it encountered a fierce storm. The tempest raged for three days, and Binh was convinced that he and his company would perish. When it was over, their ship still afloat, Binh composed a poem commemorating the occasion, "On Encountering a Storm on the Open Ocean."

As evidence of the vast immenseness in the distances of the ocean
The angels of heaven blew up a powerful storm.
The squalls of rain rose up like mountains of water,
And the peaks of the waves rose as high as the rooftops of houses.
The people holding the sails, and those holding the rudder,
Regretted their sins, and called out with laments.
It was three days before the storm ceased and we were fortunate to be given help
As the brightness before us to the east again emerged.[40]

The horrific storm so vividly described by Binh in this poem apparently scattered the convoy of ships that had been traveling with the *Saint Anne*. From this point on the English vessel sailed alone.

On May 8 Binh's vessel finally arrived at the English-controlled island of Saint Helena, off the southwestern coast of Africa, where fortune once again smiled on him and his companions. They immediately found a Portuguese vessel returning from a trading mission in Bengal, and its captain readily agreed to carry them on to Lisbon and to provide them, without charge, food and drink during the journey. On the twenty-first of May they bid farewell to the captain of the *Saint Anne* and prepared to transfer to the Portuguese ship. The English captain attempted to pay Binh and his companions something for their service in helping with the sails during the voyage, but they declined to accept his offer. Then, on the first of June, Binh's group set sail for Europe in a convoy of twenty-five English vessels, accompanied by a British naval security escort because of fear that the French might interfere along the route. The French Revolution had burst the borders of France, spilling into the sea lanes used by the British and their Portuguese allies. Indeed, not long after his arrival in Portugal, Binh would see that country itself dragged into the Napoleonic wars.

Binh in Portugal

On the twenty-fourth of July, 1796, Binh and his companions finally reached Lisbon after a journey of more than five months. Once in the Portuguese capital the men were well treated, given a place to stay, and provided with all items necessary for their residence. Binh reported their arrival to his Vietnamese colleagues in a letter dated April 25, 1800: "On the twentieth day of the sixth month of that year [Binh used the lunar calendar here], we arrived at the capital of the country of Portugal, and everything was quite calm, because the Virtuous Lord of Heaven had been merciful and had protected us and had also opened the heart of the virtuous king to be benevolent toward us. . . . They lodged us in the house of the blessed Philip Neri and gave us all the things we needed, and thus we travel about because of these benevolent kindnesses and [receive] all these things that we do not deserve."[41]

Binh and his companions were now settled in Lisbon, and they quickly began the process of adjusting to their new lives in Europe.

Even as they did so, however, events there were rapidly coming to a boil.

The Portugal in which Binh now found himself was, like the homeland he had left behind some five months earlier, mired in political uncertainty, a country in a time of transition. The eighteenth century had been marked by two major and not unrelated events in that country: the massive earthquake in 1755 that destroyed large parts of Lisbon and the rise of the Marquês de Pombal (fl. 1750–77). Taking charge in the aftermath of the enormous quake, Pombal stepped onto the political stage, where for nearly a quarter century he made his mark on the country, mixing despotism with social progress. It was Pombal, as noted earlier, who had orchestrated the demise of the Jesuit community in Portugal. The order was banned from Portugal in 1759, and its members expelled, jailed, or killed, after Jesuits were conveniently alleged to have masterminded an assassination attempt on King José I (r. 1750–77).[42] Pombal had also contributed greatly to the eventual papal dissolution of the entire order in 1773. He could not, however, survive the demise of his patron, King José, and when the Portuguese monarch died in 1777, Pombal himself was brought down. With his death a brief period of political calm returned during the beginning of the regency of Maria I (1777–99), but it was not to endure.

Maria I governed in the name of her young son (the future prince regent John) but became mentally unstable in the last years of her life, contributing to growing political unrest in the 1790s. Moreover, toward the end of this period Portugal was unable to avoid being dragged into the turmoil that was spilling out of France. After initially allying itself with Spain and England in an effort to contain the revolution within France's borders, Portugal found itself under considerable pressure to abrogate this alliance. The Spanish regime was forced to make concessions to the French and was then strongly pressed to influence Portugal to halt its support for the anti-French alliance with England. The Portuguese equivocated and while reducing the degree of their commitment to the English alliance, continued to permit some British access to their ports.

Against this political backdrop Binh and his companions settled into their new lives in Portugal at the Jesuit order house of Saint Philip Neri.[43] Binh wasted little time, however, in pursuing his chief objective, and just two weeks after making landfall he was granted an audience with the Portuguese ruler, the soon-to-be prince regent John.[44] The date was the seventh of August, 1796. At a practical level the meeting with the ruler was very useful, for the men had arrived in Portugal with very little in the way of cash or possessions, and they were assured at this time that they would be provided for. In a second audience on September 22, the ruler said to Binh, "Do not worry. With regard to all matters allow me to tend to them."[45] In this same month Binh was told by a high-ranking official that the court had been able to find an imperial order by King John V, dated November 20, 1745, ordering that a bishop be selected for the mission in Annam. This bishop had apparently never been sent, and the court intimated that the order could now be executed to fulfill Binh's request. This series of events lifted Binh's spirits, suggesting as they did that the Portuguese were concerned about this matter at the highest levels.[46]

Even as he waited to find a means to fulfill his primary mission, Binh sought to establish himself within the Portuguese ecclesiastical community. On October 10, 1796, the patriarch (of the Portuguese Church?) granted Binh permission to hear confessions and to perform the Mass, a very rare privilege for a cleric from a mission region. Binh noted that this permission was given despite the fact that he had no papers certifying his training or ordination in Annam. Then, however, his situation became difficult. Perhaps upset at this apparent irregularity, two clergymen spread stories about him or at least tried to interfere with Binh's position. Consequently all priests were banned from hearing Binh's own confessions.[47] Unfortunately Binh does not make clear the nature of this conflict (if indeed he understood it).

Despite this personal setback, Binh continued to push for the achievement of his primary objective, and in early 1797 the situation looked even more promising. The Portuguese ruler and his chief minister had decided to act on Binh's request to send a bishop to Annam. But then, as Binh wrote, "the Spanish enemy arrived with ships and attacked Portugal. For this reason all other matters at that time were put aside to worry about affairs of the nation."[48] It was the beginning of the direct Portuguese involvement in the wars spilling out of revolutionary France.

Several months earlier, in August 1796, Spain and France had signed the Treaty of San Ildefonso, which brought the Spanish into the French camp, and in October the Spanish declared war on their former allies, the British. Negotiations in Paris were designed to ensure Portuguese neutrality in this war, but apparent Portuguese assistance to the British led to the expulsion of the Portuguese envoy in Paris, and the French then applied pressure on the Spanish to invade Portugal itself.[49] Binh's sole journal entry for the year 1797 was succinct: "During this year, because there was an enemy, although I was able to enter into audience with the king many times, I did not dare to say anything about my own matters."[50] For the next several years circumstances would continue to prevent the fulfillment of Binh's mission, but he did not lose sight of his chief objective.

Binh's patience was apparently rewarded when the Portuguese ruler again took up the matter and in 1801 finally appointed a new bishop for Tonkin, Manuel d. S. Gualdino. Gualdino (or "Fr. Manuel" as Binh referred to him), however, proved to be a complete disaster in terms of advancing Binh's objectives. Gualdino was dispatched to Macao, where instead of bolstering the spirits of the former Jesuit community on whose behalf Binh had lobbied at the Portuguese court, he immediately sided with Binh's bitter rivals, the apostolic vicars of the MEP. Gualdino furthermore commenced a letter-writing campaign to the Jesuit adherents in Việt Nam, urging them to forget their hopes of a Jesuit resurrection and to submit to the authority of the secular clergy.[51] Word of this reached Binh in Lisbon, and he was outraged at Gualdino's actions. In his writings Binh noted that Gualdino used money from the Jesuit accounts in Macao to support the secular clergy; Binh called him a thief and a man of "great inhumanity."[52] Moreover, he criticized Gualdino for disobeying the orders of the king and for sending the two Vietnamese Jesuit representatives in Macao back to Việt Nam.[53] Clearly this was not the man whom Binh had hoped for, nor was it the figure the former Jesuits in Việt Nam had long been awaiting.

During this period, in which he sought to complete his primary mission, Binh continued to adapt to life in Portugal even as he was forced to deal with setbacks. By the spring of 1800, Binh was living at "Real Caza de N. Senhora das Necessidades," a home he and his companions soon had to abandon, albeit temporarily.[54] In July of that same year, Binh and his compatriots all became ill and were advised to go to a local spa for treatment. Taking this recommendation to heart, the men traveled to Caldas, a hot-springs area near Lisbon, where they spent a month taking the waters before returning to the capital.[55] Although Binh and two of his companions were able to recover, given time and medical attention, the fourth Vietnamese cleric was not so fortunate. Father Nhân, also known as Thomé Vicente, died on November 23, 1802, despite having received a rigorous course of medications and treatments.[56] He had entered the religious community in Nghệ An at the age of twelve and served the church in various ways until his death at the age of forty-two.[57]

The Portuguese ruler was upset at Nhân's death and ordered the saying of many masses for his soul. He also granted Bình's request that the remaining Vietnamese be given Western-style clothing suitable for outdoor wear. Apparently on their arrival the ruler had provided the men with Western clothing appropriate to their residence but had not made further arrangements. With the death of Nhân, Bình reported that he and his compatriots found themselves going out much more frequently and thus preferred Western-style clothing suitable for traveling about the city. The ruler granted this request with the proviso that Bình and his colleagues continue to wear their Vietnamese vestments when attending royal audiences. Bình noted that the ruler wished to show off the Vietnamese men in the garb of their homeland to impress visitors with the international character of his court.[58]

In the meantime the political situation in Portugal had become even more precarious. In 1801 France and Spain declared war on Portugal, which was still allied with Great Britain. In 1803, however, coming under increasing pressure from both France and Spain, the Portuguese ruler agreed to declare his country's neutrality, effectively severing the formal alliance with Great Britain. This concession was not enough, however, in the face of the ambitions of both Napoleon and the Spanish imperial favorite, Manuel de Godoy, and the French continued to demonstrate their interest in Portugal. However, not until 1807 did forces allied with Napoleon actually invade. In October 1807, Napoleon sent his general Junot to occupy Portugal, promising the southern half of the country to Godoy.

What Napoleon had anticipated would be a relatively simple matter of occupying Spain and Portugal, however, became a complicated mess. The Spaniards resisted, giving the British time to land troops at Lisbon in anticipation of the Spanish-French attack. Nonetheless, in November Junot's forces entered Portugal, and in response the Portuguese court gathered its possessions, piled them into ships, and hastened to Brazil, where the ruler was to remain until 1821.[59] In the same year, though a few months earlier (June 19, 1807), Binh and his colleagues moved to the House of the Virtuous Lord and Holy Spirit (Nhà Đức Chúa Espirito Santo) at the order of the king.[60] The move was probably a response to the impending French invasion, though it is not clear where this new residence was located.

Although the advancing British army was dealt a defeat by the French forces, British troops were still stationed at Lisbon, their number increasing to twenty-five thousand by 1809, supported by an additional sixteen thousand Portuguese soldiers. The British commander Wellesley arrived in Lisbon in April 1809, prepared to open a new round of attacks. In addition the Portuguese were able to establish a defensive line—the "Lines of Torres Vedras"—running just north of Lisbon, to defend southern Portugal. In 1810 Napoleon ordered the Spanish general Masséna to take sixty thousand men and destroy Wellesley's forces, a campaign seen as the key to victory on the Iberian Peninsula. By September of that year, Masséna's troops had dealt a considerable defeat to Wellesley, who led his forces back to the Lines of Torres Vedras.

Here the French pursuit stalled, and Napoleon's armies suffered a bitter winter, unable to advance through these lines, and they finally retreated in March 1811. Another Spanish attack in May was also unsuccessful. Wellesley increased his control in Portugal, marching toward the border with Spain, where his forces captured two key fortresses. In June 1812, with Napoleon away leading the campaigns against Russia, Wellesley began the decisive campaign into Spain that was to mark the beginning of the end of Napoleon's influence on the peninsula. We do not know where Binh was through all this, but he was not in Lisbon. He did not return to the Portuguese capital until 1811, after the French forces had been withdrawn.

The end of the Napoleonic campaign on the Iberian Peninsula was an important event for the Vietnamese clerics, but an even more important one was soon to follow. On August 7, 1814, Pope Pius VII made a pilgrimage of sorts to Il Gesù, the Jesuit order's spiritual center in Rome, and solemnly proclaimed the restoration of the Company of Jesus. Binh was tremendously excited at the news that the Jesuits had been restored after more than half a century: "In Rome, in that very year, on the fourteenth of November, forty novices entered, among whom were twenty priests, many of whom were university professors . . . and D. Manuel Carlos, the king of Sardinia, stepped in like the holy Franz von Borja. Is this not wonderful? And in the same year, 1814, the Jesuits traveled to the lands of the Moors to preach to the believers, and the king of Tunis gave them a college. Is this not wonderful?"[61]

He hoped, of course, that Jesuits would soon be sent back to Việt Nam. He wrote another letter imploring the religious hierarchy to send a group of Jesuits to his homeland, assuring them that "the Jesuits [were] awaited by the people like Christ himself."[62]

But as Binh soon discovered, it was not such a simple matter. Although the Jesuits had been restored with great pomp in Rome, they were not so readily welcomed by the public, and most made their way back onto the scene very quietly—"on tip-toe," as Jean Lacouture puts it.[63] And indeed, their presence in Europe remained an uneasy one. The Jesuits were expelled from France no less than three times in the period from their restoration to the end of the nineteenth century.[64] They were also expelled from Holland in 1818, from Russia and Spain in 1820, and from Mexico in 1821. In fact, they were not permitted to return to Binh's Portugal until 1829, only a few years before his death.[65] In the meantime Binh found himself with one less Vietnamese companion, for Father Francisco Ngân died on May 21, 1817, after repeatedly suffering from fever and chills. This was, Binh reported, a product of the very different climate that the men had encountered in Lisbon, and one to which Father Ngân had never fully adapted.[66]

Moreover, the political situation in Portugal remained uncertain. From his home in Lisbon, Binh witnessed the rise of a constitutionalist movement in the first decade of the nineteenth century that sought to bring an end to the absolutist monarchy, and which complicated the return of the royal family in 1821. The final three years of his life, 1830–32, saw a bitter civil war within Portugal that involved most of the major European powers and that ended only shortly after Binh's death.

Awaiting Binh's Return

While Binh was living through the tumult of Napoleonic Europe, vainly attempting to carry out his commission, his colleagues and their followers back in Tonkin continued to await his triumphant return. Binh had been sent to Europe as their emissary and constituted their best hope for a revival of the Jesuit order and mission in their midst. The available evidence suggests that Bỉnh was a man of considerable stature within the northern Vietnamese Catholic community, something reflected both by his selection for the mission to Europe and by the descriptions of his following in Việt Nam, particularly after his departure. Moreover, Bỉnh's writings too suggest a man of determination and strength, willing to defend himself and his beliefs, and unfazed by the many transitions of his life.

One also gets the sense that Bỉnh frequently encountered controversy, was quick to defend himself, and was often stubborn in his beliefs and interactions with critics. At one point, commenting on a period early in his religious career, he wrote the following in the bold strokes of his distinctive hand: "There are people who think that the Virtuous Father Phê did not like me, or that I committed some sort of fault in that house, and that [because of this] people chased me out. Or that I developed hatred because that person liked someone better than me, and that it was for those reasons that I left that house. As for all of these things, they are not true."[67]

Given his sometimes belligerent personality, it is perhaps not surprising to find that Bỉnh was frequently in conflict with the other religious orders in northern Việt Nam. In particular the secular missionaries of the MEP were troubled by Bỉnh's defiant loyalty to the Jesuit order as well as by his stature within the community of Vietnamese Jesuit converts even after his departure for Europe.

The MEP missionaries were constantly reminded of this now larger than life figure, whose memory among the Vietnamese Jesuit following remained vivid. As one of that group's clerics wrote in 1801 about the arrival of one of Bỉnh's letters from Lisbon:

He is encouraging the Christians not to imitate the Israelites, who seeing Moses very much delayed in descending from the Mountain were adoring the golden calf (he is no doubt Moses, and we are the vile animal that he is prohibiting them from worshipping). As for the rest, we are quite distant from engaging the Christians in carrying out any sort of act of adoration for our consideration, and at the same time are not without doubts about the intentions of exhorting the Christians to hold true during the schism, but there are still those who are seduced by these letters, true or false, and await his return somewhat like the Jews await the Messiah . . . I believe that the blessed Seat would do well to . . . confine him in a monastery for the rest of his days.[68]

Clearly the Vietnamese who had been touched by Binh and his considerable force of personality hoped they would soon witness his triumphant return.

Although the community was concerned about his extended absence, this did not seem to undermine their faith in their envoy. In 1804 another MEP letter indicated that the secular missionaries were still confronting the ghost of Binh among the former-Jesuit loyalists in the north: "Ever since Father Binh and his followers left Tonkin in 1795, many Christians of the former society have said to me that they ask only three years in order to receive news from the said Father Binh. I reply to them that if they wished to wait thirty years, I would not have the strength to force them to submit to the legitimate authority, and that the kingdom is full of pagans among whom I deplore this blindness."[69]

In the same year yet another MEP missionary, Philippe Sérard, wrote the following about those awaiting Binh:

Nothing remains but to comment on the aftermath of the revolt that the letters of Father Binh have assured. On his departure from Tonkin for Macao, he left behind a stamp for the chief of the schismatics, which is like a seal by which to judge and to assure the veracity of his letters. All the others that do not carry this said vile mark must be rejected as false. . . . Finally, the two young men returned from Macao some months later, serving as the bearers of letters from the said Father Binh to some in particular: to a former blind preacher who is in the district where I am at present, and one to a catechist in chief in that house where earlier lived a Portuguese preacher named Augustin Carneiro, who died two years and some months ago, at the age of ninety.[70]

From this it is clear that Binh recognized the complexity of the ongoing struggles with the secular missionaries in Tonkin, and that he was determined to prevent his name being used by other clergy to manipulate his considerable following.

As noted earlier, Manuel d. S. Gualdino, who had been named bishop to Tonkin in late 1801, had, in fact, actively sought to discourage the hopes of the Tonkinese awaiting Binh and more generally awaiting the Jesuit leaders they soon hoped to see. In his last known letter to the remaining Vietnamese Jesuit community, Gualdino made a final attempt to discourage this die-hard group, reporting that Binh and his colleagues had been expelled from Portugal in that year (1805) by the king himself. As Georg Schurhammer comments, "To what

extent this news was true, we do not know."[71] What we do know is
that Bỉnh was still (or back) in Portugal by 1811, so although it is possible that he had been forced to leave the country, it seems unlikely
that such an event would have received absolutely no mention in his
writings. More likely this report was a ploy on the part of Gualdino or
possibly even the result of poor information reaching him in distant
Macao from an unsettled Portugal about to be immersed in
Napoleon's Iberian campaigns.

Through the first years of Bỉnh's absence, the Vietnamese Catholic
community continued to hope for his return, a hope that appears to
have been justified, for it does not appear that Bỉnh originally
intended to remain in Europe. Rather, circumstances forced this exile
on him. In a letter dated April 25, 1800, he wrote to his colleagues in
Việt Nam that he still held out hope "that in the future [they would]
be able to return in order to meet one another."[72] Later Bỉnh recorded
in his journals, "When we first arrived, those of the order [i.e., the local Jesuits] thought that [we would remain here] one year or perhaps
two, and then our task would be completed and we would return to
Annam."[73] This turned out, of course, to have been a very optimistic
assessment, and instead Bỉnh remained in Portugal for more than
thirty-five years. Had he succeeded in his mission to arrange for
Jesuits to be sent to his homeland, Bỉnh would almost certainly have
returned to Việt Nam.

Bỉnh and His Writings

Although his primary mission was repeatedly stymied by circumstances outside his control, Bỉnh did not sit idly in Lisbon awaiting a
change in his fortunes. He occupied himself instead with writing and
copying books at a furious pace. Indeed, these writings underscore an
already remarkable life. Bỉnh was not the first Vietnamese Catholic to
leave behind a body of writing. Rather, he belonged to a small but
highly significant lineage of literate Vietnamese Catholics who produced writings in both *chữ nôm* (Vietnamese demotic script) and *quốc
ngữ* (romanized Vietnamese) dating as far back as the middle of the
seventeenth century. Although most of these early texts were religious tracts, a few dealt with secular matters: one was a collection of
poetry and another a brief history of Việt Nam.[74] A small number
were even produced by female converts. What sets Bỉnh's writings

apart within this tradition is their sheer volume and the diversity of their contents. His surviving works, all preserved in bound, handwritten volumes, comprise more than ten thousand pages in Vietnamese (mostly in *quốc ngữ*) and several other languages, far exceeding the combined literary output of his coreligionist predecessors. Moreover, he wrote not merely religious texts and histories but also detailed descriptions of events in his life and observations of life in Portugal and Europe more generally during the many years he spent in Lisbon.

Binh's is thus an extremely unusual case of a Vietnamese man who lived in the precolonial era and outside the Confucian scholarly tradition yet left behind a substantial body of writings. Although he was not a part of the traditional Vietnamese literary culture of his time, he was highly literate and quite knowledgeable about the events and cultures of his age; thus we cannot say that Binh's writings represent the perspective of the "common person." He almost certainly came from a peasant family (though it is not entirely clear from his writings), but he entered a career that emphasized learning and the literary arts. His was not by any means a perspective free of ideological constraints. Indeed, Binh's view was that of an extremely devout Catholic and perhaps even more importantly and specifically, a devoted champion of the Jesuit tradition. Binh nevertheless consistently transcended the parochialism frequently found in writings of other Vietnamese Catholics, and although religion remained a constant element in his writings, it did not prevent his consideration of a wide range of secular topics.

Given the sheer volume of his writings, a study of this length cannot do more than make some general observations about Binh's works and their form and content. First, Binh clearly had a capacity for learning languages, for although he wrote chiefly in *quốc ngữ*, he also wrote in *nôm*, as well as in Chinese, in Portuguese, and in Latin. Although his Portuguese has been described as rather poor, he wrote fluidly in *quốc ngữ* and indeed may be seen as a major figure in the early evolution of the romanized form of vernacular Vietnamese.

Second, Binh was a compulsive keeper of records and information, obsessed with minutia and detail. He was also an extremely organized man, and one whose writings were produced with a considerable amount of thought. These characteristics are reflected in the incredible amount of information crammed into the pages of his notebooks. It is also revealed in the form of his writings. He did not merely write seven-, eight-, nine-hundred page volumes. He provided tables of contents for each. He also indexed many of his handwritten volumes in great detail, alphabetically by topic, occasionally cross-referencing entries with his other books. In the introduction to his *Sách số sang chép các việc*, he explained his logic in providing such indexes: "[In this book] I have recorded many things, and so I have called it the 'Notebook That Transmits.' It does not have distinct parts such as other books do, and for this reason I have created an index divided into three parts in order that things might be more easily found. Thus, anyone who wishes to find a particular matter, can look in the index to find where that section is located. The first index speaks of various things regarding the Jesuit order. The second index speaks of things relating to me and my friends. The third index records all other matters."[75] This statement directly addresses another important issue concerning Binh's writings—namely, what his intention in producing them was.

It is clear from this statement and other comments scattered throughout his writings that everything Binh wrote was produced with the idea that it would serve as a source of information and instruction for his fellow Vietnamese. For example, in the introduction to his *Truyện Anam* (Tales of Annam), he offered his reasons for producing that particular text:

As for historical records of events in Annam, the king has already recorded numerous matters in our country, but when the teacher Alexander went to spread the faith, he produced a book of tales that was printed in Rome in Latin, Italian, and French in order that all the priests who traveled later would be aware of the matters in our country. Likewise, the English arrived to conduct commerce, and they also composed books of tales about our country, which they also published in their own language, telling of various other customs, along with the appearance [of the land] and [local] products, that all the merchants from their country would know these things and go there to carry out commerce. But the history of the kings we cannot see, and the tales of the teacher Alexander we cannot understand because they are in a foreign language, and moreover from then until now much has happened, because two hundred years have passed. For this reason, I am writing these tales in our language, so that every person can know them.[76]

Clearly Binh saw his writings both as a continuation of the works of his Jesuit predecessors and as a record in his own language, that his fellow Vietnamese might draw edification from the history and experiences of the European missionary work in their country. Even the diary and recordings of miscellanea were not simply private musings. Binh apparently intended that this journal, along with his poetry and collected letters, be returned to his homeland and distributed among his coreligionists. His meticulous indexing of his various texts reinforces the idea that he intended them to be used by others.

As noted earlier, at one time Binh contemplated carrying these texts back to Việt Nam himself. Although it eventually became clear that he was unlikely ever to return to his homeland, he continued to produce his texts at a torrid pace, hoping that somehow they might finally be carried to Việt Nam to serve their intended purpose. As he himself wrote at the end of a list of his own writings: "As for the many other printed books, I will create a listing of them along with all the [hand]written books and will bequeath them to the father superior of the Jesuit order before I die, for afterward someone must send a Jesuit teacher over to Annam so that my brothers may use them."[77] Although in some regards the instructional nature of his writings was intended to make Vietnamese aware of life in Europe, in other cases his descriptions were much more practical. Thus, he concluded the *Sách sổ sang chép các việc* (Notebook That Transmits and Records All Matters) with a five-page section titled "Instructions in the Manner of Making Printing Machines to Print Pictures," which he wrote "in order that [Vietnamese] carpenters may see this and be able to make [them]." The text provides detailed descriptions of how to construct movable printing presses, complete with drawings of a large and a small printing press.[78]

Finally, in addition to his commitment to making his books useful to future readers, Binh had very strong views about authorship and the responsibilities that came with it. He insisted that when one wrote books of whatever kind, one should take responsibility for these writings: "It should be the custom that on this earth any time someone writes any sort of book, he must write his name in that book so that everyone will know who it was. If one writes a book and does not write his name in it, then this person is a scoundrel, and for this reason I will write my name here in order that everyone will know who produced this book." He then proceeded to write in very large script: "I am the priest Philiphê Bỉnh."[79] This may have been a reaction to older literary traditions, particularly those found in Việt Nam, where anonymous texts were not uncommon, or a sense that anonymous texts might be used to distort messages to and within the Vietnamese Christian community.

The Content of the Writings

Most of Philiphê Bỉnh's writings are about matters of religion, and even his extensive descriptions of political events in Europe revolve around the implications of these events for the future of the Jesuit order. Despite this emphasis on religion, one still finds a considerable range of topics addressed in his various writings. Major themes found in his writings include: (1) histories of religious figures; (2) histories of the Catholic missions in Asia (Việt Nam and China); (3) general writings on religious practice: sermons, masses, prayers; (4) personal journals and miscellanea; (5) translations and linguistic tools.

Bỉnh wrote primarily in the religious idiom, and even the writings I classify as nonreligious—his journal and his recordings of miscellanea and a few other works—are strongly infused with religious observations and orientations. His religious writings include sermons, prayers, and liturgies. They also include lengthy histories (some of them copies by Bỉnh from older works) of the popes, various saints—including Francis Xavier and Ignatius of Loyola—and histories of specific missionaries and missionary activities more generally in Việt Nam and China. His nonreligious writings include translations of various texts, including the *Voyages of Mendes Pinto* and a version of Alexandre de Rhode's famous multilingual dictionary, *Dictionarium Annamiticum Lusitanum, et Latinum.*

This last category of nonreligious items also includes the two volumes serving as the chief sources of information about his own life: the *Sách sổ sang chép các việc* and the *Nhật trình kim thư khát chính Chúa Giáo.* This last volume was apparently only one of four that he wrote with the same title. The other three, covering similar topics, were written in other languages. Two were in Portuguese and one in Chinese. It is not clear whether those have survived, for they do not appear in the Vatican catalogs. As Bỉnh described the surviving volume: "This first volume in our Anamite language, is a summary of all my affairs, and records the year, month and day of all that we encountered in our travels."[80] Although this volume is labeled the first, it was clearly written over an extended period of time, for it contains many blank pages, which were probably to be filled in later, and was written with several different writing instruments. These latter works functioned as a combination of diary, field notes, general records, and monetary ledgers. They provide a fascinating glimpse into the observations, life, and perspectives of a man who had made two large leaps in his life: taking on an alien religion and then traveling to an alien land. These works describe both his life in Việt Nam after his ordination and his journey to Europe.

Of these writings perhaps none are more interesting than his observations on the ordinary elements of life around him in Portugal. There is no shortage of European explications and impressions of "the East," beginning with Marco Polo and continuing and accelerating through the period of expanding European trade and eventual colonialism. We have far fewer writings by people traveling from Asia and describing their reactions to and observations of "the West" (phương Tây), as Binh called it. There are, of course, later descriptions and reactions by Asian visitors to Europe, but these date largely to the end of the nineteenth century and the early part of the twentieth. Binh's writings offer glimpses of European life and politics through the eyes of a late eighteenth- and early nineteenth-century visitor.

Binh wrote of the daily habits of the Europeans he saw around him, including the foods they ate, the ways in which they prepared their tea, and the patterns of their eating and drinking. He also wrote about what people wore, how they fed, dressed, and schooled their children, how the Western calendar worked and how the day was divided. He observed, for example, that unlike in Việt Nam, Portuguese mothers never prechewed food for their children or fed them mouth to mouth.[81] He noted that Europeans liked to add sugar and sometimes milk to their tea, while Vietnamese, like him, preferred to drink it plain.[82] He observed that in general Europeans liked sweet foods, and that while he initially continued to prefer less sweet foods, he eventually came to enjoy the sweeter European dishes.[83] He wrote quite extensively in fact about European food and food habits, the number and size of European meals, the size of Portuguese cattle, and the manner of their slaughter in the streets of Lisbon.[84]

He also wrote in some detail about families and children. In addition to his observations about the manner in which children were fed, he also commented on pregnancy rates in Portugal, noting that many women had a child every year, some waiting even less than a year. He observed that women in Portugal led far easier lives than those in his homeland and that he frequently saw them lounging on beds.[85] He described how children were named in accordance with saints' days, with male saints' names feminized for girls.[86] He noted the types of education offered boys and girls and the care with which parents took their children out of the house. For instance, he noted, "If a child is speaking too loudly, then its mother takes a finger and puts it in front of her mouth, meaning that the child should stop talking."[87] It is to us a banal observation, but to Binh it was one more piece of useful information about the habits and customs of these strange Europeans whom he had placed under careful scrutiny.

Binh was also a fastidious recordkeeper with regard to monetary transactions. He recorded all his own expenditures as well as money he collected for the future missions in Việt Nam and more generally the costs of various items of dress and food in early nineteenth-century Lisbon. He recorded how much cakes cost and the price of a cup of tea or coffee at a local cafe.[88] He commented on the expenses involved in hiring carriages, in consulting physicians, in filling prescriptions.[89] He noted the salaries of his European counterparts and their expenditures with regard to clothing. He told about how wealth was transmitted when people died, noting that those who died without wills had their property turned over to the king.

In recording such observations Binh was writing of things possibly never before deemed worthy of notice by an educated Vietnamese. His decision to comment on such things was probably the result of his exposure to Europeans and his training in European-organized religious schools. Whatever their origin, his writings reflect a critically comparative mind that contrasted the European with the Vietnamese in an observant manner. Binh's observations constitute a marvelous parallel to the fascinated observations of early European travelers to Asia, with their detailed descriptions of various aspects of daily life. Indeed, Binh's written comments appear far more dispassionate and perhaps even less ethnocentric than the observations of many earlier visitors to his own continent.

Bình and Poetry

Finally, in addition to his many other writings, Philiphê Bình also wrote forty-four poems of which we know. These were crafted between 1793 and 1802, often reflect on his journeys, and include reactions to storms at sea, attacks by pirates, and his arrival at various destinations. All his poems were written in the classic *luật thi* form of eight seven-syllable lines in which typically the first, second, fourth, sixth, and eighth lines have an ending rhyme.[90] These poems also place Bỉnh in a long tradition of Vietnamese who wrote poems while on journeys outside of their country. The best-known poems in this genre were those produced by court officials who traveled to China on embassies to the Chinese court, poems that commented most frequently on the scenery but also on events of the journey. Bỉnh's poetry thus places him squarely in existing Vietnamese literary traditions. What is striking about these poems, however, is not the fact that they adhered to the ancient *luật thi* poetic form or that they belong to the lineage of Vietnamese travel poetry. Rather, it is that they were written in *quốc ngữ*. These poems constitute one of the earliest bodies of *quốc ngữ* poetry of any form and are particularly significant in that they combine the very classical *luật thi* poetic form with the romanized script of the Vietnamese vernacular.

Although these may not be great poems aesthetically, they are useful for providing further insights into Philiphê Bỉnh's life, feelings, and experiences. Moreover, unlike the Vietnamese tradition of travel poetry, Bỉnh's verse constitutes a commentary not merely on his life but also on the political and military events of the turbulent Europe of his time. That is, Bỉnh also used poetry to discuss events to which he was not witness but about which he heard while in Lisbon. Thus, he wrote a series of poems between early 1798 and 1799 commenting on these events: "A Poem on France Attacking the City of Rome," "A Poem on the King of Naples Assisting the Blessed Church in Attacking France," and "A Poem on the Exalted Russian Leaders Successfully Attacking France."

His poetry constitutes a window (perhaps the best one) into his personal feelings during what was arguably the most tumultuous period of a full life. They reflect not only the adventures, disappointments, and elations associated with his departure from Tonkin, but also his numerous voyages and his arrival and subsequent events in Portugal and Europe. Earlier I presented translations of poems written by Bỉnh on encountering pirates and a powerful storm on the Indian Ocean. He wrote several other poems reflecting other aspects of this trip, and although space does not permit the translation of all of them, I want to offer one more here. This poem, written somewhat earlier than the storm poem (though on the same trip), was composed while Bình's vessel was anchored in a harbor on the Malay Peninsula:

A Poem on Reaching the Land of Mã Lai

Time has passed and flown already to the end of the second month,
We have arrived at a place called the land of Mã Lai
At the edge of the forest are sprinkled about ten huts of grass
Out in the bay are sparsely scattered fishing nets
Some are selling young coconuts, while others catch fish.
Some are searching for streambeds, as others dig for taro.
In scattered clumps, the strangers mix with the local people
Who knows which one understands the language of the other?[91]

Bình observed the world around him with a clear eye and developed the capacity to record what he saw. In both prose and poetry he left behind the record of a life that mingled experience with written expression.

The End

The bulk of Bình's historical and religious writings were composed between 1811 and 1822, even as he continued to maintain his journal and his recording of miscellanea. His personal writings also make it clear that even in his later years, Bình continued to think of those he had left behind in Việt Nam. As he wrote in the closing pages of his *Sách sổ sang chép các việc* in 1822: "This year, as I write this book, I am already sixty-three years of age, and surely I cannot live much longer. I request that my brothers also keep my soul in their remembrances, because as long as I am still alive I cannot forget my brothers. Amen."[92] Then, in 1830, at seventy-one years of age, he apparently found the energy and perhaps the need to write one more volume: the 626-page *Truyện bà thánh Anna* (Tales of Saint Anne). He also continued to perform numerous masses on behalf of his fellow Vietnamese back in Việt Nam, diligently recording the numbers in his records: 41 in 1825, 145 in 1826, 54 in 1827, 31 in 1828, 98 in 1829, 110 in 1830, 105 in 1831, each year recorded in a hand that was losing energy as the words were entered more faintly and with less steadiness. Then, for 1832 he was able to record only the year, without the subsequent register of masses and monies received for performing them. His death in that same year was recorded in 1833 by a compatriot, who noted simply that "in 1832 Philiphê Bỉnh crossed over into the eternal homeland."[93]

Perhaps Bỉnh's journey to Portugal was, as some have suggested, a fool's errand. C. R. Boxer, in a study of the Portuguese overseas empire, referred to Bỉnh as a "rather pathetic figure" who represented the last Indochinese defender of the Padroado mission.[94] Yet even as Bỉnh seemingly failed in his primary mission, he continued to write in the hope that his works might some day find their way back to his homeland and there serve as sources of both liturgical and practical knowledge. Despite the great disappointments his life clearly held, one cannot agree with Boxer's assessment of Bỉnh as "pathetic." Indeed, nothing in Bỉnh's writings reveals such a person. He was acutely aware of the disappointments he suffered and yet did not wallow in self-pity, continuing instead to look toward a future to which he hoped his writings could contribute. We should view Bỉnh as the remarkable figure he was: a man of keen awareness, of vision, and of hope who left a mark on his own age if in no other way than in the hope he inspired among his fellow Catholics in Việt Nam. He also left a mark that survived him in the legacy of his writings.

Notes

1. I use the term Việt Nam here for convenience. Although the country was known as ĐạiViệt when Bỉnh was born, when the Nguyễn dynasty came to power in the early nineteenth century the name was changed to Việt Nam.

2. For the text of the expulsion decree, see Ross, *Vision Betrayed*, 93.

3. Borri, *Cochin-China*.

4. For more on Rhodes's life and mission work, see P. C. Phan, *Mission and Catechesis*.

5. Schurhammer, "Annamitische Xaveriusliteratur," 305. The Padroado mission was specifically created by the authority of the Portuguese monarchy, while the Propaganda order was answerable to Rome.

6. Teixeira, *Macau e a sua diocese*, 371–77.

7. Ibid., 383.

8. Ibid., 382–83.

9. Fôrest, *Les missionaires français au Tonkin et au Siam*, 2:209–10.

10. Ibid., 207–8.

11. Ibid., 208.

12. Ibid., 214.

13. Teixeira, *Macau e a sua diocese,* 492–93, for example, gives a list of thirty-one Vietnamese who entered the order between 1640 and 1652.

14. Bình, "Sách số sang chép các việc," 1–2. This and all other translations of Bình's writings are my own.

15. See, e.g., Phan Huy Chú, *Hoàng Việt địa du chí,* 95–97.

16. See, e.g., Roux to Blandin, June 16, 1786. Archives of the Société des Missions Étrangères de Paris (hereafter cited as AMEP), 691:735; other estimates are more cautious, but the famine was by all accounts a severe one.

17. Longer to l'Etondal, July 17, 1791, AMEP, 700:1473.

18. La Mothe to Boiret, June 19, 1793, AMEP, 692:450; quotation from Eyot to Blandin, June 19, 1793, AMEP, 692:444.

19. Gerard to Blandin, June 5, 1793/May 28, 1794, AMEP, 692:517.

20. Bình, *Sách số,* 29–30, 87.

21. See Schurhammer, "Annamitische Xaveriusliteratur," 306; and Teixeira, *Macau e a sua diocese,* 280, about the status of European Jesuits in Tonkin at this time. Bình in his *Sách số,* 29, appears to suggest that the Jesuits who had encouraged him both died in 1789 and that those who subsequently ordained him and the others had been sent from Rome and were not Jesuits.

22. E.g., Philiphê Bình, "Truyện Anam, quyển I," 423–25.

23. Ibid., 427.

24. See, e.g., Bình, *Nhật trình kim thư khất chính Chúa Giáo,* 315–80, which includes Bình's accounts of some of these journeys.

25. See, e.g., Juăo Baotista Nghiên, undated letter, AMEP, 691:305; Dụng Toà Án et al., July 21, 1785, AMEP, 691:608–9.

26. Lacouture, *Jesuits,* 262–71.

27. Ibid., 265–68.

28. Boxer, *Portuguese Seaborne Empire,* 228.

29. Teixeira, *Macau e a sua diocese,* 485.

30. Poivre, "Journal de voyage du vaisseau de la compagnie le Machault à la Cochinchine," 439.

31. Poivre himself pointed this out to the Chúa. The Chúa replied that if this was the case, then Poivre might as well collect his craftspeople from among these exiles who had "abandoned their king, their parents and their country" (ibid.).

32. For a description of these men, see Poivre, "Journal de voyage du vaisseau de la compagnie le Machault à la Cochinchine," 366–67.

33. Bình, *Nhật trình kim thư,* 2. The first ten pages of this volume are a brief year by year description of events in his life between 1793 and 1802.

34. Ibid.

35. Bình, *Truyện Anam,* 1:468; also idem, *Nhật trình kim thư,* 4.

36. Bình, *Nhật trình kim thư,* 5.

37. It is unclear from Bình's account whether these men accompanied him from Việt Nam or were already located in Macao.

38. Bình, *Nhật trình kim thư,* 29.

39. Ibid., 6–7.

40. Ibid., 440.

41. Ibid., 220. Dating events in Binh's writings can be confusing, since he switches between solar and lunar calendars throughout his writings, but he does appear to be very consistent. The date given here for their arrival, the twentieth day of the sixth month (of the lunar year), corresponds precisely with the solar calendar date of July 24, 1796, which he gives in a letter in his *Nhật trình kim thư*, 227–28.

42. Livermore, *New History of Portugal*, 230. My account of Portuguese political and military events here largely draws on Livermore's work.

43. Letter from Binh to Việt Nam, dated April 25, 1800, *Nhật trình kim thư*, 220.

44. Binh refers to the ruler as "king" (*vua*), though strictly speaking John was the second son of the ruling queen, Maria I, and was acting in her name.

45. Binh, *Nhật trình kim thư*, 9.

46. Ibid., 9–10.

47. Ibid., 10.

48. Ibid.

49. Livermore, *New History*, 245–46.

50. Binh, *Nhật trình kim thư*, 11.

51. Schurhammer, "Annamitische Xaveriusliteratur," 307.

52. Binh, *Sách sổ*, 104.

53. Ibid.

54. Letter of April 25, 1800, Binh, *Nhật trình kim thư*, 222. This may be a reference to the Convent of Necessidades, which was founded in 1750. It was apparently established within a palace of the same name. In 1801 Southey described it in part: "The Necessidades' garden is inaccessible to women. Lead us not into temptation! It is laid out in shadowed walks, like the spokes of a wheel that center on fountains. The spaces between the walks are occupied with fruit trees—apricot—almonds—lemons—oranges" (*Journals of a Residence in Portugal*, 14).

55. Binh, *Nhật trình kim thư*, 14.

56. Binh, *Sách sổ*, 131–32.

57. See Binh, *Nhật trình kim thư*, 28–30, for a brief biography of Nhân.

58. Binh, *Sách sổ*, 168–70.

59. Livermore, *New History*, 250.

60. Binh, *Sách sổ*, 133.

61. Schurhammer, "Annamitische Xaveriusliteratur," 308.

62. Ibid.

63. Lacouture, *Jesuits*, 331.

64. Tombs, *France*, 92–93.

65. Schurhammer, "Annamitische Xaveriusliteratur," 308.

66. Binh, *Sách sổ*, 133.

67. Ibid., 82.

68. Gortyne to l'Etondal, November 17, 1801, AMEP, 701:465–66.

69. Gortyne to Toulon, February 14, 1804, AMEP 701:539.

70. Sérard to Toulon, August 3, 1804, AMEP, 701:573.

71. Schurhammer, "Annamitische Xaveriusliteratur," 307.

72. Bình, *Nhật trình kim thư*, 220–22.

73. Bình, *Sách sổ*, 153.

74. Bento Thiện wrote a *quốc ngữ* history of Việt Nam, "Lịch sử᠎ nước Annam," in 1659. See Whitmore, "*Chung-hsing* and *Cheng-t'ung* in Texts," 131.

75. Ibid., 1.

76. Bình, *Truyện Anam*, 2.

77. Bình, *Sách sổ*, 599.

78. Ibid., 618–22.

79. Bình, *Nhật trình kim thư*, i.

80. Ibid., v.

81. Bình, *Sách sổ*, 393.

82. Ibid., 551–52.

83. Ibid., 568.

84. Ibid., 555–56.

85. Ibid., 398–99.

86. Ibid., 391–92.

87. Ibid., 395.

88. Ibid., 548.

89. Ibid., 130–31.

90. *Luật thi* is the Vietnamese equivalent of the Chinese *lu-shi* form, also known in Vietnamese as *thơ Đường luật,* reflecting its origins in the Tang dynasty. For more on Vietnamese poetic forms, see Huỳnh Sanh Thông, *Anthology of Vietnamese Poems*, 1–25.

91. Bình, *Nhật trình kim thư*, 439.

92. Bình, *Sách sổ*, 597.

93. Schurhammer, "Annamitische Xaveriusliteratur," 308.

94. Boxer, *Portuguese Seaborne Empire*, 247.

9

Strangers in a Foreign Land
Vietnamese Soldiers and Workers in France during World War I

KIMLOAN HILL

In World War I about ninety-nine thousand men from Indochina were recruited to serve in France as soldiers and workers. In the English-speaking world a few scholars, such as Virginia Thompson, Joseph Buttinger, and David Marr, have claimed that these men were conscripted labor and were treated as slaves, and it is widely believed that they were "rounded up, taken in chains, and shipped to France."[1] In the French-speaking world, since the 1980s there have been some discussions about these men in a few scholarly works such as those of Lê Hữu Khoa, Marie-Eve Blanc, and Henri Eckert.[2] However, none of these works deal with the claim made by the English-speaking scholars.

An examination of archival materials finds a different picture of their experiences. It shows that a majority of them were volunteers from diverse backgrounds: there were active soldiers and reservists; French citizens; members of the families of high-ranking court officials; civil servants in the colonial and imperial bureaucracies; migrant workers; and peasants. Their everyday experiences in France were also diverse. The soldiers participated in famous battles, such as the battle at Chemin des Dames, and served in the Balkans. The workers endured wartime economic hardships, joined the labor protest movements, and were both victims and perpetrators of ethnic and racial discrimination. The majority of them had opportunities to do what they could never have dreamed of doing when they lived in Indochina. They learned to speak French, went to social clubs, dated French women, and participated in labor demonstrations. Those circumstances give rise to a number of questions. How did the French treat the recruits? How did the recruits respond to their new working and living environments? What long-term impact did such an environments have on their lives? What were their views about themselves and others? What became of them at the end of the war? Finally, what effect did this have on the Franco-Indochinese relationship in the postwar era?

To answer those questions, this study draws from a large body of sources, including presidential and ministerial decrees and regulations, official communications among different organs of the metropolitan government and between the governments in Paris and Indochina, reports and diaries, personal letters, newspaper articles, statistics, and monographs written in both English and French. Primary sources written in *quốc ngữ* about the recruiting enterprise do not exist for this period because it was not made a national language until 1917 and writing in *quốc ngữ* did not become popular until the 1920s. Until then, imperial records were written in *chữ nôm* or *chữ nho*, neither of which I can read, and colonial official records were written in French. To be sure, a few newspapers were published in *quốc ngữ*, but the accounts of Vietnamese participation in the war were written in French-language newspapers such as *Le Courrier d' Haiphong* or *l'Avenir du Tonkin*.

Rallying under the French Flag

Prior to World War I, France faced a manpower shortage stemming from slow population growth. Between 1850 and 1910 the French population increased only by about 3.4 million, while the German population increased by about 31 million, and the British by 18 million. During the war France faced a labor crises. As Gordon Wright pointed out: "Of the eight million men mobilized, five million were killed or wounded. The dead alone amounted to 10 percent of the active male population."[3] To get the manpower it needed to sustain its economy as well as to meet the demands of the war machine, France mobilized women, hired European workers, and recruited labor in its colonies in Asia and Africa for its military, factories, and public works. The Ministry of Agriculture recruited laborers from Spain, Italy, Belgium, Portugal, and Greece; and the Ministry of Armaments recruited workers from the colonies in North Africa, Madagascar, China, and Indochina.[4] A total of 242,000 soldiers and 222,763 workers from Africa and Asia went to work in public and private establishments: munitions factories, administrative services, engineering, agriculture, mining, road works, and other places of business.[5] Among them were about ninety-nine thousand men from Indochina, including at least a dozen members of the families of high-ranking court officials, more than a thousand French Indochinese (European and naturalized citizens), and tens of thousands of natives. A few thousand were active soldiers in the colonial army and reserve, but most were volunteers.[6]

Various factors motivated the volunteers. Many young men joined up because they sought adventure: stories about France in newspapers and told in the letters of workers who left for France in 1915 as members of a trial group had aroused their curiosity. More importantly, many were attracted by the terms of the contracts offered by the ministries, which offered a temporary escape from the ongoing economic crises and social disorder in Tonkin and Annam in the decade immediately before the war. Annam contributed more than one-third of the labor force that went to France during the war—nineteen thousand by the end of 1915 and eighteen thousand more between January and March 1916. On the whole about seven-eighths of all the Indochinese who took part came from Tonkin and Annam.[7]

The mobilization of manpower in Indochina took place in several stages. All French military and reservist personnel were mobilized on March 29, 1915, and all French-born and naturalized citizens on July 1, 1915. Indigenous reservists of the classes of 1900, 1901, 1905, 1906, 1907, and 1909 were called to active military duty on November 22, 1915. A campaign to recruit native soldiers and workers began on December 17, 1915. On January 20, 1916, the Vietnamese court at Huế issued a royal edict to reinforce this appeal by offering each volunteer a bonus of two hundred francs, about eighty piasters, if he passed a medical examination and was incorporated into the colonial troops. A final wave of mobilization took place between October 1916 and July 1917.[8]

The volunteers were paid according to a system of base pay and allowances, including bonuses for volunteering, which varied according to their professional skill and military status, and their families received a monthly allowance. Volunteers also received health care, compensation and unemployment benefits when they were ill or injured, and a pension if they became disabled. If they died, their families would receive their pensions. Each volunteer for combat received the same wages as serving soldiers and reservists, although their bonus package was different. The base pay of all workers was the same irrespective of skill or occupation, but bonuses and allowances varied significantly. If they died or became disabled while serving, they received the same type of pension and benefits as soldiers.[9]

The payment of bonuses, wages, and pensions, and of allowances to their families, is not consistent with the men having been unwilling conscripts and indicates that they were volunteers. This conclusion is further supported by the fact that, on at least one occasion, when the bonus on offer proved too low to attract sufficient recruits, it was increased from twenty-five francs to fifty-three francs.[10] Moreover, when some overzealous officials did coerce men into becoming recruits, the officials were disciplined and the men released from service. At the beginning of the recruiting campaign, officials in Mỹ Tho, Gò Công, Tây Ninh, Sa Đéc, and Trà Vinh arrested a number of "unwanted elements in the village," chained them together, and forced them to sign employment contracts. Some peasants fled their villages; others reacted violently by using sticks and scythes to break down the *đình*, vandalized it, and chased the notables away. When the news of these abuses and unrest reached the office of the governor of Cochinchina, disciplinary action was taken against R. Striedter, the chief of the recruiting center, and native officials in those provinces. They faced reprimands and were either removed from their posts or demoted.[11]

Not all who signed up were admitted to the colonial army. They first had to undergo a series of medical examinations; only those who were fit to serve went on to induction centers and officially joined the colonial army. Those selected received some training for the jobs they were hired to do. When the time to depart for France came, they were assembled at quarantine centers to await passage to France. The voyage took at least a month, with stops at various ports to refill water tanks, load coal, replenish food supplies, hospitalize the sick, and give the troops a rest. At Djibouti the recruits could go ashore and roam through the city while their ships were anchored in the harbor.[12]

The transoceanic journey was a testing ground for the recruits. It tested their will, their strength, and their endurance. Heat, sanitary deficiencies, overcrowding, and inadequate living quarters during the voyage inevitably caused diseases. Outbreaks of cholera, beriberi, bronchitis, and pneumonia were frequent; some deaths occurred on nearly every voyage, and many sufferers were hospitalized along the way. Between May and October 1916, about 140 men died of illness during their transoceanic trips from Indochina to France. On April 5, 1916, thirty-six people on the *Porthos* were hospitalized at Colombo and eleven at Djibouti. On December 7, 1916, sixty-two travelers on the *Meinam* who were suffering from beriberi were hospitalized at Tor. On the same date, seventeen were ill on the *André Lebon* and were hospitalized at Djibouti.[13]

Battles at sea were another major cause of death during the voyages. The *Meinam* was torpedoed twice, on December 14, 1915, and September 12, 1917. When the *Athos* was torpedoed on March 1, 1917, 752 people died, of whom 37 were Indochinese. The *Porthos* was attacked on September 24, 1917. On December 22, 1918, the *Australien*, which carried mail and money orders that Indochinese soldiers and workers sent to Indochina, was torpedoed. All the mail and money orders were lost. The government in Paris had to trace all buyers of the money orders and reimburse them. The bodies of those who died while their ships were sailing were buried at sea with no fanfare and perhaps with only a brief requiem. Those who died while their ship anchored at a city port were buried in the ground.[14]

Above all, the voyages from Indochina to France were long and dangerous. They were also emotionally draining. No doubt the manner in which the Indochinese died and were buried had a great psychological impact on the minds of the surviving recruits because *chết mất xác,* or dying without leaving a trace, was seen as a family curse in traditional Việt Nam. These voyages were also eye-opening experiences for the recruits whose lives, until then, had been sheltered, being confined behind the *lũy tre xanh,* or bamboo hedge.

On the Western Front

After arriving in France the soldiers formed nineteen *bataillons de l'infanterie coloniale*, or infantry battalions (hereafter BIC)—four combat battalions and fifteen labor battalions—and were stationed throughout France as support and labor units.[15] Although the majority of them had experienced cold weather in Tonkin and Annam, the winters of northern France were far colder than anything they had been exposed to. "It was so cold," one soldier wrote, "that my saliva immediately froze after I had spit it on the ground."[16] Another complained: "The chill of winter pierces my heart." To keep the colonial troops warm, besides issuing quilt vests, long underwear, wool coats, sheepskin jackets, boots, wool blankets, and wool socks, the military authorities also provided beds that were large enough to accommodate four soldiers. The hope was that, by sharing the same bed, the men would keep one another warm. Cochinchinese soldiers were treated differently, they were sent to the Midi to escape the harsh winter in the North.[17]

During the war, although civilians frequently faced fuel shortage, soldiers received a daily ration of heating fuel if they were stationed in civilian homes. Civilians, therefore, often invited soldiers to station in their homes because they would benefit from the soldiers' fuel supplies. But the fuel shortage affected soldiers as well. At Saint-Raphaël, members of BIC 3 had to walk fourteen kilometers to buy wood for their cooking and heating stoves. Sometimes, even though they had money, they could not buy wood. Once, they cut down trees in nearby residential areas and had to pay four hundred francs compensation to the owners of the trees.[18]

As the war escalated, national food production declined, and France had to depend on food supplies from overseas. However, as the battles on the sea intensified, shipments of food supplies arrived only sporadically. Like the French people, the Vietnamese soldiers eventually experienced the impact of food shortages. In 1916 they still bragged about the "fluffy white rice" and the wonderful food that they had daily. "In France," one wrote, "we lacked nothing except *nước mắm* [fish sauce]."[19] By mid-1917, when inflation was high and food was in short supply, they began to talk about "suffering" in their letters. Adjutant Dương Đoàn complained that wood, charcoal, and bread were scarce. Moreover, rice supplies no longer arrived regularly. Even the little food that they were given no longer suited their taste." It tastes like food for animals. Dogs would not want to eat the food we are eating." By early 1918, they had only "stale bread and salted fish to celebrate Tết" on the front lines. However, although they did not have enough to eat, they probably had more than the local civilians. Toward the end of the war, when civilians experienced hunger but soldiers were fed, Vietnamese soldiers were afraid to leave their camps because, according to soldier Thuận, they "might trigger the anger of the local people who are facing a famine." So, to kill time Thuận and his fellow soldiers usually went to a British military camp nearby and mingled with the British troops. Sometimes even soldiers did not have food to eat. They "ate roots and leaves, and chewed on bark." One soldier told his parents that he hated each day he had to live.[20]

Inadequate nutrition combined with harsh winters weakened the Vietnamese recruits' immune systems, causing a large number of them to fall ill easily. Passages from the journal of BIC 23 reveal that, as soon as the winter set in, the number of soldiers registered at military clinics and hospitals increased markedly. Influenza, ear infections, and bronchitis were especially prevalent. On October 11, 1917, thirty-five men visited the battalion clinics; on October 24, forty-four. By December the number of soldiers who visited medical clinics had reached sixty-six in one day, causing the battalion commander to voice his fear that his colonial soldiers would not be able to endure another winter. Apparently medical staff also faced shortages of medical supplies, and facilities were woefully inadequate: according to the journal, when the battalion commander heard that the American medical unit was leaving, he immediately hoped that the medical staff could "use their abandoned clinics and their equipment."[21]

Despite hardship letters from Vietnamese soldiers on the frontline indicate that they adapted well to the brutality of war and learned quickly that they had to kill or be killed. On the western front, the open ground separating the two enemies was known as "no man's land" and could be anywhere from fifty to five hundred yards wide. Sometimes soldiers on both sides would burrow underground toward the enemy's trenches. Two Germans made such an attempt in 1918 when Corporal Phạm Gốc was standing guard in a trench. They knocked him down and he was seriously wounded, but he was able to kill them.[22] Sometimes patrols from both sides would creep out of their trenches to venture into no man's land. Occasionally they would encounter an enemy patrol and engage in hand-to-hand combat. Private First Class Bùi Như Tĩnh always volunteered to go on patrol because he liked the thrill of fighting the enemy face to face.[23] The prospect of winning medals and rewards also motivated the men to volunteer for dangerous missions. In September 1918 Corporal Phạm Văn Lương encountered an enemy patrol. His men opened fire with their machine guns and took the Germans by surprise. The next day he was "promoted to the rank of a sergeant and awarded the Croix de Guerre."[24]

Since the Vietnamese soldiers' main duties had been to maintain the munitions supply lines, clean up the trenches, and clear the conquered territory, they usually did not suffer heavy casualties on the battlefield like the French. That changed in Aisne. In April 1917 at the battle of Aisne the French suffered 107,854 casualties in an unsuccessful attempt to retake the Chemin des Dames. None of the Vietnamese soldiers were wounded or killed in that battle.[25] Despite such a heavy loss, General Robert Nivelle ordered a second wave of attacks on May 5. Over the course of the next few days, members of BIC 7 took part in the fighting, which was often heavy, especially on May 7, when the Germans attempted to counterattack.[26] According to the journal of the battalion, 22 Vietnamese men were killed, 69 were missing, and 104 were wounded. Meanwhile, BICs 9 and 26 were also deployed as labor battalions in Aisne. From BIC 9, 24 men were killed, 68 were missing, and 119 others were wounded; from BIC 26, 3 men were killed and 28 others were wounded. A few soldiers in all three battalions received the Croix de Guerre, the highest award of the French army, while many received other military honors and citations.[27]

The journal of BIC 7 indicates that the Vietnamese and the American soldiers worked effectively together before the Americans emerged as a powerful army, sometimes participating in joint reconnaissance missions and coming to each other's assistance during battles. The letters of the Vietnamese soldiers in this period reveal that the Americans earned both the respect and the admiration of the colonial soldiers. Soldier Thanh at Chemin de Fer du Nord declared that the U.S. Army was the "strongest and the most powerful among the Allies." According to another Vietnamese soldier, the Americans were "fierce fighters." Still another commented: "The presence of the Americans on the battlefield restored the confidence of the Vietnamese."[28]

Members of labor battalions went wherever they were needed. They worked on construction projects, repaired roads and railroads, dug trenches, fixed telegraph lines, and built underground tunnels. They also transported munitions and troops and took care of the wounded and the sick. Although they did not engage in combat, they also had brushes with death while serving on the frontlines. Members of BIC 16, for example, repaired roads, guarded the train station, and provided security for the public in Froissy. Between September and December 1916 the train station in Froissy was subjected to frequent and often heavy air raids. Railroad tracks and buildings were damaged or destroyed, and a raid in December killed three Indochinese soldiers and wounded eight. After living through those events, Trực of the Sixth Engineering Corps wrote to his family: "It's horrible to see so many deaths! It's pitiful to see so many lose their legs and arms!"[29]

The military commanders reported that the Vietnamese troops performed extremely well during these operations. "They were remarkable in their performance . . . , steadfast in their resistance against the enemy. Although they were tired and had to fight under scorching heat and on a treacherous terrain, they ceded not an inch of their territory." Recalling the manner in which the members of BIC 7 had fought in the battle, the battalion commander later wrote: "The soldiers have shown that they are excellent combatants who have remarkable courage and are capable of taking the place of French soldiers in the front lines."[30] His comment echoed a comment made by one of the Indochinese troops in a letter: "We participated in the battle on a par with the French. Many of us died and many were wounded."[31]

From the letters of the Vietnamese men and official reports, we get a glimpse of their thoughts and their feelings about the war and about the respective qualities of the French, the Germans, and the Americans. For some the war was "brutal." For others it was like a "cockfight; although the adversaries were worn and bled, they went on pecking at each other, and neither side wanted to back down." One soldier observed: "Day and night they [the Germans, the French] . . . fought each other with grenades, shells, and poison gas." During the day the airplanes of both armies engaged in "dogfights," looking like "bamboo leaves whirling in the wind of a typhoon." At night troops from both sides tried to penetrate the enemy's trenches. One soldier told his parents: "We lived in constant fear." When there was no bombing, no artillery attack, and no gunfire, "living in the trenches was like living in a cemetery."[32]

In their letters readers also can detect a change of attitude toward the French people and France, which was seen as having lost its place as a great power. The French were not only "cowards but also lacked talent because they had only one-tenth of the Germans' military skill." The Americans, by contrast, stood out like *vua* [Kings] because they had fought well and ultimately brought victory. Soldier Sửu at Vincennes suggested: "France should pay tribute to the Americans and honor them as *Thầy* [Master]." Another man wrote: "God should let them occupy the throne of the world." In effect these Vietnamese believed that the Americans had gained a mandate to be the king of kings as a result of being the saviors of the world. Since a new king could name his prize, in his letter to his parents, Phụng of BIC 21 inquired if "the Americans had landed in Indochina to establish their protectorate."[33]

Moreover, as we have seen, the Vietnamese had shown themselves to be excellent soldiers, capable of replacing French troops on the front line. As a result, although some of them showed disdain for the French and admiration for the Americans, others bragged that the Vietnamese were the "brave ones": they "marched in the front, while the French cowardly followed." Not everybody agreed with those observations, however. In the view of soldier Thanh, who served at Chemin du Nord, the Vietnamese soldiers "were good only for eating and demanding good pay."[34] Quách Văn Khai offered an even more critical assessment: "Every time they [Vietnamese soldiers] went to the battlefield, they waved the white flag and went over to the enemy's side." Those comments contradict the evidence discussed earlier that generally the Vietnamese fought well, at least on a par with the French. Nonetheless, the Vietnamese also suffered heavy casualties: "Their bodies piled in heaps on the battlefield," wrote a Corporal Chấn of BIC 3. Many more were wounded or missing in action.[35]

It is also clear that these factors—the perceived poor performance of the French soldiers against the Germans, the excellent performance of the Vietnamese soldiers, and the superiority of the Americans— resulted in a loss of respect for the French to the extent that the Vietnamese no longer regarded themselves as inferior. This change of attitude, I will argue in one of following sections, contributed to the eventual downfall of French rule in Indochina.

On the Home Front

In September 1914, at the battle of the Marne, the Paris government realized that to win the war it needed to increase its production of weapons and munitions. The industrial sector was militarized, and industrial production was shifted toward armaments.[36] The shift toward armaments, however, faced an obstacle: a severe shortage of labor. Three-fourths of the industrial labor force was already mobilized to the front; and all able men between eighteen and forty-five had been called up.[37] As part of a solution to its labor problem, the Paris government turned to the colonies to recruit workers for their factories.

In 1915 it tested that idea by hiring a trial group of skilled Vietnamese workers. After seeing that their performance was satisfactory, it decided to hire more workers from Indochina to do the tasks that required little training and little or no knowledge of the French language. The Americans also hired them as laborers in construction projects and maintenance workers in military camps. Most of the skilled workers had a labor contract with their prospective employers before they left Indochina: after arriving in France they went to work immediately after passing a medical examination. Others had to take professional aptitude tests to determine their skills before the government's Job Placement Service and the Bureau of Agricultural Labor placed them with appropriate employers.[38] In effect the French government served as an employment agency, recruiting and channeling Vietnamese workers to prospective employers. It also served as the protector of these workers' rights and benefits. For example, its agents in the Control Services frequently visited workers' sites to provide workers with moral support and to make sure employers did not violate the terms of the labor contract and abuse workers. Moreover, it also made sure that unemployed workers received medical care (at its expense) and received physical rehabilitation and monetary compensation if they were disabled due to work-related accidents.[39] Apparently Vietnamese workers in France enjoyed certain rights and privileges, a contrast to the exploitative and oppressive treatment practiced by the French colonists in Indochina.

Like all foreign workers, the Vietnamese workers were issued IDs, which served as work permits. Each time a worker moved to a new job location, he had to turn in his ID and travel permit to the local police, who would give him a receipt; this receipt served as both a work and a travel permit. When the worker got a new job, he presented his labor contract to the police and got his personal documents back. A worker could quit his job if he found a better one. However, according to a government directive, if a worker changed jobs too frequently he would be sent back to Indochina.[40]

In accordance with the terms of the workers' contract, employers had to provide the men with lodging, food, and medical care. Official documents and personal letters reveal that the living and working conditions of Vietnamese workers differed from region to region and employer to employer, and workers responded in a variety of ways to their new living and working environments. Workers in Challuy, Nièvre, and Cazeaux slept on cold cement floors in unheated barns. In the winter, since each had only a light blanket, they put their beds together to form one long common bed and slept side by side, hoping that their combined body heat would keep them warm at night.[41] At military camps in Saint-Raphaël workers lived in brick buildings with tin roofs. Only a few workers had beds, while most slept on straw mattresses on dirt floors with no pillow. Their blankets were pillows in the summer and sleeping bags in the winter. They too slept side by side to keep their bodies warm.[42]

The living conditions of workers in naval centers like La Ciotat and Toulon on the coast of the Mediterranean seemed much better. In La Ciotat workers of the Société Provençale lived comfortably on the upper level of a two-story building, which had a separate dining room and kitchen. Each man had a bed with a headboard, a mattress, and a pillow. Their sleeping quarters were heated in the winter. Two of them cooked for the group and went shopping every day to buy fresh meat and vegetables for Vietnamese-style meals. Their employers even imported *nước mắm* [fish sauce] for them.[43] In Toulon workers also had a comfortable lifestyle, living on the fourth and fifth floors of a building. Their living arrangements were the same as those of French sailors—they slept in hammocks, which could be put away in their personal storage spaces during the day. Bathrooms and shower rooms had hot and cold water.[44]

In some cases living conditions were obviously substandard. At Poudrerie Lannemezan workers on a canal construction project had to live in wooden shacks and breath dust daily.[45] At Clermont-Ferrand the living space was overcrowded—each building was supposed to house only 175 men, but 225 resided there. Every day the workers had to walk 1.5 kilometers to get their meals. The plumbing in the residential quarters did not always work, and the men sometimes had no water for days at a time. In the winter they did not have sufficient coal or wood to heat their sleeping quarters.[46]

According to a directive of the Ministry of War, each worker was entitled to a daily allowance of 800 grams of rice, 250 grams of meat, 100 grams of bread, some vegetables, butter or lard, coffee, wine, and tea.[47] In practice, the portion of each item varied with the availability of local resources, the amount of money employers paid their employees for food allowances, and inflation, especially toward the end of the war when food and fuel were scarce. For example, workers at Marseille, Saint-Cyr, Vitry-sur-Seine, and Toulouse received the full amount of rice, meat, and bread while workers at the Poudrerie X were given only 600 grams of rice but received 250 grams of bread and 300 grams of meat. Some workers did not like the food they were given. In Tarbes, workers went on a hunger strike because the rice was usually undercooked. Workers in Pau found a way to supplement their diet: they used their leftovers to raise their own pigs in order to get the meat they wanted.[48]

By 1918, when France was economically devastated and faced a food crisis, some workers complained in their correspondence that the quality and quantity of their meals had declined. Trần Văn Phương in Toulouse observed that "food for workers was like food for pigs." In some places workers were "famished" and left work in search of food. Sometimes, even if they had money, they "could not find any food to buy" because the military authority prohibited local merchants from selling food to soldiers and government workers in order to save it for civilians.[49]

From the beginnings of their sojourn in France, the Indochinese workers lacked sufficient clothes. Two years after they arrived, some workers had only "tattered uniforms." A majority had no boots, no sandals, no work uniform, and no leggings although their contracts stipulated that these items be supplied to them. At one point there were only two hundred pairs of leggings for twenty-four hundred men, and all of them were given to nurses, soldiers, and commanders, who had priority over workers.[50]

According to prewar labor legislation, French workers had to work ten hours a day and six days a week.[51] The same law was applied to the Indochinese workers. In practice their working hours varied with the employers' demands. In Angoulême they worked in three shifts, one of which was eleven hours long. Workers on that shift were paid overtime of 0.50 francs per day. In Lyon workers in a department store worked nine hours, while hospital workers in Bergerac worked eight hours and workers in the manufactories of explosive powder ten hours.[52]

Over all, French employers seemed pleased with the performance of Vietnamese workers because "the Annamites" were hard working and diligent. The owner of a boot factory in Langlèe even replaced his entire French labor force with Indochinese workers. The employer preferred Vietnamese workers because they could produce more and better quality boots; moreover, their wages were lower.[53]

Socialization

Although the Vietnamese workers and soldiers worked long hours and were living under conditions of war, they had time for entertainment and other activities. In their free time they went to coffee shops, strolled on the streets, played soccer, attended night classes, and mingled with other ethnic and social groups.

In Marseille, dressed in khaki uniform and English-style tunics, they flocked to the Cercle Indochinois [Indochinese Club] after 6 p.m. to meet their countrymen.[54] At the club they could get pens, paper, and envelopes to write letters at no cost; they could also socialize with one another over puffs of free tobacco and free cups of tea. Beer, wine, hot chocolate, café au lait, and lemonade were not free, however. Wine, in particular, was limited to only one quart for every four persons. The club provided these men with magazines and newspapers published in *quốc ngữ* and French to read, and beds in which to nap in the gathering room. On most weekdays about 90 people frequented the club. On Sundays and paydays the number rose to between 200 and 250. On holidays it could be as high as 350. The club's customers came not only from Marseille but also from other areas in the department of Bouches du Rhône, such as Gironde, Aude,

Hérault, La Charente-Inférieure, Saint-Médard, La Ciotat, and Lyon-Venissieux.[55]

Instead of going out, some spent their evenings taking French and/or *quốc ngữ* lessons offered by volunteers, who were members of the Alliance Française. Although today the objective of the Alliance Française is to promote French culture and language, when it was founded by Albert Sarraut in 1915 its principal goal was "to provide social services and organize Vietnamese cultural activities" for Vietnamese soldiers and workers in France.[56] It organized night classes to teach them *quốc ngữ* and French, using French and Vietnamese volunteers who often were former teachers. Textbooks in French and *quốc ngữ* and school supplies such as pens, pencils, ink, and paper were imported from a dealer in Sài Gòn. By the end of the war about twenty-five thousand men had benefited from this educational program.[57]

Many preferred to stay in their compound and gamble. In Marseille card games were organized every night in some workers' compounds and even attracted Chinese, Arab, and North African workers. Some, like Sergeant Nhung, played only for fun. Others, like Sergeant Lương, played with passion. To borrow Anthony Reid's words, to expect these men to play cards "simply to pass the time without gambling would have been inconceivable."[58] Sometimes not only did these gamblers lose their whole paycheck, they also had to sell their clothing to pay their debts. Sergeant Lương had to ask his family in Indochina to send him some money so he could survive. Persistent losses led to disputes and even violence among players. According to Yên at Saint-Raphaël, a Senegalese worker stabbed him with a knife after losing a lot of money. Earlier Yên himself had injured a Senegalese and a Vietnamese named Bảy Lé in a fight after a card game.[59]

Although some people lost their earnings and went into debt, a majority of the Indochinese recruits used their earnings to buy treasury bonds, put their money in savings accounts, and sent some of it to their families in Indochina. According to one official report, by early 1918, 36,715 workers had bought treasury bonds valued at 411,030 francs, put 271,887 francs in saving banks, and sent a total of 5,261,026 francs to their families in Indochina. In addition some workers and soldiers often included money orders in the letters they sent to their families.[60]

Romance and Reality

The Indochinese workers and soldiers also had considerable interaction with French people and society. They frequented the homes of the local people, fell in love with French women, had French mistresses, and fathered mixed-blood children. Hence the Franco-Vietnamese relationships in France were the exact opposite of those that occurred in the colonial setting, where the men were French and the women Vietnamese. The French government consistently expressed concern about such attachments, ostensibly on the ground that differences between French and Indochinese attitudes about the role of women in the family and society were too great for French women to overcome. Consequently the authorities took steps to prevent couples from pursuing such relationships, and in the event that the relationships were established, they made it difficult for French women to go to Indochina to join their fiancés or their husbands.

The principal way that French officials learned about relationships between French women and Vietnamese men was through censorship of the mail. Postal censors read their letters and reported on the content. Sometimes they retained the letters, hoping that such relationships would wither from lack of communication between the two parties. Both the French women and the Indochinese men, however, were aware that the government opened and read their letters. A number of them stopped sending letters; some Indochinese men used French names to receive letters at local addresses.[61]

Local mayors also were instructed to report on any Indochinese men in their jurisdiction who were courting local women. Sometimes the woman's parents reported the man who was courting their daughter to local authorities. In turn the mayor reported him to military authorities in order to have him transferred to a different region. In one such a case a man who had impregnated an eighteen-year-old girl was imprisoned at the instigation of her parents. At his request the girl told the authority that a "white" man had made her pregnant. The man escaped being court-martialed but was kept in confinement for fifteen days for "daring to fall in love with a French girl."[62]

True love did exist between Vietnamese men and French women. Trường disobeyed his parents' orders and converted to Catholicism to marry his girlfriend. In one case a man was involved with two women at the same time. When one of the women realized that she was being deceived, she reported him to the military authorities.[63] In another instance the woman's parents welcomed their daughter's fiancé into their home and treated him as if he were a member of their family, only to learn later that he was already married and had children in Indochina. They were able to learn this because the governor general of Indochina had ordered a background check on all applicants who asked for permission to marry a French woman.[64]

Although the metropolitan government tried to deter French-Indochinese marriages, when it realized that a couple was serious, it found ways to help them realize their dream. Invariably, though, there was a price to be paid. In one case a man was given permission to marry a French woman and became a French citizen; however, on becoming a French citizen he was stripped of his rank and lost all his benefits as a noncommissioned officer in the colonial army. Worse yet, he was immediately incorporated into the metropolitan army as a "simple foot soldier." He wrote to a friend, saying: "In a few days, I will leave Castres with a happy heart and an awareness that my future will be filled with memories of my dear fiancée. Yes, Loulou will be mine soon. For more than a year we have suffered together. Together we have shed many tears to fight for only one goal: to be united. She has cried a lot because of me. [On the other hand,] I am a betrayer, the worst betrayer [of my country]. [But] I already swore my allegiance to my love. Alas, neither the difference in our races nor the vicious attack by people could take me away from her."[65]

By 1918 250 French-Indochinese couples were legally married in France. In addition, according to French records 231 couples lived together and 1,132 had love affairs. In Saint-Médard-en-Jalles, there were fifty mixed-blood children.[66]

The stories of these Franco-Vietnamese romances and marriages demonstrate that the Vietnamese men encountered and established relationships with people of all types and from various socioeconomic backgrounds. They had dealings with the local people in shops and restaurants and went to their homes for meals, for example. It is likely, therefore, that regular interaction with French people and society helped strip away the mystique surrounding the French in the eyes of the Indochinese, revealing them as ordinary men and women, not significantly different from and certainly not inherently superior to themselves.

Racialization and Proletarianization

Racial conflict between the French and men from the colonies, and between men from different parts of the French Empire, was not uncommon during the war. From the beginning the policy of the metropolitan government in the recruiting enterprise was not to let people from different ethnic backgrounds work together, fearing that the differences would lead to conflict. Nonetheless, the demand for workers in the military and private sectors ultimately determined the distribution of workers, and segregation of ethnic groups was not enforced. Consequently tension among workers from different parts of the French Empire emerged, resulting from cultural differences and language barriers.

Sometimes friction produced only mild irritation, as in the case of "blackening teeth," which, according to Anthony Reid, was a widespread practice in Southeast Asia, designed to decorate one's body and make it attractive.[67] However, in France it aroused widespread public curiosity. European coworkers and acquaintances bombarded the Vietnamese with the same question: "Why are your teeth black?" Since they lacked the words to explain in social and cultural terms, they came up with a simple answer, which Europeans could understand but which was not true: "We lacquer our teeth to prevent them from having cavities and being decayed."[68]

On a few occasions ethnic and cultural tension led to more serious incidents. European soldiers and officers often falsely accused Indochinese soldiers of wrongdoing, harassed them, and even physically abused them. The Vietnamese had no way to defend themselves but to react with violence. In one incident twelve military workers assaulted a French sergeant but did not kill him. They were court-martialed and executed. One of their countryman lamented: "We left our fathers and mothers to come here [to France] only to be executed by the people whom we try to save."[69] Ethnic tension and conflict were also evident among the Vietnamese and other ethnic groups. On All Saints Day (November 1) 1917, the courtyard of a factory in Saint-Chamas became a war zone where the workers from Cochinchina and Tonkin fought each other with fists and knives. The men from Cochinchina were outnumbered and lost. Sometimes the Vietnamese men sided with the French against other ethnic minorities. In November 1917 a fight broke out between the French and the

Chinese. The men from Cochinchina and Tonkin sided with the French to defeat the Chinese.[70]

In some cases ethnic tension led to outbreaks of violence between men from different French colonies. The 1918 Senegalese massacre of Vietnamese workers at Camp Sandet in Pau was the bloodiest such event. The massacre left fourteen Vietnamese workers dead and eighteen others seriously wounded. Three died in a hospital two days later. In addition the munitions depot was vandalized, and workers' barracks were demolished. More than four hundred Vietnamese workers were dispersed to different regions for fear that if they stayed together they would plot revenge for the deaths of their countrymen. In the aftermath of the event one French officer and three noncommissioned officers were given fifteen days in prison for failing to act properly. Interestingly only one Senegalese faced a criminal charge.[71]

In 1917 the heavy loss of lives and economic crises triggered waves of soldiers' mutinies and workers' protests. At the front French soldiers refused to go to the trenches despite government threats. On the home front workers staged protests to demand better working conditions, better pay, and immediate peace. In 1915 there were 98 strikes; in 1917 that number increased to 696. The workers' principal complaints were insufficient pay, overwork, and abuse by foremen.[72]

These developments did not escape the attention of the Vietnamese soldiers and workers. Trinh at Sorgues wrote to Thược in Marseille: "Let me tell you why the French workers are so powerful. They filed complaints against the managers of the shops, when they were not paid enough. [If they were not happy], they quit their jobs. There are no more French workers around here. These French workers are powerful. They set a fine example [for us]."[73]

It is unclear whether Vietnamese soldiers participated in the 1917 mutinies led by French soldiers. Vietnamese workers, however, soon began to participate in the labor movement. Between December 20 and 25, 1917, workers at École d'Aviation in Chartres refused to go to work because their workplaces were not heated. On January 15, 1918, workers in Tarbes refused to eat their meals because their cooks did not cook the rice properly. On February 24, 1918, "at the instigation of French women workers," the men at Bergerac went on strike to demand better wages. Two months later 150 workers in Bordeaux walked out on their jobs to protest bad living conditions and demand one extra day off each month. In July another group of workers walked out on their jobs to demand a three-day vacation every four months.[74] Toward the end of the war, the workers participated in demonstrations and strikes not only to protest bad treatment but also to advance political demands: Vietnamese workers in Bourges and Toulouse went on strike to demand a cease fire and an end to the war.[75]

It is reasonable to conclude that the examples of French soldiers refusing to fight and of a militant workforce confronting employers and the government contributed to a realization among Vietnamese workers and soldiers that the French were not a superior race and that French institutions, private and public, were not invulnerable. The participation of Vietnamese workers in industrial action demonstrates an awareness that they did not have to accept the status quo but could take action to promote their interests. This radicalization of Vietnamese workers and soldiers had consequences for Vietnamese society and French rule in Indochina: as discussed later, Vietnamese veterans of the war participated in industrial action and demonstrations in Việt Nam during the 1920s and 1930s and, in some cases, turned labor disputes into political unrest.

Demobilization and Homecoming

When the armistice was signed, 43,430 Vietnamese were serving in military units in France and about 5,500 were serving in the French army outside France. There were approximately 49,000 Vietnamese workers in France and about 2,000 outside France. By September 1919 the number of soldiers was reduced to 13,370—7,000 nurses, 370 clerical workers, and 6,000 drivers. By July 1920 only 4,000 remained in the French army, stationed in Germany, China, the Levant, Syria, Lebanon, Morocco, and the Balkans.[76] The demobilization of workers did not take place on a large scale until mid-1919, because they were needed in reconstruction projects, but it took place rapidly in the last six months of 1920. On June 1, 1920, 18,879 workers still remained in France. By December the number had fallen to 331.[77] Each of the veterans received a discharge bonus (250 francs for all workers and soldiers up to the rank of captain) and a payment ranging from 15 to 20 francs for each month they had served under the French flag.[78]

A small number of soldiers like Vũ Văn Qui, Mle 1431, reenlisted in the Army; and some workers like Bùi Văn Thược, Mle 83, renewed their labor contracts. A soldier or worker could stay in France if he found employment, if he was admitted to a professional school or an institution of higher education, if he was legally married to a French woman and had children with her, or if he had a sponsor who would pay for his education and living expenses.[79] Under the sponsorship of the government in Indochina, a selected number of Indochinese stayed in France to obtain a higher education or more training at professional schools. In such cases the colonial government paid their tuition, living expenses, and transportation back to Indochina when their studies and training were completed. In return they had to sign a note promising that they would return to Indochina. The professional training program lasted only six months, while the educational program could last longer. In 1918 55 Indochinese were admitted to institutions of higher learning, while 549 became apprentices at various undertakings. Arrangements were also made with the Confédération Général du Travail, or French Trade Union, and the Ministries of Marine and War, for 1,100 men to receive professional training in metallurgy, electrical work, mining schools, and naval construction.[80]

In the end, close to 2,900 Vietnamese soldiers and workers gained permission to remain in France to work, to study, or to get married. Of that number about 850 were students; 100 were skilled workers; 725 were sailors; and the rest were employed as domestic servants and manual laborers.[81] Those who remained in Europe formed the earliest Indochinese colonies in France and paved the way for the arrival of more immigrants from Indochina in postwar time.[82] In the 1920s the Indochinese immigrants formed a significant political block. Together they actively sought social recognition and admission to French schools and the job market.

Of those who returned to Indochina, a small number reenlisted in the colonial territorial army. The majority, however, returned to civilian life. A man who wanted to farm received between six and ten hectares of land, a buffalo, seed, and tools; during the first three years of residence on the land, he was also given 120 kilograms of rice and eight piasters per month. If he had children, each child received one piaster per month.[83] Some, like Corporal Nguyễn Văn Ba, returned to their villages, using their knowledge of modern technology to improve the lives of peasants. Tôn Đức Thắng, a sailor on a French ship during the war, who later became president of the Democratic Republic of Việt Nam, used his knowledge of organized labor to found the

Association of Workers of the Sài Gòn Arsenal in 1920 to advance workers' causes.[84]

With the help of the colonial government, about twelve thousand former unskilled workers who returned from France found employment in the industrial sector; thousands of others were hired as civil servants, as workers in government projects, and as village teachers, replacing the French teachers who were drafted during the war and did not return. The total number of veterans employed in the government and private sectors is not available, but there is evidence that those who were so employed formed a distinctive part of the modern labor force and were "better paid" than the majority of the wage laborers throughout Indochina.[85]

Although this might suggest that the veterans received fairly favorable treatment and encountered some success in the postwar era, the Indochinese who remained in Europe often faced prejudice from French workers. When the war was over, French soldiers returned home to reclaim their places on the factory floor and in business establishments. As a result of postwar social and economic instability, many were concerned that the presence of foreign workers might hurt their chances of finding a good job and/or depress the wages they might be paid.[86] To protect their interests, French workers lobbied to restrict foreign workers' access to the metropolitan job market and to deny them admission to labor unions. Fearing that these workers would stir up unrest, the Paris government granted some of their demands. In February 1921, for example, it prohibited French merchant marine companies from employing non-French citizens to work on their ships. French labor unions also acted. In 1922, for example, the syndicates of French sailors and workers on merchant marine ships refused to admit any Vietnamese into their unions. They argued that since the unemployment rate in the postwar period was high, French workers should have priority over foreign workers in obtaining jobs. In taking this action they hoped also to deter shipowners from hiring Vietnamese workers.[87]

Facing discrimination and threats to their livelihood, Vietnamese workers adopted the institutional arrangements and techniques of the French labor organizations that opposed them—that is, to form their own labor organizations—to champion workers' rights and to protect and promote their economic interests. Between 1923 and 1927 a number of Vietnamese workers' associations emerged: Association

Amicale des Travailleurs Indochinois (Friendly Association of Indochinese Workers), Association de Laqueurs (Association of Lacquer
Workers), and Association Mutuelle des Travailleurs (Workers'
Mutual Association). In addition in 1928 the Comité de Défense des
Travailleurs Annamites (Committee to Defend Annamite Workers)
was established to protect Vietnamese workers' rights and to assist
them in legal matters.[88]

To get political support Vietnamese workers rallied under the ban-
ners of the Ligue des Droits de l'Homme (League of Human Rights),
the Union Intercoloniale (Intercolonial Union), and the Club International des Marins (Sailors' International Club), all of which were
affiliated with the French Communist Party (PCF). Students formed
their own associations, such as the Union Fédérale des Étudiants and
the Association Générale des Étudiants Indochinois, which were also
under the umbrella of the PCF.[89] Under the sponsorship of the PCF,
workers and students published underground literature and engaged
in other illegal political networking. Not surprisingly their participation in these political organizations not only led to the development of
a small but effective political bloc in France but also eventually contributed to the development of political unrest in Indochina in the
1930s. Sailors, for example, were the international liaisons between
the Vietnamese communists in France and in Indochina; students and
workers who had returned from France used their new knowledge
and experiences to lead and shape the labor movement in Indochina.[90]

In Indochina one found tension, resentment, disappointment, and
distrust in the ranks of the veterans. Earlier I discussed how Vietnamese workers and soldiers in France were radicalized by the example of
a militant French workforce, and how some Vietnamese workers had
themselves engaged in industrial action. I also noted how the veterans
no longer saw the French as superior to themselves. Many were no
doubt also traumatized by their experiences in war. It is not surprising, therefore, that the veterans who returned to Indochina struck
others as difficult and decidedly different men. In the words of a contemporary reporter of *Le Courrier d'Haiphong*, "they were often violent, picking fights with other customers at restaurants, and causing
serious injuries to some." Some also showed disdain for local authority and instigated trouble in the village. When villagers were dissatis-
fied with local officials, veterans encouraged them to file complaints
with the French government and even volunteered to act as their

interpreters.[91] In the 1930s officials reported "widespread discontent among former soldiers and workers of World War I." Seventeen World War I veterans were among the participants in a military mutiny at Yên Báy. The veterans were among strikers in Hà Nội, Vinh, and Bến Thủy, waving the communist flag in demonstrations in May 1929, 1930, 1931, and 1933.[92]

One reason for the discontent felt by veterans was the difficulty they had in finding employment comparable with the work they had done in France. When they returned to Indochina, they expected to find the same kinds of jobs and make the same wages as they had in France. However, the number of factories in Indochina was relatively small, and production methods there continued to rely on human labor rather than on the power of machines. Hence there were few jobs for the "specialists."[93] Those who were able to find the jobs they wanted probably did not make as much money as they had made in France. As is also the case today, the wage scale in Indochina was much lower than in France. In addition, since Indochina's labor market was saturated with surplus labor, low wages were inevitable, while the opposite was true of the labor market and wage scale in France. Consequently the veterans experienced a decline in their incomes and a decline not only in their own standard of living but also in that of their families, whose standard of living had risen with the increase in family income during the war.

Postwar economic instability was also a major cause of the veterans' discontent. Most of them had saved as much money as they could while they were in France. They used their earnings to buy treasury bonds, put their money in saving accounts, and sent some of it to their families in Indochina. Unfortunately for them, postwar inflation and currency depreciation devalued their savings. The value of the franc steadily declined against the value of the piaster, from 4 francs to 1 piaster in 1918 to 27.50 francs to 1 piaster in 1926.[94] The veterans were losing money when their savings were converted from francs to piasters.

National economic disaster further fueled their discontent. In 1923 and 1924 Tonkin suffered great floods that caused a decline in rice production. The average amount of rice yield per capita between 1920 and 1927 was about 200 kilograms, not enough to feed the local population. According to Pierre Gourou, in normal times each peasant consumed about 277 kilograms of rice per year.[95] To make matters worse, the price of rice in the world market decreased steadily, from 38 piasters per 100 kilograms in 1919 to 14.25 piasters per 100 kilograms in 1929 and to only 6.2 piasters per 100 kilograms in 1934. At the same time domestic food prices kept rising due to inflation. The situation in Annam was particularly serious. In Nghệ An between 1910 and 1939, there were only four good harvests: 1915, 1918, 1924, and 1926.[96]

The year 1930 was the breaking point. Prices in the world market dropped markedly. Many companies went out of business. Metropolitan investment declined. Tens of thousands of Chinese immigrants left Indochina to return to China. Massive layoffs occurred. Close to one-third of the labor force in Việt Nam became unemployed. Many people committed suicide because they had lost their jobs. Among government workers 14 percent were laid off, while the rest had to accept a 30 percent cut in their salaries or volunteer to retire early. Workers' wages also declined between 30 and 80 percent. In Chợ Lớn, for example, a skilled worker made approximately 2.50 piasters daily in 1929. By 1934 he made only 1 piaster, that is, 60 percent less.[97] To make the situation worse, in 1932 the Red River Delta experienced a great flood. The water in the Red River reached the forty-foot mark, burying villages, submerging rice fields, destroying livestock, and killing many people.[98]

The early 1930s was a period marked by a series of violent protests, some led by the communists. In Cochinchina, demonstrations by business owners, Europeans and natives alike, against bankers were frequent. At the peak about fifteen thousand Europeans held demonstrations, blaming the Bank of Indochina for their misfortunes. Leading communist figures such as Nguyễn Văn Tạo and Trần Văn Thạch even spoke at their rallies.[99] In Annam, meanwhile, after a long period of drought and famine farmers in Nghệ An and Hà Tĩnh, where the largest number of veterans were located, vented their anger through violence. They looted government offices, burned tax records, and murdered local officials. The protest movement was widespread throughout Indochina. There were disruptions too in a number of major modern industrial and commercial establishments in Hà Nội, Hải Phòng, Sài Gòn, Chợ Lớn, Cần Thơ, and several other cities.[100]

A close examination of the pattern of Indochina's labor movement in the early 1930s reveals that it resembled French-style labor protests in which collective action, violence, and work stoppages were the means by which the workers and peasants asserted their demands and otherwise applied pressure to their employers. This was a departure from the historical pattern of conduct by disgruntled Vietnamese peasants and workers: it seems likely, therefore, that some veterans also had a role in organizing these protests, using their experience as workers and soldiers in France to shape the activities of the labor protests in Indochina in the 1930s.

Two main conclusions can be drawn from the evidence presented in this paper. First, contrary to what some previous commentators have argued, the great majority of the Vietnamese who went to France were not unwilling conscripts but rather volunteers. This is apparent from the financial and other benefits that they and their families received, and from the fact that generally they enjoyed wages and living and working conditions similar to those of French workers and soldiers. They were also able to mix more or less freely in French society and to become familiar with its social, political, and legal systems.

Second, it is apparent that the First World War marked a turning point in the history of the Franco-Indochinese relationship. In part it was almost a case of familiarity breeding contempt. The Indochinese soldiers and workers who answered the metropolitan government's call for a "sacred union" shared many difficult experiences with the French people. Like them the Indochinese endured hunger and hardship caused by a lack of food and fuel and by inflation. They fought the Germans on a par with French soldiers, worked long hours side by side with French workers, and joined the French workers in the labor movement. Without doubt these experiences changed their perceptions about the French and about the relationship between the metropole and the colonies as well as their attitudes toward the established order in Indochina. They no longer felt inferior to the French and began to question and resent French dominance.

In part it was also because workers returning from France had to some extent been radicalized by their experiences and were less inclined to be the docile workers traditionally associated with Indochina. In France they had seen what a unionized and militant workforce could achieve in defending and advancing the interests of workers. That experience gave rise to a new social class that was not content to return to the prewar status quo but was eager to claim a new place in society and prepared to challenge the established order. As we have seen, various factors caused discontent and unrest among those veterans who participated in strikes and demonstrations. In the final analysis there is no way to measure fully the extent to which the war transformed the lives of the veterans and their families in Indochina during and after the war. It is certain, however, that the workers who had been radicalized by their experience in France were not content simply to accept inferior living and working conditions. It is not surprising, therefore, to find them among the ranks of worker demonstrators in the 1920s and 1930s demanding better treatment and better pay. It is also not farfetched to suggest that they used the knowledge and experience gained during their time in France to advance workers' causes in those years. Of course, the development of worker and peasant movements in Việt Nam in the late 1920s and the 1930s, as the late Harry Benda eloquently argued more than three decades ago, was not exclusively a response to Western colonial rule. It was also a reaction to "social *malaise*" and started with demands for the redress of specific grievances, that is, suffering stemming from economic hardship.[101]

Finally, World War I led to the development of an Indochinese diaspora in France, whose members used their knowledge of the French political and legal system to establish themselves in French society and bring changes to the colonial structure in Indochina. Their anticolonial activities in France during the next few decades contributed to the eventual downfall of French rule in Indochina.

To summarize, the French decision to recruit the Vietnamese as soldiers and workers to serve in France during World War I had a profound effect on the development of the relationships between France and Indochina. It contributed to the development of worker and peasant movements in Indochina and of an anticolonial movement in both countries, both of which ultimately led to the downfall of French rule in Indochina.

Abbreviations

ACCM	Archives de Chambre de Commerce et d'Industries de Marseille
ADBR	Archives Departmentales des Bouches du Rhône (Marseilles)
BCCM	*Bulletin de Chambre de Commerce et d'Industrie de Marseille*
CP	Contrôle Postal (Postal Censorship Reports)

DCM	La Dépêche Coloniale et Maritime (Paris)
JMO	Journal de Marches et d'Operation du Bataillon Tirailleurs Indochinois
JOIF	Journal Officiel de l'Indochine Français
JORF	Journal Officiel de La République Française
NF	Nouveau Fond
PA	Papiers d'Agent (Albert Sarraut's files)
SLOTFOM	Service de Liason avec les Originaires des Territoires de la France d'Outre Mer
SHAT	Service Historique de l'Armée de Terre (Paris)

Archival Collection

Archives de Chambre de Commerce et d'Industries de Marseille. Valuable chiefly for business development and transaction in Marseille and between Marseille and the colonies.

Archives Departmentales des Bouches du Rhône. Little value on social and political activities of Vietnamese immigrants.

Archival sources such as Contrôle Postal reports, Nouveau Fond, and Albert Sarraut's papers are located at Centre des Archives d'Outre Mer (Aix-en-Provence) and Service Historique de l'Armée de Terre (Paris). Nouveau Fond and Service de Liason avec les Originaires des Territoires de la France d'Outre Mer are of great importance for interofficial communication between the Ministries of War and of the Colonies, as well as between the Ministry of the Colonies and the office of the governor general of Indochina, and reports of official inspectors concerning the everyday activities of government offices and of the immigrants in France.

Notes

1. Thompson, *French Indo-China,* 90, 480; Buttinger, *Vietnam,* 1:96, 490; Marr, *Vietnamese Tradition on Trial,* 5.

2. Lê Hữu Khoa, *Les Vietnamiens en France;* Marie-Eve Blanc, "La pratique associative vietnamienne"; Henri Eckert, "Les militaires indochinois au service de la France."

3. Mitchell, *International Historical Statistics,* 4, 8, 92, 95, 101–2. Between 1851 and 1911 the French population increased from 35,783,000 to 39,192,000; the German population, excluding the population in areas ceded by Austria, Denmark, and France between 1860–1871, increased from 33,413,000 to

64,926,000. The population in England and Wales increased from 17,928,000 to 36,070,000; see Wright, *France in Modern Times*, 306.

4. Oualid and Picquenard, *La guerre et le travail*, 63–66; Magraw, *History of the Working Class*, 2:132–33; Cross, *Immigrant Workers in Industrial France*, 34–40; Nogaro and Weil, *La main d'oeuvre étrangère et coloniale pendant la guerre*, 32–35; Albert Sarraut, *La mise en valeur des colonies françaises*, 41–43.

5. Cross, *Immigrant Workers*, 34–36; Nogaro and Weil, *La main d'oeuvre étrangère*, 32–35.

6. See Amireaux 1893–1934: The number ninety-nine thousand also included a few hundred Cambodians and a little more than a thousand French citizens; *JORF* 343 (1915); 10 SLOTFOM 6, "Liste nominative des gens de la famille royal d'Annam dans des bataillons indochinois" and "Liste nominative des gens de la famille royale d'Annam, comptant au 73e battailon sénégalais," March 15, 1919.

7. 9 PA 13, Memo from the governor of Cochinchina and the resident superiors of Tonkin, Annam, and Cambodia regarding the total number of soldiers and workers in France during World War I, June 2, 1918; NF 226, "Rapport sur la situation politique de l'Annam," April 12, 1916.

8. Sarraut, *La mise en valeur*, 42–43; Emanuel Bouhier, "Les troupes coloniales d'Indochine en 1914–1918," 69–81; *JOIF*, March 29, July 1, November 22, 1915, January 26, February 2, 1916.

9. Amireaux 1884, État Major, "Instructions générales sur le recrutement et l'incorporation des contingents indigènes fournis par l'Indochine en exécution des prescriptions de câblogrammes ministérielles no. 991 du 27 Novembre et no. 1056 du 13 Décembre, et du décret du 18 Décembre 1915"; 1 SLOTFOM 1, dossier 6, "Action de l'autorité militaire, rapport sur le recrutement indigène demandé à l'Indochine de Août à Décembre 1915"; SHAT 7N2121, "Rapport présenté à la Commission des Pensions militaires," n.d; 9 PA 13, "Le délégations d'ouvriers indigènes," *Le Courrier d'Haiphong*, September 12, 1917.

10. Amireaux 1883, Cablegram 406 from the Minister of the Colonies Doumergue to the Governor General of Indochina in Hà Nội, April 5, 1916.

11. 1 SLOTFOM 4; Amireaux 7599, Report by Inspector Saurin, October 12, 1916; Explanation from the Acting Governor Rivet, October 21, 1916; Dossier 6, "Action de l'autorité militaire: rapport sur le recrutement indigène," 9 PA 13/3 Memo from the governor of Cochinchina, superior residents of Tonkin, Annam, and Cambodia regarding the total number of soldiers and workers contributed to France during the war, June 2, 1918.

12. NF252, Circonscription administrative de l'Indochine, 1916; Ministère de la Guerre, "Instructions générales sur le recrutement et l'incorporation des contingents indigènes," January 3, 1916; Extrait 153 de l'instruction spéciale, January 11, 1916; ADBR, 531 U 414 and 531 U 417, "Rapports de mer," 1916.

13. ACCM, "Rapport de mer" by the captain of the *Meinam*, December 6 and 7, 1916. Amireaux 1883, Cablegram from the minister of the colonies to the governor general in Indochina, April 5, 1916; Journal de Marche et d'Opération du 13e Bataillon Tirailleurs Indochinois.

14. ADBR 531 U 417 and 531 U 419; ACCM "Rapport de mer" by the captain of the *Meinam* on line Marseille-Hải Phòng-Marseille; NF 246, Circulaire 56,868–5/8 Direction to all commanders of the colonial troops; ACCM, "Rapport de mer" by captain of the *Athos,* December 7, 1916.

15. Exposition Coloniale de Paris, *Les armées françaises d'outre-mer,* 72–97.

16. From this point forward, all translations in the text are mine.

17. NF 227, CP January 1918; Eckert, "Les militaires indochinois," 20–525; 10 SLOTFOM 5, Note for the Council of War on the question of wintering for Indochinese soldiers, September 5, 1917; 16 N 196, Report by Lt. Mangin in the First Bureau, Army Zone 6, 16, March 18, 1917; Marquet, *Lettres d'annamites,* 32.

18. Eckert, "Les militaires indochinois," 520–25; 10 SLOTFOM 5, NF 227, Reports by Dupuy-Volny and Tri Phủ Vinh, August 31, 1918.

19. NF 227, Sergeant Đỗ Văn Tâm.

20. 1 SLOTFOM 8, CP November 1917; NF 227, CP January and March 1918.

21. JMO of BIC 23; "Les Annamites en France pendant la guerre," *DCM,* June 20, 1916; 10 SLOTFOM 5, Report by Tri Phủ Nguyễn Văn Vinh about his visit to the Third and the Seventh Battalions at Saint-Raphaël and letter from Dupuy-Volny to Pierre Guesde, the superior resident of the Worker Control Services.

22. 10 SLOTFOM 4, Decorations of War.

23. Buchan, *History of the Great War,* 3:457–61; Koeltz, *La guerre de 1914–1918,* 267–75, 379; 10 SLOTFOM 4, Decorations of War.

24. NF 227, CP November 1917.

25. JMO of BIC 7; Buchan, *History of the Great War,* 3:465–76; Koeltz, *La guerre de 1914–1918,* 345–59.

26. JMO of BIC 7.

27. JMO of BICs 7, 9, 26; 10 SLOTFOM 4, Decorations of War.

28. 1 SLOTFOM 8, Report by Josselme, July 1919; NF 246, 3 SLOTFOM 93; 10 SLOTFOM 5, 1 SLOTFOM 8, CP May 1918–June 1919.

29. JMO of BIC 16.

30. Exposition Coloniale Internationale de Paris, *Les armées françaises d' outre mer,* 95, 96; JMO of BIC 7.

31. 1 SLOTFOM 8.

32. NF 227, 1 SLOTFOM 8, June and September 1918.

33. 1 SLOTFOM 8, CP March, May, and June 1918.

34. 1 SLOTFOM 8, CP September 1918.

35. NF 227, CP March, June 1918.

36. Hardach, "Industrial Mobilization" 60; Grenville, *History of the World,* 95.

37. Hardach, "Industrial Mobilization," 57–59; Clark, Hamilton, and Moulton, *Readings in the Economics of War,* 189; Magraw, *History of the Working Class,* 2:133.

38. Dương Văn Giao, "l'Indochine pendant la guerre de 1914–1918," 125–30; NF 226 and 244, Ministère de La Guerre, "Situation numérique d'effectifs

des groupements au 1 Fevrier, 1 Mars, 1 Avril, 1 Juin, 1 Juillet 1918"; 10 SLOT-FOM 4, "Les Indochinois en France"; 1 SLOTFOM 4, "Note sommaire sur le service de contrôle et d'assistance des Indochinois en France"; "La main-d'oeuvre indochinoise en France," *DCM*, September 7, 1915, and January 28, 1916; 9 PA 13, "La main d'oeuvre agricole dans la métropole," *l'Opinion*, August 28, 1917; JOIF, "Main d'oeuvre étrangère et coloniale en France," August 22, 1916; Decree concerning the recruitment, distribution, and surveillance of foreign and colonial workers in France in "Correspondances et documents," BCCM, nos. 143–44 (April 28–May 5, 1917).

39. 1 SLOTFOM 4, Summary of the role of the agents of the Worker Control Services 16 N 1507, Memo from the War Council to the commanders of colonial workers on the subject of workers' compensation, April 21, 1916; NF 226, Policy on sick leave by General Aube, the director of the Colonial Troops, July 12, 1918.

40. "Main d'oeuvre étrangère et coloniale en France," *JOIF*, August 22, 1916; Decree concerning the recruitment, distribution, and surveillance of foreign and colonial workers in France in "Correspondances et documents," *BCCM*, nos. 143–44 (April 28–May 5, 1917).

41. 10 SLOTFOM 3 and 5, Reports by Lamarre, January 21, 30 and February 27, 1918; NF 250, NF 246/249, Report by Przyluski, May 1918.

42. 10 SLOTFOM 5, Reports by Tri Phủ Vinh and Dupuy Volny, January and April 1918.

43. 9 PA 13, "Les Indochinois en France," *Le Courrier d'Haiphong*, June 25 and 26, 1917.

44. "Le groupement des travailleurs indochinois employés à l'arsenal de Toulon," *Le Courrier d'Haiphong*, March 28, 1917.

45. 10 SLOTFOM 3, Report by Lammare, July 8, 1918.

46. 10 SLOTFOM 5, Reports of 1917 and 1918.

47. Ministry of War, Notice No. 4686–5/8, August 1916.

48. "Les Indochinois en France," *Le Courrier d'Haiphong*, June 25, 26, 1917; "Les ouvriers annamites en France," *l'Avenir du Tonkin*, March 24, 1917; NF 249, Note from Pierre Guesde to the governor general of Indochina, December 1917; "Les ouvriers annamites en France," *l'Avenir du Tonkin*, March 24, 1917.

49. 10 SLOTFOM 5, February 1918 report.

50. 10 SLOTFOM 4, June 1917 and January, March, and June 1918 reports.

51. Dubesset, Thébaud, and Vincent, "Female Munition Workers of the Seine," 92.

52. 10 SLOTFOM 3, June 1917 report.

53. 10 SLOTFOM 4, February 1918 report; "Des travailleurs employés par la Société Provençale des Constructions Navales," *Le Courrier d'Haiphong*, June 25, 26, 1917.

54. "Les Indochinois en France," *l'Opinion*, November 27, 1918.

55. 1 SLOTFOM 2, Report by G. du Vaure, August 4, 1916; "Correspondances et documents," *BCCM*, 3eme Année, nos. 81–82 (February 19–26, 1916): 181–83; and "Inauguration du cercle des travailleurs indochinois,"

BCCM, nos. 94–95 (May 20–27, 1916); 1 SLOTFOM 4, Report by J. Bosc, April 28, 1917; Amireaux 1882, Memo dated November 8, 1918.

56. I SLOTFOM 1, from the report of the Budget General of Indochina, 1919.

57. Ibid.; NF 258 and 264; 9 PA 13, Phạm Gia Thuỷ, "Les ouvriers annamites en France," *l'Avenir du Tonkin,* March 24, 1917.

58. Reid, *Southeast Asia in the Age of Commerce,* 1:197.

59. 1 SLOTFOM 8, CP November 1917; NF 227, CP January 1918; 3 SLOTFOM 93; 10 SLOTFOM 5.

60. NF 226, 227, 246/249; 3 SLOTFOM 93; 10 SLOTFOM 5.

61. NF 227, CP Report, March 1918.

62. Ibid.

63. 1 SLOTFOM 8, CP Reports, March 1917 and November 1918; 7 N 97, CP Report, August 1917.

64. 3 SLOTFOM 93, Report by Przyluski, June 1918; "Circulaire confidentiale de Sceaux," 1918; Cablegram from Albert Sarraut to the minister of the colonies, March 1919.

65. NF 227, Lê Văn Nghiệp, CP Report, March 1918.

66. 10 SLOTFOM 5, 1918 report; Rives and Deroo with Pinaeau, *Les Linh Tap,* 63.

67. Reid, *Southeast Asia in the Age of Commerce,* 1:75.

68. 1 SLOTFOM 8, 1916 report.

69. 10 SLOTFOM 5, November 1918 official reports; 3 SLOTFOM 93, CP report, July 31, 1918.

70. 10 SLOTFOM 5, Memo from the Service for Organization of the Colonial Workers in France to the Minister of the Colonies on Angoulême; 1 SLOTFOM 8, 1918 report.

71. 10 SLOTFOM 5, Report by Paul Chassaing on incident at Pau, November 7, 1918; Note 367 from Pierre Guesde, the superior resident of the Worker Control Services, November 14, 1918; Report by Colonel Briand, commander of Senegalese Camp at Sendet, November 16, 1918; Report by Tri Phu Vinh, November 6, 1918; Note 101 from the minister of the Colonies to the president of the War Council, February 13, 1919; Note from the president of the War Council to the minister of the colonies, March 6, 1919.

72. Oualid and Picquenard, *La guerre et le travail,* 24, 330–48; Dubesset, Thébaud, and Vincent, "Female Munition Workers of the Seine," 203. See also Smith, *Between Mutiny and Obedience.*

73. NF 227.

74. 10 SLOTFOM 3, NF 227 and 246, February, March, and April 1918 reports.

75. NF 246, CP May 1918.

76. Sarraut, *La mise en valeur,* 44; 10 SLOTFOM 4–5, Note from the Ministry of War to the Ministry of the Colonies, March 4, March 22, July 1, 1919; 10 SLOTFOM 6; 12 SLOTFOM 1 and 2; Eckert, "Les militaires indochinois," 96.

77. 10 SLOTFOM 4, Report from the Bureau of the Colonial Troop Control Services.

78. "Acte de la métropole," *JOIF*, July 16, 1919.

79. Interministerial memo on the demobilization of colonial soldiers and workers, other than Algerians and Tunisians, who petition to stay in France, April 4, 1919; Addendum to the interministerial memo of 4 April 1919, Erratum to the interministerial memo of April 4, 1919 and to the addendum of April 16, 1919, Rectification to the interministerial memo on April 4, 1919, by the Bureau of Military Services, December 7, 1919.

80. 10 SLOTFOM 4, Cablegram from the governor general of Indochina to the minister of public education, October 30, 1918.

81. 1 SLOTFOM 4, Dossier 6, Report from the Worker Control Services, 1932.

82. See SLOTFOM series 1, 3, 12; and McConnell, *Leftward Journey*.

83. Robequain, *Economic Development of French Indochina*, 59, 65–71; Gourou, *Peasants of the Tonkin Delta*, 242–43; Dương Văn Giao, "l'Indochine pendant la guerre," 133–44.

84. Marquet, *Lettres d'annamites*, 68–69; Brocheux and Hémery, *Indochine*, 204. See also Giebel, "Tôn Đức Thắng and the Imagined Ancestries of Vietnamese Communism."

85. 10 SLOTFOM 4, Note in file; Brocheux and Hémery, *Indochine*, 201; "l' ouvriers indigènes en France," *Le Courrier d'Haiphong*, October 13, 1918; Murray, *Development of Capitalism in Colonial Indochina*, 224.

86. 10 SLOTFOM 6, Note in file on the subject of "The Maintaining of the Indochinese Labor Force in France," 1918.

87. 10 SLOTFOM 8 and 9, Letters from the under secretary of state to the minister of public works and the general controller of Indochinese workers, April 25 and May 9, 1922; Note from the governor general of Indochina, April 29, 1922; 6 SLOTFOM 8, letters from SR agent Jolin on the subject of Indochinese soldiers who entered France illegally, May 17, 1922.

88. 1 SLOTFOM 4; 3 SLOTFOM 1–4, 32, A. S. de la Colonie Indochinoise de Paris, December 1929; Extrait de la lettre no. 2277 du Délégué du C. A. I. à Marseille, Note sur la propagande révolutionnaire, July 22, 1929; 3 SLOTFOM 53, Letter from the police Commissioner of Marseille to the prefect of the department of Bouches du Rhône, May 21, 1928, and February 5, 1930.

89. 3 SLOTFOM 32, A. S. de la colonie indochinoise de Paris, December 1929.

90. 3 SLOTFOM 5, Leaflets distributed to Indochinese workers by the French Communist Party during the demonstrations in Paris in 1930, "Appel du S. R. I pour la libération de tous les emprisonnés," *l'Humanité*, July 8, 1929; Brocheux and Hémery, *Indochine*, 201.

91. "Un état d'esprit nouveau: grave barrage, les ONS contre tirailleurs," *l'Opinon*, November 8, 1918; "Barrage sanglante," *Le Courrier Saigonnais*, November 8, 1918; Dương Văn Giao, "l'Indochine pendant la guerre," 133–44.

92. 3 SLOTFOM 22; 3 SLOTFOM 7.

93. R. Helgé, "Problème de demain," *Le Courrier d'Haiphong*, May 9, 1917.

94. *JOIF*, June 1919–November 1920; Courdurie and Miège, *Histoire du commerce et de l'industrie de Marseille*, 374.

95. Pierre Gourou, *l'utilisation du sol en Indochine* (Paris: n. p, 1940), quoted in Tạ Thị Thúy, "Rice Cultivating and Cattle Raising," 92.

96. Tạ Thị Thúy, "Rice Cultivating and Cattle Raising," 88–91; Jean-Dominique Giacometti, "Wages and Consumer Prices for Urban and Industrial Workers in Vietnam under French Rule," 113–19; and idem, "Bases for Estimation of Agriculture in Central Vietnam before 1954," 211–14.

97. Huỳnh Kim Khánh, *Vietnamese Communism*, 143–47; Hémery, *Révolutionnaires vietnamiens et pouvoir colonial en Indochine*, 226–31.

98. Gourou, *Peasants of the Tonkin Delta*, 77.

99. Huỳnh Kim Khánh, *Vietnamese Communism*, 143–47; NF 2635, 2636, 2639.

100. Huỳnh Kim Khánh, *Vietnamese Communism*, 143–47; Hémery, *Révolutionnaires vietnamiens et pouvoir colonial*, 231–47; Brocheux and Hémery, *Indochine*, 304–10.

101. Benda, "Peasant Movements in Colonial Southeast Asia," 221–24.

10

Recasting Pigneau de Béhaine

Missionaries and the Politics of French Colonial History, 1894–1914

JAMES P. DAUGHTON

For many scholars of French colonialism, the figure of Pigneau de Béhaine, bishop of Adran, represents a critical moment in the history of the French presence in Southeast Asia. History books—from scholarly texts to more popular narratives—commonly recount how the young missionary brokered an agreement at Versailles between his king, Louis XVI, and Nguyễn Ánh, the leader (*chúa*) of the struggling family in Cochin China.[1] Pigneau most often emerges in these accounts as a patriotic Frenchman, motivated in large part by a love of country and a desire to see France take an active role in Indochina. The bishop's supplying, training, and leading of Nguyễn Ánh's troops in their clashes with Tây Sơn forces foreshadowed French involvement to come: in the wake of military victory Pigneau and a handful of French advisors helped Nguyễn Ánh consolidate his rule over Việt Nam. Such were the origins, according to this narrative, of France's political, economic, and cultural ties to Indochina.

More specific studies of Pigneau's role in Nguyễn Ánh's struggle for power suggest a number of problems with this common account of the bishop's deeds. Looking at archival material, including Pigneau's own correspondence, historians such as Pierre-Yves Manguin and Frédéric Mantienne have pointed out that Pigneau was motivated far less by hopes of expanding France's empire than by a desire to protect the region from the influence of Protestant powers such as England and Holland.[2] This picture of Pigneau shows him first and foremost to be a missionary, driven to protect his life's work, spreading Catholicism. Because France was a Catholic power, Pigneau sought his country's support, but his primary allegiance remained to God and church, not king and country.

These contrasting historical portraits of Pigneau de Béhaine raise an important question: how did the bishop of Adran, a missionary whose own correspondence reveals a fundamental commitment to Catholic evangelizing, become a patriot of France and a champion of French colonial expansion? In other words, when and under what circumstances did historical accounts of Pigneau de Béhaine acquire such patriotic flourishes and begin to downplay his religious zeal? In addressing these questions, this study is concerned less with exploring Pigneau de Béhaine's actual motivations in turning to Louis XVI's government for assistance in 1787 than with examining how a variety of journalists, historians, and commentators portrayed and even redefined the bishop's goals and accomplishments over the course of the century after his death.

Interest in the historical significance of Pigneau's life blossomed in the 1890s when Catholic missionaries and a handful of colonists agreed to raise funds to erect a statue of the bishop in front of Sài Gòn Cathedral. The planned ceremony, which celebrated the centenary of his death, gave the Catholic mission the opportunity not only to revisit the accomplishments of the late-eighteenth century missionary but also to reassess the role of twentieth-century missionaries in the colony. As Patrick Tuck has shown, in the 1890s and early 1900s the Catholic mission in Indochina increasingly faced attack.[3] Pressure came from both radical left-wing colonists in Indochina who rejected religious proselytization as detrimental to republican colonial aims and from anticlerics in France spurred by the polemics of the Dreyfus Affair. Anticlericalism posed a real threat to the mission: politicians in

France and colonists abroad called for banning Christian missions in France's overseas possessions, ending a centuries-old tradition.

In this quarrelsome political atmosphere, the centenary commemoration of Pigneau de Béhaine's death, with its biographies, articles, speeches, and unveiling ceremony, allowed missionaries to assert their commitment to French colonial expansion and disarm accusations that they lacked patriotism. In short, at the turn of the twentieth century, missionaries rehabilitated and recast a historical figure— Pigneau de Béhaine, bishop of Adran—to give meaning to their present predicament and to safeguard their future proselytizing work. This rhetorical campaign, however, did not go unchallenged: the centenary also brought forth critics of the mission who openly questioned both Pigneau's and contemporary missionaries' loyalty to France. In the debates that followed, the image of Pigneau became a symbol around which a variety of Frenchmen—from missionaries to radical Freemasons—debated the definition of French patriotism as well as the nature and moral justification of French colonialism in Indochina.

Pigneau de Béhaine and "French" Involvement in Cochin China

In April 1897, at a meeting presided over by the governor general of Indochina, a group of organizers committed themselves to raise a monument in Sài Gòn to mark the centenary of Pigneau's death; "from the head of the colony and its functionaries and officers to the colonists and missionaries, all, without distinction of party or religion," agreed to raise money.[4] Indeed, support for the project did not come simply from *religieux*. The director of posts, for example, assumed the presidency of a committee in Tonkin to raise money for the monument, aided by a wide array of colonists, from a banker and a member of the chamber of commerce to a doctor and a military man.[5] Financial support came from Vietnamese sources as well; at least seventy Vietnamese bureaucrats, teachers, and students gave money for the monument, which would include a statue of Prince Cảnh.[6] The Vietnamese government at Huế also recognized Pigneau's role in the formation of colonial Việt Nam, requesting that a copy of his portrait be hung at the royal court.[7] As an apostolic vicar in Sài Gòn observed, Pigneau de Béhaine brought together "all the French and Annamite patriots of Indo-China."[8]

Who was Pigneau de Béhaine, and why did he garner such apparent admiration from all sides? Born in the Aisne in 1741, Pierre-Joseph-Georges Pigneau left for Southeast Asia in 1765, where he was a teacher in Hon Dat, in the gulf of Cambodia.[9] Later arrested by invading Siamese troops, Pigneau was forced to flee to India, where he was named bishop of Adran in 1771.[10] Five years later, he again went east, this time to Cochin China, a region in the throes of civil war. The ruling Nguyễn family was in disarray, threatened by the Tây Sơn uprising. Rebels killed the head of the Nguyễn family and his eldest son at Huế and sent the family's entourage fleeing south. Nguyễn officials called on various European officers in Asia— Portuguese, Dutch, and British—throughout the late 1770s, informally asking for assistance in their fight against Tây Sơn forces. The British offered assistance, though their plans for involvement aimed to aid British merchants more than the Nguyễn. In 1776 or 1777, Pigneau de Béhaine met and befriended Nguyễn Phước Ánh, the eldest living male in the Nguyễn family, on Phú Quốc Island, where the two had sought haven from the fighting in Cochin China. Pigneau agreed to act as intermediary in 1781 between Nguyễn Ánh and European powers in India. At first Nguyễn Ánh requested only material aid, which he ultimately received, though it did little good. On the brink of defeat Nguyễn Ánh finally asked for formal help from Europe in 1785, turning again to his friend Pigneau to assist him.[11]

Exactly what followed was to become the topic of much debate among historians, commentators, and politicians at the end of the nineteenth century. What is certain is that in 1787 Pigneau returned to Paris, accompanied by Nguyễn Ánh's five-year-old son, Prince Cảnh, to secure troops and arms from Louis XVI. The young Cảnh proved to be popular at court, so admired for his kind nature that the queen's hairdresser, the famous Léonard, even created a man's hairstyle, *"au prince de Cochinchine."*[12] Though Louis's monarchy faced its own problems, the French king agreed to support Nguyễn Ánh's attempt to take power. The treaty of November 28, 1787, promised troops, arms, and ships for Cochin China in exchange for French control of the island of Puolo Condor and the port of Tourane as well as commercial privileges for French merchants.[13] The treaty, however, though full of symbolic value, failed to help the Nguyễn cause. France proved too preoccupied with its own civil strife to offer help in distant Cochin

China; the official promise of men and arms offered by the treaty went unfulfilled.

Pigneau returned to Cochin China, where in late 1788 Nguyễn Ánh had begun to push back the Tây Sơn. With fighting stalled in the south of Cochin China, Pigneau organized a group of French officers and soldiers from Pondichéry without the official cooperation of the French monarchy. More important than men and equipment, the Frenchmen offered technical assistance and instruction in the use of artillery, ships, and fortifications. Pigneau himself led a successful raid of Tây Sơn forces in the south. The victory helped turn the conflict, and Nguyễn Ánh—who took the reign name Gia Long once the Tây Sơn were defeated—ultimately took power in Huế in 1801. Until his death in 1799, Pigneau remained a friend and close advisor to the Nguyễn leader. For his funeral Gia Long built for the bishop an elaborate tomb and delivered a eulogy at the graveside. "I had a wise man," Gia Long began, "the intimate confidant of all my secrets, who, despite the distance of thousands and thousands of leagues, came to my country, and never left me, even when fortune abandoned me."[14]

Pigneau de Béhaine's reasons for turning to France for help remain far less clear than this account suggests. Most suspect was the claim—made by missionaries, as we shall see, a century after his death—that Pigneau was motivated by patriotism and by a desire to see French colonial involvement in Indochina. In the mid-1780s, an array of powers, including England, Portugal, Spain, France, and Holland, could have potentially helped Nguyễn Ánh's cause. When Nguyễn Ánh asked Pigneau's advice, the bishop's first concern was to find a suitable Catholic nation to help. As Frédéric Mantienne has pointed out, despite later accounts, neither man specifically sought help from France; in fact, Pigneau's first request went to the Spanish in Manila.[15] In early 1785, he turned to the French in Pondichéry for help, only to be harshly rejected. In a letter to the Missions Étrangères, the bishop described the Frenchmen he encountered there as "impious" and "enemies of religion"; ultimately, he determined that asking for their help would do as much damage to the mission as "any other heretic nation" would.[16]

Pigneau turned next to Macao and then to Goa in search of Portuguese assistance. Negotiations lasted more than a year but failed to secure a commitment. Still without military support in 1786, Pigneau finally determined to turn to France. Even with the bishop talking to

Louis XVI, Nguyễn Ánh continued to discuss his plight with the Portuguese through merchants in Macao and Goa. In letters aimed at winning money and supplies, Nguyễn Ánh himself wrote to Macao speaking of how "the people of Portugal and Vietnam . . . are like children in the same family."[17] The treaty Nguyễn Ánh offered the Portuguese was almost identical to the one Pigneau had signed in Versailles, suggesting that the two men were more concerned with terms and results than with which country would assist their cause.[18]

At the forefront of Pigneau's thinking was certainly religion. Since 1659 the Congregation for the Propagation of the Faith in Rome repeatedly reminded missionaries to have no national allegiances and to avoid meddling in all forms of politics.[19] Such activity, Rome believed, detracted from a missionary's one true goal: to spread the word of God. Missionaries such as Pigneau, however, did become involved in political struggles, but for reasons of promoting Catholicism rather than for national gains. As Adrien Launay noted in his 1894 history of the Missions Étrangères, all members of the society in that period dreamt of Catholicism reigning the world over. Nguyễn Ánh, though he never converted to Catholicism, appeared to Pigneau as potentially a "new Constantine, king of all of Annam, prostrate with his subjects at the foot of the conquering and sovereign cross."[20]

Despite the apparent limitations of his patriotism, Pigneau de Béhaine slowly emerged in French political and historical accounts as a symbol of the origins of "French" interests and influence in Việt Nam. Reference to Pigneau de Béhaine's work surfaced during periods of French political or military conquest in the region, from midcentury forward, adding historical legitimacy to the colonial project. As one historian has remarked, "as with her other colonies, France successfully raked history for proofs of her interest in Indo-China."[21]

In 1863, for example, a writer in the center-right *Moniteur Universel* was one of the first to credit Pigneau with forging a union between France and Việt Nam.[22] In the wake of a treaty securing French influence over Cochin China, and with French interest in Cambodia mounting, the author noted that "very few people . . . know the origins of France's relations with Cochin China, the first treaty, concluded in 1787 between the two kingdoms, and the considerable services then rendered *by France* to Cochinchina in executing this treaty."[23] The author ignored the fact that a French commission set up in 1857 to examine the Versailles treaty had found it to be legally null and void.[24] Instead, what the author lacked in historical fact, he made up for with patriotic rhetoric. Accordingly, Pigneau—a "great and patriotic Frenchmen, as well as great and pious bishop"—knew that Gia Long could seek help from the British, Dutch, or Portuguese but felt, according to the author, that the "glory of a restoration" must be given to France, "his *patrie*."[25]

The article established a direct historical link between Pigneau's work and France's present colonial aspirations. Unfazed by the fact that France never fulfilled its obligations under the treaty of 1787, the *Moniteur Universel* author spoke of *France's* decisive contribution to Gia Long's plight. "When the goal is achieved," the writer asked, "what does it matter if it's by a volunteer army or the regular army?" "The king of Cochin China was established?—Yes. By whom?—By France. Do we not see in this event the signature, the flag, the gold, the blood, and, in the end, the glory of France?"[26] After this "French" victory, he continued, Gia Long did not act without the consent of Pigneau. And the bishop's sage counsel still shaped Vietnamese respect for the French nearly seventy-five years later; the *Moniteur* biography quoted various reporters who claimed that all Vietnamese were still full of "the warmest sympathy" for the French, whom they saw as the "children of the great master"—the term of endearment the Vietnamese gave Pigneau.[27]

Another account, from a few years later, went into slightly more detail about Pigneau's deal making but remained clear that the bishop was an agent of France. Michel Đức Chaigneau's 1867 *Souvenirs de Hué* was based on the experiences of the author's father, who had accompanied Pigneau de Béhaine to Cochin China and stayed on after his death as an advisor to Gia Long. Though less overtly patriotic than the *Moniteur Universel* article, Chaigneau did not complicate his narrative with the intricacies of Pigneau's negotiations at Pondichéry and Macao, opting instead to portray the bishop's return to Versailles as the inevitable act of a Frenchman in need of assistance. Nor was Chaigneau bothered by Pondichéry's refusal to honor the treaty upon Pigneau's return from Versailles. In this account, like the *Moniteur Universel*, the author attributed little importance to the difference between a French government-sponsored project and an ad hoc collection of officers, merchants, and soldiers.[28]

The first real biography to appear on Pigneau was Alexis Faure's 1891 book, *Les Français en Cochinchine au XVIIIe siècle: Mgr Pigneau de Béhaine, Évêque d'Adran* (The French in Cochin China in the Eighteenth Century: Monsignor Pigneau de Béhaine, bishop of Adran). From the title of the book, Faure made clear his simple argument: Pigneau was the first Frenchman to secure his nation's influence in the region. The biography was a meticulously researched history of Pigneau's interaction with Nguyễn Ánh during the Tây Sơn uprising. After a brief biographical chapter on Pigneau's early life, the book examined the political machinations of a region of the world inhabited by a complex set of characters from a variety of countries. A detailed and— compared to later accounts of Pigneau—relatively well-balanced piece, Faure's book did address the troubles Pigneau experienced in Pondichéry. But it also emphasized the bishop's allegiance to France at key points throughout the text. "To speak frankly, the bishop of Adran pursued a politico-religious idea in Cochin China . . . the intervention of France and the triumph of the Christian religion." Other missionaries, especially Jesuits, in the region preferred Portuguese involvement. But Pigneau resolved, Faure wrote, "to pursue with all the energy of which he was capable the realization of his projects by calling on France, and nothing but France."[29]

Early references to the historical significance of Pigneau's action in Cochin China were not promissionary as much as they were procolonial. Even the stalwart republican Jules Ferry, in defending the French invasion of Tonkin in the mid-1880s, made reference to Pigneau's pioneering work in establishing French relations with the region.[30] And other republican colonialists, including prominent historians such as Alfred Rambaud noted with ease that French involvement in Indochina began with the Versailles Treaty of 1787.[31] The political ironies of this cut at many levels: republicans put aside two of their deepest political convictions—a suspicion of Catholic power and rejection of monarchism—by praising the bishop and his treaty with Louis XVI. Such were the awkward alliances of colonialism. Nonetheless, a pattern had started to develop. In general, authors made little attempt to explore how Pigneau sought Portuguese help for Nguyễn Ánh. Pigneau's identity as a Frenchmen tended to outshine his commitment to the church. Similarly, Nguyễn Ánh's identity changed: French writers viewed him as a "king" who sought to retake his "throne" and reestablish the "Nguyễn dynasty" in Việt Nam. In all these works, to prove France's historical claim to "influence" in

these works, to prove France's historical claim to "influence" in Indochina, authors argued that Pigneau was not only of French origin but
an agent working for the interests of his *mère-patrie*; further, Nguyễn
Ánh was the legitimate, if ousted leader of Cochin China and not
simply one of a number vying for power.

The Mission Finds a Patriot

Just as colonialists drew on Pigneau as a historical basis for France's
colonial aspirations in the region, missionaries adopted him to defend
their role within colonial politics. The occasion of the centenary of the
bishop's death brought his legacy into focus like never before. By
1901, the politics of religion and the demands of colonialism defined
the details of Pigneau's legacy more than concern over historical accuracy. Now the radical republican threat to Catholicism in the colonies
led missionaries in both Indochina and France to remake Pigneau in
an image that suited them best. The Third Republic had few colonial
heroes to model the new Pigneau after; Gallieni, Lyautey, and other
colonial figures who would ultimately win national fame and have
streets and Paris Métro stops named in their honor were still midca-
reer. As a result, the mission's first biographical pieces on Pigneau
sketched out a formula—French patriotism as an allegiance to commerce, republican politics, and a "civilizing" colonial rule—that
would later become standard missionary rhetoric for defending their
colonial presence.

The shift in the missionary interpretation of Pigneau between the
1880s and 1890s can be seen in two books by the same author, Adrien
Launay, official historian of the Missions Étrangères de Paris. Launay
wrote a history of Annam in 1884 that mentioned Pigneau de Béhaine
only in passing in its discussion of the Tây Sơn uprising. In this book,
Launay ultimately considered Pigneau's work a failure as it did nothing to help the Catholic Church.[32] A decade later, however, the same
author paid close attention to Pigneau in his *Histoire générale* of the
society; here, a new Pigneau emerged who embodied both a "love of
patrie" and a deep commitment to his religion. There was no question
that the bishop would turn to France, as England and Holland offered
nothing but heresy, and Portugal represented disorganization and
potential disaster.[33] Though he tempered his characterization of
Pigneau's patriotism, Launay's emphasis on the inevitability of the

bishop's trip to Versailles signaled an important turn from fact to myth in the historical discourse. As the recognized historian of the society, Launay had access to Pigneau's letters, archived at the Missions Étrangères, which documented the variety of options the bishop pursued, and the frustrations that finally led him back to France. As Launay's book became a key source, this omission would shape historical interpretations that followed. Launay, however, cannot be faulted for the rhetoric of patriotism that filled the pages of later accounts.

In anticipation of the centenary of Pigneau's death, Louis-Eugène Louvet, another Missions Étrangères historian, published his biography as part of a broader project that included the erection of the statue and the "religious and national ceremony" commemorating Pigneau's contribution to French-Indochinese relations.[34] In a rousing preface to an otherwise straightforward biography, Louvet considered Pigneau's current-day importance in a way that contrasted even more starkly with the traditional image of the missionary. Just a decade earlier Missions Étrangères publications had focused on the 1884–85 massacres of Christians in Tonkin and Annam as proof of their missionaries' selfless commitment to God. Now Louvet's preface did not even mention conversion, nor did it even explicitly associate Pigneau's work with bringing Christianity to Việt Nam. Instead, Louvet emphasized the bishop's work as a civilizer and politician. "Nation" shared equal prominence with "God" in most of Louvet's formulations. Pigneau — like missionaries in 1896 — strove "to continue and achieve civilizing work." Thanks to the bishop, Louvet argued, France could harvest the fruit "of his wise politics."[35]

One of the more striking departures from tradition was Louvet's veneration of Pigneau's work as a facilitator of French commercial interests in the region. Aside from wrenching Việt Nam from the grips of "civil war and anarchy," Pigneau "opened the ports of Annam to [France], despite the ill will and avarice of [our] rivals for influence in the seas of China: the English in India, and the Spanish of Manila."[36] Associating Pigneau with France's commercial hopes reflected the political and economic concerns of Louvet's era as much as Pigneau's. Within the broad context of European relations in the 1890s, Britain emerged as France's chief competitor, both on the Continent and in the colonies. By mentioning Pigneau's concerns with the British in India, Louvet touched on anxieties as pertinent in 1897 as in

1787. And in Indochina itself, the 1890s witnessed the French administration undertaking a vigorous period of *mise-en-valeur* in the hopes
of making investment in the colony pay off.

By the time of Louvet's publication, anxiety over the colony's
economic viability took the form of numerous antimissionary accusations. In colonial newspapers, colonists—many of whom were radical
Freemasons—denounced missionaries for exploiting their Vietnamese
neophytes to the detriment of the colony. In 1893 the condemning
editorials in the *Courrier de Haiphong* grew so hateful that the apostolic
vicar of West Tonkin appealed to the governor general to intervene
for the sake of the colony.[37] The critiques leveled at the mission, in
addition to conforming to anticlerical rhetoric in France at the time,
gave voice to anxiety over disappointing financial returns of colonial
businesses. Mgr. Mossard, the apostolic vicar of West Cochin China,
described commonly held, antimissionary criticisms in these terms:
missionaries worked "first, to enrich themselves, [and] second, to
dominate and exploit the indigenous." In this view, missions were
little more than "vast commercial and industrial companies" that
used converts "in order to operate in the best possible condition."[38]
With the local population enslaved and ignorant, so the argument
went, missionaries accumulated vast personal wealth and threatened
to put honest colonists out of business.

Louvet's biography gave the Missions Étrangères the opportunity
to address accusations that the mission was detrimental to the
colonial economy. By the 1890s, missionaries increasingly defended
themselves by asserting that Christian education and the teaching of
French developed local colonial populations into responsible colonial
citizens and labor forces. The missionaries' moral lesson in the colonies—one in which, according to Mossard, "religious morality and
civic morality are one"—was the same that brought such unparalleled
progress to Europe over the previous fourteen hundred years, linking
economic gain directly to Christianity.[39] Through religious education,
local populations learned moral and regimented behavior, in turn
making them effective members of the workforce. The proposed
Pigneau ceremony promised a useful way to promote the mission's
rhetoric that it assisted economic development. Mgr. Dépierre—
the apostolic vicar of West Cochin China who first suggested the
statue be mounted, and whose reflections on Pigneau were reproduced as part of Louvet's preface—wrote that Pigneau's contribution

to Việt Nam was "the gift of Christian faith, source of all true civilization and all prosperity, even material." Dépierre's formulation took
aim at French critics more than at potential Vietnamese converts.[40]
Either way, the message was clear: evangelizing paid off in more
ways than one.

The centenary of Pigneau de Béhaine's death also gave missionaries in Indochina the opportunity to redefine the political goals of both
the bishop and their project. If there was a single theme to the centenary it was patriotism. In his first preface to Pigneau's biography, Louvet used the word itself in its various forms more than once per page.
The theme of patriotism even changed the title of Louvet's book. In
Louvet's first French edition of the biography, published in Paris in
1900, the publisher dropped the lackluster title *Mgr d'Adran, notice
biographique* for the more poignant *Mgr d'Adran, missionnaire et
patriote.*[41]

In defining Pigneau's patriotism, Louvet and others not only recast
the bishop of Adran as a national hero; they gave shape to a new form
of missionary patriotism that inextricably linked a love of God with a
love of France. Louvet rejected what he termed *"laic"* claims that
Pigneau's religious career minimized his patriotism. In the biography,
he elaborated: "The bishop of Adran [is] no less a good patriot for
taking before all other considerations his duty as bishop and missionary. Such [did] not impede him at all, moreover, from serving his
country, as we will see."[42] Thus, Louvet again challenged missionary
traditions as well as both moderate and radical republican ideas of
national identity. Symbolizing "the indissoluble alliance of patriotism
and religion," Pigneau worked for the "reign of God" and opened "to
French influence this rich and populous peninsula of Indochina."[43]

The image of patriotism that emerged around Pigneau was also
closely tied to the colonial aspirations of the French nation. For
Louvet and other commentators' pieces reproduced in the various
editions of the biography, Pigneau's crafting of the Versailles treaty
was a model of colonialism: it reestablished the king of Việt Nam,
civilized a society in the grips of "profound anarchy," and secured
territorial and economic benefits for France.[44] "This, it must be recognized, was truly Christian and civilizing politics"—the kind of politics, Louvet added, that "present-day governments rarely show us,
respectful of people's rights and the honor of the weak." In rendering
services and clarifying duties, Pigneau's work offered a recipe for

peaceful colonial existence: his political goals, "far from oppressing and dividing hearts, brought together two civilizations, until then strangers and enemies, by opening to them magnificent prospects of prosperity and grandeur."[45] For enriching the colony in so many ways, France owed Pigneau "the debt of national gratitude and patriotism."[46]

Such a portrayal of the civilizing and pacifying work of Christian missions responded not only to anticlericalism in France but also to suggestions by critics in Indochina that the mission actively undermined the political stability of the colonial regime. From the 1880s forward, colonial administrators and colonists leveled accusations at individual missionaries for working with "pirates" and "rebels." This was particularly true of missionaries stationed in isolated rural or mountainous regions of the country that remained outside the reach of French influence long after "pacification" was complete.[47] For example, in Nghệ An province in 1889, one colonial official observed that missionaries were exercising pressure over rebels as well as mandarins in an attempt to gain power in a part of Annam still largely autonomous.[48] Such accusations would be recycled again and again by critics of the mission for some twenty years. Though French rhetoric confidently held that colonial control was complete by the 1890s, officials remained anxious, vigilantly pursuing a wide range of threats to social stability, including political activism.[49] Louvet's depiction of Pigneau's patriotism tried to dispel criticisms that missionaries undermined colonial control. As Frenchmen in Indochina dealt with nascent anticolonial political movements in the late 1890s and early 1900s, the mission positioned itself as an integral part of the colonial effort.

Though shaped by the exigencies of colonial relations among missionaries, a variety of colonists, and the Vietnamese population, the mission's reevaluation of Pigneau's historical role was also influenced by the metropolitan political culture of the mid-1890s. After the failure of Boulangism in 1889, the conservative right wing in France divided. With the Third Republic looking ever more permanent, many Catholics, in the words of one commentator, had become "exiles in their own country."[50] As Réné Rémond points out in his classic study of the Right in France, conservative Catholics—many of whom were faithful monarchists—faced the unlikelihood of ever seeing another restoration. The Pope's commitment to *ralliement* in 1892 essentially sent legitimists and other conservatives on two paths: one that accepted the papal decree and moved to conservative republicanism, and those who resisted the order and embraced extremist, right-wing nationalism.[51] By the mid-1890s, conservative republicans, also known as *ralliés,* had become essential partners of moderates in government—an alliance that held off radical, anticlerical demands on the Far Left.[52]

The rhetoric of Louvet and other promissionary commentators in the 1890s gave form to a colonial conservative republicanism. When Louvet noted that Pigneau's figure "glorified two things which to [me are] the most valuable over [here]: the church and France," he was describing a distinctly post-*ralliement* Catholic vision of republican colonialism in which Catholicism and republicanism worked together.[53] Formerly legitimist and aristocratic, the newly republican *ralliés* melded two conflicting historical traditions. The missionary community's exaltation of a past bishop who showed allegiance to Louis XVI was not necessarily at odds with republican colonialism, especially since it helped justify expansion.

But the missionary assertion that Pigneau de Béhaine was both a missionary and a patriot was not without controversy. Radicals, who reviled all clerics as a source of counterrevolutionary conspiracy, continued to argue for the outlawing of missionary organizations in the colonies. Louvet's central claim—that the life of Pigneau de Béhaine proved that French patriots must be religious and that *religieux* were by definition patriots—challenged not only the radical political agenda, but also the Left's very definition of French national identity. In the radical view, clerics were not patriots; they were enemies.

Finally, the redefinition of Pigneau de Béhaine did not end with the bishop's commitment to French commerce and patriotism. Ultimately, the biographies and other commentaries presented a historical overview of French involvement in Southeast Asia that lent moral justification to republican colonial policies. Louvet's biography replaced a history of battles and conquest with a process of "domination, at once both pacific and civilizing."[54] In bringing French influence to Việt Nam, Pigneau was responding to Vietnamese requests—a half-truth, considering Gia Long's dire circumstances. In a commentary reproduced in one of Louvet's biographies, M. Le Myre de Vilers—a former deputy of Cochin China and avid supporter of Catholic missionaries— mirrored this idea: "Despite certain appearances, the Vietnamese people are not ungrateful. . . . They know that Mgr. d'Adran was, a century ago, the friend, the confidant, and the savior of their king. They know that it was because of him alone that the dynasty of the Nguyễn was able to regain the throne of its fathers; they have not forgotten that in a time of trouble and of national calamity, the bishop was the pacifier of their country and the benefactor of all, pagans as well as Christians."[55]

For missionaries and politicians alike, Pigneau seemed to embody the paradoxes that helped justify a republican vision of colonial domination. Pigneau both saved the Nguyễn dynasty and paved the road for colonial control. He liberated the Vietnamese people from the oppression of the Tây Sơn by bringing them under French control. And in this era of colonial rule, Pigneau stood as a reminder of Vietnamese indebtedness to the good will of France. Le Myre de Vilers, Dépierre, Mossard, and others emphasized how eager all Vietnamese were to recognize the benefits of "the great bishop" not simply as an aide to a struggling empire but as a sign of French assistance to come. Dépierre envisioned Pigneau's monument as a lesson to future generations of how France became the dictator of the Vietnamese. In return, he wrote, the Vietnamese people would be proud to see "honors rendered to the savior of their country, to the man . . . who never had another goal or preoccupation than to assure them a great destiny in the future."[56]

Rejecting Pigneau and Missionary Work: The Radical Reply

Not everyone in Indochina, however, was willing to accept the mission's new vision of Pigneau. Louvet's book alone would certainly not close the political divide between anticlerical republicans and missionaries. From the moment the mission announced plans for the Pigneau monument and centenary, the project met with varying degrees of dissent. Though the governor general authorized the monument, he did little to support the project. His office pledged only ten piasters to the monument, less than any other branch of the administration, even dictation.[57] Furthermore, though Governor General Doumer attended the ceremony, he had initially refused the invitation. A radical republican, Doumer tempered his distaste for the mission while serving the generally moderate Colonial Ministry. But

he refused to celebrate past missionary glories. Only after Mgr.
Mossard appealed directly to him and offered to set the date of the
ceremony at his convenience did Doumer agree to come to the
ceremony.[58] The most distinguished French guest at the event, however, sat silently in his seat and left the speech making to others.

Perhaps the greatest challenge came in 1897, before the pedestal for
the statue was even built. The year after Louvet's publication in Sài
Gòn of his *Notice biographique,* a contingent of radical colonists hit the
mission with a barrage of articles in the Freemason-owned newspaper
Le Mékong. With typical anticlerical panache, articles in the early
summer claimed that nuns in Indochina had quit their posts to take
up prostitution, that priests were teaching obscene songs to be sung in
church, and that missionaries were murdering locals. Exasperated by
the disparagement, Dépierre wrote the editor of the paper, Ulysse
Leriche, to insist that the lies stop. Dépierre's letter was not without
its own accusatory flair: "Don't force respectable people to expose all
your misdeeds and avoid you like a mangy dog or a putrid corpse. . . .
How dare you of all people, Ulysse Leriche, give us lessons in patriotism, morality and devotion to worthy causes!" Worst of all, in the
bishop's estimation, Leriche's journalism exposed ugly divisions
between Frenchmen, "[shaming] our country in native eyes."[59] In
June, the bishop took his threats a step further by writing to the justice
ministry in Sài Gòn demanding something be done to stop the Freemasons; nothing ever was.

A number of the articles appearing in *Le Mékong* were by Camille
Pâris, a postal administrator and rabidly anticlerical Freemason who
made a career of baiting missionaries.[60] In general, Pâris's criticisms
were in keeping with other anti-clerical accusations that radical Freemasons made both in France and Indochina.[61] The traditional enemies
of monarchism and the extreme Right, Freemasons played a prominent role in republican politics from the advent of the Third Republic.
Until the First World War, some 40 percent of civilian ministers in
the republic were lodge members.[62] Though moderates like Jules
Ferry were Masons, a radical wing of Freemasonry developed from
the 1860s, committed to moral law, scientism, and avidly anti-Catholic
policies.[63] By the 1890s, right-wing nationalists had become the radical
Freemasons' enemy of choice in France, and the rancor on both sides
of the polemic was violent. In radical eyes, Catholicism was superstitious,
intolerant, and counterrevolutionary. To nationalists, Freemasons were

godless Jews and "guttersnipes" bent on robbing true Frenchmen blind.[64] The only thing they agreed on was that their enemies were anti-French.

Much of Camille Pâris's writing stuck close to the radical script, importing many ready-made accusations to the colonial context. In 1897, however, he built his claims around the historical question of Pigneau de Béhaine. Pâris took on not only the proposed memorial but the bishop of Adran himself. One of Pâris's polemics appeared in the June 3, 1897, edition of *Le Mékong*, starting with characteristic bombast: "The proposed monument to the bishop of Adran will be the glorification of the deplorable conduct of the missions in Indochina." For Pâris, it revealed once again "the incomparable ability of missionaries to attribute to themselves sublime roles when they are nothing but mercenaries," while also proving "Frenchmen's incomparable ignorance of history."[65] From these first sentences, Pâris's "historical" account of "Pigneaux" showed itself to be as shaped by politics as Louvet's preface to his biography: "What services did the bishop of Adran render to the *patrie*, to humanity? What did he do to establish French influence in Annam? . . . Did he get from [Gia Long] the smallest island, the least peninsula, commercial rights for our nationals? Nothing. His work is this in sum: By his religious intolerance, he strongly accentuated the Vietnamese hatred of the European, hate that his predecessors had given birth to, and that his successors pushed to paroxysm."[66]

Pâris's newspaper article was not simply a slandering of the mission; he reinterpreted eighteenth-century Vietnamese history with remarkable facility and creativity. Having rejected the idea that Pigneau was a patriot, Pâris moved on to denounce Nguyễn Ánh as a fraud and a torturer. Nguyễn Ánh was not the legitimate heir to the throne, Pâris argued, because he was only the nephew of the Emperor Nguyễn Duê Tông, who was executed by the Tây Sơn. In so claiming, Pâris recast the Tây Sơn rebellion to look suspiciously like France's revolutionary past. Nguyễn Ánh was the cruel, illegitimate emperor in the clutches of the conniving bishop, and the Tây Sơn were a "secular dynasty" not unlike the Republic. Far from saving Việt Nam, Pigneau helped conquer it for his own benefit. Among other acts he instructed Nguyễn Ánh to levy heavy taxes on Buddhists to help augment Catholic conversion. And if his politics were not reprehensible enough, Pigneau was a torturer to boot. On one occasion, Nguyễn

Ánh and the bishop of Adran sentenced a captured daughter of a Tây Sơn leader to a slow, painful death that included genital mutilation and dismemberment.[67] Pigneau committed such horrific deeds in the name of Catholicism, Pâris hastened to add, for the bishop's sole concern was the "extension of this religion by bloody means."

In a final statement, Pâris revealed the extent to which colonial history was linked to French identity both in the colonies and in France. Worse than what Pigneau represented in Indochina was what a statue in his honor meant for the *mère-patrie*. Pâris concluded that republican France would never want to glorify such conduct as Pigneau's with a public statue.[68] It is likely that the animosity Pâris directed at the mission was intended to rouse the mission to condemn republicanism. But the mission did not revert to the diatribe of conservative nationalism. The combined threats of anticlerical journalists like Pâris in Indochina and radical republicans calling for outlawing congregations in France had the effect of strengthening the resolve of missionaries. They would write more pamphlets, make more speeches, in short, argue ever more vehemently that they were both Catholics and Frenchmen, committed to the Republic.

Pigneau de Béhaine—and Missionaries— at the Center of Sài Gòn

Just as Louvet and other commentators created patriotic images with text, the unveiling of Pigneau's statue brimmed with visual and ceremonial symbolism. In the early morning of March 10, 1901, a considerable crowd of colonists, French and Vietnamese dignitaries, and local Christians gathered in front of the Sài Gòn Cathedral. One witness reported it was "one of those beautiful days in the Far East, when the light of the sun brings a special clarity." Flowers and palms as well as countless French flags covered the pavilion set up for the occasion. At exactly seven o'clock, Governor General Paul Doumer arrived and was first greeted by Mgr. Mossard, who hosted the event, and then joined other guests such as the mayor of Sài Gòn, admirals, commandants, and members of the administration. A military band and a church chorus played patriotic music as the guests took their places. Then the veil covering the statue fell to the ground, revealing the nearly three-meter tall figure of Pigneau and his young companion, Prince Cảnh. For the mission in Cochin China, it was the most important day of the year.[69] According to the Missions Étrangères's journal, "It was France saluting one of its illustrious children."[70]

What is striking about the centenary of Pigneau de Béhaine's death—in text, stone, and ceremony—is just how *republican* it was. Commemorations and monuments were central to republican culture in the 1880s and 1890s. Up until the failure of Boulangism, moderate republicans were continually on the defensive in France against threats from both the monarchist Right and the radical Left. Moderates— aptly called opportunists because they made alliances where necessary to hold power—endeavored not only to secure their political positions but to make their republican ideals part of France's national culture. They embraced the image of the Revolution of 1789 with its promise of liberty, justice, and power of the people—and rejected the violent populism evoked by the memory of 1793. Public ceremonies and monuments gave shape to this vision. In 1880, 14 *Juillet* became a national holiday, celebrating the unity of the Fête de la Fédération of 1790, not the mobs that took the Bastille in 1789.[71] From the 1880s on, busts of a woman in a Phrygian cap—"Marianne," symbol of the republic—began appearing in town halls across France, and statues of heroes of the nation were erected in squares and parks.[72] With the death and entombment of Victor Hugo, hero of the republic, the Pantheon became the undisputed secular church of the nation, thus dividing republican "great men" from religious and royal ones.[73] Such statues and landmarks, as one historian has observed, turned the nation into a "great outdoor classroom, bristling with moral lessons for youth."[74]

The centenary of Pigneau's death performed a similar function, but it was tailored to the politics of colonialism and religion. As France had become a classroom of the Republic, missionaries now proposed to create a classroom of the Republic abroad; as past republican heroes gave historical meaning to contemporary politics in France, Pigneau's statue explained France's presence in Indochina. Louvet wrote: "At a time when in all parts of France statues . . . are being raised, it seems that the statue of the bishop of Adran has its natural place on this land of Annam, where he introduced us, in this city of Sài Gon, where he passed a great part of his apostolic life, at the foot of this beautiful cathedral, indisputable testimony of the success of his work, both religious and patriotic."[75] The ceremony—an opportunity for selective remembering and forgetting—made "natural" the political relations of the present. More than anything else, the statue of Pigneau de Béhaine made sense of divided allegiances. It literally and figuratively linked France with its colonies: the statue itself, delayed by production problems, was exhibited first at the Exposition of 1900 in Paris before making the journey to Sài Gòn.[76] And symbolically, Pigneau's figure brought together commerce and morality, patriotism and Catholicism, and France and Việt Nam.

With the dropping of the statue's veil emerged a new image of Catholic missionaries in colonial and French politics. Pigneau's statue embodied a vision of the Catholic mission as a bridge between France and its colonial peoples, a symbol of a love of nation inextricably mingled with a love of God, and even a model of republican political ideals buttressed by Christian charity. The tall statue had Pigneau standing straight in a bishop's robe and cross, his right hand extended from his body, holding a copy of the Treaty of Versailles he had brokered in 1787. In his other hand, he guided the young Prince Cảnh, Pigneau's travel companion to Louis's court. Pigneau's massive figure nearly enveloped the small prince; the sculptor ambiguously placed Pigneau behind Cảnh but with his foot and hand forward, as if also guiding the young Vietnamese prince.

The speeches given that morning were stitched with the symbolism of the statue. Pigneau was a Frenchman supporting and leading a generation of Vietnamese; he was a missionary upholding the laws of France. Mgr. Mossard, a gifted political negotiator, was the mission's speaker. He began his remarks by recounting the history of Pigneau de Béhaine, saying the bishop was a sign of the intervention of divine providence—of morality and justice overcoming abuses of power. Addressing the ambiguity of the statue's figural arrangement, Mossard explained that Pigneau had appeared to the Vietnamese "as the most perfect model of a master, as a loyal, wise, and devoted friend." His soul was full of "loyalty, courage and respect for the established power."[77] Pigneau saved the life of Nguyễn Ánh, the bishop said, and inspired his followers. And he united France and Cochin China, obtaining "for his royal *protégé* the help of his country of origin, of the generous nation, France, always helpful in hardship, for centuries protector of civilization and the Catholic apostolate."[78]

Mossard's speech, however, was not only about France's accomplishments in Việt Nam. After his opening remarks he addressed contemporary French domestic conflicts as much as colonial struggles. In addition to France's success in the Far East, Mossard said that the Pigneau statue represented Frenchmen's ability to put aside political differences and work together. The statue of Pigneau ceased to be of an individual missionary; rather, it became a historical marker of French unity: "We salute this statue: it will be like an open book and future generations will be able to read from it one glorious page. . . . It will say aloud that the battles of parties, the political dissensions, in a word, all that excites the spirits these days in the *mère-patrie*, cannot divide, in this colony, the hearts of true Frenchmen. Yes, gentlemen, it will say that we all were united to offer this bronze to an illustrious compatriot, the bishop of Adran, a name long famous and henceforth the most honored and the most popular in Cochin China."[79]

Ever-aware of the political climate at home—the Dreyfus Affair was in full swing, Waldeck-Rousseau's government teetered, and the French assembly was on the verge of making a strong shift to the radical Left—Mossard's comments were a white flag to a republican administration increasingly intolerant of all things clerical. Mossard understood that the political shift to the left in France would threaten the mission's work abroad; in fact, he once commented that the mission "had the privilege of feeling almost instantaneously the *contre-coup* of events that result from religious political fighting in France."[80] In Pigneau, Mossard saw an opportunity to express the mission's commitment to *ralliement*. Pigneau was a religious man, one who was meant foremost to bring Frenchmen together—a compatriot of all Frenchmen. In France, religious and political division was possible, but the colonies were different. Mossard's missionary rhetoric—stripped of all talk of God and conversion—spoke of reconciliation, of a missionary project willing to join, rather than challenge, republican colonialism. "For us, Frenchmen abroad, who anxiously follow the marching of the national flag across the world . . . we salute this man of large and fertile ideas who wanted that, in this Far East, the name of Frenchmen be synonymous with progress, civilization, and true liberty."[81]

No longer interested in fighting the colonial project, Mossard emphasized that missionaries accepted with pride the expansion of France abroad. But Mossard's equation was not without its challenge to republican patriots. First of all, he insisted that missionaries were patriots, concerned with the greatness of France as much as with the reign of God. Considering that republican administrators continued to accuse missionaries of treason until the First World War, this was a significant claim. Second, to drive this point further, Mossard argued that anyone abroad who failed to put aside the divisions of French politics was not a true Frenchman. To challenge the work of missionaries and patriots like Pigneau de Béhaine was itself an unpatriotic act—an act not in France's best interest.

Finally, when Mossard spoke he both invoked concepts at the heart of French republican patriotism and challenged the words' very meanings. The image of Pigneau, with his patriotic ambitions to open Việt Nam to French commercial and political influence, allowed missionaries to recast their project as committed to "progress, civilization, and true liberty." But rather than achieving goals based on revolutionary ideals, Pigneau was motivated by Christianity. Mgr. Dépierre had first outlined this argument in his 1896 letter to Louvet. In his role as missionary, and bishop Pigneau acted with a mixture of force and goodness, wisdom, moderation, and prudence that made him "a model of a politician of good standing [bonne marque] and truly Christian." This combination of political know-how and Christian morality allowed him to exercise a "lasting influence."[82] France entered Indochina, Dépierre noted, in the wake of Pigneau's work. France, like Pigneau, was on "a mission of peace and progress, of justice and fairness"; in short, it was "politics inspired by Christian faith." The "superior men" who subscribe to these ideas and who understood colonial issues knew "that Christianity is the great factor of all true civilization." Catholicism, Dépierre wrote, brought to barbarous people a "great, large, civilizing, and disinterested politics."[83]

Thus, when Mossard took the stage that clear day in March 1901, he used words and ideas that had been redefined with both Christian and republican significance. Informed by a host of missionary commentators, Mossard echoed the rhetoric of Jules Ferry's famous 1884 speech in which he called on France to spread its ideas, language, and genius around the world. Now, little more than a decade after Ferry spoke the words, missionaries had adopted the republicans' language to describe their own project. In 1896, Dépierre parroted Ferry's famous formulation with an added word or two: the honor of noble France, the bishop wrote, was not to exploit the people it conquered but "to bring before them all [France's] ideas, its civilization, and its faith."[84] In the early 1880s, such a formulation would have been unthinkable for either a missionary or a republican. Ironically, a decade of conflict and critique—both in Indochina and France—had driven missionaries like Dépierre and Mossard to wax patriotic in a way both moderate republicans and *religieux* could accept.

Jean de Lanessan and Colonialism's Gift to Humanity

In 1907, another book critical of the mission was published in France. Radical republican and Freemason Jean Marie-Antoine de Lanessan was a one-time governor general of Indochina, minister of the Navy, deputy, professor at the Faculté de Médecine in Paris, and a prolific writer on a host of subjects from politics to colonialism to botany. Though clearly antimissionary, while in the governor general's office, de Lanessan did not use his influence in the colony to undermine significantly the position of the mission. But a decade after the debate began in Indochina over the memory of Pigneau de Béhaine, he published *Les missions et leur protectorat* (The Missions and Their Protectorate), in which he explored whether missionaries helped or injured French relations with colonial populations. His central concerns were, first, whether it was conceivable that missionaries worked for France and, second, whether their work benefited the colonial effort. His conclusions were clear: in this era after Dreyfus and the separation of church and state, it was time for the role of missionaries in the colonies to be greatly minimized.[85]

Though the book drew widely from de Lanessan's knowledge of foreign affairs (more than half of the study examined the Levant), he dedicated a chapter to Indochina and took special care to address the legacy of Pigneau de Béhaine. De Lanessan started his examination of Pigneau by linking him to a decadent past. He attributed Pigneau's success at court to "snobbism," exemplified by the aristocracy's quaint fascination with young Prince Cảnh. Yet even in this remote past, de Lanessan found unfortunate links with the present: Pigneau found success at Versailles because "all our [French] foreign policy was then, but not more than today, in the hands of the religious congregations." Then as now, de Lanessan argued, the missionaries had but one goal in mind, the spread of the Catholic Church. Adeptly quoting from Launay's history of the Missions Étrangères, he wrote, "It was the 'conquering and sovereign cross' that they see in their dreams, not France extending its influence in the Far East." Even if Pigneau had been sympathetic to the monarchy, with the revolution in France he broke any ties to his former nation and gave voice to his true motivations. Again, drawing on Launay's history, de Lanessan reiterated Pigneau's dying words: "Precious cross . . . the French have thrown you out and knocked you down from their temples; come to Cochin China. . . . I wanted to plant you in this kingdom, upon the throne of kings. . . . Plant it here yourself, O my Savior, and build your temples upon the debris of demons. . . . Reign over the Cochin Chinese!"[86]

For de Lanessan, Pigneau's words dealt a final blow to the argument that the bishop was a patriot. "I am not criticizing; I am noting. I do not blame the conduct of the bishop of Adran, who was a man of valor, intelligent and bold [hardi], but it is impossible for me not to observe that, from one end of his life to the other, he was before all else a bishop and worked above all else, if not exclusively, for his church."[87] A final, condemning reference to a missionary's work—this time to Louvet's biography of Mgr. Puginier, the prominent late nineteenth-century apostolic vicar in Hà Nội—expanded the criticism of Pigneau de Béhaine into a statement about missionaries in present-day Indochina. Despite his claims about Pigneau's patriotism, Louvet wrote in his study of Puginier that there were many apostolic vicars and missionaries who did not wish to see the colonial expansion of France. "I would say further," wrote Louvet, "a great number of our brothers . . . even though excellent patriots, dreaded to see France installed here because of the suspicions and hatred that the presence of foreigners had fatally excited against the Christians."[88] For de Lanessan, this was proof, from the very pen of a *religieux*, that the missionary served his mission, his religion, himself, but not his nation. "After the conquest, as before, missionaries had but one goal: to make Christians. Is this surprising? Is this not why they became missionaries?"[89]

Just as de Lanessan's observations moved chronologically from Pigneau de Béhaine to Puginier and the missionaries of contemporary Indochina, so too did they move geographically from a focus on Southeast Asia to the French colonial world as a whole. De Lanessan found it hard to accept Louvet's claim that missionaries were patriots who spread "in pagan areas, entirely closed to Europeans, our ideas, our morals, our civilization, and our faith." De Lanessan pointed to a number of examples in Indochina where converts refused to give up their independence; in this way they "were in agreement with pirates in resisting [French] authority."[90] Missionaries, he continued, repeatedly tried to assert control over French soldiers and officers. And they interfered with foreign affairs, as when missionaries converted a Vietnamese prince in the royal family and then attempted to stage a coup so that the prince could take power. In de Lanessan's assessment, Christian evangelizing inevitably caused social breakdown, because pagans viewed conversion as a fall into shame. The humility and division caused by missionaries turned into passions of hostility toward Europeans. Failing even to teach French, not to mention French civilization, missionaries were "far more harmful than useful."[91]

De Lanessan's book was more than a condemnation of Christian proselytization by a radical republican. It revealed the extent to which the debate over missionaries in the colonies took on a strongly moral dimension, evolving into a debate over the ethics of colonialism. In contrast to the alleged evil wrought by missionary practices, de Lanessan's book put forward a humanitarian vision of republican colonialism. By ridding the colonies—and potential areas of influence such as China—of missionaries, new regions would open to business and civilization. De Lanessan suggested that the turmoil caused by evangelization would abate, and resistance to foreign invasion would fade. Laic schools, unlike their missionary predecessors, would teach French, helping the "yellow peoples" of the world in the future.[92] The final result, he concluded, would be a relationship based on mutual admiration and respect for progress.[93]

Within this model, de Lanessan's colonizers took on the role of protectorate of local cultural heritage. For an example, he turned to personal experience; as governor general of Indochina, de Lanessan had helped rebuild the pagoda of Trần Vũ. At the celebration marking the reopening of the temple, de Lanessan had been moved by the joy and warm sentiments expressed by the Vietnamese people. He had seen the satisfaction of a people whose national religion had been "the object of [French] contempt and incessant *profanations*," and who were once again able to make ritual *hommages* to their ancestors as their traditions dictated. The experience proved to de Lanessan what an error the colony made in allowing missionaries to continue their work. That day at the Trần Vũ pagoda was "a profitable lesson for France"—applicable to the colonial project as a whole.[94] "Our first duty," he wrote, "is to respect, in an absolute manner, the traditional beliefs of the indigenous." Missionaries, he argued, undermined the Third Republic's ability to accomplish this task. De Lanessan's opposition to missionaries not only promised to rid the colonies of enemies of the state; it would also allow republican officials to defend the rights of local populations. Thus, to de Lanessan, missionaries represented far more than political or cultural adversaries. When he demanded that the republic renounce the protectorate of missionaries, he claimed to do so "in the name of peace and of the tranquility of humanity."[95]

The Colonial Histories of a Divided France

The missionary version of Pigneau de Béhaine—perhaps because it was more palatable to French audiences hungry for stories of France's history of "civilizing" work abroad—weathered the many challenges from the radical Left. In 1907, when de Lanessan's work on missionaries came and went, a book called *Héros trop oubliés de notre épopée coloniale* (Forgotten Heroes from Our Colonial Era) had already been through multiple printings in France, garnering awards from the Académie Française and the Académie de Lyon.[96] Sponsored by the Oeuvre de la Propagation de la Foi, Valérien Groffier's *Forgotten Heroes* intertwined the history of the French colonies with the history of Catholic missionaries. In its pages, Pigneau de Béhaine was not simply a warrior of the church but a national hero of France; a photo of his statue in Sài Gòn decorated the title page of the chapter on French influence in Indochina.[97] This version of Pigneau soon became accepted doctrine among missionary commentators. The heroism of the bishop even gave rise to a nationalistic play written by a *religieux*.[98]

Nonmissionary interests also exalted Pigneau's patriotism. In 1914, the Société de Géographie de Paris—one of the leading geographic societies in France and a laic, procolonial organization—purchased Pigneau's childhood home and opened it as a museum, honoring the man who first took French politics to Việt Nam. The inspector-general of schools in Indochina, as well as Le Myre de Vilers, was on hand for the museum's inauguration.[99] During the First World War, scholars in France and the colony showed great concern that the Germans would destroy the home, which had been designated a historic monument, to weaken French national resolve.[100] Most recently, in March of 1983,

the government of Việt Nam officially returned the remains of
Pigneau de Béhaine to France, where they were placed in the crypt at
the Missions Étrangères. Though ostensibly a gesture of good will, its
symbolism remains poignant: the figure associated with first bringing
France to Việt Nam had finally been sent home.[101]

Debates over the history of Indochina that took place in the 1890s
and early 1900s reveal the deep political rifts that divided Frenchmen,
both at home and abroad, over colonial expansion. Some of the most
vociferous personalities in this conflict came from Catholic missionaries and their supporters, on the one hand, and from radical republicans and Freemasons, on the other. The debates were not without
voices from extreme nationalist quarters that defended missionary
work with anti-Semitic and antiparliamentarian vitriol.[102] But the
major missionary organizations, following the lead of the Oeuvres de
la Propagation de la Foi, avoided the reactionary rhetoric of *La Croix*,
La Libre Parole, and other far-right publications. Instead, most missionaries adopted the language of republican *ralliement*. Nonetheless,
radical critics denounced missionary work abroad with the same
vigor as they decried clericalism on French soil. In certain instances,
radical colonists' attacks on the missions—replete with stories of
whorish nuns and murderous priests—were without evidence, pull-
ing the exchange down into the mire of propaganda.

What emerged from these brawls was a body of historical literature
in which fact and fiction, moderation and hyperbole were inextricably
entangled. Of all the assessments of Pigneau de Béhaine to emerge
around the time of his centenary celebration, Jean de Lanessan's offered the most convincing historical argument. His main point that
Pigneau de Béhaine was motivated more by religious conviction than
national pride showed a depth of understanding of missionary traditions notably lacking—ironically—in the rhetoric of Catholics bent on
rehabilitating the bishop as a patriot par excellence. Driven by concern that domestic and colonial strife would spell the end of their
work, missionaries abandoned a centuries-old tradition of identifying
themselves as homeless soldiers of God and asserted their tradition of
spreading, like republican colonizers, "*civilisation*."

On both sides, rhetoric was aimed largely at the moderate republican center, which until 1902 controlled the French government and
continued to hold influence over colonial policy even after radicals
gained power. The parliamentary shift to the radical Left in 1902 pre-

sented the missionary community with its greatest challenge to date. Radicals instituted a general policy of *laïcisation*, forcing nuns out of military hospitals, priests out of state schools, and cutting government funding to missionary projects such as schools, hospitals, leper colonies, and orphanages. Moderate republicans did not, however, ultimately support radicals' desire to ban missionaries from the colonies altogether. If this fact says anything about the rhetorical war waged from the 1890s forward, it suggests that missionaries were more convincing that they were committed to the *patrie* than their radical adversaries who accused them of being enemies to colonial expansion. After 1905, with the passage of laic reforms limiting the power of the clergy in French society in place, anticlericalism became a dead issue for most republicans.[103] Some radicals, like de Lanessan and Pâris, continued to fight. But increasingly their denunciations were drowned out by the patriotic chants of missionaries.[104]

More important, the writing of colonial history at the turn of the twentieth century represented a broader cultural process whereby Frenchmen from a variety of backgrounds sought to explain and justify historically, politically, and morally French colonial expansion. The formulations that emerged on all sides reveal deep reservations about, and—at times—even critique of the impact of colonization on local populations. References to the "civilizing domination" of France, a "pacific empire" of missionaries, and the "tranquility" and "humanity" provided by radical republicanism all suggest the lengths to which men and women would go to defend their individual "French" projects, even while condemning their adversaries' behavior.[105] All sides preserved various ideas about French "civilization." All sides espoused plans to improve the moral, intellectual, and material conditions of indigenous populations. And all sides found in their adversaries the reasons why liberty and redemption—the by-products of very different forms of French proselytization—were as yet unattained.

Archival Collections

Archives de la Société des Missions Étrangères de Paris (AMEP)
Centre National de Documentation et d'Archives Missionnaires, Lyon
Centre des Archives d'Outre Mer, Aix-en-Provence (AOM)

Trung Tam Luu Tru Quoc Gia–1 (National Archives of Việt Nam, 1),
Hà Nội (TTLT)

Notes

1. See, for example, Montagnon, *La France coloniale*; Pluchon, *Histoire de la colonisation*, vol. 1; Bouche, *Histoire de la colonisation française*, vol. 2; Aldrich, *Greater France*; Haudrère, *l'Empire des rois*.

2. Manguin, *Les Nguyên, Macau et le Portugal*, 53–54; and Mantienne, "Le recours des états de la péninsule indochinoise à l'aide européene dans leurs relations," 73–74.

3. See Tuck, *French Catholic Missionaries*, especially chap. 6.

4. Trung Tâm Lưu Trữ Quốc Gia 1, Hà Nội (National Archives of Việt Nam, no. 1) (henceforth TTLT), Résidence Supérieur du Tonkin (henceforth RST), 39,040: Souscriptions pour l'érection d'un monument à la mémoire de l'évêque d'Adran, 1898; Letter from M. Escobet, Administrateur-Conseil à M. le Résident Supérieur de Tonkin à Hanoi, no. 71. Giadinh, le 29 Décembre 1897. All translations are my own unless otherwise noted.

5. TTLT, RST, 39,040: Letter from M. Fourès, Résident Supérieur au Tonkin à M. le Directeur des Postes et Télégraphes à Hanoi, no. 141, Hanoi, le 16 Février 1898.

6. Centre des Archives d'Outre Mer, Aix-en-Provence (henceforth AOM), Indochine: Gouvernement Général de l'Indochine (henceforth GGI), 5680: Souscription publique aux monuments Richard et Pigneau de Béhaine; Report "Souscription pour l'érection d'un groupe à la Grandeur Monseigneur Pigneau de Béhaine, évêque d'Adran et à son altesse le prince Cảnh."

7. AOM, GGI, 9760: "Demande aux missions étrangères du portrait de l'Évêque d'Adran"; Report from le Résident Supérieur de l'Annam à M. le Gouverneur Général, Hué, le 25 Août 1896.

8. AOM, GGI, 5680: Letter from l'évêque titulaire de Benda, Vic. Apost. de Saigon Dépierre à M. Doumer, Gouverneur Général de l'Indo-Chine à Saigon, Saigon, le 24 Février 1897.

9. L. E. Louvet, historian for the Missions Étrangères, initially spelled Pigneau's name "Pigneaux" in his 1885 history of Catholicism in Cochin China. In his later biography, at the time when Pigneau's life was reexamined, the *x* was dropped, perhaps in an attempt to shed the aristocratic pretensions of the original spelling. See Louvet, *La Cochinchine religieuse*, 379.

10. "Inauguration de la statue de Monseigneur Pigneau de Béhaine, évêque d'Adran, vicaire apostolique de Cochinchine," *Annales de la Société des Missions-Étrangères* (1902): 146.

11. Mantienne, "Le recours des états," 73–74.

12. De Lanessan, *Les missions et leur protectorat*, 59.

13. Devillers, *Français et Annamites*, 28.

14. The original "Texte du discours prononcé par le roi Gia-Long aux funérailles de Mgr. Pigneau de Béhaine, le 16 Décembre 1799" hangs in the reading room at the Archives de la Société des Missions Étrangères de Paris; a

French translation was reprinted in "Inauguration de la statue," *Annales de la Société des Missions-Étrangères,* 158.

15. Mantienne, "Le recours des états," 74.

16. This letter remained in the archives of the Société des Missions Étrangères de Paris. Manguin, *Les Nguyên,* 54, esp. n. 19. Pigneau reiterated this point in a letter to the Senate of Macao, July 8, 1785; reprinted in Manguin, *Les Nguyên,* 198–99.

17. Manguin, *Les Nguyên,* 92.

18. Portugal demanded too much in the end, including suzerainty over the Vietnamese empire, and the Treaty of Versailles became the best deal Nguyễn Ánh could make. Mantienne, "Le recours des états," 74–75.

19. Goyau, *La France missionnaire dans les cinq parties du monde,* 1:307–8.

20. Launay, *Histoire générale de la Société des Missions Étrangères,* 2:252.

21. Roberts, *History of French Colonial Policy,* 2:421.

22. The *Moniteur Universel* was at this time the official newspapers reporting on government policies in France. See Bellanger, Godechot, Guiral, and Terrou, *Histoire générale de la presse française,* 3:191.

23. *Histoire de Pigneau de Béhaine, Évêque d'Adran,* 4. This pamphlet, an "Extrait du *Moniteur Universel* du 16 Février 1863," is in the collection of the Bibliothèque Asiatique of the Société des Missions Étrangères de Paris. My italics.

24. Devillers, *Français et Annamites,* 28.

25. Histoire de Pigneau, 8.

26. Ibid., 19–20.

27. Ibid., 18–19.

28. Chaigneau, *Souvenirs de Hué,* 5–7.

29. Faure, *Les Français en Cochinchine,* 59.

30. See Ferry's introduction to *Le Tonkin et la mère-patrie.*

31. See, for example, the "Indo-Chine Française" chapter by Bounais and Paulus in Rambaud's influential *La France coloniale, histoire, géographie, commerce,* 410–11. Bounais and Paulus describe the work of Pigneau de Béhaine and the treaty and note that when Pigneau died, "the fortune of our compatriots declined." Acknowledging that the "successors of Gia-Long were not as favorable to European enterprises," the narrative skips ahead to the first war with Annam in 1858. The only apparent link between the two events is that the French government in 1858 responded to the "torture of several missionaries." On the significance of Rambaud in constructing an early republican stance on colonialism, see Girardet, *l'idée coloniale,* 88–89.

32. Launay, *Histoire ancienne et moderne de l'Annam, Tong-King et Cochinchine,* 189.

33. Launay, *Histoire générale,* 2:230–31.

34. Louvet, *Mgr d'Adran, notice biographique,* preface.

35. Ibid.

36. Ibid.

37. See the 1893 exchange between de Lanessan and Mgr. Gendreau in Tuck, *French Catholic Missionaries,* 250–51.

38. Archives of the Société des Missions Étrangères de Paris (henceforth AMEP), no. 757 (v. 2), Cochinchine Occidentale, 1901–12: Mgr. Lucien Mossard, "A Monsieur C., Réponse à Monsieur X," 10. This document, which took the form of a letter, addressed a variety of criticisms leveled against the mission. It described several common criticisms of missionaries in Indochina and outlined possible responses to each.

39. AMEP, no. 757 (v. 2): Mossard, "À Monsieur C.," 12–13.

40. From Dépierre's letter (Sài Gòn, June 19, 1896) to Louvet, which was reprinted in the front of *Mgr d'Adran, notice biographique*, iii.

41. *Mgr d'Adran, missionnaire et patriote* went through at least two editions in the first year and another in 1902.

42. Louvet, *Mgr d'Adran, missionnaire et patriote*, 111.

43. Louvet, *Mgr d'Adran, notice biographique*, preface.

44. From a letter from Mossard reprinted in Louvet, *Mgr d'Adran, missionnaire et patriote*, i–ii.

45. Ibid., 156.

46. Louvet, *Mgr d'Adran, notice biographique*, preface.

47. Marr, *Vietnamese Anticolonialism*, 72–73. Marr notes the hypocrisy of French colonizers deeming those outside their grasp "pirates."

48. AOM, GGI, 9234: Affaire du Père Magat, 1889: Letter from M. Hector, Résident Supérieur en Annam à M. Gouverneur Générale de l'Indo-Chine, Saigon, no. 614, Hué, le 21 Août 1889.

49. By the 1890s, for example, the colonial administration passed Article 91 outlawing a wide range of political crimes, as distinct from criminal ones, suggesting concern over growing anticolonial activities. See Zinoman, *Colonial Bastille*, 108–9.

50. Tertullian, quoted in Agulhon, *French Republic*, 56.

51. Rémond, *Right Wing in France*, 208–12.

52. This was especially true during the ministries of Charles Dupuy, Alexandre Ribot, and Jules Méline (between 1894 and 1898). As Larkin notes, "The Catholic Ralliés had some thirty to forty seats in the Chamber of Deputies which, when added to the two-hundred-and-fifty-odd moderate republicans, gave these governments a comfortable majority against the radicals and Socialists, as well as marginalizing still further the fifty or so members of the dissident Right" (*Religion, Politics and Preferment in France*, 7).

53. Louvet, *Mgr. d'Adran, notice biographique*, preface.

54. Ibid.

55. Le Myre de Vilers is quoted in the epilogue of Louvet, *Mgr. d'Adran, missionnaire et patriote*, 2nd ed., 313–14.

56. Quoted in ibid., 318.

57. AOM, Indo, GGI, 5680: Report "Souscription pour l'érection d'un groupe à la Grandeur Mansiegneur Pigneau de Béhaine, évêque d'Adran at à son altesse le prince Cảnh." A handwritten note from the governor general's office asked that the list of administrative donations for the ceremony be redrafted to combine the ten piasters given by the government with the seventy-five raised among the Colonial Council. Perhaps embarrassed by the

meager amount it contributed to the fund, the Governor-General's office asked that a single amount of eighty-five piasters from the colonial government be put on record.

58. The colonial administration's approval of the monument but refusal to participate in the unveiling is discussed in Mossard's obituary. See "Nécrologe," 94.

59. This exchange is in Tuck, *French Catholic Missionaries*, 253–54.

60. In addition to newspaper articles Pâris wrote three longer works condemning the missionaries. Pâris and Barsanti, *Les missionnaires d'Asie;* and C. Pâris, under the pseudonym "Protée," the pamphlet *Du rôle néfast joué par les missions en Annam* (Hanoi: La Fraternité Tonkinoise, 1897), which was originally written in 1889; and a follow-up book *Réponse à "l'oeuvre néfaste" du père Guerlach.*

61. On anti-clerical Freemasons in Indochina, see Tuck, *Catholic Missionaries.* And for a flavor of the Freemasons' positions regarding missionaries in the 1890s, see "Nicolas," *Le rôle des missionnaires religieux en Extrême-Orient;* and documents at the Bibliothèque Nationale de France, Fonds Maçonnique: Rés. FM(2) 142; folders for Haiphong and Saigon.

62. Nord, *Republican Moment*, 15.

63. Ibid., 23–25.

64. Rémond, *Right Wing in France*, 213.

65. Reprinted in Pâris and Barsanti, *Les missionnaires,* 52.

66. Ibid., 53.

67. Ibid., 55.

68. Ibid., 56.

69. ASME, 757 (v. 2), 1902, doc. 95: Compte-rendu, vicariat apostolique de Cochinchine occidentale, Saigon, le 5 Octobre 1902.

70. "Inauguration de la statue de Monseigneur Pigneau de Béhaine," *Annales de la Société des Missions-Étrangères* (1902), 152, 153–54.

71. Guildea, Past in French History, 38.

72. See Agulhon, *Marianne au pouvoir.*

73. Mona Ozouf, "The Panthéon: The École Normale of the Dead," in Nora, *Realms of Memory,* 3:326.

74. Nord, *Republican Moment*, 191.

75. Louvet, *Mgr D'Adran, notice biographique,* preface.

76. Louvet, *Mgr d'Adran, missionnaire et patriote,* 2nd ed, 317.

77. "Discours de S. G. Mgr. Mossard . . . prononcé à l'inauguration de la statue de Mgr Pigneau de Béhaine, le 10 mars 1902," *Annales de la Société des Missions-Étrangères* (1902): 155.

78. Ibid., 156.

79. Ibid.

80. Quoted in "Nécrologe,"94.

81. "Discours," 156.

82. In Louvet, *Mgr. Pigneau, notice biographique,* ii.

83. Ibid., vii.

84. Ibid.

85. De Lanessan, *Les missions*, vi.

86. Ibid., 59, 60, 61.

87. Ibid., 61.

88. Ibid., 62–63, quoting Louvet, *Viede Mgr Puginier*, 508.

89. De Lanessan, *Les missions*, 68.

90. Ibid., 64, 65.

91. Ibid., 197, 201.

92. Ibid., 218–21.

93. Such a "philanthropic" view of colonialism signaled somewhat of a departure from de Lanessan's earlier, "scientistic" work; in books such as *l'Indo-Chine française* (1887) and *Principes de colonisation* (1889), de Lanessan drew on racialist theories of superior and inferior peoples to explain colonization as a by-product of human nature. See Todorov's brief discussion of de Lanessan in *On Human Diversity*, 256–57.

94. De Lanessan, *Les missions*, 70.

95. Ibid., 213, 216.

96. *Annales de la propagation de la foi* 79 (1907): 350.

97. Groffier, *Héros trop oubliés*, 272.

98. Philannam, *Saigon-Versailles*.

99. *Annales de la propagation de la foi* 86 (1914): 346–47.

100. See the short article in *Bulletin des Amis du Vieux Hué* 6, no. 4 (October–December 1919): 525–26.

101. Pluchon, *Histoire de la colonisation*, 765.

102. See, for example, Archives Nationales (Paris), F 19, 6214, Comptabilité; vic apost; correspondence et rapports. Police des cultes (1843–1900): Pamphlet by P. Hilaire de Barenton, *La guerre contre congrégations, ou le bienfaits du laicisme. Ce que feront les religieux?* 2nd ed. (Vannes: Imprimerie Lafolye Frères, 1903), 39. Hilaire de Barenton's pamphlet primarily addresses the law of July 1, 1901, and assesses its impact on congregations in France. He uses the example of the missionaries to show how the enemies of religion in France were also enemies of the *patrie*. Antimissionary policies, he argued, threatened France's position abroad. "All [the missionaries'] work profits the Catholic religion first, civilization next, and finally France" (37).

103. See Gildea, *Past in French History*, 220.

104. Pravieux's book *À quoi servent les missionnaires* reflects the extent to which the strategy of defending the mission that began with writers like Louvet had become a formula by the eve of the First World War. The chapters of the book possessed such predictable titles as "Les missionnaires et la prospérité commerciale de la France"; "Les missionnaires et la civilisation"; "Services rendus à la science par les missionnaires"; and "Services rendus à la France par les missionnaires."

105. Louvet, Mgr d'Adran, notice biographique, preface; Pâris and Barsanti, missionnaires d'Asie, 11; De Lanessan, Les missions, 216.

Glossary
Bibliography
Contributors
Index

Glossary of Chinese, Nôm, and Sino-Vietnamese Terms

Annan Ying	安南營
ấp	邑
Bá Đa Lộc	百多祿
bản thôn thượng hạ	本村上下
bất quân	不均
bầu hậu	裒後
Bi Nhu quận công phương tích lục	悲柔郡公芳績
bột đạo	孛悖
Bửu Châu (Bảo Châu)	寶州
Cẩm Thanh	錦青
Chiêm Động	占洞
Chiêm Thành	占城
Chiên Đàn	栴檀
chong	銃
chúc thư văn khế cữu chỉ	囑書文契舊紙
chúc thư	囑書
chữ nôm	**字字喃**
chúa tiên	主仙
chúng tử	眾子

Cổ Luỹ	古壘
công	公
Cù Lao Chàm	岣勞山
Da Đô Bi	妬悲
dinh	營
Dinh Chiêm	占
dinh trấn	營
Da AnnanYing	大安南營
dachong baizi huoqi	大銃百子火器
da jiangjun chong	大將軍銃
Dương Văn An	楊文安
Đà Nẵng	沱㶞
Đại Chiêm Châu	大占州
Đại Chiêm Của Môn	大占口門
Đại Nam nhất thông chí	大南一通志
Đại Nam Thực Lục	大南實綠
Đại Nam thực lục tiền biên	大南寔綠前編
Đại Việt	大越
Đại Việt sử ký toàn thư	大越史記全書
Đàng Trong	塘中
Điện Bàn	尊磐
điền tích	田積
đinh	丁
đình	亭
đô ngự sử	都御史
Đồng Dương	桐陽
duanjian	短箭
feimache	飛馬車
feiqiang	飛槍
fenwen	幩

giáp	甲
Giám Mục Sư	監牧師
Hà Hỉ Văn	何喜文
hải phỉ	海匪
họ	姓
Hổ bì xứ	虎皮處
hộ	戶
Hoá Châu	化州
Hoàn Vương	環王
Hội An phố	會安浦
hội đồng hương chính	會同鄉正
hội đồng kỳ hào	會同其豪
hội đồng kỳ mục	會同其牧
hội đồng tộc biểu	會同族表
Hồng Đức Thiện Chính Thư	洪德善政書
huochong	火銃
huojian	火箭
huopao	火砲
huo pentong	火噴筒
huoqi	火器
huotong	火筒
hương lão	鄉老
hương ước	鄉約
hương hỏa	香火
huynh đệ	兄弟
jiangjun shi	將軍石
jiangjun shizi	將軍石子
Khâm Sai Chưởng Cơ	差掌奇
Khâm Sai Cai Cơ	差該奇
Khâm Sai Cai Đội	差該隊

khẩu (unit of measurement)	口
làng	郎
lệ làng	例 郎
lianzhu pao	連珠砲
Long Hưng	龍興
lügong che	呂公車
lý trưởng	里長
Man	蠻
Man ô ê	麻怒
mẫu (unit of measurement)	畝
mẫu điền sản	母田
miếu	庙
minh hương	明香
mu ma zi	木馬子
Mỹ Sơn	美山
nam tiến	南進
Nguyễn	阮
Nguyễn Ánh Gia Long	阮映嘉
Nguyễn Hoàng	阮潢
Nguyễn Huệ Quang Trung	阮文惠光中
Nguyễn Phước Châu (Phúc Chu)	阮福週
Nguyễn Phước Nguyên	阮福原
Nguyễn Văn Tồn	阮文存
nhất xã nhất thôn	一社一村
nông	農
Ô Châu cận lục	烏州近綠
pao	砲
phó hương hội	付 鄉 會
phủ	府
Phú Xuân	富春

phụ điền sản	父田產
pilipao	霹靂砲
quan viên	官 員
Quảng Nam	廣南
quận công	郡公
quân phân	均分
Quốc Sử Quán	國史館
Quốc Triều Hình Luật	國朝刑律
Sài Giang	柴江
shenchong	神銃
shenji chong	神機銃
shenji huoqiang	神機火槍
shenji jiangjun	神機將軍
shenji qiangpao fa	神機槍砲法
shenji ying	神機營
shenjian	神箭
shenqiang	神槍
shen qiang jian	神槍箭
shouba chong	手把銃
sĩ	士
sông thị	江市
tân mại điền sản	新賣田
Tân Ninh	新冰
tiên thổ	先土
Thái Tử Thái Phó	太子太傅
Thần Nông(Shen Nong)	神農
Thiên Y A Na (or Bà Mụ)	天依阿哪
thôn	村
Thu Bồn	秋盆
thương	商

tỉ muội	姊妹
tỉnh	省
tông	宗
Trà/Chà	茶
Trà Kiệu	茶蕎
trấn	鎮
triều đình	朝廷
Triệu Phong	肇豐
Trịnh	鄭
Trịnh Hoài Đức	鄭怀德
Trương Sĩ Tải	張士載
Trường Sơn	長山
tử tôn	子孫
Tư Vinh	思榮
tương phân	相分
Vinh Ma Ly	榮麻離
Võng Nhị	綱貳
wankou chong	碗口銃
xã	社
xã trưởng	社長
xianren dong	仙人洞
xiangyang pao	襄陽砲
Xiao Annan Ying	小安南營
xiao fei pao	小飛砲
xứ	處
yemingguang huoyao	夜明光火藥
Yueqiao shu	越嶠書
yunti	雲梯

zhankou jiangjun pao	盞口將軍砲
zhanpeng	戰棚
zhuli heichi	侏離黑齒

Bibliography

Agulhon, Maurice. *The French Republic, 1879–1992.* Translated by Antonia Nevill. Oxford: Blackwell, 1993.

———. *Marianne au pouvoir: l'imagerie et la symbolique républicaines de 1880 à 1914.* Paris: Flammarion, 1989.

———. *Marianne into Battle: Republican Imagery and Symbolism in France 1789–1880.* Cambridge: Cambridge University Press, 1981.

al-Ahmadi, Abdul Rahman. "Champa in Malay Literature." In *Proceedings of the Seminar on Champa: University of Copenhagen on May 23, 1987,* edited by Pierre-Bernard Lafont, translated from the original French (Paris, 1988) by Huynh Dinh Te, 100–109. Rancho Cordova, CA: Southeast Asia Community Resource Center, 1994.

Aldrich, Robert. *Greater France: A History of French Overseas Expansion.* New York: St. Martin's Press, 1996.

Andaya, Barbara Watson. *Perak, the Abode of Grace: A Study of an Eighteenth-Century Malay State.* New York: Oxford University Press, 1979.

———. *To Live as Brothers: Southeast Sumatra in the Seventeenth and Eighteenth Centuries.* Honolulu: University of Hawaii Press, 1993.

Anderson, Benedict. *Imagined Communities: Reflections on the Origins and Spread of Nationalism.* London: Verso Press, 1983.

Annan zhiyuan [Records of Annam]. Hanoi: Imprimérie d'Éxtrême Orient, 1932.

Arima Seiho. *Kaho no kigen to sono denryu* [The Origin of Firearms and Their Transmission]. Tokyo: Yoshikawa Kobunkan, 1962.

Bá Đa Lộc Bi Nhu [Pierre Pigneaux de Béhaine]. *Tự vị Annam Latinh* [Dictionarium anamitico-latinum]. Translated into quốc ngữ by Hồng Nhuệ and Nguyễn Khác Xuyên. Hanoi: Nhà Xuất Bản Trẻ 1999.

Bai Shouyi. "Mingdai kuangye de fazhan" [The Development of the Mining Industry during the Ming Dynasty]. *Beijing Shifan Daxue xuebao* 1 (1956): 95–129.

Baron, Samuel. "A Description of the Kingdom of Tonqueen, by Samuel Baron, a Native Thereof." In *Collection of Voyages and Travels,* 6:1–40. London: A. & W. Churchhill, 1732.

Barrow, John. *A Voyage to Cochinchina.* Kuala Lumpur: Oxford, 1975.

Bassino, Jean-Pascal, Jean-Dominique Giacometti, and Konosuke Odak, eds. *Quantitative Economic History of Vietnam, 1900–1990.* Tokyo: Institute of Economic Research Hitosubashi University, 2000.

Bế Viết Đẳng. *Các Dân tộc ít người ở Việt Nam.* 2 vols. Hanoi: Nhà Xuất Bản Khoa Học Xã Hội, 1978, 1984.

Bế Viết Đẳng and Nguyễn Khắc Tụng. *Người Dao ở Việt Nam.* Hanoi: Nhà Xuất Bản Khoa Học Xã Hội, 1971.

Becker, Jean-Jacques. *The Great War and the French People.* Translated by Arnold Pomerans. Dover, NH: Berg, 1985.

Bellanger, Claude, Jacques Godechot, Pierre Guiral, and Fernand Terrou, eds. *Histoire générale de la presse française.* Vol. 3, *De 1871 à 1940.* Paris: Presses Universitaires de France, 1972.

Ben-Amos, Avner. *Funerals, Politics, and Memory in Modern France, 1789–1996.* Oxford: Oxford University Press, 2000.

Benda, Henry. "Peasant Movements in Colonial Southeast Asia." In *Continuity and Change in Southeast Asia: Collected Journal Articles of Harry Benda,* edited by Harry Benda, 221–35. Monograph Series, no. 18. New Haven, CT: Yale University Southeast Asia Studies, 1972.

Bento, Thiện. "Lịch sử nước Annam." Jap/Sin vol. 81:248–50. Archivum Romanum Societatis Iesu. Unpublished manuscript, 1659.

Bernhardt, Kathryn. "The Inheritance Rights of Daughters: The Song Anomaly?" *Modern China* 21, no. 3 (July 1995): 269–309.

———. *Women and Property in China.* Stanford, CA: Stanford University Press, 1999.

Berteloot, Joseph. *La franc-maçonnerie et l'église Catholique.* Lausanne: Éditions du Monde Nouveau, 1947.

Betts, Raymond. *Assimilation and Association in French Colonial Theory, 1890–1914.* New York: Columbia University Press, 1960.

Bhabha, Homi. *The Location of Culture.* New York: Routledge, 1994.

Bielenstein, Hans. "The Chinese Colonization of Fukien until the End of the Tang." In *Studia Serica: Bernhard Karlgren Dedicata,* compiled by Soren Egorod and Else Glahn, 98–122. Copenhagen: Ejnar Munkgaard, 1959.

Bình, Philiphê. "Nhật trình kim thư khát chính Chúa giáo" [Daily Records, Current Letters, and Supplications to the Lord Teacher]. MS Borgiana Tonchinese 7. Biblioteca Apostolica Vaticana.

———. "Sách sổ sang chép các việc" [Notebook That Transmits and Records All Matters]. MS Borgiana Tonchinese 3. Biblioteca Apostolica Vaticana.

———. "Truyện Anam," quyển I [Tales of Annam, book 1]. MS Borgiana Tonchinese 1. Biblioteca ApostolicaVaticana.

———. "Truyện Anam," quyển II [Tales of Annam, book 2]. MS Borgiana Tonchinese 2. Biblioteca Apostolica Vaticana.

Birge, Bettine. *Women, Property and Confucian Reaction in Sung and Yuan China (960–1368).* Cambridge: Cambridge University Press, 2002.

Blagden, C. O., and E. D. Edwards. "A Chinese Vocabulary of Cham Words and Phrases." *Bulletin of the School of Oriental and African Studies* 10 (1940–42): 53–91.

Blanc, Marie-Eve. "La Pratique associative vietnamienne, tradition et modernité: Tuong Te Hoi." PhD diss., Département de Sociologie, Université de Provence, 1995.

Borri, Cristoforo. *Cochin-China*. London, 1633. Facsimile reprint, New York: Da Capo Press, 1970.

———. *Cochin-China: Containing Many Admirable Rarities and Singularities of That Countrey.* Translated from the original Italian by Robert Ashley. London: Robert Raworth, 1633.

Bouche, Denise. *Histoire de la colonisation française. Vol. 2, Flux et reflux (1815–1962).* Paris: Fayard, 1991.

Bouhier, Emanuel. "Les troupes coloniales d'Indochine en 1914–1918." In *Les troupes coloniales dans la Grand Guerre,* edited by Claude Carlier and Guy Pedroncini, 69–81. Paris: Economica, 1997.

Bounais, A., and A. Paulus. "Indo-Chine Française." In *La France coloniale, histoire, géographie, commerce,* edited by Alfred Rambaud, 410–529. Paris: A. Colin, 1886.

Boxer, C. R. "Asian Potentates and European Artillery in the 16th–18th Centuries: A Footnote to Gibson-Hill." *Journal of the Malayan Branch of the Royal Asiatic Society* 38, no. 2 (1965): 156–72.

———. *The Portuguese Seaborne Empire.* Manchester: Carcanet Press, 1991.

Bradley, Mark Phillip. *Imagining Vietnam and America: The Making of Postcolonial Vietnam, 1919–1950.* Chapel Hill: University of North Carolina Press, 2000.

Braudel, Fernand. *The Mediterranean and the Mediterranean World in the Age of Philip II.* Translated by Sian Reynolds. New York: Harper & Row, 1972.

Briffaut, Camille. *La cité annamite.* 3 vols. Paris: Librairie Coloniale & Orientaliste, Emile Larose, 1909–12.

———. *Études sur les biens cultuels familiaux en pays d'Annam, Huong-Hoa.* Paris: Librairie de la Société du Recueil J.-B. Sirey & du Journal du Palais, 1907.

Brocheux, Pierre. *The Mekong Delta: Ecology, Economy, and Revolution, 1860–1960.* Madison: University of Wisconsin–Madison, Center for Southeast Asian Studies, 1995.

Brocheux, Pierre, and Daniel Hémery. *Indochine: La colonisation ambigué, 1858–1954.* Paris: Édition la Découverte, 1995.

Bronson, Bennet. "Exchange at the Upstream and Downstream Ends: Notes toward a Functional Model of the Coastal State in Southeast Asia." In *Economic Exchange and Social Interaction in Southeast Asia: Perspectives from Prehistory, History, and Ethnography,* edited by Karl Hutterer, 39–52. Ann Arbor: University of Michigan, Center for South and Southeast Asian Studies, 1977.

Buchan, John. *A History of the Great War.* Vol. 3. New York: Houghton Mifflin, 1922.

Bùi Huy Đáp. *Văn minh lúa nước và nghề trồng lúa Việt Nam.* Hanoi, 1995.

Bùi Quang Chiêu. *La polygamie dans le droit annamite.* Paris: Rousseau & Cie, 1933.

Bùi Thị Tân. *Về hai làng truyền thống Phú Bài và Hiền Lương.* Hue: Nhà Xuất Bản Thuận Hóa, 2000.

Bùi Văn Thịnh. *l'usufruit familial et la veuve en droit Vietnamien.* Saigon: Imprimerie de J. O., 1949.

Bùi Văn Vượng. *Làng nghề thủ công truyền thống Việt Nam.* Hanoi: Nhà Xuất Bản Văn Hóa Dân Tộc, 1998.

Bùi Xuân Đính. "Bàn Về mối quan hệ giữa làng và xã qua qui mô cấp xã thời phong kiến." In *Nghiên cứu Việt Nam: một số vấn đề lịch sử, xã hội, kính tế, văn hóa,* edited by Đình Xuân Lâm and Dương Lan Hải. Hanoi: Nhà Xuất Bản Thế Giới, 1998.

———. *Hương ước và quản lý làng xã.* Hanoi: Nhà Xuất Bản Khoa Học Xã Hội, 1998.

———. *Lệ làng phép nước.* Hanoi: Pháp Lý, 1985.

———. *Lịch sử xã Đông La.* Hanoi, 1995.

Buttinger, Joseph. *A Dragon Defiant: A Short History of Vietnam.* New York: Praeger, 1971.

———. *Vietnam: A Dragon Embattled.* Vol. 1. London: Pall Mall Press, 1967.

Cadière, Léopold M. "Les Européens qui ont vu le vieux Hué: Cristoforo Borri." *Bulletin des Amis du Vieux Hué* 18, nos. 3–4 (July–December 1931): 261–65; 409–32 (plus 28 leaves).

———. "Les Français aux service de Gia-Long III: Leurs nôms, titres, et appellations annamites." *Bulletin des Amis du Vieux Hué* 7, no. 1 (1920): 137–76.

———. "Les Français aux service de Gia-Long XI: Nguyễn Ánh et la mission, documents inédits." *Bulletin des Amis du Vieux Hué* 13, no. 1 (1926): 1–49.

Cadière, R. L., and Paul Pelloit. "Première étude sur des sources annamites de l'histoire d'Annam." *Bulletin de l'École Française d'Extrême Orient* 4 (1904): 617–71.

Cẩm Trọng. *Người Thái ở tây bắc Việt Nam.* Hanoi: Nhà Xuất Bản Khoa Học Xã Hội, 1978.

Cannsu Kamani Sankram. *Jan May rajavan* [Chiang Mai Chronicle]. Unpublished palm leaf. Burma Microfilm Series. University of Michigan Graduate Library.

Cao Huy Thuần. *Les missionnaires et la politique coloniale française au Vietnam 1857–1914.* New Haven, CT: Council on Southeast Asia Studies, Yale Center for International and Area Studies, 1990.

Cao Xuân Dục, comp. *Đại Nam nhất thông chí* [Unified Gazetteer of Great South]. 1909. Original Hán with quốc ngữ translation. Saigon: Nhà Văn hoá, Bộ Quốc gia Giáo Dục, 1964.

———. comp. *Đại Nam nhất thông chí* [Unified Gazetteer of Great South]. 1909. Translated into quốc ngữ by Phạm Trọng Điềm. Hanoi: Nxb. Thuận Hoá, 1997.

Cao Xuân Huy, ed. *Một vài sử liệu về Bắc Bình Vương Nguyễn Huệ.* Glendale,
CA: Đại Nam, 1992.

Carlier, Claude, and Guy Pedroncini, eds. *Les Troupes Coloniales dans la Grand
Guerre.* Paris: Economica, 1997.

Chaigneau, Michel Đức. *Souvenirs de Huế.* Paris: Imprimerie Impériale, 1863.

Chan Hok-lam (Chen Xuelin). "Mingdai Annan ji huanguan shishi kaoshu—
Jin Ying, Xing An." In *Mingdai renwu yu shiliao* [Essays on Ming Person-
ages and Historical Sources], 205–63. Hong Kong: Chinese
University of Hong Kong, 2001.

Chatterjee, Partha. *The Nation and Its Fragments: Colonial and Post-Colonial Histories.* Princeton, NJ: Princeton University Press, 1993.

Chen Chingho (Chen Jinghe), ed. *Đại Việt sử ký toàn thư* ⊚⊚[Complete Book of
the Historical Record of Dai Viet]. Tokyo: Tokyo Daigaku Toyo Bunka
Kenkyujo, 1984–86.

———. *Historical Notes on Hoi-An (Faifo).* Carbondale: Center for Vietnamese
Studies, Southern Illinois University, 1974.

———. "Les missions officielles dans les Ha châu ou 'contrées meridionales'
de la première periode des Nguyên." *Bulletin de l'École Française d'
Extrême-Orient* 81 (1994).

Chen Jiarong, comp. *Gudai Nanhai diming huishi* [Compendium of Topogra-
phy for Ancient Southeast Asia]. Beijing: Zhonghua shuju, 1986.

Chen Zongfan. *Yandu congkao* [Studies of the Capital Beijing]. Beijing: Beijing
Guji Chubanshe, 1991.

Cheng Dong and Zhong Shaoyi, eds. *Zhongguo gudai bingqi tuji* [Ancient Chinese Weapons: A Collection of Pictures]. Beijing: Jiefangjun Chubanshe,
1990.

Chevalier, Pierre. *Histoire de la Franc-Maçonnerie Française. Vol. 3, La Maçon-
nerie: Église de la République (1877–1944).* Paris: Fayard, 1975.

Choi Byung Wook. *Southern Vietnam under the Reign of Minh Mạng
(1820–1841): Central Policies and Local Response.* Ithaca, NY: Southeast Asia
Program, Cornell University, 2004.

Cholvy, Gérard, and Yves-Marie Hilaire. *Histoire religieuse de la France contem-
poraine.* 2 vols. Toulouse: Privat, 1985.

Chu Hữu Quý. "Trang trại gia đình một hiện tương kinh tế xã hội mới xuất
hiện trên một số vùng nông thôn nước ta." In *Việt Nam Học Kỷ Yếu Hội
Thảo Quốc Tế Lần thư nhất,* edited by the Center for Social Sciences of Humanities of the Hà Nội National University. Hanoi: Nhà Xuất Bản Thế
Giới, 2000.

Chu Quang Trú. *Kiến trúc dân gian truyền thống Việt Nam.* Hanoi: Nhà Xuất
Bản Mỹ Thuật, 1996.

———. *Sáng giá chùa xưa.* Hanoi: Nhà Xuất Bản Mỹ Thuật, 2001.

———. *Tìm hiểu làng nghệ thủ công điêu khắc cổ truyền.* Hue: Nhà Xuất Bản
Thuận Hóa, 1997.

Chử Văn Lâm. *Hớp tác hóa nông nghiệp Việt Nam.* Hanoi: Sự Thật, 1991.

"Chúc thư văn khế cửu chỉ" [Ancient Wills, Testaments, and Contracts]. Hán
original. MS A.2917. Institute of Hán-Nôm Studies, Hanoi.

Ciyuan [Word Origins]. 4 vols. 1915. Rev. ed. Beijing: Shangwu shuju, 1979–84.

Claeys, Jean Yves. "Introduction à l'étude de l'Annam et du Champa." *Bulletin des Amis du Vieux Hué* 21, no. 1/2 (1934): 11–132.

———. "Inspections et reconnaissances en Annam: Quang-nam." *Bulletin de l'École Française d'Extreme Orient* 28 (1928): 596–98.

Clark, Hugh R. *Community, Trade and Networks: Southern Fujian Province from the Third to the Thirteenth Century.* Cambridge: Cambridge University Press, 1991.

Clark, Maurice, Walton H. Hamilton, and Harold G. Moulton. *Readings in the Economics of War.* Chicago: University of Chicago Press, 1996.

Coedès, Georges. *Histoire ancienne des états hindouisés d'Extrême-Orient.* Hanoi: EFEO, 1944. Third edition translated by Susan Brown Cowing as *The Indianized States of Southeast Asia.* Honolulu: University of Hawaii Press, 1967.

"Công án Tra Nghiệm Bí Pháp." MS A.1760. Institute of Hán-Nôm Studies, Hanoi.

Công Huyền Tôn Nữ Nha Trang. "The Traditional Roles of Women as Reflected in Oral and Written Vietnamese Literature." PhD diss., University of California, 1973.

Cooke, Nola. "Colonial Political Myth and the Problem of the Other: French and Vietnamese in the Protectorate of Annam." PhD diss., Australian National University, 1992.

———. "The Myth of the Restoration: Dang-trong Influences in the Spiritual Life of the Early Nguyen Dynasty (1802–47)." In *The Last Stand of Asian Autonomies,* edited by Anthony Reid, 265–96. Basingstoke: Macmillan, 1997.

———. "Regionalism and Nguyen Rule in Seventeenth-Century Đàng Trong (Cochinchina)." *Journal of Southeast Asian Studies* 29, no. 1 (March 1998): 122–61.

Copin-Albancelli, Paul. *La Franc-maçonnerie et la question religieuse.* Rev. ed. Paris: Perrin, 1905.

Cosserat, H. "Documents A. Salles III: Philippe Vannier." *Bulletin des Amis du Vieux Hué* 22, no. 2 (1935): 121–86.

———. "Documents A. Salles IV: Laurent Barizy." *Bulletin des Amis du Vieux Hué* 26, no. 3 (1939): 173–236.

———. "Note au sujet de la mort de Ma no ê (Manuel) et de un officer irlandais." *Bulletin des Amis du Vieux Hué* 7, no. 4 (1920): 454–58.

Courdurie, Marcel, and Jean-Louis Miège. *Histoire du commerce et de l'industrie de Marseille xix–xxe siècle: Marseille colonial face à la crise de 1929.* Marseille: Chambre de Commerce de d'Industrie Marseille-Provence, 1991.

Crawfurd, John. *Journal of an Embassy from the Governor General of India to the Courts of Siam and Cochin-China.* 1828. Reprint, Kuala Lumpur: Oxford University Press, 1967.

Cross, Gary. *Immigrant Workers in Industrial France.* Philadelphia: Temple University Press, 1983.

Cục Thông Kế. *Niên giam thông kế 1999* [Statistical Almanac, 1999]. Hanoi: Cục Thông Kế, 2000.

Cupet, Le Capitaine. *Mission Pavie, Indo-Chine 1897–1895: Géographie et voyages. Vol. 3, Voyages au Laos et chez les sauvages du sud-est de l'Indo-Chine.* Paris: Ernest Leroux, 1900.

Cushman, Jennifer. *Fields from the Sea.* Ithaca, NY: Southeast Asia Publications, Cornell University, 1993.

"Đại Việt sử ký tục biên." MS A.1189. Institute of Hán-Nôm Studies, Hanoi.

Dalrymple, Alexander. *Oriental Reportory.* London: East-India Company, 1808.

Daney, Charles. *Quand les Français découvraient l'Indochine.* Paris: Editions Herscher, 1981.

Đẳng Cộng Sản Việt Nam: Ban nông nghiệp trung ương. *Kinh tế xã hội nông thôn Việt Nam ngày nay.* 2 vols. Hanoi: Tư Tưởng Văn Hóa, 1991.

Đặng Nghiêm Vạn and Cầm Trọng. *Các dân tộc Gia-Lai Công Tum.* Hanoi: Nhà Xuất Bản Khoa Học Xã Hội, 1981.

Đặng Nghiêm Vạn et al. *Những nhóm dân tộc thuộc ngữ hệ Nám Á ở tây bắc Việt Nam.* Hanoi: Nhà Xuất Bản Khoa Học Xã Hội, 1972.

———. *Về tín ngưỡng tôn giáo Việt Nam hiện nay.* Hanoi: Nhà Xuất Bản Khoa Học Xã Hội, 1998.

Đăng Phương Nghi. "Triều đại Vua Quang Trung dưới mất các nhà truyền giáo tây phương." In *Một vài sử liệu về Bắc Bình Vương Nguyễn Huệ,* edited by Cao Xuân Huy, 231–74. Glendale, CA: Đại Nam, 1992.

Đăng Thu, ed. *Di dân của người Việt từ thế kỷ X đến giữa thế kỷ XIX* [Migration of Vietnamese from the Tenth to the Nineteenth Centuries]. Hanoi: Viện Sử Học, 1994.

Đặng Văn Lung, Nguyên Sông Thao, and Hoàng Văn Trụ. *Phong tục tạp quán dân tộc Việt Nam.* Hanoi: Nhà Xuất Bản Văn Hóa Dân Tộc, 1999.

Đặng Văn Tu. "Danh nhân Ngô Sĩ Liên" [A Noted Person, Ngô Sĩ Liên]. In *Ngô Sĩ Liên và Đại Việt sử ký toàn thư* [Ngô Sĩ Liên and the Đại Việt sử ký tòan thư], edited by Phan Đại Doãn. Hanoi: Nhà Xuất Bản Chính trị quốc gia, 1998.

Đặng Xuân Viễn. "Hương Chính Cải Lương." *Nam Phong* 141 (1929).

Đào Duy Anh. *Việt Nam văn hóa sử cương.* Hue: Quan Hải Tùng Thư, 1938. Translated into Chinese as *Yuenan lidai jiangyu* [Vietnam's Territories throughout History] by Zhong Minyan (Dai Kelai). Beijing: Shangwu Yinshuguan, 1973.

Đào Thế Tuấn. *Khảo sát các hình thức tổ chức hợp tác xã của nông dân nước ta hiện nay.* Hanoi: Nhà Xuất Bản Chính Trị Quốc Gia, 1995.

———. *Kinh tế hội nông dân.* Hanoi: Nhà Xuất Bản Chính Trị Quốc Gia, 1997.

Delacroix, Simon, ed. *Histoire universelle des missions catholique.* Paris: Librairie Grund, 1957.

de Lanessan, Jean Marie-Antoine. *La colonisation française en Indo-Chine.* Paris: F. Alcan, 1895.

———. *l'expansion coloniale de la France: Étude économique, politique et géographique sur les establissements français d'outre-mer.* Paris: F. Alcan, 1886.

———. *l'Indo-Chine francaise: Étude politique, économique et administrative sur la Cochinchine, le Cambodge, l'Annam et le Tonkin*. Paris: F. Alcan, 1889.

———. *Les missions et leur protectorat*. Paris: F. Alcan, 1907.

Delaplace, F. *La révérende mère Anne-Marie Javouhey, fondatrice de la congrégation de Saint-Joseph de Cluny*. 2 vols. Paris: V. Lecoffre, 1886.

Déloustal, Raymond. "La justice dans l'ancien Annam." *Bulletin de l'École Française d'Extreme Orient* 8 (1908): 177–220; 9 (1909): 91–122, 471–91, 765–86; 10 (1910): 1–60, 349–505; 11 (1911): 25–66; 12 (1912): 1–33; 13 (1913): 1–59; 19 (1919): 1–81; 22 (1922): 1–35.

Devillers, Philippe. *Français et annamites: Partenaires ou ennemis? 1856–1902*. Paris: Denoel, 1998.

Diệp Đinh Hoa. *Làng Nguyễn: Tìm hiểu làng Việt II*. Hanoi: Nhà Xuất Bản Khoa Học Xã Hội, 1994.

Đinh Gia Khánh and Lê Hữu Tầng. *Lễ hội truyền trong đời sống xã hội hiện đại*. Hanoi: Nhà Xuất Bản Khoa Học Xã Hội, 1993.

Đinh Khắc Thuân. "Contribution a l'histoire de la dynastie des Mặc au Việt Nam." PhD diss., Université de Paris, 2002.

———. *Văn bia thời Mặc*. Hanoi: Nhà Xuất Bản Khoa Học Xã Hôi, 1996.

Đinh Thái Sơn. *Nam kỳ phong tục nhơn vật diễn ca* [Ballades on the Customs and People of Southern Việt Nam]. Saigon: Phát-Toàn, Librarie-Imprimeur, 1909.

Đỗ Bang. *Phố cảng Thuận-Quảng thế kỷ 17 và 18* [The Ports of Thuận-Quảng in the Seventeenth and Eighteenth Centuries]. Hue: Nhà Xuất Bản Thuận Hoá, 1996.

———. "Relations between the Port Cities in Đàng Trong and Pho Hiên in the Seventeenth–Eighteenth Centuries." In *Phố Hiến: The Centre of International Commerce in the XVIIth–XVIIIth Centuries*, compiled by the Association of Vietnamese Historians, 195–203. Hanoi: Thế Giới Publishers, 1994.

Đỗ Chi Lan. *La mère et l'enfant au Vietnam et d'autrefois*. Paris: Harmattan, 1996.

Đỗ Đức Hùng. "Góp phần tìm hiểu tiểu sử và hành trang của Ngô Sĩ Liên" [A Short Biography of Ngô Sĩ Liên and His Achievements]. In *Ngô Sĩ Liên và Đại Việt sử ký toàn thư* [Ngo Si Lien and the Dai Viet su ky toan thu], edited by Phan Đại Doãn. Hanoi: Nhà Xuất Bản Chính trị quốc gia, 1998.

Đỗ Khải Đại. *Hương Ước xã Nam Trung*. Hanoi, 1996.

Đỗ Nguyên Phương. *Những vấn đề chính tri—xã hội của cơ cấu xã hội—giai cấp ở nước ta*. Hanoi: Chính Trị Quốc Gia, Khoa Học & Kỹ Thuật, 1993.

Đỗ Thiện. "Cải Lương Hương Chính." *Nam Phong* 99 (1925).

"Đông khê thôn khoán ước" [Regulations of Đông Khê (Village)]. MS A.2875. Hán-nôm original. Institute of Hán-Nôm Studies, Hanoi.

Đồng Phố. *Lịch Sử khẩn hoang miền Nam*. Saigon: Sơn Nam, 1973.

Donoghue, John. *My Thuan, a Mekong Delta Village in South Vietnam*. Saigon: Michigan State University, Vietnam Advisory Group, 1961.

Doumer, Paul. *l'Indo-Chine française (souvenirs)*. Paris: Vuibert & Nony, 1905.

———. *La situation de l'Indo-Chine, 1897–1901*. Hanoi: F. H. Schneider, 1902.

Dourisbourne, Pierre. *Les sauvages Ba-Hnars, souvenir d'un missionnaire*. Paris: Le Coffre, 1875.

Duara, Prasenjit. *Rescuing History from the Nation.* Chicago: University of Chicago Press, 1995.

Dubesset, Mathilde, Françoise Thébaud, and Catherine Vincent. "The Female Munition Workers of the Seine." In *The French Home Front, 1914–1918,* edited by Patrick Fridenson, 183–218. Oxford: Berg, 1992.

Dương Văn An, comp. *Ô Châu cận lục* [A Record of Ô Châu and Environs]. Ca. 1555. Translated into quốc ngữ by Bùi Lương. Saigon: Văn Hóa Á Châu, 1961.

———, comp. *Ô Châu cận lục* [A Record of Ô Châu and Environs]. Ca. 1555. Original Hán with quốc ngữ translation by Trịnh Khác Mạnh and Nguyễn Văn Nguyên. Hanoi: Nhà Xuất Bản Khoa Học Xã Hội, 1997.

Dương Văn Giao. "l'Indochine Pendant la Guerre de 1914–1918." PhD diss., Faculté de Droit, Université de Paris, 1925.

Dutton, George. "The Tây Sơn Uprising: Society and Rebellion in the Late Eighteenth Century Việt Nam, 1771–1802." PhD diss., University of Washington, 2001.

Ebrey, Patricia. *The Inner Quarters: Marriage and the Lives of Women in the Sung Period.* Berkeley: University of California Press, 1993.

Eckert, Henri. "Les militaires indochinois au service de la France, 1859–1939." 2 vols. PhD diss., Université de Paris IV–Sorbonne, 1998.

Exposition Coloniale de Paris. *Les armées françaises d'Outre-Mer: Les contingents coloniaux du soleil et de la gloire.* Paris: Imprimerie Nationale, 1931.

Faure, Alexis. *Les Français en Cochinchine au XVIIIe siècle: Monsigneur Pigneu de Béhaine évêque d'Adran.* Paris: A. Challamel, 1891.

Ferry, Jules. *Tonkin et la mère-patrie.* Paris: Victor Havard, 1890.

Fforde, Adam. *The Agrarian Question in North Vietnam, 1974–79.* Armonk, NY: M. E. Sharpe, 1989.

Finot, Louis. "Les études indochinois." *Bulletin de l'École Française d'Extreme Orient* 8 (1908): 177–99.

Fitzgerald, Frances. *Fire in the Lake: The Vietnamese and the Americans in Vietnam.* Boston: Little, Brown, 1971.

Ford, Thadeus, and Chadin Ford, trans. and ed. *The Dynastic Chronicles, Bangkok Era.* Tokyo: Centre for East Asian Cultural Studies, 1978.

Fôrest, Alain. *Les missionaires français au Tonkin et au Siam, XVIIe–XVIIIe siècles: Analyse comparée d'un relatif succés et d'un total échec.* Vol. 2, *Histoires du Tonkin.* Paris: l'Harmattan, 1998.

———. *Les missionaires français au Tonkin et au Siam, XVIIe–XVIIIe siècles: Analyse comparée d'un relatif succés et d'un total échec.* Vol. 3, *Organiser une église, convertir les infidèles.* Paris: l'Harmattan, 1998.

Garnier, Francis. *Voyage d'exploration en Indochine.* Paris: Editions La Découverte.

Gaspardone, Emile. "Annamites et Thai au XVe siècle." *Journal Asiatique* 231 (1939): 405–36.

———. "Le Quy-ly." In *Dictionary of Ming Biography, 1368–1644,* edited by L. Carrington Goodrich and Chaoying Fang, 1:798. New York: Columbia University Press, 1976.

Giacometti, Jean-Dominique. "Bases for Estimation of Agriculture in Central Vietnam before 1954: The Examples of Thanh Hóa and Nghệ An Provinces." In *Quantitative Economic History of Vietnam, 1900–1990,* edited by Jean-Pascal Bassino, Jean-Dominique Giacometti, and Konosuke Odaka, 105–24. Tokyo: Institute of Economic Research Hitosubashi University, 2000.

————. "Wages and Consumer Prices for Urban and Industrial Workers in Vietnam under French Rule, 1910–1954." In *Quantitative Economic History of Vietnam, 1900–1990,* edited by Jean-Pascal Bassino, Jean-Dominique Giacometti, and Konosuke Odaka, 163–214. Tokyo: Institute of Economic Research Hitosubashi University, 2000.

Giebel, Christoph. "Tôn Đức Thắng and the Imagined Ancestries of Vietnamese Communism." PhD diss., Cornell University, 1996.

————. *Imagined Ancestries of Vietnamese Communism: Ton Duc Thang and the Politics of History and Memory.* Seattle: University of Washington Press in association with the National University of Singapore Press, 2004.

————. "Tôn Đức Thắng and the Imagined Ancestries of Vietnamese Communism." PhD diss., Cornell University, 1996.

Gildea, Robert. *The Past in French History.* New Haven, CT: Yale University Press, 1994.

Girardet, Raoul. *l'idée coloniale en France de 1871 à 1962.* Paris: La Table Rond, 1972.

Goggin, Joyce, and Sonja Neef, eds. *Travelling Concepts I: Subjectivity, Hybridity, Text.* Amsterdam: ASCA, 2001.

Gonçalez, Blas Ruiz de Hernan. "Relation des affaires du Campā." Translated by Pierre-Yves Manguin. *Bulletin de l'École Francaise d'Extreme-Orient* 70 (1981): 258–59.

Gosselin, Charles. *l'empire d'Annam.* Paris: Perrin & Cie, Libraires-Editeurs, 1904.

Gouin, Eugène. *Dictionnaire vietnamien-chinois-français.* Saigon: Imprimerie d'Extrême-Orient, 1957.

Gourou, Pierre. *Les paysans du delta Tonkinois: étude de géographie humaine.* Paris: Les editions d'art et l'histoire, 1936.

————. *The Peasants of the Tonkin Delta: A Study of Human Geography.* 1936. Translated by Richard Miller. New Haven, CT: Human Relations Area Files, 1955.

Goyau, Georges. *La Franc-maçonnerie en France.* Paris: Perrin, 1899.

Grenville, J. A. S. *A History of the World in the Twentieth Century.* Cambridge, MA: Belknap Press, 1994.

Groffier, Valérien. *Héros trop oubliés de notre épopée coloniale.* Lyon: Emmanuel Vitte, 1906.

Grossheim, Martin. "Kontinuität und Wandel in nord-vietnamesischen Dorfgemeinschaften vom Beginn der Kolonialzeit bis zum Ende der Vietnam Kriege." PhD diss., Passau University, 1995.

————. "Local Government in Pre-colonial and Colonial Vietnam." In *Beyond Hanoi: Local Government in Vietnam,* edited by Benedict T. Kerkvliet and

David G. Marr, 54–89. Singapore: Institute of Southeast Asian Studies, 2004.

———. "Das vietnamesische Dorf und seine Transformation in der franzözischen Kolonialzeit" [The Vietnamese Village and Its Transformation during the French Colonial Period]. Passau: Passau Contributions to Southeast Asian Studies.

Gu Yingtai. *Mingshi jishi benmo* [History of the Ming Arranged by Events]. Taiwan: Sanmin Shuju, 1956.

Gudai Zhong Yue guanxi shi ziliao xuanbian [Selected Materials on the Ancient Sino-Vietnamese Relations]. Beijing: Zhongguo Shehui Kexue Chubanshe, 1982.

Guerlach, J. B. *"l'oeuvre néfaste." Réponse à l'oeuvre néfaste du R. P. Guerlach, par C. Paris.* Haiphong: Éditions du Courier d'Haiphong, 1906.

Gueyfier, René. *Essai sur le régime de la terre en Indochine.* Lyon: Bosc Frères & Riou, 1928.

Guildea, Robert. *The Past in French History.* New Haven, CT: Yale University Press, 1994.

Hà Văn Tấn. *Chùa Việt Nam.* Hanoi: Nhà Xuất Bản Khoa Học Xã Hội, 1993.

———. *Đình Việt Nam.* Ho Chi Minh City: Nhà Xuất Bản Thành Phố Hồ Chí Minh, 1998.

Hage, Ghassan. *White Nation: Fantasies of White Supremacy in a Multicultural Society.* Annandale, NSW: Pluto, 1998.

Hall, Kenneth R. "Economic History of Early Southeast Asia." In *Cambridge History of Southeast Asia,* edited by Nicholas Tarling, 1:252–60. Cambridge: Cambridge University Press, 1992.

———. *Maritime Trade and State Development in Early Southeast Asia.* Honolulu: University of Hawaii Press, 1985.

———. "The Politics of Plunder in the Cham Realm of Early Vietnam." In *Art and Politics in Southeast Asian History: Six Perspectives,* edited by Robert van Neil, 5–32. Center for Southeast Asian Studies Paper 32. Honolulu: University of Hawaii, Center for Southeast Asian Studies, 1989.

Hardach, Gerd. "Industrial Mobilization in 1914–1918: Production, Planning and Ideology." In *The French Home Front,* edited by Patrick Fridenson, 57–88. Providence, RI: Berg, 1992.

Haudrère, Philippe. *l'empire des rois, 1500–1789.* Paris: Denoel, 1997.

Hazelton, Keith. *A Synchronic Chinese-Western Daily Calendar, 1341–1661 A.D.* Minneapolis: Ming Studies, History Department, University of Minnesota, 1984.

Heidhues, Mary Somers. *Bangka Tin and Mentok Pepper: Chinese Settlement on an Indonesian Island.* Singapore: Institute of Southeast Asian Studies, 1992.

He Mengchun. *He Wenjian shuyi* [Memorials by He Mengchun]. Memorials presented 1496–1524. Reprint, Taipei: Taiwan Shangwu Yinshuguan, 1973.

Hémery, Daniel. *Révolutionnaires Vietnamiens et Pouvoir Colonial en Indochine: Communistes, Trotskystes, Nationalistes à Saigon de 1932 à 1937.* Paris: François Maspero, 1975.

Henry, James B. *The Small World of Khanh Hau.* Chicago: Aldine, 1964.

Henry, Yves. *l'économie agricole de l'Indochine*. Hanoi: Imprimérie d'Extrême Orient, 1932.

Hickey, Gerald Cannon. *Kingdom in the Morning Mist: Mayréna in the Highlands of Vietnam*. Philadelphia: University of Pennsylvania Press, 1988.

———. *Nghiên cứu một cộng đồng thôn xã Việt Nam, xã hội học* [The Study of a Vietnamese Rural Community, Sociology]. Translated from English into quốc ngũ by Bùi Quang Đa and Võ Hồng Phúc. Saigon: Tháng Giêng, 1960.

———. *Sons of the Mountains: Ethnohistory of the Vietnamese Central Highlands to 1954*. New Haven, CT: Yale University Press, 1982.

———. *Village in Vietnam*. New Haven, CT: Yale University Press, 1964.

Histoire de Pigneau de Béhaine, évêque d'Adran, négociateur et signateur du traité de 1787 entre la France et la Cochinchine. Paris: Typographie E. Panckoucke & Cie, 1863.

Hồ Đặc Diễm. *La puissance paternelle dans le droit annamite*. Paris: Jouve & cie, 1928.

Hồ Đức Thọ. *Lệ làng Việt Nam*. Hanoi: Nhà Xuất Bản Hà Nội, 1999.

Hồ Sĩ Giàng. *Từ thổ Đôi Trang đến xã Quỳn Đôi*. Vinh, 1988.

Hoàng Côn. "Chiêm Thành khảo" [A Study of Champa]. MS A.970. Institute of Hán-Nôm Studies, Hanoi.

Hoàng Hồng. "Tư tưởng sử học của Ngô Sĩ Liên" [Historical Thought of Ngô Sĩ Liên]. In *Ngô Sĩ Liên và Đại Việt sử ký toàn thư* [Ngo Si Lien and the Đại Việt sử ký toàn thư], edited by Phan Đại Doãn. Hanoi: Nhà Xuất Bản Chính trị quốc gia, 1998.

Hoàng Hữu Đôn. "Cải Lương Hương tục." *Nam Phong* 37 (1927).

Học Viện chính trị quốc gia Hồ Chí Minh. *Cộng đồng xã Việt Nam hiện nay.* Hanoi, 2001.

Hội Đồng lý luận tung ương. *Các chương trình khoa Học xã hội cấp nhà nước 1991–2000*. Hanoi, 1998.

Holmgren, Jennifer. "Myth, Fantasy or Scholarship: Images of the Status of Women in Traditional China." *Australian Journal of Chinese Affairs* 6 (July 1981): 147–70.

Hong, Lysa. *Thailand in the Nineteenth Century: Evolution of the Economy and Society*. Singapore: Institute of Southeast Asian Studies, 1984.

"Hồng Đức thiện chính" [The (Book) of Good Government]. Ca. sixteenth century. Nineteenth-century hand-copied Hán manuscript. MS A.330. Institute of Hán-Nôm Studies, Hanoi.

Hồng Đức thiện chính thư [The Book of Good Government]. Translated from the Hán into quốc ngũ by Nguyễn Sĩ Giắc, with original Hán manuscript. Saigon: Đại Học Viện Sài Gòn, Trường Luật Khoa Đại Học, 1959.

Houtart, François. *Sociologie d'une commune vietnamienne*. Louvain la Neuve: ICRSR Université Catholique de Louvaine, 1981.

Huang Fu. "Huang Zhongxuangong wenji" [Collection of Writings of Huang Fu]. In *Siku Quanshu cunmu congshu*, 198–442. Tainan, Taiwan: Zhuangyan Wenhua Shiye Youxian Gongsi, 1997.

Hucker, Charles O. *China's Imperial Past: An Introduction to Chinese History and Culture.* Stanford, CA: Stanford University Press, 1975.

Hui Lu. *Pingpi baijin fang* [The Washerman's Precious Salve]. 1st ed. after 1626. Reprint, ca. 1844.

Hunter, W. C. *The "Fan kwae" at Canton before Treaty Days, 1825–1844.* 1882. Reprint, Taipei: Ch'eng-wen, 1965.

Hurlbut, Floy. "The Fukienese: A Study in Human Geography." PhD diss., University of Nebraska, 1930. Muncie, IN: Floy Hurlbut, 1939.

Huỳnh Công Bá. "Tìm hiểu cộng cuộc khai khẩn vùng Bắc Quảng Nam dưới thời Trần" [Investigation into the Great Task of Opening the Region of Northern Quảng Nam in the Time of Trần]. *Nghiên cứu lịch sử* 2 (1961): 46–49.

Huỳnh Kim Khánh. *Vietnamese Communism, 1925–1945.* Ithaca, NY: Cornell University, 1994.

Huỳnh Lứa. *Góp phần tìm hiểu vùng đất nam Bộ các thế kỷ XVII, XVIII, XIX.* Hanoi, 2000.

———. *Lịch sử khai phá vùng đất Nam Bộ.* Ho Chí Minh City: Nhà Xuất Bản Thành Phố Hồ Chí Minh, 1987.

Huỳnh Ngọc Trang, Trương Ngọc Tường, and Hồ Tường. *Đình Nam Bộ.* Ho Chí Minh City: Nhà Xuất Bản Tín Ngưỡng và Nghi Lễ, 1993.

Huỳnh Sanh Thông. *An Anthology of Vietnamese Poems from the Eleventh through the Twentieth Centuries.* New Haven, CT: Yale University Press, 1996.

Hy Văn Lương. *Revolution in the Village.* Honolulu: University of Hawaii Press, 1992.

Innes, Ralph. "The Door Ajar: Japan's Foreign Trade in the Seventeenth Century." PhD diss., University of Michigan, 1980.

———. "Trade between Japan and Central Vietnam in the Seventeenth Century: The Domestic Impact." Unpublished manuscript, 1988.

Ishii Yoneo, ed. *The Junk Trade from Southeast Asia: Translations from the Tosen Fusetsu-gaki, 1674–1723.* Canberra: Research School of Pacific and Asian Studies, Australian National University; Singapore: Institute of Southeast Asian Studies, 1998.

Iwao Seiichi. "Annan koku tokou Chosenjin Cho Wan-byok ni tsuite (On the Biography of Cho Wan-byok, a Korean Who Sailed to Annam)." *Chosen gakuho* 6 (1954).

Jamieson, Neil. *Understanding Vietnam.* Berkeley: University of California Press, 1993.

Johnson, Wallace. *The Tang Code.* Vols. 1–3. Princeton, NJ: Princeton University Press, 1979.

Kawahara Masahiro. "Teiburyo no sokui nendai ni tsuite" [A Study on the Year of Đinh Bộ Lĩnh's Ascension to the Throne]. *Hosei Daigaku Bungakubu Kiyo* 15 (1970): 32–37.

Kelley, Liam C. "Vietnam through the Eyes of a Chinese Abbot: Dashan's *Haiwai Jishi* (1694–95)." Master's thesis, University of Hawaii at Manoa, 1996.

Kerkvliet, Benedict. *Land Struggles and Land Regimes in the Philippines and Vietnam during the Twentieth Century.* Amsterdam: CASA, 1993.

———. *State-Village Relations in Vietnam: Contested Co-operatives and Collectivization.* Clayton, Victoria: Center for Southeast Asian Studies, Monash University, 1990.

Kerkvliet, Benedict, and Gareth Porter. *Vietnam's Rural Transformation.* New York: Westview Press, 1996.

Keyes, Charles F. *The Golden Peninsula: Culture and Adaptation in Mainland Southeast Asia.* New York: Macmillan, 1977.

Kham dinh Viet su thong giam cuong muc [The Text and Commentary of the Complete Mirror of Vietnamese History as Ordered by the Emperor]. Taipei: Guoli Zhongyang Tushuguan, 1969.

Kleinen, John. "Sự Đáp ứng với Việc chuyển biến kinh tế ở một làng Bắc Bộ Việt Nam." In *Làng xã châu Á và ở Việt Nam,* edited by Mạc Đường. Ho Chi Minh City, 2000.

———. "The Village as Pretext: Ethnographic Praxis and the Colonial State in Vietnam." In *The Village in Asia Revisited,* edited by Jan Breman, Peter Kloos, and Ashwam Saith, 353–95. Delhi: Oxford University Press, 1997.

Ko, Dorothy. *Teachers of the Inner Chambers.* Stanford, CA: Stanford University Press, 1990.

Kobata Atsushi and Matsuda Mitsugu. *Ryukyuan Relations with Korea and South Sea Countries: An Annotated Translation of Documents in the Rekidai Hoan.* Kyoto: Atsushi Kobata, 1969.

Koeltz, L. *La guerre de 1914–1918.* Paris: Édition Sirey, 1966.

Koo Bum-Jin. "Betunam jinjo (1225–1400) mollak ui il yoin: Sanhwangje wa hwangsil gunchinhon wonchik ui bungkwe" [One Reason for the Fall of the Tran Dynasty (1225–1400): The Breakdown of the Senior Emperor System and Royal Endogamy]. *Seoul National University Papers on Asian History* 20 (1996): 18–25.

Kresser, Pierre. *La commune annamite en Cochinchine: Le recrutement des notables.* Paris: Domat Chrétien, 1935; Saigon, 1948.

Lacouture, Jean. *Jesuits: A Multibiography.* Washington, DC: Counterpoint, 1995.

Lafont, Pierre-Bernard, ed. *Les frontières du Vietnam: Histoires et frontières de la peninsule indochinoise. Ouvrage collectif.* Paris: Editions l'Harmattan, 1989.

———. "New Patterns on the Ethnic Composition of Champa." In *Proceedings of the Seminar on Champa: University of Copenhagen on May 23, 1987,* edited by Pierre-Bernard Lafont, 41–42, 69. Rancho Cordova, CA: Southeast Asia Community Resource Center, 1994.

———. ed. *Proceedings of the Seminar on Champa: University of Copenhagen on May 23, 1987.* Translated from the original French (Paris, 1988) by Huynh Dinh Te. Rancho Cordova, CA: Southeast Asia Community Resource Center, 1994.

"Lam sơn thực lục" [Veritable Records of the Lâm-sơn Rebellion]. MS VHV 4088. Institute of Hán-Nôm Studies, Hanoi.

"Lam sơn thực lục tục biên" [Sequel to the Lam sơn thực lục]. MS VHV 1384.
    Institute of Hán-Nôm Studies, Hanoi.
Larkin, Maurice. *Religion, Politics and Preferment in France since 1890: La Belle
    Epoque and Its Legacy.* Cambridge: Cambridge University Press, 1995.
Launay, Adrien. *Les cinquante-deux serviteurs de Dieu, français, annamites,
    chinois mis à mort pour la foi en Extrême-Orient de 1815–1856.* Paris: Téqui,
    1893.
———. *Histoire ancienne et moderne de l'Annam, Tonkin et Cochinchine, depuis
    l'année 2,700 avant l'ère chrétienne jusqu'à nos jours.* Paris: Challamel Ainé,
    1884.
———. *Histoire de la mission de Cochinchine 1658–1823: Documents historiques.*
    Paris: Indes Savantes, 2000.
———. *Histoire générale de la Société des Missions-Étrangères.* 3 vols. Paris:
    Téqui, 1894.
———. *Les Missionnaires français au Tonkin.* Paris: Delhomme & Briguet, 1900.
Lê, Nicole-Dominique. *Les Missions-Étrangères et la penetration française au Viêt-
    Nam.* Paris: Aubin, 1975.
Lê Đình Chân. *Cuộc đời oanh liệt của Tả Quân Lê Văn Duyệt.* Saigon: Phổ
    Thông, 1956.
Lê Hữu Khoa. *Les Vietnamiens en France: Insertion et identité.* Paris: Édition
    l'Harmattan, 1985.
Lê Quý Đôn. *Đại Việt thông sử* [A General History of Đại Việt]. Translation
    from the classical Chinese into quốc ngữ by Lê Mạnh Liệu. Saigon: Bộ Văn
    hóa giáo dục và thanh niên, 1973.
———. *Kiến văn tiểu lục.* Quốc ngữ translation. Hanoi: Khoa Học xã hội, 1977–
    78.
———. *Phủ biên tạp lục* [Miscellaneous Records of Pacification in the Border
    Area]. Ca. 1776. Hán with quốc ngữ translation by Lê Xuân Giáo. Reprint,
    Saigon: Phủ Quốc vụ khanh đặc trách Văn hóa, 1973.
———. *Phủ biên tạp lục* [Miscellaneous Records of Pacification in the Border
    Area]. Ca. 1776. Quốc ngữ translation Hanoi: Khoa Học xã hội, 1977–78.
Lê Tấn Nẫm. *Lễ hội cổ truyền.* Hanoi, 1992.
Lê Thành Khôi. *Histoire de l'Asie du Sud-Est.* 1959. Paris: P.U.F., 1967.
———. *Histoire du Việt Nam: Des origines à 1858.* 1971. Paris: Sudestasie, 1984.
———. *Histoire du Việt Nam: Des origines à 1858.* Paris: Sudestasie, 1987.
———. *Histoire du Việt Nam: Des origines à 1858.* Paris: Sudestasie, 1992.
"Lê triều hội điển" [Statutes of the Lê Dynasty]. MS A.52. Institute of Hán-
    Nôm Studies, Hanoi.
Lê Văn Hồ. "La mère de famille annamite." PhD diss., Université de Paris,
    1932.
Lejosne, Jean-Claude. *Le journal de voyage de Gerrit van Wuysthoff et de ses assis-
    tants au Laos (1641–1642).* Metz: Centre de documentation et d'information
    sur le Laos, 1993.
Li Bin. "Yongle chao he Annan de huoqi jishu jiaoliu" [The Exchange of Fire-
    arm Technologies between the Ming and Vietnam during the Yongle
    Reign]. In *Zhongguo gudai huoyao huoqi shi yanjiu* [Studies of the History of

Gunpowder and Firearms in Ancient China], edited by Zhong Shaoyi, 147–58. Beijing: Zhongguo Shehui Kexue Chubanshe, 1995.

Li Tana. "An Alternative Vietnam? The Nguyễn Kingdom in the Seventeenth and Eighteenth Centuries." *Journal of Southeast Asian Studies* 29, no. 1 (March 1998): 111–21.

———. *Nguyễn Cochinchina: Southern Vietnam in the Seventeenth and Eighteenth Centuries.* Studies on Southeast Asia 23. Ithaca, NY: Southeast Asia Program Publications, Cornell University, 1998.

Li Tana and Anthony Reid, eds. *Southern Vietnam under the Nguyễn: Documents on the Economic History of Cochinchina (Đàng Trong), 1602–1777.* Singapore: Institute of Southeast Asian Studies, 1993.

Li Wenfeng. *Yue qiao shu* [Records of Vietnam]. Introduction in 1540. Reprint, 1940.

Li Xu. *Jiean Laoren manbi* [Notes of the Jiean Laoren]. Beijing: Zhonghua Shuju, 1982.

Lieberman, Victor, ed. *Beyond Binary Histories: Re-imaging Eurasia to c. 1830.* Ann Arbor: University of Michigan Press, 1999.

———. "Local Integration and Eurasian Analogies: Structuring Southeast Asian History, c. 1350–c. 1830." *Modern Asian Studies* 27, no. 3 (1993): 475–572.

———. "Transcending East-West Dichotomies: State and Culture Formation in Six Ostensibly Disparate Areas." In *Beyond Binary Histories,* edited by Victor Lieberman, 19–102. Ann Arbor: University of Michigan Press, 1999.

Liu Kun. *Nanzhong zashuo* [Miscellanies of the Nanzhong Region]. Ca. 1680. Reprint, Taipei: Yiwen Yinshuguan, 1970.

Liu Zhenren. "Mingdai weisuo zhidu yanjiu" [A Study of the *weisuo* System of the Ming Dynasty]. PhD diss., Taiwan Guoli Zhengzhi Daxue Zhengzhi Xuexi, 1998.

Livermore, H. V. *A New History of Portugal.* 2nd ed. Cambridge: Cambridge University Press, 1976.

Lo Jung-pang (Luo Rongbang). "The Decline of the Early Ming Navy." *Oriens Extremus* 5, no. 2 (1958): 149–68.

———. "The Emergence of China as a Sea Power during the Late Song and Early Yüng Periods." *Far Eastern Quarterly* 14, no. 4 (1955): 489–504.

———. "Intervention in Vietnam: A Case Study of the Foreign Policy of the Early Ming Government." *Tsing Hua Journal of Chinese Studies,* n.s., 7, no. 2 (1969): 154–82.

Lochore, R. A. *History of the Idea of Civilization in France (1830–1870).* Bonn: Ludwig Rohrscheid, 1935.

Lockhart, Bruce M. "Colonial and Post-colonial Constructions of 'Champa'." Paper presented at the NUS–UNSW workshop "Ways of Seeing," Sydney, January 2000.

———. "Competing Narratives of the *Nam tien.*" Unpublished manuscript.

Louvet, Louis-Eugène. *La Cochinchine religieuse.* 2 vols. Paris: E. Leroux, 1885.

———. *Mgr d'Adran, notice biographique.* Saigon: Imprimerie de la mission. 1896.

———. *Mgr d'Adran, missionnaire et patriote.* 2nd ed. Paris: Delhomme & Briguet, 1900.

———. *Viede Mgr Puginier.* Hanoi: F. H. Schneider, 1894.

Lurô, Eliacin. *Cours annamite.* Saigon, 1872.

———. *Cours d'administration annamite.* Saigon: Collège des Stagiares, 1875.

———. *Le pays d'Annam.* Paris: E. Leroux, 1878.

Ma Khánh Bằng. *Người Sánh dìu ở Việt Nam.* Hanoi, 1983.

Mabbett, Ian, and David Chandler. *The Khmers.* Oxford: Blackwell, 1995.

Mặc Đường. *Các dân tộc miền núi Bắc Trung Bộ.* Hanoi: Nhà Xuất Bản Văn Hóa, 1964.

Mục lục châu bản Triều Nguyễn [Catalogue of the Nguyễn Archives]. Vol. 2. Hanoi: Văn Hóa Dân Tộc, 1998.

Magraw, Roger. *A History of the Working Class.* Vol. 2. Cambridge, MA: Blackwell, 1992.

Mai Thị Tú. "The Vietnamese Woman, Yesterday and Today." *Vietnamese Studies* 10 (1966): 7–59.

Mai Thị Tú and Lê Thị Nhầm Tuyết. *La femme au Vietnam.* Hanoi: Éditions en langues etrangères, 1976.

Maitre, C. E. "Critique sur M. Briffaut, *Étude sur les biens cultuels en pays d'Annam.*" *Bulletin de l'École Française d'Extreme Orient* 8, no. 1 (1908): 235–49.

———. "Introduction à l'ouvrage du M. Deloustal." *Bulletin de l'École Française d'Extreme Orient* 8, no. 1 (1908): 177–99.

Malarney, Shaun K. *Culture, Ritual and Revolution in Vietnam.* London: Routledge Curzon, 2002.

———. "Ritual and Revolution in Vietnam." PhD diss., University of Michigan, 1993.

Manguin, Pierre-Yves. *Les Nguyên, Macau et le Portugal: Aspects politiques et commerciaux d'une relation privilégiée en mer de Chine, 1773–1802.* Paris: École Française d'Extrême-Orient, 1984.

———. *Les Portugais sur les côtes du Vietnam et du Campa.* Publications de l'École Française d'Extrême-Orient, vol. 81. Paris: l'École Française d'Extrême-Orient, 1972.

Mann, Susan. *Precious Records: Women in China's Long Eighteenth Century.* Stanford, CA: Stanford University Press, 1997.

Mantienne, Frédéric. *Mgr Pierre Pigneaux, évêque d'Adran, dignitaire de Cochinchine.* Paris: Églises d'Asie, 1999.

———. "Le recours des états de la péninsule indochinoise à l'aide européenne dans leurs relations (XVIème–XVIIIème siècles)." In *Guerre et paix en Asie du Sud-Est,* edited by Nguyên Thê Anh and Alain Fôrest, 55–84. Paris: l'Harmattan, 1998.

Mao Qiling. *Mansi hezhi* [A Comprehensive Record of the Aboriginal Chieftains]. Taipei: Guangwen Shuju, 1968.

Mao Yuanyi. *Wu bei zhi* [Treatise on Military Defense]. Prefaced in 1621. Reprint, Beijing: Jiefangjun Chubanshe & Liaoshen Shushe, 1987.

Marquet, Jean. *Lettres d'annamites: Lettres de guerre, lettres de paix.* Hanoi: Édition du Fleuve Rouge, 1929.

Marr, David G. "The 1920s Debate on Women's Rights." *Journal of Asian Studies* 36, no. 3:371–89.

———. *Vietnamese Anticolonialism, 1885–1925.* Berkeley: University of California Press, 1971.

———. *Vietnamese Tradition on Trial, 1920–1945.* Berkeley: University of California Press, 1981.

Marrison, G. E. "The Chams of Malaka." *Journal of the Malaysian Branch Royal Asiatic Society* 24, no. 1 (1951): 90–98.

Maspéro, Georges. *The Champa Kingdom: The History of an Extinct Vietnamese Culture.* Bangkok: White Lotus Press, 2002.

———. *Un empire colonial français: l'Indochine.* 2 vols. Paris: Editions G. Ban Oest, 1929.

———. *Royaume de Champa.* Paris: Editions G. Van Oest, 1928.

Massot-Marin, Catherine. "Le rôle des missionnaires français en Cochinchine aux XVIIè et XVIIIè siècles: Fidélité à Rome et volonté d'indépendance." PhD diss., Université Paris IV–Sorbonne, UFR d'Histoire Moderne, 1998.

Maxwell, Kenneth. *Pombal: Paradox of the Enlightenment.* Cambridge: Cambridge University Press, 1995.

McAlister, John T., and Paul Mus. *The Vietnamese and Their Revolution.* New York: Harper & Row, 1970.

McConnell, Scott. *Leftward Journey: Vietnamese Students in France, 1919–1939.* New Brunswick, NJ: Transaction, 1989.

McHale, Shawn. *Print and Power: Confucianism, Communism, and Buddhism in the Making of Modern Vietnam.* Honolulu: University of Hawaii Press, 2004.

McLeod, Mark W. *The Vietnamese Response to French Invasion, 1862–1874.* New York: Praeger, 1991.

McNeill, William H. *The Age of Gunpowder Empires, 1450–1800.* Washington, DC: American Historical Association, 1989.

Meyer, Charles. *La vie quotidienne des français en Indochine, 1860–1910.* Paris: Hatchette, 1985.

Ming shi [The History of the Ming]. Beijing: Zhonghua Shuju, 1974.

Ming shilu leizuan—Junshi shiliao juan [Categorical Compilation of the *Ming shilu*—The Volume of Historical Sources on Military Affairs]. Wuhan: Wuhan Chubanshe, 1993.

Ming shilu leizuan—Shewai shiliao juan [Categorical Compilation of the *Ming shilu*—The Volume of Historical Sources on Foreign Relations]. Wuhan: Wuhan Chubanshe, 1991.

Ming shilu youguan Yunnan lishi ziliao zhaichao [Historical Records on Yunnan in the *Ming shilu*]. Kunming, Yunnan: Yunnan Renmin Chubanshe, 1959–63.

"Minh Đô Sử" [History of the Enlightened Capital]. MS VH285. Hà Nội Institute of History.

Misaki Shigehisa. "Nghiên Cứu làng Tran Liệt (huyện Tiên Sơn, tinh Bắc Ninh)." PhD diss, Kanda University for Foreign Languages.

Mitchell, B. R. *International Historical Statistics: Europe, 1750–1988.* 3rd ed. New York: Stockton Press, 1992.

Miyazawa Chihiro. "Nghiên Cứu làng Diễm Xá." PhD diss.

Momoki Shiro. "10–15 seiki Betonamu kokka no minami to nishi" [Vietnamese Policy toward Its Southern and Western Neighbors from the Tenth to the Fifteenth Centuries]. *Toyoshi kenkyu* 51, no. 3 (1992): 158–91.

———. "Dai Viet and the South China Sea Trade: From the Tenth to the Fifteenth Century." *Crossroads: An Interdisciplinary Journal of Southeast Asian Studies* 12, no. 1 (1998): 1–34.

———. "Was Champa a Pure Maritime Polity? Agriculture and Industry Recorded in Chinese Documents." Presented at 1998 Core University Seminar, Kyoto University and Thammasat University, "Eco-history and Rise/Demise of the Dry Areas in Southeast Asia," Kyoto University, Japan, October 13–16, 1998.

———. "Was Dai Viêt during the Early Lê Period (1428–1527) a Rival of Ryukyu within the Tributary Trade System of the Ming?" Presented at the Euro-Japanese International Seminar "Trade and Navigation in Southeast Asia," Institute of Asian Culture, Sophia University, October 1–4, 1997.

Montagnon, Pierre. *La France coloniale: La gloire de l'empire.* Paris: Pygmalion, 1988.

Mossard, Lucien. *Lettre de Mgr Mossard sur l'education donnée par la mission de Cochinchine.* Saigon: Imprimerie de la Mission, 1903.

Mote, Frederick W. "The T'u-mu Incident of 1449." In *Chinese Ways in Warfare,* edited by Frank A. Kierman Jr. and John K. Fairbank, 243–72. Cambridge, MA: Harvard University Press, 1974.

Moussay, Gérard. *Dictionnaire çam-vietnamien-français.* Phan Rang: Centre culturel Cam, 1971.

Murray, Dian. *Pirates on the South China Coast, 1790–1810.* Stanford, CA: Stanford University Press, 1987.

Murray, Martin J. *The Development of Capitalism in Colonial Indochina, 1870–1940.* Berkeley: University of California Press, 1976.

"Nécrologe." In *Compte-Rendu de la Société des Missions-Étrangères.* Paris, 1920.

Needham, Joseph. *Science and Civilisation in China.* Vol. 5, *Chemistry and Chemical Technology,* pt. 7, "Military Technology: The Gunpowder Epic." Cambridge: Cambridge University Press, 1986.

Ng Chin-keong. *Trade and Society: The Amoy Network on the China Coast, 1683–1735.* Singapore: Singapore University Press, 1983.

Ng, R. C. "The Geographical Habitat of Historical Settlement in Mainland Southeast Asia." In *Early South East Asia: Essays in Archaeology, History and Historical Geography,* edited by R. B. Smith and W. Watson, 262–72. New York: Oxford University Press, 1979.

Ngô Đức Thịnh. *Đạo mẫu ở Việt Nam.* 2 vols. Hanoi: Nhà Xuất Bản Văn Hóa Thông Tin, 1990.

Ngô Đức Thịnh and Cầm Trọng. *Luật tục Thái ở Việt Nam: Tạp quán pháp.* Hanoi: Nhà Xuất Bản Văn Hóa Dân Tộc, 1999.

Ngô Đức Thịnh and Chu Thái Sơn. *Luật tục Êđê: Tạp quán pháp*. Hanoi: Nhà Xuât Bản Chính Trị Quốc Gia, 1996.

Ngô Sĩ Liên, comp. *Đại Việt sử ký toán thư* [The Historical Record of Đại Việt, the Complete Books]. Edited by Ch'en Ching-ho. Tokyo: Tōkyō Daigaku Tōyō Bunka Kekyūjo Fuzoku Tōyōgaku Bunken Sentā, 1984.

———, comp. *Đại Việt sử ký toàn thư*. Vol. 1. Hanoi: Nxb Khoa học xã hội Việt Nam, 1993.

Ngô Thị Sĩ. "Đại Việt sử ký tiền biên" [Early Part of the Historical Record of Đại Việt). MS A.2. Institute of Hán-Nôm Studies, Hanoi.

Ngô Vi Liễn. *Nomenclature des communes du Tonkin*. Hanoi: Imprimérie Mạc Đình Tư & Lê Văn Tần, 1928.

Nguyễn Cảnh Minh and Đào Tố Uyên. *Công cuộc khẩn hoang thành lập huyện Kim Sơn*.

Nguyễn Chí Bền. *Kho tang lễ hội cổ truyền Việt Nam*. Hanoi: Nhà Xuất Bản Văn Hóa Dân Tọc, 2000.

Nguyễn Công Bình, Lê Xuân Diễm, and Mạc Đường. *Văn hóa cư dân đồng song Cửu Long*. Ho Chí Minh City: Nhà Xuất Bản Khò Học Xã Hội Thành Phố Hồ Chí Minh, 1990.

Nguyễn Danh Phiệt. "Ý thức hệ tư tưởng chính thống và tính khách quan lịch sử trong *Đại Việt sử ký toàn thư*" [Orthodoxy and Historical Objectivity in the *Đại Việt sử ký toàn thư*]. In *Ngô Sĩ Liên và Đại Việt sử ký toàn thư* [Ngo Si Lien and the *Đại Việt sử ký toàn thư*], edited by Phan Đại Doãn. Hanoi: Nhà Xuất Bản Chính trị quốc gia, 1998.

Nguyễn Đình Đầu. *Nghiên cứu địa bạ Triều Nguyễn: Thừa Thiên*. Ho Chi Minh City: Nhà Xuất Bản Thành Phố Hồ Chí Minh, 1997.

———. *Tổng kết nghiên cứu địa bạ: Nam Kỳ lục tỉnh*. Ho Chi Minh City: T. P. Hồ Chí Minh, 1994.

Nguyễn Đình Đầu, Trần Văn Giậu, and Hà Tiên, eds. *Nghiên cứu địa bạ triều Nguyễn: Biên Hòa*. Ho Chí Minh City: Nhà Xuất Bản Thành Phố Hồ Chí Minh, 1994.

Nguyễn Đức Diệu, ed. *Đô thị cổ Hội An* [Ancient Town of Hội An]. Hanoi: Nhà Xuất Bản Khoa Học Xã Hội, 1990.

Nguyễn Đức Nghinh. "Chợ chùa ở thế kỷ XVII." *NCLS* 4 (1979).

———. "Mấy nét phác thảo chợ lang qua những tư liệu của các thế kỷ XVII–XVIII." *NCLS* 6 (1998).

Nguyễn Duy Hình. *Tín ngưỡng Thành Hoàng Việt Nam*. Hanoi: Nhà Xuất Bản Khoa Học Xã Hội, 1996.

Nguyễn Hồng Phong. *Xã-thôn Việt Nam*. Hanoi: Văn Sử Địa, 1959.

Nguyễn Hữu Khang. *La commune annamite*. Paris: Receuil Sirey, 1946.

Nguyễn Huy Lai. *Les régimes matrimoniaux en droit annamite*. Paris: Les Editions Domat Montchrestien, 1934.

Nguyễn Khắc Tụng. *Nhà cứu các dân tộc ở trung du Bắc Bộ*. Hanoi: Nhà Xuất Bản Khoa Học Xã Hội, 1978.

Nguyễn Khắc Viên. *Vietnam: A Long History*. Hanoi: Thế Giới, 1993.

Nguyễn Mạnh Tường. *l'individu dans la vieille cité annamite*. Montpellier: Imprimérie de la Press, 1932.

Nguyễn Ngọc Huy and Tạ Văn Tài, trans. *The Lê Code: Law in Traditional Viet-nam (a Comparative Sino-Vietnamese Legal Study with Historical-Juridical Analysis and Annotations)*. 3 vols. Athens: Ohio University Press, 1987.

Nguyễn Như Ngọc. "Bàn góp Về vấn đề Cải lương hương chính." *Nam Phong* 41 (1920).

Nguyen On Khe. "*Phủ man tạp lục* ou notes diverse sur le pacification de la region des Möi." *Revue Indochinoise* (1904): no. 7: 445–69; no. 8: 641–48; no. 9: 706–16; no. 10: 789–96.

Nguyen Phu Đức. *La veuve en droit vietnamien: Contribution à l'étude du patri-monie familial en droit vietnamien*. Saigon: Ministère de l'education nation-ale, 1964.

Nguyễn Phương Đỗ. *Thực tràng và xu thế phát triển có cấu xã hội nước ta trong giai đoạn hiện nay*. Hanoi: Chương Trình Khoa Học Công Nghệ Cấp Nhà Nước, 1995.

Nguyễn Quang Ngọc. *Cơ cấu xã hội trong quá trình phát triển của lịch sử Việt Nam*. Hanoi, 1995.

———, ed. *Tiến trình lịch sử Việt Nam* [The Evolution of Vietnamese History]. Hanoi: Nhà Xuất Bản Giáo Dục, 2000.

———. *Về một số làng buôn ở đồng bằng bắc bộ thế kỷ XVIII–XIX*. Hanoi: Hội sử học Việt Nam, 1993.

Nguyễn Sinh Duy. "Danh xưng Hội An xưa" [The Ancient Place Names for Hội An]. *Xưa Này* (Hà Nội, s.d.): 19–21.

Nguyễn Thế Anh. "Le Nam Tien dans les textes vietnamiens." In *Les frontières du Vietnam: Histoire des frontières de la péninsule indochinoise*, edited by P. B. Lafont, 121–27. Paris: l'Harmattan, 1989.

———. "The Vietnamization of the Cham Deity Po Nagar." In *Essays into Viet-namese Pasts*, edited by Keith Taylor and John Whitmore, 42–50. Ithaca, NY: Cornell University Southeast Asia Publications, 1995.

Nguyễn Thị Phương. *Bảng tra thần tích theo địa danh làng xã*. Hanoi: Trung Tâm Khoa Học Xã Hội và Nhân Văn, 1996.

Nguyễn Trãi. *Uc Trai tap* [A Collection of the Writings by Nguyễn Trãi]. Saigon: Phu quoc-vu khanh dac-trách van-hóa, 1972.

Nguyen, Tri An. "Ninh Phúc Temple: A Study of Seventeenth-Century Bud-dhist Architecture in Vietnam." PhD diss., University of California, Berke-ley, 1999.

Nguyễn Tùng. *Mong Phu, un village du delta du fleuve Rouge (Vietnam)*. Paris: l'Harmarttan, 1999.

Nguyễn Văn Hầu. *Thoại Ngọc Hầu và những cuộc khai phá miền Hậu Giang*. Saigon: Hương Sen, 1972.

Nguyễn Văn Huyên. *La civilisation annamite*. 1945. Reprint, Hanoi: Thế Giới, 1995.

———. *Contribution à l'étude d'un génie titulaire annamite Li Phu Man*. Paris: École Française d'Éxtrême Orient, 1938.

———. *Le culte des immortels en Annam*. Hanoi: Imprimérie d'Éxtrême Orient, 1944.

———. *Les fêtes de Phù Đông: Une bataille céleste dans la tradition annamite.* Hanoi: Imprimérie de l'École Extrême Orient, 1938.

———. *Le problème de la paysannerie annamite au Tonkin.* Hanoi, 1939.

———. *Récherche sur la commune annamite.* Hanoi, 1939.

Nguyễn Văn Khoan. *Essai sur le Dinh et le culte du génie titulaire des villages au Tonkin.* Hanoi: Imprimérie d'Extrême Orient, 1930.

Nguyễn Văn Phong. *La Société Vietnamienne de 1882 à 1902 d'après les écrits des auteurs français.* Paris: Presse Universitaires de France, 1971.

Nguyễn Văn Siêu. *Đại Việt địa du toàn biên* [A Complete Record of the Territory of Đại Việt]. Quốc ngữ translation by Tổ Biên Dịch Viện Sử Học. Hanoi: Viện Sử Học & Nhà Xuất Bản Văn Hóa, 1997.

Nguyễn Văn Vĩnh. "Le village annamite." *Annam Nouveau* (1931): vol. 8; vol. 14; vol. 16; vol. 18.

Nhất Thanh. *Đất là quê thói.* Saigon: Đại Việt, 1968.

"Nicolas" [Le franc-maçon]. "Le rôle des missionnaires religieux en Extrême-Orient." Conférence faite à la tenue du 21 Février 1893. Paris: Imprimerie Alexandre Pichon, 1893.

Ni Tui. *Dian Yun linian zhuan* [A General History of Yunnan]. Prefaced in 1737. Reprint, Kunming: Yunnan, 1914.

Nogaro, B., and Lucien Weil. *La main d'oeuvre étrangère et coloniale pendant la guerre.* New Haven, CT: Yale University Press, 1926.

Nora, Pierre, ed. *Realms of Memory.* Translated by Arthur Goldhammer. 3 vols. New York: Columbia University Press, 1996–98.

———. *The Republican Moment: Struggles for Democracy in Nineteenth-Century France.* Cambridge, MA: Harvard University Press, 1995.

Nord, Philip. *The Republican Moment: Struggles for Democracy in Nineteenth-Century France.* Cambridge, MA: Harvard University Press, 1995.

Ô Thiện. "Cải lương hương Chính." *Nam Phong* 99 (1925).

O'Connor, Richard A. "Agricultural Change and Ethnic Succession in Southeast Asian States: A Case for Regional Anthropology." *Journal of Asian Studies* 54, no. 4 (1995): 968–96.

O'Harrow, Stephen. "Vietnamese Women and Confucianism: Creating Spaces from Patriarchy." In *"Male" and "Female" in Developing Southeast Asia,* edited by Wazir Jahan Wahid, 161–80. Washington, DC: Berg, 1995.

———. "Nguyen Trai's *Binh Ngo Dai Cao* of 1428." *Journal of Southeast Asian Studies* 10, no. 1 (March 1979): 159–74.

Ory, Paul. *La commune annamite au Tonkin.* Paris: A. Challamel, 1894.

Oualid, William, and Charles Picquenard. *La guerre et le travail: Salaires et tarifs, conventions collectives et grèves.* Paris: Les Presses Universitaires de France, 1928.

Ozouf, Mona. "The Panthéon: The École Normale of the Dead." In *Realms of Memory: The Construction of the French Past.* Vol. 3, *Symbols,* edited by Pierre Nora, translated by Arthur Goldhammer, 325–48. New York: Columbia University Press, 1998.

Pâris, Camille. *Colon en Annam.* Saigon: Imprimérie Commerciale, 1907.

————. *Réponse à "l'oeuvre néfaste" du père Guerlach.* Qui Nhon: Editions du Courrier d'Haiphong, 1906.

Pâris, Camille, and A. Barsanti. *Les missionaires d'Asie: Leur oeuvre néfaste.* Paris: Imprimerie "le Papier," 1905.

Pelley, Patricia. *Postcolonial Vietnam: New Histories of the National Past.* Durham, NC: Duke University Press, 2002.

Perry, Elizabeth J. "Worshipers and Warriors: White Lotus Influence on the Nian Rebellion." *Modern China* 2, no. 1 (1976): 4–22.

Phạm Đình Khiêm. "Đi tìm địa-điểm và di-tích hai thành cổ đầu thế-kỷ XVII" [In Search of the Two Old Cities of the Early Seventeenth Century]. *Việt-nam Khảo-cổ tập-san* (Saigon), no. 1 (1960): 171–96.

Phạm Hữu Công, "Mười một khẩu đài bác bằng đồng thời Nguyễn tại bảo tạng lịch sử Việt Nam T. P. Hồ Chí Minh" [The Eleven Copper Cannons Cast in the Nguyễn Dynasty, Now Held in the Museum of Ho Chi Minh City]. In *Những vấn đề văn hóa xã hồI thời Nguyễn* [Some Cultural and Social Aspects of the Nguyễn Dynasty], edited by Mạc Đường et al., 221–32. Ho Chi Minh City: KHXH, 1992.

Phạm Văn Sơn. *Việt sử tân biên: Thượng cổ và trung cổ thời Đại.* 7 vols. Saigon: NXB, 1954–72.

Phan Bội Châu. "Việt Nam quốc sử kháo." Hanoi: Văn Sử Địa, 1957.

————. *Việt Nam vong quốc sử* [History of the Loss of Việt Nam]. 1909. Reprint, Saigon: Dai Nam, 1958.

Phan Đại Doãn. "Mấy khía cạnh triết lịch sử của Ngô Sĩ Liên" [Several Points of View on Ngô Sĩ Liên's Philosophy of History]. In *Ngô Sĩ Liên và Đại Việt sử ký toàn thư* [Ngo Si Lien and the *Đại Việt sử ký toàn thư*], edited by Phan Đại Doãn. Hanoi: Nxb Chính trị quốc gia, 1998.

————, ed. *Ngô Sĩ Liên và Đại Việt sử ký toàn thư* [Ngo Si Lien and the *Đại Việt sử ký toàn thư*]. Hanoi: Nhà Xuất Bản Chính trị quốc gia, 1998.

Phan Du. *Quảng Nam qua các thờ dài* [Quảng Nam across the Ages]. Da Nang: Cổ Học tùng thư, 1974.

Phan Huy Chú. *Hoàng Việt địa dạ chí* [Record of the Imperial Việt Territories]. Translated into quốc ngữ by Phan Đang Ngư. Hue: Nhà Xuất Bản Thuận Hóa, 1997.

————. "Lịch triều hiến chương loài chí." MS VHC807. Institute of Hán-Nôm Studies, Hanoi.

————. *Lịch triều hiến chương loài chí.* Saigon: Nha In Bao-vinh, 1957.

Phan Huy Lê, Đình Chiến, and Nguyễn Quang Ngọc. *Bổm Bát Tràng / Bát Tràng Ceramics.* Hanoi: Thế Giới, 1995.

Phan Huy Lê. "Làng xã cổ truyền của người Việt: tiến trình lịch sử và kết cấu kinh tế xã hội." In *Tìm về cội nguồn*, vol. 1. Hanoi: Nhà Xuất Bản Văn Hóa Thông Tin, 1999.

Phan Huy Lê, Nguyễn Đức Nghinh, and Philippe Langlet. *Địa bạ Thái Bình.* Hanoi: Thế Giới, 1997.

Phan Huy Lê, Vũ Minh Giang, and Phan Phương Thảo. *Chế độ ruộng đất và kinh tế nông nghiệp thời Lê sơ.* Hanoi: Văn Sử địa, 1959.

———. *Địa bạ Hà Đông*. Hanoi: Đại Học Quốc Gia Hà Nội, 1995.

———. "Kẻ Giá, một làng chiến đấu tiêu." *Tạp chí dân tộc học* 2 (1985).

———. "Structure des villages vietnamiens traditionels." *Revue Inter-Monde* (Université Ramkamhaeng) 2, no. 3 (1991).

———. "The Vietnamese Traditional Village: Historical Evolution and Socioeconomic Structure." *Vietnam Social Sciences Review* 1 (1991).

Phan Huy Lê et al. *Một số trận quyết chiến chiến lược trong lịch sử dân tộc.* Hanoi: Quân Đội Nhân Dân, 1976. Translated into Chinese as *Yuenan minzu lishi shang de jici zhanlue juezhan* [Several Strategic Decisive Battles in Vietnamese History] by Dai Kelai. Beijing: Shijie Zhishi Chubanshe, 1980.

Phan Kế Bính. "Phong tục Việt Nam." *Đông Dương Tạp Chí,* vols. 24–49, 1913–14.

Phan Khoang. *Việt sử xứ Đàng Trong, 1558–1777, cuộc nam tiến của dân tộc Việt Nam.* Saigon: Khai Trí, 1970.

Phan Văn Các and Claudine Salmon. *Épigraphie en Chinois du Vietnam.* Hanoi: EFEO, 1998.

Phan Xuân Biên. *Văn hóa và xã hội người Raglai ở Việt Nam.* Hanoi: Nhà Xuất Bản Khoa Học Xã Hội, 1998.

Phan Xuân Biên, Phan An, and Phan Văn Dốp. *Văn Hóa Chàm.* Ho Chí Minh City: Nhà Xuất Bản Thành Phố Hồ Chí Minh, 1991.

Phan, Peter C. *Mission and Catechesis: Alexandre de Rhodes and Inculturation in Seventeenth-Century Vietnam.* Maryknoll, NY: Orbis Books, 1998.

Philannam, R. P. *Saigon-Versailles ou Monseigneur Pigneau de Béhaine évêque d'Adran,* "Drame missionnaire en 4 actes." Lyon: Aux Missions Catholiques, n.d.

"Phô Đà Sơn bi kí." Ca. 1640. Institute of Hán-Nôm Studies, Hanoi.

Pires, Tomé. *The Suma Oriental of Tomé Pires, an Account of the East, from the Red Sea to Japan, Written in Malacca and India in 1512–1515.* London: Hakluyt Society, 1944.

Pluchon, Pierre. *Histoire de la colonisation.* Vol. 1, *Le premier empire colonial, des origins à la restauration.* Paris: Fayard, 1991.

Poivre, Pierre. "Journal de voyage du vaisseau de la compagnie le Machault à la Cochinchine depuis le 29 Aout 1749, jour de nôtre arrivée, au 11 Fevrier 1750." Reproduced by H. Cordier in *Revue de l'Extrême Orient* 3 (1887): 81–121, 364–510.

Pravieux, Jules. *À quoi servent les missionnaires.* Paris: P. Lethielleux, 1912.

Puangthong Rungswasdisab. "Siam and the Control of the Trans-Mekong Trading Networks." In *Water Frontier: Commerce and the Chinese in the Lower Mekong Region, 1750–1880,* edited by Nola Cooke and Li Tana, 101–18. New York: Rowman & Littlefield, 2004.

Qi Jiguang. *Jixiao xinshu* [New Treatise on Efficient Military Training]. Beijing: Zhonghua Shuju, 2001.

Qiu Jun. *Daxue yanyi bu* [Supplements to the *Daxue yanyi*]. 1487. Reprint, 1971.

————. *Pingding Jiaonan lu* [An Account of the Pacification of Annam]. In *Jilu huibian* [Collection of Records], vol. 47. Shanghai: Shangwu Yinshuguan, 1937.

Quách-Langlet, Tâm. "The Geographical Setting of Ancient Champa." In *Proceedings of the Seminar on Champa: University of Copenhagen on May 23, 1987*, edited by Pierre-Bernard Lafont, translated from the original French (Paris, 1988) by Huynh Dinh Te. Rancho Cordova, CA: Southeast Asia Community Resource Center, 1994.

Quốc Sử Quán Triều Nguyễn. *Đại Nam liệt truyện tiền biên*. Hanoi: Nhà xuất bản khoa Học xã hội, 1995.

————. *Đại Nam nhất thông chí* [The Unification Records of Đại Nam]. Translated from Hán into quốc ngữ by Phạm Trọng Điềm. 5 vols. Hue: Nhà Xuất Bản Thuận Hóa, 1996.

————. *Đại Nam thực lục* [Veritable Records of the Nguyễn Dynasty]. Vol. 1. Tokyo: Keio Institute of Linguistic Studies, 1963.

————. *Đại Nam thực lục tiền biên* [Veritable Records of Đại Nam, Ancestral Compilation]. Tokyo: Oriental Institute, Keio University, 1961.

————. *Đại Nam thực lục tiền biên* [Veritable Records of Đại Nam, Ancestral Compilation]. Quốc ngữ translation. Hanoi: Viện Sử Học, 1962–78.

————. *Đại Nam thực lục tiền biên* [Veritable Records of Đại Nam, Ancestral Compilation]. Hán original. Microfilm, no. A.2714. l'Ecole Français d'Extrême-Orient, Paris.

————. *Đại Nam thực lục chính biên đệ nhất kỷ*. Quốc ngữ translation. Hanoi: Nhà Xuất Bản Sử Học, 1983.

————. *Mục lục châu bản Triều Nguyễn*. Quốc ngữ translation. Hue: Đại Học Huế, 1960.

"Quốc triều hình luật" [The Penal Code of the (Lê) Dynasty]. Original Hán. MS A.341. Institute of Hán-Nôm Studies, Hanoi.

"Quốc triều quan chế điện lệ" [Governmental Organizations of the (Lê) dynasty]. MS A.56. Institute of Hán-Nôm Studies, Hanoi.

Reid, Anthony. "Chams in the Southeast Asian Maritime System." In *Charting the Shape of Early Modern Southeast Asia*, edited by Anthony Reid, 39–55. Chiang Mai, Thailand: Silkworm Books, 1999.

————. *Europe and Southeast Asia: The Military Balance*. Townsville, Queensland: Centre for Southeast Asian Studies, James Cook University of North Queensland, 1982.

————. ed. *The Last Stand of Asian Autonomies*. London: Macmillan, 1997.

————. "Slavery and Bondage in Southeast Asian History." In *Charting the Shape of Early Modern Southeast Asia*, 181–216. Chiang Mai, Thailand: Silkworm Books, 1999.

————. "Southeast Asia before the Nation-State: An Economic History."

————. *Southeast Asia in the Age of Commerce, 1450–1680*. Vol. 1, *The Lands beneath the Winds*. New Haven, CT: Yale University Press, 1988.

————. *Southeast Asia in the Age of Commerce, 1450–1680*. Vol. 2, *Expansion and Crisis*. New Haven, CT: Yale University Press, 1992.

————. ed. *Southeast Asia in the Early Modern Era: Trade, Power, and Belief.* Ithaca, NY: Cornell University Press, 1993.

Rémond, René. *The Right Wing in France, from 1815 to de Gaulle.* Translated by James M. Laux. Philadelphia: University of Pennsylvania Press, 1966.

Rey, L. "Voyage from France to Cochin-China, in the Ship Henry, Captain Rey, of Bourdeaux, in the Years 1819 and 1820." In *Schoolcrafts Journals: Voyages and Travels,* no. 5, vol. 4, 105–28. London, 1821.

Rhodes, Alexander de. *Histoire du royaume de tunquin et des grands progrés que la predication de l'évangile y a fait en la conversion des infidelles, dépuis l'année 1627 jusques à l'année 1646.* Translated into French by Henry Albi. Lyon: Chez Jean Baptiste Devenet, 1651.

————. *Rhodes of Viet Nam: The Travels and Missions of Father Alexander de Rhodes in China and Other Kingdoms of the Orient.* Westminster, MD: Newman Press, 1966.

Rives, Maurice, and Eric Deroo with the collaboration of Frédéric Pinaeau. *Les Linh Tap.* Paris: Charles-Lavauzelle, 1999.

Robequain, Charles. *The Economic Development of French Indo-China.* 1944. Translated by Isabel A. Ward. New York: Oxford University Press, 1974.

Roberts, Stephen H. *History of French Colonial Policy, 1870–1925.* Vol. 2. London: P. S. King & Son, 1929.

Ross, Andrew. *A Vision Betrayed: The Jesuits in Japan and China, 1542–1742.* Maryknoll, NY: Orbis Books, 1994.

Rouilly, Marcel. "La commune annamite." PhD diss., Université de Paris, 1929.

Russell-Wood, A. J. R. *World on the Move: The Portuguese in Africa, Asia and America, 1415–1808.* Manchester: Carcanet Press, 1992.

Sakurai Yumio. *Betonamu sonorakai no keisei* [The Formation of the Vietnamese Village]. Tokyo: Sbunsha, 1987.

Sallet, Albert. *Jean-Baptiste Chaigneau et sa famille.* Hue: Amis du Vieux Hué, 1922.

————. "Les souvenirs Chams dans le folk-lore et les croyances annamites du Quang-Nam." *Bulletin des Amis du Vieux Hué* 10e anée, 2 (April–June 1923): 201–28.

————. "Le vieux Faifo." *Bulletin des Amis du Vieux Hué* 6e année, 3–4 (October–December 1919): 501–19.

Samran Wangsapha. "Pu'n san samai boran thi lamphun." *Sinlapakon* 20, no. 3 (1976): 64–66.

Sansom, Robert. *The Economics of Insurgency in the Mekong Delta of Vietnam.* Cambridge: M.I.T. Press, 1970.

Sarraut, Albert. *La mise en valeur des colonies françaises.* Paris: Payot, 1923.

Scammell, G. V. "European Exiles, Renegades and Outlaws and the Maritime Economy of Asia c. 1500–1750." *Modern Asian Studies* 26, no. 4 (1992): 641–61.

Schell, Jonathan. *The Village of Ben Suc.* New York: Knopf, 1967.

Schreiner, Alfred. *Étude sur la constitution de la propriété foncière en Cochinchine.* Saigon: Menard, 1902.

———. *Les institutions annamites en Basse-Cochinchine avant la conquête fran-caise.* 3 vols. Saigon: Claude & Cie, 1900–1902.

Schurhammer, Georg, S. I. "Annamitische Xaveriusliteratur." In *Missionswis-senschaftliche Studien, Pr. Festgabe Joh. Dindinger, O. M. I.,* 300–314. Aachen, 1951.

Sejarah Melayu, or, Malay Annals. Translated by C. C. Brown. Kuala Lumpur: Oxford University Press, 1970.

Septans, Albert. *Les commencements de l'Indo-Chine française d'après les archives du ministère de la marine et des colonies.* Paris: Challamel aîné, 1887.

Shen Defu. *Wangli yehuo bian* [Unofficial Sources Written during the Wanli Reign]. First completed in 1606 but revised in 1700 and enlarged in 1713. Reprint, Beijing: Zhonghua Shuju, 1997.

Shilian Dashan. *Haiwai jishi* [Record of Travel Overseas]. 1699. Reprint, Taipei: Guangwen shuju, 1969.

Si Ma Qian. *Shi Ji.* Beijing: Zhonghua shuju, 1959.

Sim Sang Joon. "Gia đình Người Việt ở châu thổ sông Hồng và mối liên hệ của nó với các cộng đồng xã hội." PhD diss., 2001.

Singaravélou, Pierre. *l'école françáise d'Extrême-Orient, ou, l'institution des mar-ges, 1898–1956.* Paris: l'Harmattan, 1999.

Smail, John R. W. "On an Autonomous History of Southeast Asia." *Journal of Southeast Asian History* 2 (1961): 77–102.

Smith, Leonard V. *Between Mutiny and Obedience: The Case of the French Fifth Infantry Division during World War I.* Princeton, NJ: Princeton University Press, 1994.

Sommer, Matthew. "The Uses of Chastity: Sex, Law, and the Property of Wid-ows in Qing China." *Late Imperial China* 17, no. 2 (1996): 77–130.

Sơn Nam. *Đồng bằng sông Cửu Long* [The Mekong Delta]. Ho Chi Minh City: Hochiminh City Press, 1993.

———. *Đồng bằng sông Cửu Long hay văn minh miệt vườn.* Saigon: An Tiên, 1970.

Song Jeong Nam. "Làng Yên Sơ, truyền thống và Đổi mới." PhD diss., 1998.

Soothill, William, and Lewis Hodous. *A Dictionary of Chinese Buddhist Terms.* London: K. Paul, French Frubè & Co., 1937.

Southey, Robert. *Journals of a Residence in Portugal 1800–1801 and a Visit to France 1838.* Edited by Adolfo Cabral. Oxford: Oxford University Press, 1960.

Spence, Jonathan. *The Question of Hu.* New York: Vintage Books, 1989.

Stuart-Fox, Martin. *The Lao Kingdom of Lan Xang: Rise and Decline.* Bangkok: White Lotus, 1998.

Sun Laichen. "Transfers of Military Technology from Ming China to Northern Mainland Southeast Asia, c. 1390s–1527." *Journal of Southeast Asian Studies* 34, no. 3 (2003): 495–517.

Tạ Chí Đại Trường, "Góp thêm về phổ hệ Tây Sơn." In *Một vài sử liệu về Bắc Bình Vương Nguyễn Huệ,* edited by Cao Xuân Huy, 72–73. Glendale, CA: Đại Nam, 1992.

Tạ Phong Châu, Nguyễn Quang Vinh, and Đa Văn Nghiêm. *Truyện các ngành nghề.* Hanoi: Lao Động, 1977.

Tạ Thị Thúy. "Rice Cultivating and Cattle Raising." In *Quantitative Economic History of Vietnam, 1900–1990,* edited by Jean-Pascal Bassino, Jean-Dominique Giacometti, and Konosuke Odaka. Tokyo: Institute of Economic Research Hitosubashi University, 2000.

Tạ Văn Tài. "The Status of Women in Traditional Vietnam: A Comparison of the Code of the Lê Dynasty (1428–1788) with the Chinese Codes." *Journal of Asian History* 15, no. 2 (1981): 123–50.

———. "Women and the Law in Traditional Vietnam." *Vietnam Forum* 3 (1984): 23–53.

Taboulet, Georges. *La geste française en Indochine.* Paris: Adrien-Maisonneuve, 1955.

Tăng Bá Hoành. *Nghề cổ truyền.* 2 vols. Hai Hung: Sở Văn Hóa Thông Tin Hải Hưng, 1984, 1987.

Tay nam bien tai luc [Record of the Frontier Passes to the West and South].

Taylor, Keith W. "Authority and Legitimacy in Eleventh-Century Vietnam." In *Southeast Asia in the Ninth to Fourteenth Centuries,* edited by David G. Marr and A. C. Milner, 139–76. Singapore: Institute of Southeast Asian Studies, 1982.

———. *The Birth of Vietnam.* Berkeley: University of California Press, 1983.

———. "The Early Kingdoms." In *The Cambridge History of Southeast Asia,* edited by Nicholas Tarling, vol. 1, pt. 1, 137–86. Cambridge: Cambridge University Press, 1999.

———. "Nguyen Hoang and the Beginning of Vietnam's Southward Expansion." In *Trade Power and Belief,* edited by Anthony Reid, 42–68. Ithaca, NY: Cornell University Press, 1993.

———. "Surface Orientations in Vietnam: Beyond Histories of Nation and Region." *Journal of Asian Studies* 57, no. 4 (November 1998): 949–78.

———. "Vietnamese Studies in North America." Keynote speech to the First International Conference on Vietnamese Studies, Hanoi, July 1997.

Taylor, Keith W., and John Whitmore, eds. *Essays into Vietnamese Pasts.* Ithaca, NY: Southeast Asia Publications, Cornell University, 1995.

Teixeira, P. Manuel. *Macau e a sua diocese, XIV, as missões portuguesas no Vietnam.* Macao: Imprensa Nacional, 1977.

Thạch Phương Hồ, Lê Huỳnh Lứa, and Nguyễn Quang Vinh. *Văn hóa dân gian Người Việt ở Nam Bộ.* Hanoi: Nhà Xuất Bản Khoa Học Xã Hội, 1992.

Thanh Lãng. Introduction to Philiphê Bỉnh's *Sách sổ sang chép các việc.* Saigon: Viện Sử Họ Đà Lạt Xuất Bản, 1968.

"Thiên nam dư hạ tập" [Collection of Works Written during Leisure Time in the South]. MS A.334. Institute of Hán-Nôm Studies, Hanoi.

Thompson, Virginia. *French Indo-China.* New York: Macmillan, 1937.

Thongchai Winichakul. "Writing at the Interstices: Southeast Asian Historians and Postnational Histories in Southeast Asia." In *New Terrains in Southeast Asian History,* edited by Abu Talib Ahmad and Tan Liok Ee, 3–29. Athens: Ohio University Press, 2002.

Thurgood, Graham. *From Ancient Cham to Modern Dialects: Two Thousand Years of Language Contact and Change.* Honolulu: University of Hawaii Press, 1999.

Tìm hiểu tính chất dân tộc. Hanoi, 1963.

Toan Ánh. *Con Người Việt Nam.* 1965. Reprint, Ho Chi Minh City: Xuân Thu, 1992.

———. *Nếp cũ hội hè đình đám.* Saigon: Nam Chí Tùng Thư, 1968.

———. *Nếp cũ tín ngưỡng Việt Nam.* Saigon: Xuân Thu, 1966.

———. *Nếp cũ xóm làng.* Saigon, 1968. Reprint, Ho Chí Minh City, 1992.

Todorov, Tzvetan. *On Human Diversity: Nationalism, Racism, and Exoticism in French Thought.* Translated by Catherine Porter. Cambridge, MA: Harvard University Press, 1993.

Tombs, Robert. *France, 1814–1914.* New York: Longman, 1996.

Tống Phúc Ngoan, Dương Văn Châu, and Nhầm Văn, eds. *Xiêm La quốc lộ trình tập lục* [A Collection of Routes to the Kingdom of Siam]. Introduced by Chen Chingho. Hong Kong: New Asia Institute, Chinese University of Hong Kong, 1966.

Trần Đức. *Nền văn minh Song Hồng xưa và nay.* Hanoi: Nhà Xuất Bản Khoa Học Xã Hội, 1993.

Trần Kỳ Phương and Vũ Hữu Minh. "Của Đại Chiêm thời vương quốc Champa thế kỷ 4 đến 10" [Great Cham Harbor under the Cham Kingdoms from the Fourth through Tenth Centuries]. In *Đô thị cổ Hội An* [Ancient Town of Hội An], edited by Nguyễn Đức Diệu, 125–34. Hanoi: Nhà Xuất Bản Khoa Học Xã Hội, 1991).

Trần Lâm Biền. *Chùa Việt.* Hanoi: Nhà Xuất Bản Văn Hóa Thông Tin, 1996.

Trần Mỹ Vân. "The Status of Women in Traditional Việt Nam." In *Asian Panorama: Essays in Asian History, Past and Present,* edited by K. M. De Silva and Sirima Kiribamune, 274–83. New Delhi: Vikas, 1990.

Tran, Nhung Tuyet. "Vietnamese Women at the Crossroads: Gender and Society in Seventeenth- and Eighteenth-Century An Nam." PhD diss., University of California, Los Angeles, 2004.

Trần Quốc Vương. "Hội An-Đà Nẵng, Đà Nẵng và Hội An trong bối cảnh địa văn hoá-lịch sử xứ Quảng Nam" [Hội An-Đà Nẵng, Đà Nẵng, and Hội An in the Context of the Culture and History of Quảng Nam]. *Văn hoá mỹ thuật* 8 (1998): 15–19.

———. *Truyền thống phụ nữ Việt Nam.* Hanoi: Nhà Xuất Bản Văn Hóa Thông Tin, 2001.

———. *Văn hóa Việt Nam, tìm tới và suy ngẫm.* Hanoi: Nhà Xuất Bản Văn Hóa Dân Tộc, 2000.

Trần Quốc Vượng and Đỗ Thị Hảo. *Nghề thủ công truyền thống và các vị tổ nghề.* Hanoi: Nhà Xuất Bản Văn Hóa Dân Tộc, 1996.

Trần Trọng Kim. *Việt Nam sử lược.* 1920. Reprint, Ho Chí Minh City: Nhà Xuất Bản Văn Hóa Thông Tin, 1999.

———. *Yuenan tongshi* [A Brief History of Vietnam]. Translated into Chinese by Dai Kelai from the *Việt Nam sử-lược.* Beijing: Zhonghua Shuju, 1992.

Trần Từ. *Cơ cấu tổ chức của làng Việt cổ truyền ở Bắc Bộ*. Hanoi: Nhà Xuất Bản Khoa Học Xã Hội, 1984.

Trần Văn Chương. *Essai sur l'esprit du droit sino-annamite*. Paris: Montpellier, 1928.

Trần Văn Giàu, Trần Bạch Đăng, and Nguyễn Công Bình, eds. *Địa chí văn hóa Thành Phố Hồ Chí Minh* [A Cultural Gazette of Hochiminh City]. Ho Chí Minh City: Nhà Xuất Bản Thành Phố Hồ Chí Minh, 1987.

Tran V. Tam Tinh. *Dieu et Caesar: Les catholiques dans l'histoire du Vietnam*. Paris: Sudestasie, 1978.

Trinh Hoài Đức. *Gia Định thành thông chí* [Gia Định Gazetteer]. Saigon: Phủ Quốc vụ khanh đặc trách Văn hóa, 1972.

———. *Gia Định thành thông chí*. Hanoi: Giáo dục, 1998.

Trocki, Carl. "Chinese Pioneering in Eighteenth-Century Southeast Asia." In *The Last Stand of Asian Autonomies*, edited by Anthony Reid, 83–101. London: Macmillan, 1997.

Trung Tâm Khoa Học Xã Hội van Nhân Văn Quốc Gia. *Hội Thảo quốc tế về Việt Nam học (Tóm tắt báo cáo) / International Conference*. Hanoi: Thế Giới, 1998.

———. *Việt Nam học, kỷ yếu hội thảo quốc tế lần thứ nhất*. Vol. 3. Hanoi: Thế Giới, 2001.

Trung Tâm Nghiên Cứu Việt Nam Đông Nam Á. *Văn hóa Nam Bộ trong không gian xã hội Đông Nam Ă*. Saigon, 2000.

Trương Bửu Lâm. *Colonialism Experienced: Vietnamese Writings on Colonialism, 1900–1931*. Ann Arbor: University of Michigan Press, 2000.

———. *Patterns of Vietnamese Response to Foreign Intervention: 1858–1900*. New Haven, CT: Yale Southeast Asia Studies, 1967.

Trương Bửu Lâm and Bửu Cầm. *Hồng Đức bản đồ* [The *Hồng Đức* Maps]. Saigon: Bộ Quốc Gia Giáo Dục, 1962.

Trương Hữu Quỳnh. *Chế độ ruộng đất ở Việt Nam thế kỷ XI–XVIII*. 2 vols. Hanoi: Nhà Xuất Bản Khoa Học Xã Hội, 1982, 1983.

Trương Lưu, ed. *Văn hóa người Khmer vùng đồng Bằng sôn Cửu Long*. Hanoi: Văn Hóa Dân Tộc, 1993.

Trương Sĩ Tải [Petrus Jean-Baptiste Trương Vĩnh Ký], ed. *Bi Nhu quận công phương tích lục*. Hong Kong, 1897. MS A.1178. Institute of Hán-Nôm Studies, Hanoi.

Trương Văn Ngọc. "Đình Chiên Đàn" [The Communal Hall of Chiên Đàn]. *Dất Quảng* 118 (1996): 68–73.

Trương Vĩnh Ký. *Gia Định phong cảnh vinh* [Odes to Gia Định]. 1882. Introduced by Nguyễn Đình Đầu. Reprint, Ho Chí Minh City: Nhà Xuất Bản Thanh Niên, 1997.

Tuck, Patrick. *French Catholic Missionaries and the Politics of Imperialism in Vietnam, 1857–1914: A Documentary Survey*. Liverpool: Liverpool University Press, 1987.

Ungar, Esta. "Vietnamese Leadership and Order: Dai Viet under the Le Dynasty." PhD diss., Cornell University, 1983.

Van Dyke, Paul. "The Canton-Việt Nam Junk Trade in the 1760s and 1770s: Some Preliminary Observations from the Dutch, Danish, and Swedish Re-

cords." Paper for the international workshop "Commercial Việt Nam:
Trade and the Chinese in the Nineteenth-Century South,"
December 1999, Hong Kong.

Van Raveschot, E. L. G. *La Franc-Maçonnerie au Tonkin en Extrême-Orient et les agissements des missionnaires en extrême-orient.* Paris: E. Comprègne, 1906.

Văn Tân. *Cách mạng Tây Sơn.* Hanoi: Văn sử địa, 1958.

"Viêm bang niên biểu" [Chronology of the Trần Dynasty]. MS A.2346. Institute of Hán-Nôm Studies, Hanoi.

Viên Kinh Tế Học. *45 Năm kinh tế Việt Nam, 1945–1990.* Hanoi: Nhà Xuất Bản Khoa Học Xã Hội, 1991.

Viện Nghiên Cứu Văn Hóa Dân Gian. *Lễ hội truyền thống.* Hanoi: Nhà Xuất Bản Khoa Học Xã Hội, 1992.

———. *Luật tục Mường.* Hanoi, 1998.

Viện Sử Học. *Lịch sử Việt Nam* [History of Việt Nam]. 2 vols. Hanoi: Nhà Xuất Bản Khoa Học Xã Hội, 1971, 1988.

———. *Nông thôn và nông dân Việt Nam thời cận Đại.* 2 vols. Hanoi: Nhà Xuất Bản Khoa Học Xã Hội, 1990, 1992.

———. *Nông thôn Việt Nam trong lịch sử: nghiên cứu xã hội nông thôn truyền thống.* 2 vols. Hanoi: Nhà Xuất Bản Khoa Học Xã Hội, 1977, 1978.

———. *Tổng mục lục tạp chí nghiên cứu lịch sử 1954–94.* Hanoi: Trung Tâm Khoa Học Xã Hội và Nhân Văn, 1995.

Viện Thông Tin Khoa Học Xã Hội. *Thư mục hương ước Việt Nam thời cận Đại.* Hanoi: Viện Khoa Học Xã Hội, 1991.

Viraphol, Sarasin. *Tribute and Profit: Sino-Siamese Trade, 1652–1853.* Cambridge, MA: Council on East Asian Studies, Harvard University, 1977.

Vo Duc Hanh, Etienne. *La place du catholicisme dans les relations entre la France et le Viet-Nam de 1851 à 1870.* Leiden: Brill, 1969.

———. *La place du catholicisme dans les relations entre la France et le Viét-Nam de 1870 à 1886.* New York: P. Lang, 1992.

Vũ Huy Phúc. *Tìm hiểu chế độ ruộng đất Việt Nam nửa đầu thế kỷ XIX.* Hanoi: Nhà Xuất Bản Khoa Học Xã Hội, 1979.

Vũ Ngọc Khánh. *Lược truyện văn hóa truyền Việt Nam.* Hanoi: Nhà Xuất Bản Giáo Dục, 1998.

Vũ Tự Lập. *Văn hóa và cư dân đồng bằng song Hồng.* Hanoi: Nhà Xuất Bản Khoa Học Xã Hội, 1991.

Vũ Từ Trang. *Nghề cổ nước Việt Nam.* Hanoi: Nhà Xuất Bản Văn Hóa Dân Tộc, 2001.

Vũ Văn Hiền. *La propriété communale du Tonkin.* Paris: Les Presses Modernes, 1939.

Vũ Văn Mẫu. Introduction to *Hồng Đức thiện chính thư.* Translated by Nguyễn Sĩ Giắc, x–xvii. Saigon: Trường Luật Khoa Đại Học, 1959.

———. "Les successions testamentaires en droit vietnamien." PhD diss., Université de Paris, 1948.

Vũ Xuân Quốc. "Philiphê Bình và sách quốc ngữ viết tay: Nhật trình kim thu khát chính Chúa Giáo" [Philiphê Bình and a Handwritten Book in Quốc

Ngữ: Daily Records, Current Letters, and Supplications to the Lord Teacher]. *Nghiên Cứu Lịch Sử* 3, 298 (V–VI, 1998): 52–58.

Wada Sei. *Ming dai Menggu shi lun ji* [Collection of Essays on the History of the Mongols during the Ming Dynasty]. Translated by Pan Shixian. Beijing: Shangwu Yinshuguan, 1984.

Wade, Geoff. "Melaka in Ming Dynasty Texts." *Journal of the Malaysian Branch, Royal Asiatic Society* 70, no. 1 (1997): 31–69.

Wan Sitong. "Ming shi" [The History of the Ming Dynasty]. In *Xuxiu Siku quanshu*, 324–31. Shanghai: Shanghai Guji Chubanshe, 1995.

Wang Ao. *Zhenze jiwen* [Notes of Wang Ao]. In *Ming Qing shiliao huibian*, edited by Shen Yunlong, series 1, bk. 3, 1191–336. Taipei: Wenhai Chubanshe, 1967.

Wang Ji. *Junjitang rixun shoujing* [Daily Notes at the Junzitang]. In *Congshu jicheng chubian* no. 3120, edited by Wang Yunwu. Shanghai: Shangwu Yinshuguan, 1936.

Wang Shizhen. *Annan zhuan* [An Account of Annam]. In *Jilu huibian*, vols. 48–49, pp. 14a.

Wang Zhaochun. *Zhongguo huoqi shi* [A History of Chinese Firearms]. Beijing: Junshi Kexue Chubanshe, 1991.

Wei Yuan. *Shengwu ji* [Account of the Military Affairs of the Qing Dynasty]. Beijing: Zhonghua Shuju, 1984.

Whitmore, John K. "Chung-hsing and Cheng-t'ung in Texts of and on Sixteenth-Century Việt Nam." In *Essays into Vietnamese Pasts,* edited by K. W. Taylor and John K. Whitmore, 116–36. Ithaca, NY: Southeast Asia Publications, Cornell University, 1995.

———. "Colliding Peoples: Tai/Viet Interactions in the Fourteenth and Fifteenth Centuries." Unpublished manuscript, 2000.

———. "The Development of Le Government in Fifteenth-Century Vietnam." PhD diss., Cornell University, 1968.

———. "Transforming Dai Viet, Politics and Confucianism in the Fifteenth Century." Unpublished manuscript.

———. "The Two Great Campaigns of the Hong-Duc Era (1470–1497) in Dai Viet." Paper presented at the "International Workshop on Indigenous Warfare in Precolonial Monsoon Asia," School of Oriental and African Studies, University of London, January 10–11, 2003.

———. *Vietnam, Ho Quy Ly and the Ming (1371–1421).* Lac Viet Series No. 2. New Haven, CT: Yale Center for International and Area Studies, Council on Southeast Asian Studies, 1985.

Wicks, Robert S. *Money, Markets and Trade in Early Southeast Asia: The Development of Indigenous Monetary Systems to A.D. 1400.* Studies on Southeast Asia series. Ithaca, NY: Southeast Asia Publications, Cornell University, 1992.

Wilcox, Wynn. "Allegories of Vietnam: Transculturation and the Origin Myths of Franco-Vietnamese Relations." PhD diss., Cornell University, 2002.

————. "Hybridity, Colonialism, and National Subjectivity in Vietnamese
    Historiography." In *Travelling Concepts I: Subjectivity, Hybridity, Text*, ed-
    ited by Joyce Goggin and Sonja Neef, 101–11. Amsterdam: ASCA, 2001.
Wolters, Oliver. "Assertions of Cultural Well-Being in Fourteenth-Century
    Vietnam (Part One)." *Journal of Southeast Asian Studies* 10, no. 2 (September
    1979): 435–50.
————. "Historians and Emperors in Vietnam and China." In *Perceptions of the
    Past in Southeast Asia*, edited by Anthony Reid and David Marr, 69–89. Sin-
    gapore: Heinemann for ASAA Southeast Asia Publications Series, 1979.
————. *History, Culture and Region in Southeast Asian Perspectives*. Singapore:
    Institute of Southeast Asian Studies, 1982.
————. "Le Van Huu's Treatment of Ly Than Tong's Reign (1127–1137)." In
    Southeast Asian History and Historiography, edited by C. D. Cowan and O.
    W. Wolters, 203–26. Ithaca, NY: Cornell University Press, 1976.
————. "What Else May Ngo Si Lien Mean? A Matter of Distinctions in the
    Fifteenth Century." In *Sojourners and Settlers: Histories of Southeast Asia and
    the Chinese*, edited by Anthony Reid, 94–114. St. Leonards, NSW: Allen &
    Unwin, 1996.
Woodside, Alexander B. *Community and Revolution in Modern Vietnam*. Boston:
    Houghton Mifflin, 1976.
————. *Vietnam and the Chinese Model: A Comparison of Vietnamese and Chinese
    Government in the First Half of the Nineteenth Century*. Cambridge, MA: Har-
    vard University Press, 1971.
Wright, Gordon. *France in Modern Times*. 5th ed. New York: W. W. Norton,
    1995.
Wu Xingnan. *Yunnan duiwai maoyi: Cong chuantong dao jindaihua de licheng*
    [Yunnan's External Trade: The Process from Traditional to Modern]. Kun-
    ming, Yunnan: Yunnan Minzu Chubanshe, 1997.
Wyatt, David K. *Nan Chronicle*. Ithaca, NY: Southeast Asia Program, Cornell
    University, 1994.
Wyatt, David K., and Aroonrut Wichienkeeo. *The Chiang Mai Chronicle*.
    Chiang Mai: Silkworm Books, 1995.
Xie Zhaozhe. *Dian lue* [A Sketchy Record of Yunnan]. Block print, 1600. Asia
    Library, University of Michigan.
Yamamoto Tatsuro. *Annan shi kenkyu* [Study of the History of Annam].
    Tokyo: Yamakana Shippansha, 1950.
————. *Betonamu Chugoku kankeishi* [History of Vietnamese-Chinese Rela-
    tions]. Tokyo: Yamakana Shippansha, 1975.
————. "Etsshiryaku to Taietsshiki" [*Viet su luoc* and *Dai Viet su ky*]. *Toyo Ga-
    kuho* 32, no. 4 (April 1950).
Yan Congjian. *Shuyu zhouzi lu* [A Comprehensive Record of Foreign Coun-
    tries]. Beijing: Zhonghua Shuju, 1993.
Yang Baoyun. *Contribution à l'histoire de la principauté des Nguyên au Vietnam
    méridional (1600–1775)*. Geneva: Études Orientales, 1992. Reprint, New
    York: Columbia University Press, 1996.

Young, Robert J. C. *Colonial Desire: Hybridity in Theory, Culture, and Race.* New York: Routledge, 1995.

Yu Insun. "Bilateral Social Pattern and the Status of Women in Traditional Vietnam." *Southeast Asia Research* 7, no. 6 (1999): 215–31.

———. "Cấu trúc của làng xã Việt Nam ở vùng đông bắc bộ và mối quan hệ vii nhà nước thời Lê" [The Village in Eastern Tonkin and Its Relationship with the State in the Le Period]. *Tạp Chí Nghiên Cứu Lịch Sử* 3 (2000): 22–79.

———. *Law and Society in Seventeenth- and Eighteenth-Century Vietnam.* Seoul: Asiatic Research Center, Korea University, 1990.

Zhang Hong. "Nanyi shu" [Book of the Southern Barbarian]. In *Siku Quanshu cunmu congshu.* Taiwan: Zhuangyan Wenhua Shiye Youxian Gongsi, 1997.

Zhang Jingxin. *Yu Jiao ji* [An Account of Subjugating Jiaozhi]. In *Congshu jicheng xinbian* [New Compilation of the *Congshu jicheng*], bk. 104. Taipei: Xinwenfeng Chuban Gongsi, 1984.

Zhang Jue. *Jingshi wucheng fangxiang hutong ji* [The List of the Alleys and Shops of the Five Sections in the Capital]. Beijing: Beijing Guji Chubanshe, 1982.

Zhang Xiumin. "Mingdai Jiaozhi ren yiru redi kao" [A Study of the Settlement of Vietnamese People in the Interior during the Ming Dynasty]. In *Zhong Yue guanxi shi lunwenji,* edited by Zhang Xiumin, 75–109. Taipei: Wenshizhe Chubanshe, 1992.

———. "Mingdai Jiaozhi ren zai Zhongguo zhi gongxian" [Contributions of the Vietnamese People in China during the Ming Dynasty]. In *Zhong Yue guanxi shi lunwenji,* edited by Zhang Xiumin, 45–74. Taipei: Wenshizhe Chubanshe, 1992.

———. "Zhancheng ren yiru Zhongguo kao" [A Study of Cham Immigrants in China]. In *Zhongyue guanxi shi lunwenji,* edited by Zhang Xiumin, 275–322. Taipei: Wenshizhe Chubanshe, 1992.

———. *Zhong Yue guanxi shi lunwenji* [Collection of Articles on Sino-Vietnamese Relations]. Taipei: Wenshizhe Chubanshe, 1992.

Zhang Xuan. *Xiyuan wenjian lu* [Account Written by Zhang Xuan]. Taipei: Mingwen Shuju, 1991.

Zheng Liangsheng. *Mingdai Zhong Ri guanxi yanjiu—Yi Ming shi Riben zhuan suojian jige wenti wei zhongxin* [Studies on Sino-Japanese Relations during the Ming Dynasty—Centering on Several Issues in the "Section of Japan" in the *Ming shi*]. Taipei: Wenshizhe Chubanshe, 1985.

Zheng Yongchang. *Zhengzhan yu qishou—Mingdai Zhong Yue guanxi yanjiu* [Military Expedition and Withdrawal—A Study of Sino-Vietnamese Relations during the Ming Dynasty]. Tainan: Guoli Chenggong Daxue, 1998.

Zhongguo, Riben, Chaoxian, Yuenan siguo lishi niandai duizhao biao [Comparative Tables of the Historical Chronology of the Four Countries China, Japan, Korea, and Vietnam]. Taiyuan: Shanxi Sheng Tushuguan, 1979.

Zhou, Daguan. *Zhen la feng tu ji* [The Customs of Cambodia]. Beijing: Zhonghua Press, 1981.

Zinoman, Peter. *The Colonial Bastille: A History of Imprisonment in Vietnam, 1862–1940.* Berkeley: University of California Press, 2001.
Zottoli, Brian. "Roots of Nineteenth-Century Vietnamese Confucianism: Scholarship and Statesmanship under the Gia Long Emperor." Unpublished paper presented at the Midwest Conference on Asian Studies, September 24, 1999.

Contributors

JAMES P. DAUGHTON is an assistant professor of modern European history at Stanford University. He completed his dissertation, "The Civilizing Mission: Missionaries, Colonialists, and French Identity," at the University of California, Berkeley.

GEORGE DUTTON is an assistant professor in the Department of Asian Languages and Cultures at the University of California, Los Angeles. He completed his dissertation, "The Tây Sơn Uprising: Society in Eighteenth-Century Việt Nam," at the University of Washington. He is also the author of "Verse in a Time of Turmoil: Poetry as History in the Tây Sơn Period" (*Moussons* 6 [2002]).

KIM LOAN HILL is a lecturer in Vietnamese language and history at the University of California, San Diego. She completed her dissertation, "A Westward Journey, and Enlightened Path: Vietnamese *lính thợ*, 1915–1930," at the University of Oregon. Her current research project focuses on Vietnamese diaspora in the United States and the Pacific Islands.

LI TANA is a senior fellow at the Research School of Pacific and Asian Studies, the Australian National University. She is the author of *Nguyễn Cochinchina: Southern Vietnam in the Seventeenth and Eighteenth Centuries* (SEAP, Cornell University, 1998).

PHAN HUY LÊ is a professor of history of the Hà Nội National University. He is the author of numerous monographs and articles on village society, peasant revolution, and landholding patterns in Vietnamese history. In recent years he has led several projects that published Minh Mạng's vermillion records (*Châu Bản*) in English and is a primary researcher on village registry projects. His numerous articles were recently collected in *Tìm về cội nguồn* (2 volumes, Nhà Xuất Bản Văn Hóa Thông Tin).

ANTHONY REID is a professor of history and the director of the Asia Research Institute at the National University of Singapore. He is the author of *Southeast Asia in the Age of Commerce* (2 volumes, Yale University Press).

SUN LAICHEN is an assistant professor of history at California State University, Fullerton. He completed his dissertation, "Ming-Southeast Asian Overland Interactions, 1368–1644," at the University of Michigan. He recently finished a term as a senior research fellow at the Asia Research Institute at the National University of Singapore.

NHUNG TUYET TRAN is an assistant professor of Southeast Asian history at the University of Toronto. She completed her dissertation, "Vietnamese Women at the Crossroads: Gender and Society in Seventeenth- and Eighteenth-Century An Nam," at the University of California, Los Angeles. In addition to revising her dissertation into a monograph-length study of gender in Vietnamese society, she has begun work on a cultural history of Vietnamese Catholicism.

CHARLES WHEELER is an assistant professor of Southeast Asian history at the University of California, Irvine. He completed his dissertation, "Cross-cultural Trade and Trans-regional Network in the Port of Hội An: Maritime Vietnam in the Early Modern Era," at Yale University. His other projects on transregional networks of commerce, belief and identity, and global comparisons reflect a commitment to bringing Vietnamese history into world historical perspective.

WYNN WILCOX is an assistant professor at Western Connecticut University. He completed his dissertation, "Allegories of Vietnam: Transculturation and the Origin Myths of Franco-Vietnamese Relations," at Cornell University. He is currently studying the role of myth and allegory in twentieth-century Vietnamese history and literature.

YU INSUN is a professor of Vietnamese history at Seoul National University in Seoul, Korea. He is the author of *Law and Society in Seventeenth- and Eighteenth-Century Vietnam* (Asiatic Research Center, Korea University, 1990).

Index

Vatican, 230

Vermillion Records. *See Châu bản triều Nguyễn*

Versailles, 228

Versailles treaty, agreement to aid in Vietnamese civil war, 290, 295, 296, 297, 299, 301, 309, 312

Vietnamese colonial volunteers: background check, 272; experience of French racism, 19; in the First World War, 19; in France, 256–89; gambling, 270; Indochinese involvement, 256–89; interracial romance and marriage, 271–72; political support for Vietnamese workers, 278; postwar Vietnamese population in France, 275; social lives in France, 269–75; struggles with winter in France, 261; Vietnamese workers' association, 277–78; wages and pay for, 259, 269, 274, 277, 279–81; war casualties, 260, 263; war diseases, 262; workers ID for, 267

Vietnamese culture, 10; uniqueness of, 14

Vietnamese women, 18; as the embodiment of Vietnamese identity, 18, 125–26; in the village codes, 126–27

Việt Nam History Museum, 91

Việt sử Đàng Trong, 14

Việt Sử Tân Biên, 9

Vijaya, 73, 99, 101, 104, 109, 175. *See also* Chà-bàn; Yak

village (*làng*), 8, 23–41; able-bodied men (*đinh*), 128, 143n37; administrative apparatus, 32–34; agrarian-handicraft-trading, 31; anthropological study of, life, 25; in Asian context, 17, 36, 127; autonomy and insularity, 29, 32; Board of Lineage Heads, 33; changes in, structure, 34–36; and colonial government, 24, 33; communal land, 29; conventions/regulations (*hương ước, lệ làng*), 24, 28, 33, 123, 127, 128, 143n33; as a copy of that of the Chinese, 19–20n8, 24; council of elders, 31, 32, 127, 128; cultural and beliefs, 25, 28, 34; definitions of, 28; economy, 25; development of, in Mekong Delta, 25, 27, 29, 31; ethnic minority villages, 26; heads, 32, 34, 127, 128; important role of, 8, 23, 126, 127; land ownership, 25; with particularly strong lineages (*làng-họ*), 28; organization, 25; patron "saints" (*bầu hậu*), 128; premier notable (*tiên chỉ*), 32; in Red River Delta, 27, 29, 31, 127; Reform Program, 33; as a revolutionary base, 17, 25; role of women in, 128–29; socioeconomic structures, 25, 29–32, 35; state officials (*quan viên*), 28; study of, 24–27; as a symbol of Vietnamese identity, 17, 23, 148; top and bottom sectors, 127; use of the word *làng,* 28, 142n28, 143n33; village-wide meetings, 128

Vincennes, 256

Vĩnh Lại, district, 225

Vinh Li Ma. *See* Vinh Ma Li

Vĩnh Long, 158

Vinh Ma Li, 197

virtue (*đức*), 49

Võng Nhị, 180

Vũ Đức Thắng, 134, 135

Vũ Minh Giang, 30

Vũ ng Tàu, 199

Vũ Quỳnh, 69n12

Vũ Thị Hợp, 134, 135

Vũ Thị Sơ, 136

Vũ Văn Bân, 134, 135

Vũ Văn Huân, 136

Vũ Văn Liễn, 134, 135, 136

Vũ Văn Mẫu, 141n12

Vũ Văn Qui, 275

Vũ Xuân, 137

Vũ Xuân Ban, 137

Vũ Xuân Đông, 136

Vũ Xuân Dương, 136, 137

Vũ Xuân Hoàn, 137

Vũ Xuân Liên, 137

Wako, 182

Wang Ji, 77

NEW PERSPECTIVES IN
SOUTHEAST ASIAN STUDIES

Series Editors
Alfred W. McCoy, Kris Olds (Managing Editor), R. Anderson Sutton,
and Thongchai Winichakul

Associate Editors
Warwick H. Anderson, Katherine Bowie, Ian Coxhead, Michael
Cullinane, Paul D. Hutchcroft, and Courtney Johnson

---

*Pretext for Mass Murder: The September 30th Movement and Suharto's
Coup d'État in Indonesia*
JOHN ROOSA

Việt
Edit